Latin America

Latin America

An Introduction

Gary Prevost

Harry E. Vanden

New York   Oxford

OXFORD UNIVERSITY PRESS

2011

Oxford University Press, Inc., publishes works that further Oxford University's
objective of excellence in research, scholarship, and education.

Oxford New York
Auckland Cape Town Dar es Salaam Hong Kong Karachi
Kuala Lumpur Madrid Melbourne Mexico City Nairobi
New Delhi Shanghai Taipei Toronto

With offices in
Argentina Austria Brazil Chile Czech Republic France Greece
Guatemala Hungary Italy Japan Poland Portugal Singapore
South Korea Switzerland Thailand Turkey Ukraine Vietnam

Published by Oxford University Press, Inc.
198 Madison Avenue, New York, New York 10016
http://www.oup.com

Library of Congress Cataloging-in-Publication Data

Prevost, Gary.
Latin America : an introduction / Gary Prevost, Harry E. Vanden.
   p. cm.
Includes bibliographical references and index.
ISBN 978-0-19-534006-8
1. Latin America—History. 2. Latin America—Politics and government.
3. Latin America—Social conditions. I. Vanden, Harry E. II. Title.
F1408.P727 2011
980—dc22   2010023410

ISBN: 978-0-19-534006-8 (pbk.: alk. Paper)

Printed in the United States of America
on acid-free paper

This work is dedicated to Latin America and her people.

CONTENTS

Maps and Tables

MAPS

TABLES

PREFACE

This book is born from a great love and appreciation of Latin America and a fascination with its societal interaction beginning with politics and extending to culture. It is designed to provide a contemporary, thematic understanding of the region that is grounded in Latin America's social, political, economic, and cultural past. The authors happen to both be political scientists but we embrace the view that the region can only be understood through a multi-disciplinary approach. We have both lived for extended periods of time in Latin America and been Fulbright scholars in the region. Our approach is strongly grounded in the progressive social science research of the past twenty years that has placed the voices of long ignored groups in Latin America (i.e. women, indigenous peoples, workers, peasants, gays and lesbians) at the heart of our analysis. We also stand on the shoulders of those professors who taught us about Latin America and its complexities. Gary Prevost gratefully acknowledges the import of his teacher Gary Wynia and his excellent work, The Politics of Latin American Development. Professor Prevost also acknowledges his first professor of Latin American politics, Byron Nichols of Union College. Harry Vanden expresses his profound thanks to those who guided and inspired his study of the region: C. Neale Ronning, John C. Honey, and Mario Hernández Sánchez-Barba. Both also acknowledge the influence of a great many Latin American friends, colleagues, participants in the Latin American drama and many excellent Latin Americanists from all over the world who have informed us and helped to shape our thinking.

This book gives attention to the recent political, social, and economic developments in the region, such as the failure of the neoliberal economic policies of the 1980's and 1990's to deliver promised prosperity and the related resurgence of progressive politics in the region as manifested in the election of numerous left and center-left governments and the strong role of numerous social movements in setting the region's political agenda in the new century. We also analyze the continuing power of the United States in the region as seen in the implementation of the Central American Free Trade Agreement (CAFTA), bilateral trade agreements with Chile and

Peru, and the continued funding of Plan Colombia. To understand how U.S. power is being counteracted, we analyze the role of various Latin American based initiatives, including the expansion of MERCOSUR, the Bolivarian Alliance, and The Bank of the South. We also provide ongoing analysis of the role that previously marginalized groups such as women, gays and lesbians, Afro-Latins, and the indigenous play in contemporary Latin American life, primarily through a myriad of groups and organizations that challenge Latin America's long-standing elites, taking advantage of the hard-won political openings achieved in recent years.

Many have helped us in this endeavor. The history chapters benefitted from the input of Dorothea Melcher, and Rob Buffington. Kwame Dixon assisted greatly in the sections on slavery and Afro-Latins. Brian Larkin's input on the religion chapter was invaluable. The section on gays and lesbians was primarily researched and written by Shawn Schulenberg. Important contributions to the revolution and social change chapters came from Richard Stahler-Sholk and Eric Selbin. Madeline Camara was most generous with her considerable literary knowledge and critical talents in the chapter on thought and culture. Gary Prevost is especially indebted to the office staff of St. John's University and the College of St. Benedict. Special recognition goes to Suzanne Reinert for invaluable secretarial help and to student assistant Benjamin Heiserich for preparing the charts on governmental structures. We are also indebted to Marc Grzegorzewski and Samar Hennawi of the University of South Florida for work on the tables in the book. Mr. Grzegorzewski also constructed the index for this book. Harry E. Vanden also wishes to thank Beverly G. Ward for inspiration, support, and assistance with photos and data. We hope this work will be valuable to all who read it and especially to those professors who confront the challenging task of introducing this fascinating "continent" to a new generation of students and hope that any deficiencies will not greatly limit its usefulness.

Gary Prevost
Collegeville

Harry E. Vanden
Tampa

UNITED STATES OF AMERICA

Gulf of Mexico

BAHAMAS

Atlantic Ocean

MEXICO

Havana ● CUBA

Mexico City ●

DOMINICAN REPUBLIC

BELIZE JAMAICA

HAITI

San Juan

Belmopan ●

Port-au-Prince

Santo Domingo

PUERTO RICO

GUATEMALA

HONDURAS

Guatemala City

Tegucigalpa

Caribbean Sea

BARBADOS

EL SALVADOR NICARAGUA

San Salvador ● Managua

GRENADA

TRINIDAD & TOBAGO

COSTA RICA

San José

Panama City

Caracas ●

VENEZUELA

GUYANA

SURINAME

PANAMA

Bogotá ●

Georgetown

Paramaribo ●

FRENCH GUIANA

Cayenne ●

COLOMBIA

ECUADOR

Quito ●

Pacific Ocean

PERU

Lima ●

BRAZIL

Brasília ●

BOLIVIA

La Paz ●

Sucre ●

PARAGUAY

Asunción ●

Political Map
of
LATIN AMERICA

CHILE

ARGENTINA URUGUAY

Santiago ●

Buenos Aires ● Montevideo ●

N

W E

S

Atlantic Ocean

Falkland Islands
(Islas Malvinas)

400   0   400   800 Miles

Scale 1:75,208,000

ONE

AN INTRODUCTION TO TWENTY-FIRST CENTURY LATIN AMERICA

The people are on the move in Latin America. They have mobilized by the thousands to force leaders out of office in Ecuador, Argentina, and Bolivia and force policy change in those and many other countries. A whole generation of more responsive, progressive leaders have taken the helm in the region. The traditional dominance of the United States and international financial institutions like the International Monetary Fund are being challenged throughout the hemisphere. Old norms are being put aside as Bolivia is governed by its first indigenous president, women serve as elected presidents in Chile and Argentina, and a progressive former bishop heads formerly conservative Paraguay. And Hugo Chávez and even Raul Castro respond to respectful initiatives from the Obama administration in Washington. Latin America—a term coined by a Frenchman to describe this diverse region—is not a homogeneous part of the world that just happens to lie south of the border that runs from Florida to California. It is an immense region that is striving to establish its place in the world in the twenty-first century.

A diverse area of thirty-four nations and peoples that includes Mexico, Central America, the Caribbean nations, and South America and surrounding islands, Latin America is home to some 600 million people (10 percent of the world's population) who well represent the rich racial and cultural diversity of the human family. Its people include Amero-Indians from pre-Columbian civilizations, such as the Incas, Aztecs, and Maya; Europeans from such countries as Spain and Portugal (but also England, France, Holland, Italy, Poland, and Germany); West Africans from areas such as what is now Nigeria, the Congo, and Angola; Jews from Europe and elsewhere; Arabs and Turks from countries such as Lebanon, Syria, Egypt, and Turkey; Japanese; Chinese; and different peoples from the Indian subcontinent. These and other racial and cultural groupings have combined to create modern nations rich in talent and variety. The dynamic way the races have combined in Latin America even led one observer to predict that the Latin American region would be the birthplace of the fusion of the world's major racial groupings into a new *raza cosmica*—a cosmic race.

Latin America still has some places where the siesta follows the large midday meal. More commonly, the modern Latin American has a heavy meal in an urban setting and returns to the job for a full afternoon of work. The rapid pace of globalization, urbanization, commercialization, industrialization, and political mobilization continues to radically change the face of the region. Colombia, Nicaragua, Guatemala, and Costa Rica still gear much of their economies around the export of excellent coffee. Meanwhile, Mexico is making more and more automobiles and automobile components as a result of the North American Free Trade Agreement (between Mexico, Canada, and the United States); Brazil is selling its passenger planes, jet trainers, and modern fighter aircraft in the globalized international market while it is developing a common market in the Southern Cone of South America (*Mercosur*); new clothing assembly plants are moving to Nicaragua and Guatemala; and Costa Rica is manufacturing Intel chips and exporting software for hospital administration.

Latin America and the Caribbean constitute an enormous and extremely rich region. The area ranges from the Bahamas, Cuba, and Mexico in the north to Argentina and Chile's southern tip in Tierra del Fuego some 7,000 miles to the south. *El continente*, as the region is called by many of its Spanish-speaking inhabitants, is extremely diverse in geography and population. It encompasses hot and humid coastal lowlands, steamy interior river basins, tropical rain forest, highland plateaus, coastal deserts, fertile lowlands, and high mountain peaks of almost 7,000 meters (23,000 feet).

The term *Latin America* is an ingenious attempt to link together most of this vast area. Strictly speaking, it refers to those countries in the Western Hemisphere south of the United States that speak Latin-based (Romance) languages: Spanish, Portuguese, and French.[1] In a more general sense, it also includes the English- and Dutch-speaking parts of the Caribbean and South America as well as Belize in Central America.[2] The focus of this book will be on the Latin part of the region, although the English- and Dutch-speaking countries will be included in some of the maps and tables and are occasionally referred to for the sake of comparison. Nor would we minimize their importance or the many similarities they share with the Latin part of the Americas.

Geography

Latin America is huge and diverse; it runs from 32.5° north latitude to 55° south latitude. With a total area of 20 million square kilometers (8 million square miles), it is one of the largest regions of the world. Taken on the whole, it is almost as large as the United States and Canada combined and larger than Europe.

The climatic and topographic diversity of Latin America is remarkable. Its range of environments is greater than in North America and Europe: rain forests, savanna grasslands, thorn scrub, temperate grasslands, coniferous forests, and even deserts. Plateaus extend down from the United States into Mexico and Central America. The Andes extend from the Caribbean island of Trinidad to Tierra del Fuego at the southern tip of South America and form the largest mountain chain on earth. They are most prominent as they parallel the west coast of South America. Many peaks are over 5,486 meters (18,000 feet); Mount Aconcagua in northern Argentina

TABLE 1. Basic Statistics for Latin America, Canada, and the United States

Countries	Estimated Total Population 2009 (thousands)*	Annual Population Growth Rate (2009) %*	% Urban Population (2009)*	Cities with 100,000 or More Inhabitants (2007)***	Per Capita Gross National Income (US $)*	Life Expectancy at Birth (2009)*	Literacy Rate (15+ years old)*	% of Women in Adult Labor Force (2008)**	Estimated Infant Mortality Rate (2009) (per 1000 live births)*
Argentina	40,276	1.0	92.2	34	6,040^	75.5	97.6^	41	12.8
Bolivia	9,863	1.7	66.1	8	1,260^	66.0	90.7^	44	42.6
Brazil	193,734	0.9	86.1	257	5,860^	72.7	90.0^	44	22.3
Chile	16,970	1.0	88.7	24	8,190^	78.7	96.5^	38	6.9
Colombia	45,660	1.4	74.8	58	4,100^	73.2	92.7^	36	18.0
Costa Rica	4,579	1.3	63.8	6	5,520^	79.0	95.9^	35	9.7
Cuba	11,204	0.0	75.7	12	…	78.8	99.8^	38	4.9
Dominican Republic	10,090	1.4	69.7	7	3,560^	72.7	89.1^	39	27.8
Ecuador	13,625	1.1	66.3	16	3,110^	75.3	84.2^	38	19.7
El Salvador	6,163	0.5	61.0	13	2,850^	71.7	82.0^	42	19.9
Guatemala	14,027	2.5	49.0	5	2,450^	70.5	73.2^	38	27.1
Haiti	10,033	1.6	48.2	4	520^	61.5	62.1^	43	46.7
Honduras	7,466	2.0	48.4	3	1,590^	72.4	83.6^	34	26.9
Nicaragua	5,743	1.3	57.0	2	990^	73.4	80.5^	38	20.2
Panama	3,454	1.6	74.0	2	5,500^	75.8	93.4^	37	17.2
Paraguay	6,349	1.7	60.9	7	1,710^	72.1	94.6^	39	30.7
Peru	29,165	1.1	71.5	21	3,410^	73.5	89.6^	43	20.2
Puerto Rico	3,982	0.4	98.6	7	10,950^^^~	79.0	94.1^^	42	7.0
Uruguay	3,361	0.3	92.4	1	6,390^	76.5	97.9^	44	12.5
Venezuela	28,583	1.6	93.7	26	7,550^	74.0	95.2^	39	16.3
NAFTA countries									
Canada	33,573	0.9	80.5	27	39,650^	80.9	99.0^^^	47	4.7
Mexico	109,610	1.0	77.5	47	9,400^	76.5	92.8^	36	15.5
United States	314,659	0.9	82.0	220	46,040^	79.4	99.0^^^	46	6.2

Sources: *Regional Core Health Data Initiative Table Generator System (online: http://www.paho.org/English/SHA/coredata/tabulator/newTabulator.htm).

Note: Literacy rate data for Puerto Rico, Canada, and U.S. was accessed from CIA World Factbook (online: https://www.cia.gov/library/publications/the-world-factbook/geos/us.html).

~ indicates data for 2001   ^ indicates data for 2007   ^^ indicates data for 2002   ^^^ indicates data for 2003

… = data not available

** United Nations Statistics Division. Statistics and Indicators on Women and Men. (online: http://unstats.un.org/unsd/demographic/products/indwm/tab5a.htm).

*** United Nations Statistical Division. Population of Capital Cities and Cities of 100,000 or More Inhabitants. (online: http://unstats.un.org/unsd/demographic/products/dyb/dyb2007/Table08.pdf).

reaches almost 6,982 meters (22,840 feet) and is the highest point in the Western Hemisphere. Snow-capped peaks can be found from Venezuela in northern South America to Argentina and Chile in the south. A fault line that runs from California through the middle of Mexico and Central America and down the west coast of South America and another that runs through the Caribbean make the region prone to earthquakes. Volcanoes are found in Mexico, the Caribbean, and Central and South America. Other major geographic areas include the Guiana Highlands in northern South America, the Brazilian highlands, and the Pampas in the south. River systems include the Orinoco in the north, the Río de la Plata in the south, and the mighty Amazon in the middle of the South American continent.

Even at the same latitude, one can find very different climates. *Altitudinal zonation*, as this phenomenon is called, refers to the range in altitude from sea level to thousands of meters that occurs as one travels as few as 80 kilometers (50 miles) horizontally. It makes for very different climates. Land from sea level to 915 meters (3,000 feet) is termed *tierra caliente*; from 915 to 1,930 meters (3,000 to 6,000 feet), *tierra templada*; from 1,930 to 3,660 meters (6,000 to 12,000 feet), *tierra fría*; and above 3,660 meters (12,000 feet), *tierra helada*, which experiences frost, snow, and ice through all or most of the year. Even close to the equator, the temperature cools 2.05° C (3.7° F) for each 305 meters (1,000 feet) of altitude. Although at the same latitude, Quito, the capital of Ecuador at 2,835 meters (9,300 feet), has an average annual temperature of 12.6° C (54.6° F), while Ecuador's largest city, Guayaquil, located on the coast, has an average temperature of 25.7° C (78.2° F). Each zone is suitable for different crops. Tierra caliente, when it is humid, is usually ideal for tropical fruits, while tierra templada is suited for growing crops like coffee, potatoes (which can be grown up to 3,355 meters [11,000 feet]), corn, and coca plants. Because of the temperature variation, crops requiring very different climates, such as bananas (humid, tropical lowlands) and coffee (cooler, shaded highlands), can be grown in the same Caribbean island (Jamaica) or small Central American nation (Costa Rica, Nicaragua, Honduras, or Guatemala). It is interesting to note that there are some crops that are extremely adaptive and can grow at a variety of altitudes. Corn is grown throughout Mexico, Central America, and the Andean region and formed an essential part of the classical Aztec, Mayan, and Incan economies. Coca cultivation has remained an essential part of agriculture in the area occupied by the Incan Empire (concentrated in Peru, Bolivia, and Ecuador but extending into Colombia, northern Chile, and Argentina). The cultivation and consumption of coca leaves has been an essential part of indigenous culture in most of the Andean region since pre-Incan times. The coca plant can live up to forty years and produces the best leaves for chewing when grown at altitudes of 915 to 1,220 meters (3,000 to 4,000 feet). Coca thrives in the shaded areas of the eastern Andean slopes, but it also can be grown at much higher altitudes or in the dryer mountainous regions such as the eastern Colombian Andes. It will also grow in hot, humid rain forests at much lower elevations. The leaves are not as good from these latter locations, but this is a less important consideration when they are used for a newer economic activity—the production of cocaine.

The Amazon is the second longest river in the world, carrying more water than any other. It runs from the jungles of eastern Peru for some 6,275 meters (3,900 miles) to its mouth at the Atlantic Ocean. Large riverboats and many ocean-going ships with a draft of 4.3 meters (14 feet) or less can go as far as Iquitos, Peru, where they still transport all the heavy cargo for that jungle city.

Rio Grande

Sierra Madre Occidental

Sierra Madre Oriental

Gulf of Mexico

Sierra Maestra

Caribbean Sea

Atlantic Ocean

Pacific Ocean

Orinoco River

Guiana Highlands

Equator

Galapagos Islands

Amazon River

Amazon Rainforest

ANDES MOUNTAINS

Gran Chaco

Rio de la Plata

Brazilian Highlands

Pampas

Atlantic Ocean

Falkland Islands (Islas Malvinas)

Tierra del Fuego

Physical Map
of
LATIN AMERICA

N
W   E
S

400   0   400   800 Miles

Scale 1:120,000,00

Once There Were Rain Forests

During the first century, tropical rain forests covered 2.02 billion hectares (5 billion acres) on our planet and represented 12 percent of the land surface. In the last 100 years alone, more than half that forest has been actively destroyed. The deforestation is extensive. According to one study, the size of the deforested areas rose from 78,000 square kilometers (30,110 square miles) in 1978 to 230,000 square kilometers (88,780 square miles) in 1988. By the mid-1990s, the annual deforestation rate was 15,000 square kilometers (5,790 square miles) per year and has continued to rise. In 2002, as we began the new millennium, over 20.2 million hectares (50 million acres) of tropical rain forest were lost every year. In Latin America, the Amazon basin alone houses the largest tropical rain forest in the world and contains one-fifth of the earth's freshwater, 20 percent of the world's bird species, and 10 percent of the world's mammals. More than 20 percent of the planet's oxygen is produced by the trees and plants in the area. Yet, 14 percent of the rain forest has disappeared in a recent ten-year period. This trend has not decreased.

In 1964, a military government staged a coup and displaced the civilian government in Brazil. During their two decades in power, the development-minded military leadership built the Trans-Amazon Highway and embarked on a policy of exploiting the resources in the Amazon basin and encouraging settlement. During

Rain forest in Costa Rica. *(Photo by Patrice Olsen)*

the 1960s, Peru's civilian president, Fernando Belaunde Terry, tried a similar developmentalist strategy for Peru's jungle area that lay on the eastern side of the Andes. However, most of the Peruvian settlers found the jungle's "green wall"[3] much more impenetrable than did their Brazilian counterparts. In Brazil, the migration into the Amazon was enormous. In 1960, there were 2.5 million people living in Brazil's six Amazon states. By the early 1990s, the population had grown to 10 million and continues to grow today. There are more than 18 million landless people in Brazil. Thousands of landless peasants, rural workers, urban slum dwellers, entrepreneurs, and well-heeled Brazilian and foreign businesspeople arrived each day to see how they could carve a fortune from the land and resources in the forest. The land is often crudely torn open to search for gold, iron ore, or other minerals in places like the huge open-pit gold mine at Serra Pelada. Indigenous populations like the Yanomami are pushed farther into the jungle and even shot if they resist the encroachment on their ancestral lands. When other local inhabitants, like rubber tapper Chico Mendes or enviornmental activist Sister Dorothy, try to resist the brutal destruction of the rain forest, they are often bullied by local officials, *fazenderos* (large landowners), or their hired henchmen or, as were Mendes and Sister Dorothy, assassinated.

The rain forest problem in Brazil alone is enormous. In 1998, the Brazilian government released figures indicating that destruction of the Amazon rain forest reached record levels in the mid-1990s. In 1994 and 1995, for example, an area larger than the state of New Jersey (12,610 square kilometers [7,836 square miles]) was destroyed. Indeed, according to a satellite imaging study by Brazil's National Institute of Space Research, 11,280 square kilometers (7,010 square miles) of Amazon

The immense Iguazu Falls on the Brazilian-Argentinian border. *(Cro Magnon/Alamy Images)*

rain forest were lost in 2001, and the figure increased to 15,835 square meters (9,840 square miles) in 2002. Not only is the rain forest cut down, but in classic slash-and-burn fashion, the vegetation is burned to prepare the land for agriculture or pasture. This means that not only are thousands of oxygen-producing trees lost every year, but enormous amounts of carbon dioxide are released into the atmosphere when the biomass is burned. This process is also accelerating in Central America and the rain forest in southern Mexico. Since 1960 almost 50 percent of Central American forests have been destroyed. Environmentalists see the resultant drastic reduction in oxygen production and dramatic increase in carbon dioxide as significant causal factors in the greenhouse effect linked to global warming.

As Latin America strives to develop and as its population grows, its ecosystems are put under increasing stress. In Haiti, Brazil, and elsewhere, the ecosystem has suffered severe stress because of the intense population density. In Haiti, most of the trees have been cut down for building materials and firewood, and the number of birds and other dependent species has been reduced drastically. In Haiti and elsewhere, the commercialization of agriculture, demographic pressure, and policies that favor large commercial producers over small peasant farmers are also combining to increase land degradation. This set the stage for a huge loss of life as rain and mud flowed uncontrolled down the hills and into heavily populated areas when a hurricane swept across Haiti in 2004. Deforestation, overgrazing, and over-exploitation of the land are endangering entire ecosystems throughout the region. Desertification is advancing. It has been estimated that desertification and deforestation alone have affected about one-fifth of Latin America. As early as 1995, some 200 million hectares (494 million acres) of land—almost a third of the total vegetated land—were moderately or severely degraded.

The People

Latin America is endowed with enormous human resources. Its 600 million people come from all corners of the globe and are rich in their diversity and skills. Fertility rates are high in Latin America, and population growth rates have been some of the highest in the world. Currently, these rates have declined to 2 percent per year or less. Even at this rate, the population will double approximately every thirty-five years.

The original inhabitants of the region crossed to the Western Hemisphere on the Bering land and ice bridge that once united Asia and North America. This happened some 20,000 to 35,000 years ago during the Ice Age. The Asian migration flowed into North America and then spread into the Caribbean and through Central America to South America. Varied indigenous civilizations grew up throughout the region. By the time the Spaniards and Portuguese arrived in the late 1400s and early 1500s, at least 50 million indigenous people lived in the region (some estimates are more than double this figure). Population concentrations included the Aztec civilization in central Mexico, the Maya civilization in southern Mexico and northern Central America, and the Incan Empire in the west coast central Andean region in South America. Other groupings could be found throughout the region, including the Caribs, Taínos/Arawaks, Guaraní, and

Araucanian. These peoples and their civilizations will be discussed more fully in the following chapter.

The Spanish and Portuguese were the first Europeans to arrive in Latin America. As they came in ever-increasing numbers, they began to populate the region as well. Informal and formal unions between Iberian men and indigenous women soon produced offspring, who came to be known as *mestizos*. Later, as the Amero-Indian population was drastically decimated and additional inexpensive labor was needed, Africans were brought to the hemisphere as enslaved peoples. At least 7 million survived the Middle Passage from western and southern Africa to Latin America and the Caribbean. The culture, religion, and cuisine they brought with them would forever change the face of the societies they helped to form. Indians, Europeans, and Africans populated Latin America during the first centuries. The fact that early Spaniards and Portuguese came without their families and claimed access to women in subordinate positions began a process of racial melding that continues to the present day. These pairings and their children were thrown together in dynamic new societies. *Mestizos, mulattos*, and *zambos* (the children of unions between native peoples and Africans) appeared in growing numbers.

Most Latin Americans trace their ancestry to Amero-Indian, Iberian, and/or African sources. However, by the middle of the nineteenth century, there was a general realization that new laborers, artisans, and those with other skills could add to the growing nations. Most nations had outlawed slavery by the time of the Civil War in the United States. Brazil was the last; slavery was outlawed there in 1888. Thus, other sources of abundant and inexpensive labor were often needed. Chinese laborers were brought into Peru in the latter part of the nineteenth century. Thousands of Italians were lured to Argentina and southern Brazil to supply the labor for the growing agricultural and industrial production. Workers and indentured servants from India and the Chinese mainland were brought to the British Caribbean and British South America. Many Europeans came to their colonies or former colonies or from other nations to make their way in these new societies. French, Germans, Swedes, Irish, Poles, and others from Europe arrived on Latin American shores to make a better life or as refugees from famine, war, and revolution. European Jews came to seek opportunity and escape pogroms and persecution. Japanese came to southern Brazil and to other countries like Peru for better opportunities, often with their passages paid by the Japanese government (which wanted to alleviate population pressures on the home islands). Turks and Arabs came to explore new horizons. As the United States expanded its economic sphere into Latin America and the Caribbean, some U.S. citizens chose to stay in the lands where they went to make their fortunes. One, an early aviator who came to Peru, stayed to found what was that nation's best-known private airline, Faucett. The Spanish Civil War and World War II began a new wave of immigration from Spain and other countries taken over by the Fascists. Many Jews and others targeted by the Nazis owe their lives to the liberal immigration and visa policies of Latin American nations. (Ironically, as World War II was ending, Nazis, Fascists, and accused war criminals were often able to take advantage of these same liberal immigration policies and Argentine neutrality during World War II to make their way to countries like Argentina and Paraguay.) Today, new immigrants from eastern Europe and elsewhere continue to arrive, to make their places in these dynamic new societies.

The Land

When the first Europeans arrived in the Western Hemisphere, they found abundant land and resources. Most of the native peoples incorporated the concept of the earth mother, as most notably articulated in Andean culture as the earth mother *Pachamama*, the giver of all life. The land was a sacred trust, to be used with respect and care, and was not the property of any one person. Land either existed in a state of nature or was used or owned collectively by and for the whole community. It was never to be harmed or destroyed and always to be used for the benefit of all creatures. Thus, the native people used but did not abuse the land. Early reports suggest that food was in abundance and generally well distributed to the entire population.

The regime the Iberians brought was far different. The crown, not the earth mother, was sovereign. Lands that had been inhabited by native peoples for thousands of years were unhesitatingly claimed for Spain and Portugal. Those who had been living on the land and working it were thought to have only those rights granted by the crown. Europeanization had begun. Hereafter, the land was to be used, owned, and abused for the benefit of the crown or its subjects. The native peoples, their needs, and their descendants were and would continue to be secondary and subordinate. The land and the people who lived in harmony with it would no longer be respected. There were empires to be carved and fortunes to be made.

At the time of the conquest (late 1400s and early 1500s), Spain and Portugal were very much dominated by feudal institutions. The landowning system was no exception. Both countries were dominated by huge feudal estates and powerful landlords. The peasants were poor and subordinate. This would be the basis of the system brought to the newly conquered lands. Initially, the Spanish and Portuguese monarchs gave huge land grants and grants to use the native peoples in a specific area. The *mercedes* (land grants, *sesmarias* in Brazil) and *encomiendas* (right to use the native peoples and the land on which they lived as long as the *encomendero* took responsibility for Christianizing them) were given to the *conquistadores* and others to whom the crown owed favors or debts. Thus, Europeans soon established domain over huge stretches of land and the people who lived on them. These initial grants were later turned into large landed estates, or *latifundios*, which were not too different from the huge feudal landed estates in the Iberian peninsula. Often ranging for hundreds of thousands of acres, they were frequently larger than whole counties. They were ruled over by the *patrón* and his family, who were the undisputed masters. The lowly *peon* was like a feudal serf and had little, if any, power or recourse, even after protective laws had been enacted. From colonial times to the present, the land tenure system reflected the nature and power configuration of the whole society. Well into the twentieth century the subordinate status of the peasant and agricultural laborer was maintained. Vestiges of this system were still in evidence in the 1970s. In many areas, the humble *campesino* was expected to approach the *patrón* with eyes cast down, bowing and scraping. As late as the 1960s, there were still instances (mostly in the Andes) of what had become a widespread practice in colonial times: *primera noche/prima nocta*, the landlord's right to spend the wedding night with a newly married woman on his estate.

In time, many of the *latifundios* were divided or otherwise changed and became modern-day large landholdings: *haciendas, fazendas* (in Brazil), and *estancias* (in Argentina). Still owned by one family and comprising hundreds, if not thousands, of hectares (1 hectare = 2.47 acres) these farms still control a disproportionate amount of the land and resources in the countryside. Their continued existence attests to the concentrated nature of land ownership in Latin America. Currently, land is also being concentrated in large commercial farms, including land used for soy, sugar cane, and other ethanol-producing crops.

The original indigenous population and later the *mestizos*, Africans, mulattos, *zambos*, and Europeans who became *campesinos* (anyone who owns or has control over the small or medium-sized land parcels they work) were left with the rest. Their holdings were never large and were further reduced by division through inheritance, illegal takings by large landowners, or the need to sell off part of the land to survive. The resulting small landholdings, or *minifundios*, were and are the most common type of agricultural unit. Comprising less than 10 hectares (24.7 acres), these small family farms afford a meager living during good times and near starvation during bad. In Colombia, traditionally they accounted for 73 percent of the farms, yet they covered only 7.2 percent of the agricultural area. In Ecuador in 1954, 0.04 percent of the landholdings accounted for 45.2 percent of the farmland; in contrast, the *minifundios* comprised 73 percent of the landholdings but only 7 percent of the land. In Guatemala, per the 1979 agrarian census, less than one-tenth of 1 percent of the landholdings comprised 22 percent of the land, while the largest 2 percent of the farms had 65 percent of the land. In El Salvador in 1971, 4 percent of the landowners (the *latifundistas*) owned 64 percent of the land, and 63 percent of the landowners (the *minifundistas* and *microfundistas*) had only 8 percent of the land. At the beginning of the 1980s, 40.9 percent of rural families were landless altogether; and land concentration is still continuing in many areas. In Brazil, 70 percent of the rural population did not own any land at all, but 1 percent of the country's farms (*fazendas*) occupied 43 percent of the arable land in the 1950s. This inequity continued and later engendered a growing Landless Workers Movement (Movimento dos Trabalhadores Rurais Sem Terra or MST) in the 1980s. Their occupations of unused land have often met with brutal repression by local authorities and the *fazendero's* hired gunmen (see Table 2). The conflict was so intense that some 1,600 Brazilians have been killed in land disputes since 1985.

The process of the fractionalization of small holdings has continued. The *microfundio*, a very small farm of less than two hectares (five acres), is unable to sustain a family. The food and income from this small holding must be supplemented by income from outside labor by one or more family members. The capitalization and commercialization of agriculture have put even greater stress on the *microfundistas* and many of the *minifundistas*. The reduction in demand for rural labor has forced many to abandon their holdings and flee to the cities in hope of better opportunities. In recent times, large-scale agricultural production has undergone a transformation.

TABLE 2. *Minifundios* and *Latifundios* in Select Countries: Traditional Landholding Patterns, 1970

| | Minifundios | | Latifundios | |
	% of Farms	% of Land	% of Farms	% of Land
Argentina	43.2	3.4	0.8	36.9
Brazil	22.5	0.5	4.7	59.5
Colombia	64.0	4.9	1.3	49.5
Chile	36.9	0.2	6.9	81.3
Ecuador	89.9	16.6	0.4	45.1
Guatemala	88.4	14.3	0.1	40.8
Peru	88.0	7.4	1.1	82.4

Source: Michael Todaro, *Economic Development in the Third World*. 2nd ed. New York: Longman, 1985, p. 295.

The heavy reliance on cheap labor and abundant land in the absence of mechanization is rapidly giving way to more capital-intensive production that relies on mechanization and more intensive use of irrigation (where necessary), chemical fertilizers, and the application of insecticides by aerial spraying. As has been the case in U.S. agriculture, land is also in the process of being consolidated into larger units that can most benefit from the efficiencies of large-scale production. This has signaled a move from the traditional agricultural economy to an integrated capitalist mode of production.[4] The large plantations and commercial farms devote more and more of their production to cash crops that are sold on the world market, while the production of basic foodstuffs for local consumption more frequently occurs on the small farms. Not surprisingly, the production of corn and grains for local consumption is decreasing amidst growing malnutrition. Fewer of the poor have the funds to augment their consumption of staples. Groups such as OxFam, Bread for the World, and Food First have noted the decrease in protein consumption among the poor with increasing alarm. More and more land is being used for the production of export crops like beef or soy, yet few of the poor are able to afford beef or other meats more than a few times a year.

Although Latin America is industrializing and urbanizing at an amazing rate, agriculture is still very important. In 1990, agriculture still accounted for 40 percent of the exports for the region. The capitalization and commercialization of agriculture that have buttressed the consolidation and reconcentration of the land have radically decreased opportunities for labor and sharecropping in the countryside. Thirty-nine percent of the rural population in Brazil is now landless. There is also a high incidence of landlessness in Colombia, Ecuador, Guatemala, and Peru. Consequently, there are fewer opportunities for peasants and landless laborers to sustain themselves. Currently, more than 60 percent of the rural population live in poverty. Global economic forces are driving people off the land in record numbers. In Brazil, many flee to the Amazon region to mine gold or engage in a cycle of slash-and-burn agriculture that pushes them ever farther into the virgin rain forest. More generally, new rural refugees flock to the cities, where they try to establish themselves in the growing shantytowns that ring large urban centers.

The Cities Explode: Urbanization

Latin America is no longer the land of sleepy peasants and small villages. It has changed dramatically. Some three-quarters of the population now live in urban areas (see Table 1) compared to 41.6 percent in 1950. There are three cities in Latin America that are now larger than New York City. Mexico City alone has some 22 million people and is the largest city in the world. São Paulo, Brazil, has 18 million and is the third largest city in the world, and Buenos Aires, the capital of Argentina, has more than 12 million. By 1990 Latin America had forty cities with 1 million or more inhabitants. This was more than Canada and the United States combined. More than 140 million Latin Americans live in these modern megalopolises compared to fewer than 100 million in the United States. Urban areas in

Mexico City, 2000. *(Photo by Patrice Olsen)*

Latin America continue to explode with new people as more children are born and millions flock to the bright city lights each year. Municipal services can in no way keep up with the steady stream of new arrivals. The streets are clogged with all types of vehicular traffic, and the air is polluted by thousands of cars, trucks, and buses. Mexico City has some of the most polluted air in the world. Oxygen is sold at booths on the street. Thousands suffer and many die from pollution-induced respiratory problems. Mexico City is immense and unmanageable. The quality of life for all too many of its residents is marginal. Nor is it easy to escape. It can take more than two hours to traverse it. São Paulo suffers from similar problems and, like Mexico City, has a very high crime rate. Other cities seem headed in this direction. As the growing middle class exercises its consumers' right to own private vehicles, gridlock is the norm in rush hour and parking is often nearly impossible. The impoverished masses endure long hours on crowded buses and vans. The congestion is sometimes alleviated by subways, but they rarely cover more than a few areas of the city, may be more expensive, and cannot keep up with the growing number of new neighborhoods and urban squatter settlements.

Often, a third or more of the population in the large cities live in slums and shantytowns. Of the 18 million people in greater São Paulo, close to 8 million live in the *favelas*, as the urban slums are called in Brazil. Because many of these new agglomerations often grow up quickly where unused land is illegally occupied, city services are often minimal or unavailable altogether. Living conditions are frequently horrible, with no running water, sewer, or trash collection (see Table 7 in Chapter 5). Sometimes the only electricity is provided by illegal taps to lines that run close to the neighborhood. Crime and violence are often at uncontrollable levels. Little, if any, police protection is available in most of the larger slums, and poor neighborhoods are often infiltrated, if not run by, drug gangs and other types of organized crime. The rapidly growing Mara Salvatrucha and M-18 gangs control entire neighborhoods throughout El Salvador, Guatemala, and Honduras. Gangs often assert de facto control of specific slum neighborhoods, and the police are often reluctant to enter unless as part of a concerted, massive action led by heavily armed special police. (See the Brazilian films *Cidade de Deus* and *Tropa de Elite* for graphic depictions.) Slum areas are referred to as *barriadas, colonias, pueblos jovenes, villas de miseria*, or *tugurvios* in different Spanish-speaking countries and as *favelas* or *mocambos* in Brazil. They continue to grow dramatically. In these places, there is an abundance of misery and drugs, while hope is often in short supply.

Originally, towns in Spanish America were planned around gracious central plazas, often called the *Plaza de Armas* or *Zócalo*. Here, one would find a pleasant plaza with the main church or cathedral, government buildings, and the palaces of prominent officials ringing it. Others of means and social standing would occupy neighborhoods adjacent to the center. The outskirts of the cities were reserved for the poor and marginalized. However, the once-majestic colonial centers are now generally overwhelmed with traffic problems and pollution. Towns in Portuguese America were not always planned affairs; often, they grew up around a fort or business center and then just grew. In all of Latin America, the worst slums are still generally found on the peripheries of the cities, although poor neighborhoods and scattered makeshift dwellings can also be found inside traditional cities, as is the case in Rio de Janeiro. Many of the wealthy and upper middle class have also begun to move to well-protected, gated and guarded urban high-rises, or flee the centers to populate more removed, attractive, exclusive neighborhoods characterized by gates and guards and high-walled, luxurious houses or high-rise condominiums staffed by numerous servants and well-armed private guards and with easy access to the newest in Latin American consumerism—the mall. Suburban-style *urbanizaciones* are also being constructed to cater to the housing needs of the rest of the growing middle class, which is also flocking to shopping centers and malls in growing numbers. The contrast between the lives of the urban poor and their middle- and upper-class fellow urbanites becomes ever more stark each day and increased in much of the region with the turn to neoliberal economics.

Ironically, many are afraid to shop outside of the privately guarded malls and shopping centers. Fed by deteriorating socioeconomic conditions for the poor, urban crime and delinquency have grown dramatically in recent years. One can see the homeless and the hustlers living and sleeping on the streets in most of the major cities. Many middle- and upper-class drivers are even afraid to stop at traffic lights—particularly at night—in many areas for fear they will be robbed at knife- or gunpoint or even by street children who threaten with broken shards of glass. Sometimes the merchants and the police take matters into their own hands. Brazil in particular has become infamous for the way street children have been beaten, run off, and even killed in groups to clear the area and discourage their perceived criminal activity. Some 5 percent of Brazil's children live in the streets. Of these, more than 4,000 were murdered between 1988 and 1991. Even Charles Dickens's impoverished souls would find life hard in the modern Latin American city.

Throughout Latin American society crime and violence are growing to astronomical levels. Economic and social disparities, the suffering caused by International Monetary Fund–dictated economic adjustments and austerity, the ravages of globalization, a brand of free market economic policy called "neoliberalism" (see Chapter 8), narco trafficking, and the fallout from the guerrilla wars that have raged throughout the region all add to the general level of violence, which is now very high. For instance, El Salvador has one of the highest murder rates in the world at 55 per 100,000 per annum. A few years ago Colombia was higher at 80 murders per 100,000, while Brazil has 20 per 100,000. The cost in human suffering and lives is horrendous, and the economic cost is staggering. In 1998, the head of the Inter-American Development Bank reported that violence cost the region about $168 billion per year, or 14.2 percent of the regional economic product. Just in Brazil, the cost was $84 billion, or 10.5 percent of the gross domestic product. The figure for Colombia was 24.7 percent. Nor is Central America immune to the growing crime rates. Violent crime increased by 14 percent in the first half of 2004 alone in Guatemala. Throughout northern Central America violent street gangs, or *maras*, are on the rise. They got their start when thousands of Salvadoran and other street gang members from Los Angeles and elsewhere in the United States lost their residency because of criminal convictions and were deported to their home countries. Gang activity has been so virulent in El Salvador, Honduras, and even Guatemala that their governments have engaged in heavy-handed, often violent, crackdowns on the Mara Salvatrucha, M-18, and other gangs. Yet neither the police nor judicial authorities are able to stop the rapid growth of gangs (*maras*) in the three Central American countries, where they may include as many as 100,000 members. Also on the increase are violent kidnappings and carjackings in Mexico, Central America, Colombia, and elsewhere. The resultant personal insecurity and added economic expense weigh heavily on the region's future and cloud its growing dynamism. Crime and measures to combat it are consuming more of the region's gross national product (GNP) and slowing development. Many are now fleeing the cities to heavily guarded high-rises or gated suburban communities, or leaving their countries completely. More and more of the upper and middle class leave in fear of their own countrymen and try to isolate themselves from the masses. As well as economic refugees there is a growing flow of refugees to the United States because of high levels of crime generally, and gang persecution in Central America in particular. These problems, and their causes, will need to be addressed before the region can realize its full potential.

Yet, the growing personal insecurity and environmental degradation that the region is suffering would seem to contradict an essential tenet of Latin American life—*Hay que gozar de la vida*, life is to be enjoyed. Many Latin Americans note that North Americans (meaning those who are from the United States) live to work and worry much too much about things. In contrast, Latin Americans work to live and *no se preocupan tanto*—do not worry so much. Whenever there is a bare modicum of economic security—and sometimes even when there is not—they live very well indeed. When one is free from the imminent threat of crime, kidnapping, or economic deprivation, life can be an enjoyable experience to be savored. One rarely turns down an invitation to a social gathering and frequently enthusiastically dances till dawn at a *fiesta*. Of those with any means, it is common practice to stop for a coffee or lunch with friends and family, and most business meetings begin with a *cafecito* and talk of family and friends. Indeed, work is generally not the all-consuming activity it has become in the United States, Japan, and parts of western Europe. However, when the pollution from the street makes it difficult to sit in sidewalk cafés and the frequency of attacks on nocturnal travelers makes it dangerous to go out at night, the very essence of Latin American existence is challenged. Many are even afraid to leave their houses unattended or in the hands of poorly paid servants because of the frequent break-ins and house takeovers. In countries like Colombia, Guatemala, and El Salvador, and in cities like Mexico City, any person of means or position must also live in fear of kidnapping for ransom. Thus, rapid urbanization, industrialization, and the persistence of unresolved social and economic problems such as high unemployment, exploitation, and economic injustice have combined with rapid social and cultural change to produce conditions that threaten the very essence of the Latin American lifestyle. Yet, the indomitable Latin American spirit and passion for life propel "the continent" ever onward.

Notes

1. *Latin* here refers to modern languages that were derived from classical Latin: Spanish, Portuguese, and French in this case. Haiti is included as part of the region (indeed, it was the first country to gain independence—in 1804) and receives its fair share of attention and

interest. Those areas still under French colonial rule receive much less attention. French colonies in Latin America include the Caribbean islands of Martinique, Guadeloupe, Saint Martin, and Saint Pierre and Miquelon as well as French Guiana (site of Devil's Island) on the South American continent.

2. Although we will generally not include those areas that do not speak Spanish, Portuguese, or French in our study, it should be noted that the English-speaking part of the region includes not only Belize in Central America and Guyana in South America but also the Caribbean countries of the Bahamas, Barbados, Dominica, Grenada, Jamaica, Saint Kitts-Nevis, Saint Lucia, Saint Vincent, and the Grenadines, and Trinidad and Tobago; English-speaking territories include Anguilla, Cayman Islands, Falkland Islands (which Argentina claims as the Islas Malvinas), Montserrat, Turks and Caicos Islands, British Virgin Islands, and U.S. Virgin Islands. Dutch is spoken in the South American nation of Suriname and in the Caribbean Dutch islands of Aruba, Curaçao, Bonaire, Saba, Saint Eustatius, and Saint Maarten.

3. See the award-winning 1970 Peruvian film *La Muralla Verde* (written, produced, and directed by Armando Robles Godoy with Mario Robles Godoy) for a graphic depiction of the struggle with the jungle.

4. Because of the feudal nature of the original *latifundio* system and the way many small producers were primarily subsistence farmers who sold little, if any, of their production for the world market, many spoke of a dual rural economy with aspects of both feudal and capitalist modes of production. The integration into the capitalist world system that authors such as Andre Gunder Frank emphasized in his *Capitalism and Underdevelopment in Latin America* (1967) has now become almost universal as the large farmers and plantations become ever more oriented to the production of cash crops for export and more and more of the smaller farmers are forced to sell their labor in the globalized national economy in order to survive.

Bibliography

Black, Jan Knippers, ed. *Latin America, Its Problems and Promise.* 4th ed. Boulder, CO: Westview Press, 2005.

Blouet, Brian W., and Olwyn M. Blouet. *Latin America and the Caribbean: A Systematic and Regional Survey.* 4th ed. New York: John Wiley and Sons, 2004.

Burch, Joann J. *Chico Mendes, Defender of the Rain Forest.* Brookfield, CT: Millbrook Press, 1994.

Dimenstein, Gilberto. *Brazil: War on Children.* London: Latin American Bureau, 1991.

Elkin, Judith. *The Jews of Latin America.* New York: Holmes and Meir, 1997.

Frank, Andre Gunder. *Capitalism and Underdevelopment in Latin America.* New York: Monthly Review, 1967.

Garrett, James L., ed. *A 2020 Vision for Food, Agriculture, and the Environment in Latin America.* Washington, DC: International Food Policy Research Institute, 1995.

Haralambous, Sappho, ed. *The State of World Rural Poverty: A Profile of Latin America and the Caribbean.* Rome: International Fund for Agricultural Development, 1993.

Hillman, Richard, ed. *Understanding Contemporary Latin America.* 3rd ed. Boulder, CO: Lynne Rienner, 2005.

Janvry, Alain de. *The Agrarian Question and Reformism in Latin America.* Baltimore: Johns Hopkins University Press, 1981.

Klich, Ignacio, and Jeffrey Lesser. *Arab and Jewish Immigrants in Latin America: Images and Realities.* London: F. Cass, 1998.

Levine, Robert. *Tropical Diaspora: The Jewish Experience in Cuba.* Gainesville: University Press of Florida, 1993.

Page, Joseph A. *The Brazilians.* New York: Addison-Wesley, 1995.

Place, Susan E., ed. *Tropical Rainforests: Latin American Nature and Society in Transition.* Revised and updated. Wilmington, DE: Scholarly Resources, 2001.

Preston, David, ed. *Latin American Development: Geographical Perspectives.* 2nd ed. Harlow, G.B.: Longman, 1996.

Rifkin, Jeremy. *Biosphere Politics: A New Consciousness for a New Century.* New York: Crown Publishers, 1991.

Skole, D. L., and C. J. Tucker. "Tropical Deforestation, Fragmented Habitat, and Adversely Affected Habitat in the Brazilian Amazon: 1978–1988." *Science* 260 (1993):1905–1910.

Trigo, Eduardo J. *Agriculture, Technological Change, and the Environment in Latin America: A 2020 Perspective.* Washington, DC: International Food Policy Research Institute, 1995.

Vandermeer, John, and Ivette Perfecto. *Breakfast of Biodiversity: The Truth about Rainforest Destruction.* Oakland, CA: Food First, 1995.

Vasconcelos, José. *The Cosmic Race: A Bilingual Edition.* Baltimore: Johns Hopkins University Press, 1997.

Films and Videos

Bye, Bye Brazil. Brazil, 1980. A madcap introduction to Brazil.

Cidade de Deus/City of God. Brazil, 2003. A modern classic on (very) violent gang activity in the largest slum in Rio de Janeiro.

Like Water for Chocolate. Mexico, 1992. Excellent portrait of Mexican family, food, and the daughter who stays at home to care for her mother.

Mexican Bus Ride. Mexico, 1951. Classic film by the Spanish director Luis Buñuel on Mexico, life in Latin America, and the institution of the bus in Mexico and Latin America.

La Muralla Verde/The Green Wall. Peru, 1970 (video, 1990). An excellent film about a young Lima family that fights bureaucracy and the jungle's green wall to colonize the Peruvian Amazon.

Pejote. Brazil, 1981. Gives a glimpse of the life of street children in a large Brazilian city. For a more general view of city life, see *Central Station*, Brazil, 1998.

Tropa da Elite. Brazil, 2007. Graphically depicts how an elite police unit in Rio de Janeiro operates in the city's slums.

Websites

http://lanic.utexas.edu/   Latin American Center Homepage, University of Texas.
www.blueplanetbiomes.org/   On rain forests in the Amazon.

TWO

EARLY HISTORY

For many years, people in the Western Hemisphere have widely celebrated Columbus's 1492 "discovery" of what the Europeans called the "New World." Accordingly, Columbus Day is celebrated as a national holiday in the United States. More broadly, throughout the Americas, the year 1992 was celebrated as the 500th anniversary of the discovery of the "Americas"; but not all celebrated. Many Native Americans banded together to solemnly mark the same period as 500 years of mourning because of the many injustices that the European invasion wrought on their people. Indeed, in the first 100 years of colonization, European rule attacked native religion and culture, razed temples and cultural centers to the ground, and forbade the practice of native religions. In so doing, the colonists attacked the very essence of the original Americans, called "Indians" because Columbus and the original explorers mistakenly believed they had reached the East Indies. Colonization was, as the French Antillean author Frantz Fanon suggests, a brutal, violent imposition of European on native. The effect of European rule was so devastating to the native peoples of Latin America that their numbers were reduced by as much as 90 percent during the first 100 years of European occupation.

There are several versions of how the Iberians treated the native people they encountered. The indigenous version is one of conquest, domination, and subordination. Yet Spain maintained that it brought Christianity and Western civilization to the world it found. In contrast, England long propagated the Black Legend about the cruelties of Spanish colonial rule in the Americas and attributed much of the native population's decline to the barbarities they suffered at the hands of the Spaniards. Another explanation of this precipitous decline is found in several recent studies that make an ever stronger case for the disease theory of population decline—that is, the main cause of the radical decline in population of the original Americans was not the undeniable cruelty practiced by many of the Spaniards but the unstoppable epidemics of smallpox, measles, typhus, and other diseases that swept through the native population. The first Americans had not, it seems,

Rio Grande

Gulf of
Mexico

Island Arawak

Taino

Atlantic
Ocean

Teotihuacan
Tenochtitlan

Tikal

Aztec

Maya

Caribbean Sea

Island
Carib

Carib

Pacific
Ocean

Equator

Quito

Inca

Arawak

Machu Picchu   Cusco

Tupi-
speaking

Guarani

Map of
**MAJOR GROUPINGS OF
INDIGENOUS PEOPLE**
circa 1500 A.D.

N

W   E

S

Atlantic
Ocean

Araucanian

400   0   400   800 Miles

Scale 1:75,208,000

acquired any natural immunity to these and other diseases the Europeans brought with them. Thus, they were ravaged by them. Many also argue this was the principal factor in the Spaniards' astounding conquest of millions of people with a few hundred *conquistadores*. Indeed, the diseases often spread so rapidly that they arrived before the Spaniards. Evaluating these different perspectives, one might conclude that the story does indeed sometimes change over time but that each new version adds to our understanding of the past. Not surprisingly, then, we find that our historical views of what happened in the sixteenth century are heavily colored not only by the cruelty that gave rise to the Black Legend but also by our present understanding of epidemiology.

People in the Americas before the Conquest

To understand the historical context in which political power is exercised in Latin America, we need to briefly trace the human past as it developed in the Americas. Human history did not begin when Europeans began arriving in the Western Hemisphere in large numbers after 1492. Indeed, the common ancestry of all racial groups who found their way to the Americas was neither European nor Asian. Currently, it is believed that the earliest humans emerged on the shores of Lake Victoria in East Africa some 3 million years ago. The famous Leakey family of anthropologists' discovery of tools and bone fragments from our most ancient human predecessors suggests an African birthplace for our species. From there, it is believed, humans spread south in Africa and north to the Middle East, Asia, and eventually Europe. Later, they crossed the land and ice bridge that spanned the Bering Strait during the Ice Age to move into the Americas.

INDIGENOUS CIVILIZATION

The movement of peoples from Asia to North America occurred in waves and began as early as 40,000 years ago. It continued until about 8000 B.C.E. These immigrants first populated the Western Hemisphere and were the first Americans. They swept down from Alaska and spread across North America and into the Caribbean and Central America; from there they spread down the west coast of South America and then eastward across the continent. As their productive forces increased, they moved from a nomadic existence to one of sedentary agriculture. By 1500 B.C.E., there were villages of full-time farmers. Corn, beans, and squash became staples in Mesoamerica (the southern two-thirds of Mexico, all of Guatemala, and most of El Salvador, Belize, Honduras, and Nicaragua), while potatoes, manioc, and amaranth were dominant in areas of South America. The large numbers of different ethnic groups practiced sedentary or semi-sedentary agriculture. As they further developed their productivity, they formed larger groups: tribes, chiefdoms, and states. This also led to more concentrated political power.

Native American settlements were scattered throughout the region. The population did, however, become concentrated in three areas: present-day central Mexico, southern Mexico, and northern Central America; along the Pacific Coast; and in the Andean highlands in what is now Peru, Bolivia, and Ecuador. Here, agricultural production was sufficiently advanced to sustain a large, relatively concentrated

DISPUTED BY
ENGLAND, RUSSIA
AND SPAIN

NEW
FRANCE

ENGLISH COLONIES

EFFECTIVE FRONTIER
OF SPANISH
SETTLEMENT

VICEROYALTY OF
NEW SPAIN

FLORIDA
Ceded to England,
1763–1783

ATLANTIC
OCEAN

Guadalajara • • Mexico City

HAITI
(SAINT DOMINGUE)
Ceded to France, 1697

Guatemala •

JAMAICA
Conquered by
England, 1655

Santo
Domingo

Caracas •

VICEROYALTY OF
NEW GRANADA

Bogotá •

GUIANA

Separated from
Viceroyalty of Peru,
1717, 1739

Quito •

Pernambuco •

PACIFIC
OCEAN

VICEROYALTY OF
PERU

VICEROYALTY OF
BRAZIL

Lima • • Cusco

Salvador
(Bahia)

Chuquisaca
(La Plata, Sucre)

Sao Paulo •

Rio de Janeiro
(Capital, 1763)

VICEROYALTY
OF LA PLATA
Separated from
Viceroyalty of Peru,
1776

Santiago •

ANDES MTS

Map of
COLONIAL
LATIN AMERICA

N
W   E
S

AUDIENCIA OF CHILE
Retained by
Viceroyalty of Peru,
1776

Buenos
Aires •

CLAIMED BUT
NOT SETTLED
BY SPAIN

0   500   1000 Miles

population. Each of these areas eventually developed a dominant, centralized state civilization that came to be known, respectively, as Aztec, Mayan, and Incan. Smaller political groupings developed elsewhere.

Many aspects of these empires have influenced the culture and even the political organization of subsequent polities in these areas. In that little about these civilizations is usually included in most general courses, the following section presents a rudimentary description of their key aspects.

Large draft or meat animals that could be domesticated were not available to the native civilizations. In the west coast civilization in South America, the guinea pig was domesticated as a source of food and the llama was used as a pack animal and as a source of wool and meat. The Aztecs bred a small mute dog for food in Mexico. Unlike in Europe, there were no cattle, horses, or oxen.

The use of baskets and of stone, bone, and wood gave way to the development of pottery and more sophisticated stone (obsidian) weapons and tools and eventually to the use of bronze in the Aztec and Incan empires. In the first more developed societies to emerge, such as the Olmecs and Toltecs in Mexico and the Mochica in coastal Peru, large temple-centered cities emerged. They were beautifully designed and employed sophisticated stone and adobe construction. Only in the thirteenth and fourteenth centuries did these city-centered societies begin to expand and form empires. They were still in the process of expansion when the Europeans arrived.

Our knowledge of these societies is incomplete, in part because there were few chronicles and inscriptions in Incan and pre-Incan civilizations on the west coast of South America and because many of the written texts, inscriptions, and chronicles that did exist for the Aztecs and Mayans were destroyed by the Europeans. The story of these peoples is only now being reconstructed through the laborious work of archaeologists and ethnologists from around the world.

The Maya. Mayan civilization flowered between 300 B.C.E. and 1100 C.E. During this time, Europe witnessed the disintegration of the Roman Empire, the rise of the Holy Roman Empire, and the beginning of the Middle Ages. Mayan civilization consisted of a series of city-states that developed in the Petén region of northern Guatemala, the Yucatán, and Chiapas. Their cities later spread into Belize and part of Honduras and eventually numbered about fifty. The Mayans developed what was then a very sophisticated native civilization. Their political-social organization was, however, hierarchical, with a king, nobles, and priests on top and the common people and slaves on the bottom; decision making was authoritarian.

In the original Mayan states, the common people lived in thatched roof huts, not unlike those of the poor Mayan peasants of today, and nourished themselves on a balanced diet consisting of beans, corn, and squash. These crops could be cultivated in the same field. Planting the corn first ensured that it grew upward toward the all-important sun; the beans then used the stalk of the corn to follow the same path, while the broad leaves of the squash spread out on the ground to shade the soil from the desiccating rays of the sun and inhibit the growth of weeds. Further, the beans added nitrogen to the soil as the corn and squash removed it. The Mayan calendar also specified times when the land was to lie fallow. Terraces were used in highland areas to increase land area and stop soil erosion.

It is currently believed that the Mayan peasants paid tribute to the political and religious rulers in the cities. They in turn engaged in warfare with other city-states to

Rising some 148 feet out of the jungle in the Petén region of Guatemala, the Temple of the Jaguar in Tikal is one of the greatest Mayan structures. Apparently used for ceremonial purposes, it dates from the Classical Mayan period and was constructed about 700 C.E. *(Photo by H. Vanden)*

gain more riches and obtain additional tribute. They also established extended commercial relations with civilizations to the north and even used the sea as a trade route.

In about 900 c.e., Mayan civilization suffered a rapid decline. The major cities and ceremonial centers were eventually abandoned, to be reclaimed by the jungle. Current research suggests the causes for this disaster were probably the increasing wars among the Mayan states, civil wars, and soil exhaustion from overfarming, which had been induced by what evidently became an unsustainable population density.

The Maya's accomplishments in astronomy, mathematics, ideographic writing, architecture, and art and their highly sophisticated calendar mark them as one of the most developed civilizations of their time. They had incorporated advances in timekeeping from the Toltec and Olmec and employed the resultant extremely accurate 365-day calendar of 18 months of 20 days with 5 additional days or "dead" days (which were considered unlucky). Their mathematical system used units of one, five, and twenty (which could be written as dots for ones and dashes for fives, with twenties denoted by position) and included a place value system employing a sign for zero. During their classical period, their calendar, astronomical observations, and use of zero as a place in written numbers marked their civilization as more advanced than any in Europe in these areas. Their hieroglyph-type writing recounted great events in their history and mythology and was carved or painted on their temples, pyramids, or upright stone *stelae* or recorded in their bark paper *codices*. Recent research suggests symbols for syllables were also sometimes used to phonetically sound out words. Although only four of the original glyph codices survived, an early Spanish transcription of the Quiche Mayan creation story, the Popol Vuh, is now part of world literature. Mayan civilization thrived in the classic period from 250 to 900 c.e. in the lowlands in northern Central America and southern Mexico. Great city-state centers like Tikal, Palenque, and Copan flourished.

Although there were occasional female rulers, the societies were patriarchal and the royal succession was decided through primogeniture. The kings and the nobles made up the ruling class but worked closely with the priests, who were also the astronomers and chroniclers as well as the theologians. Human sacrifice and blood-letting were integral parts of the ceremonial functions, with special importance placed on blood derived from puncturing the royal penis. The losers in a version of Mayan soccer were often beheaded or rolled down the steps of the great pyramids after being tied together as human balls.

Postclassical Mayan civilization lived on in the Yucatán centers like Chichén Itzá and Uxmal after other Mayan lands were conquered by the Spaniards beginning in 1527. As had been the case with the Aztecs, much of the remaining Mayan culture was destroyed by the Spanish authorities, who, despite some initial efforts by priests to preserve Mayan culture, eventually burned many invaluable codices as works of the devil, thus depriving the Mayan people of a good part of their history and heritage. Perhaps because of the strength and sophistication of their culture, Mayan resistance to European domination lived on in more remote areas for centuries and bubbled to the surface occasionally. The Caste Wars in the Yucatán in the nineteenth century (isolated pockets of rebellion lasted into the twentieth century), the indigenous support for some guerrilla groups in the Guatemalan highlands in the 1980s, and the Zapatista uprising in Chiapas in the 1990s were more recent manifestations. Mayan languages are still spoken in these areas, and some religious practices are still honored.

Maya stella showing Mayan glyph writing. *(Photo by Beverly G. Ward and H. Vanden)*

The Aztecs. The Aztecs replaced previous native civilizations like that of Teotihuacan and the Toltecs in central Mexico and the Olmecs in eastern Mexico and incorporated many of the values, knowledge, and technology of their predecessors' cultures. By the time Hernán Cortés arrived in central Mexico in 1519, there were perhaps 25 million inhabitants in the region (there is some controversy as to the exact number here and elsewhere in the region). The Aztecs, who migrated from northern Mexico, arrived in the Valley of Mexico in the early 1200s. They were

relegated to marshy land not occupied by any other ethnic group. There, they established their capital, Tenochtitlán, on an island in Lake Texcoco about 1325. As their
myths explain, they picked the spot because they saw the promised sign of an eagle
clutching a snake perched atop a cactus (this symbol graces the Mexican flag).

The Aztec capital became very populous; it had between 150,000 and 200,000
inhabitants by the time of the conquest. As many as 60,000 came to an open-air
market each day. Aztec civilization was characterized by military prowess, which
extended control beyond the mountains ringing the Valley of Mexico through most
of central Mexico and as far south as the Guatemalan border. Once they subjugated
other peoples, the Aztecs forced them to pay tribute but did not directly occupy
their land save in times of rebellion. Their frequent military campaigns provided
many prisoners from the loose-knit empire.

Aztec traders and merchants ranged far and wide. The thriving merchant class
lived well. There were large houses for the nobility and the priests, palaces for the
emperor, monumental limestone-covered pyramids, temples and other public buildings, and thatched roof huts for the commoners. Agriculture and trade provided the
economic base for the society, which had also developed a well-respected artisan
class. The common people consumed corn, beans, and vegetables garnished with
chili sauces as their daily meals. The nobility and emperor had diets that included
abundant fowl, venison, and the drink reserved solely for them—chocolate. Aztec
civilization excelled in engineering, architecture, astronomy, and mathematics.
Based on earlier achievements of the Toltecs and Maya, the Aztecs adopted the same
365-day calendar, divided into 18 months of 20 days, with 5 additional or "hollow"
days added. The calendar also marked the beginning and end of religious rituals. A
type of pictorial writing had been developed that was linked to some phonetic elements and was found in their codices, or paperlike books. They did elaborate metal
work in gold and silver but not iron. Like other civilizations in the Americas, the
Aztecs had not yet learned how to work hard metals and did not use the wheel, nor,
as noted before, had nature provided draft animals or beasts of burden.

Power was concentrated and vertical. The Aztec polity was a hierarchical the-
ocracy headed by an emperor who was assisted by four great lords. Next came the
politically powerful priests and nobles. The power of the ruler was not unlike that
exercised by Mexican leaders in the last two centuries. The ruler exercised power
absolutely and often despotically. The new Aztec emperor was chosen by a tribal
council, where priests, state officials, and warriors dominated. He was chosen from
among the sons, brothers, or nephews of the previous ruler. When Cortés arrived
in 1519 and began to subjugate the Aztecs, Moctezuma II was the ruler. He had succeeded his uncle.

By the late fifteenth century, the number of private estates belonging to the
nobles had begun to grow, with the subsequent conversion of small farmers into
farm workers and tenant farmers. Slavery was a recognized institution and, as
in African society, was used as a punishment for a variety of offenses. There was
continuing incentive for the frequent wars and uprisings that occurred within the
empire. The continuing conflicts provided an almost constant flow of prisoners,
who were sometimes sold as slaves to be used as forced labor but were most often
sacrificed in large numbers to Aztec deities like Huitzilopochli, the god of war.

Conflicts within the Aztec Empire hastened its demise. With the help of the Tlaxcalans and other Aztec enemies, the Spaniards (whose numbers never exceeded 600) finally defeated the last Aztec emperor, Cuauhtemoc, in 1521. This signaled the formal end of what had been a great, although autocratic, civilization. When the capital had been stripped of its gold and silver, Cortés ordered the temples burned and the city of Tenochtitlán razed. As a way of legitimizing European rule, orders were given to have Mexico City built on the ruins of the old city. It can be argued, however, that the hierarchical power configurations, brutality of those who ruled, and political patriarchy were part of the legacy that did survive and that they left indelible marks on subsequent society and the polities that emerged in the centuries that followed.

The Incas. The third great pre-Columbian civilization in the Americas at the time of the conquest was the Incan Empire. The Incas date their early development back to the 1200s but did not begin to expand into an empire until the middle of the fifteenth century. This expansion was led by a series of extremely capable rulers. Outstanding among these was Pachacuti Inca Yupanqui (ruler from the late 1400s to 1525), who many consider to be one of the great rulers and conquerors in the annals of history. The empire was centered in the Andes Mountains around the valley of Cuzco in southern Peru and eventually extended from what is now Colombia's southern border for 3,621 kilometers (2,250 miles) through Ecuador, Peru, and Bolivia into northern Chile and northwest Argentina. At its zenith in the early 1500s, it was tied together by an excellent system of often narrow stone roads, which facilitated communication and troop movement. A system of relay runners could carry messages at the rate of some 241 kilometers (150 miles) a day. The llama was used as a pack animal, but the wheel was not part of their technology. There was no written language, and history and events were kept by official memorizers. Also employed was the *kipu*, a memory device composed of a handle with cords of different colors attached to it. Knots were tied in the different color strands at different lengths to signify quantity and events.

The land was intensively tilled, and terraces were built in the highlands to improve and expand the fields. The cultivation of a variety of different types of potato (which originated in the Andes) was highly perfected, as was the cultivation of corn. The common people primarily ate potatoes and corn. The latter crop was also collected by the rulers as a form of tribute. A portion of the grain harvest was given to the state to be kept in state storehouses. It was distributed to the elderly, the infirm, and the widowed or to villages in times of famine or natural disaster. Coca leaves (which are still used today), beans, amaranth, and other crops were also grown.

The state was more developed than other pre-Columbian civilizations and ruled by a semidivine hereditary king called the *Inca*. Power was centralized in his hands, and he was assisted by other members of the royal family, the nobility, and the royal administrators, who were responsible for running the far-flung empire. A lesser nobility also existed. The artisans and agriculturists were on the bottom of the social pyramid and lived in humble, adobe-sided, thatched roof huts with simple furnishings. Priests and public officials also received grain from the storehouses, as did those pressed into public labor. The state owned or administered most of the society and could require unpaid labor on roads, other public works, or the land of the *ruler* or estate holders. Writers such as the Peruvian indigenist José Carlos Mariátegui have characterized this as a form of state socialism. Even today, there is still a strong communal heritage in the Indian villages in the Andes.

Some have also noted the importance of the collection of tribute in this system and have further suggested that, as was the case in the Aztec Empire, the tradition of tribute made it very easy for the Spaniards to also extract tribute from the indigenous population.

The Incan Empire was administratively divided into four parts, with each part subdivided into provinces. The basic unit was the *ayllu*, which was organized around the extended family. Villages were formed by a collection of *ayllus*, and a grouping of these was ruled over by a *curaca*, or ethnic lord.

Like their Mayan and Aztec counterparts, the Incas had a developed theological system. They had a pantheon of gods beginning with Viracocha, the creator, and Inti, the sun god. Also included was Tumi, the god invoked in human sacrifice. They gave special attention to events like the summer solstice, which occasioned great ceremony and feasting. This is still a major festival in the Peruvian highlands.

The Incas excelled in pottery and weaving and had the proficiency to open the skull in a form of brain surgery. Their architecture was impressive and marked by their ability to move huge stones (on wooden rollers) that weighed tons and then carefully cut and fit them together without mortar. The Cuzco fortress of Sacsahuaman is an excellent example of this. In metallurgy they were quite proficient in the production of gold, silver, and copper; and they even made some of their tools from bronze. They did not, however, utilize iron.

Less Centralized Societies. There were many other less centralized native civilizations as well. These societies were based on hunting, gathering, and agriculture. When they did grow foods, they often practiced slash-and-burn agriculture. Their social organization was much more decentralized than that of the Aztecs, Incas, or Maya. Carib (the origin of the word *Caribbean*), Taíno, and other Arawak peoples populated Antilles islands like Hispaniola, Cuba, and Puerto Rico and were the first to have contact with the Spanish explorers. At the time of Colombus's arrival, there were Arawak settlements extending from Florida to the Amazon basin. Also of importance were the Taíno, who were a native people found in Puerto Rico, Cuba, Hispaniola, and elsewhere in the Caribbean. Their treatment by the Europeans and susceptibility to disease caused them to virtually disappear during the first generation after the conquest.

Other less politically centralized groups fared better. The Mapuche (whom the Spaniards called Araucanians) of Chile and Argentina offered such spirited and sustained resistance to the European invaders that they were not completely conquered until 1883. Similarly, the Apaches of northern Mexico battled on until the last decades of the nineteenth century. The Mapuche of southern Chile continue to struggle for their cultural survival today.

The Conquest

The first clash of European and native American civilizations occurred when the Spanish explorers and *conquistadores* consolidated their power in the Caribbean in the 1490s and early 1500s. Santo Domingo and later Havana in particular had become major staging areas for expeditions to other areas. Native people in the Caribbean were rapidly subjugated, and the conquerors looked elsewhere for gold and glory. By the second decade of the sixteenth century, rumors of a rich civilization in central Mexico reached the new colonial rulers in the Caribbean.

Like many of the *conquistadores*, Hernán Cortés was a poor noble, or *hidalgo*, who came to the New World to make his fortune. Commissioned by the colonial authorities to explore the Mexican gulf coast, he led an expedition of 600 men from Cuba to Mexico in 1519. Violating orders established by the governor of Cuba, Cortés landed on the coast and soon made allies with local tribes that had been forced into tributary status by the Aztecs. He was given a resourceful native woman by one of the chiefs. Malinche (Marina), or "la Malinche" as she was called by subsequent generations, became Cortés's translator, advisor, and eventually mistress. Because of this collaboration, she has often been equated with the betrayal of Latin American culture and autonomy and is sometimes seen as a symbol of selling out to outside interests. Others note that a more complex reading of her life reveals her to be a woman trying to survive in a complex time in which both indigenous and European societies cemented relationships through the use of native women.

Cortés sent some of his force back to Cuba for more proper authorization and reinforcements and left other men installed in the newly formed municipality of Vera Cruz on the coast. He then ordered his ships burned and directed his main force toward the Aztec capital. They were greatly aided not only by their horses (which were unknown to the natives), diseases, steel swords, steel armor, guns, and cannons but also by an Aztec myth. Cortés was coming in the year that was foretold for the return of the deposed plumed serpent king Quetzalcóatl. The Spanish leader was seen by the Aztec ruler Moctezuma II as Quetzalcóatl returning to claim his throne, and his arrival was not resisted, although Aztec resistance did spring up once the avaricious nature of the Spaniards became evident and the indecisive Moctezuma was replaced by more aggressive rulers.

Christopher Columbus landed in Central America in 1502 on his fourth voyage to the Americas. After Vasco Núñez de Balboa crossed the isthmus and discovered the Pacific Ocean in 1513, settlements were set up on the Caribbean side of Panama. They were later used as transit points between the two oceans. On the Pacific coast, Panama City was not founded until 1519. As expeditions went north from Panama into what is now Costa Rica and Nicaragua, no large, centralized civilizations were encountered and the indigenous groups were soon subjugated. By the second decade of the sixteenth century, Cortés was sending expeditions south from Mexico. By this time, the Maya in Central America were not highly organized in city-states, although there were heavily populated areas in Guatemala. Guatemala City, founded in 1524, eventually became the administrative center for the part of Central America north of Panama. From the time of the earliest European arrivals, there were rivalries among different groups and leaders and a great deal of conflict. Indeed, within two years of the founding of the cities of Granada and León in present-day Nicaragua, the two centers were engaged in a conflict that might be best described as a civil war. This pattern of behavior has persisted in most of the Central American isthmus to the present.

After reports of the riches of the empire to the south had reached the Spanish settlement in Panama, considerable interest in conquest developed. After going back to Spain for special authorization to colonize the great civilization in South America, Francisco Pizarro sailed from Panama with a band of some 200 *conquistadores*. They landed on the Peruvian coast in 1532. The Incan Empire was then at the height of its territorial expansion and encompassed more than 10 million people. However, it was engaged in civil war. The last *Inca* Huayna Capac, had died without naming his successor, and his two sons, Huáscar and Atahualpa, were both competing for the throne. Atahualpa had just captured Huáscar as the Spaniards arrived, but many followers of the latter were still ready to continue the conflict. Pizarro arranged a meeting with the victor in Cajamarca but used the occasion to capture Atahualpa and slaughter many of his surprised followers. Atahualpa ordered the execution of Huáscar lest he mobilize his supporters and soon offered his Spanish captors a surprising ransom to gain his freedom. Realizing the Spaniards' obsession with gold, he offered to buy his freedom by filling the room where he was kept with gold and silver to the height of his raised arm. As pack trains of llamas were bringing the ransom from the far corners of the empire, Atahualpa's cruel captors nonetheless executed him by garrote. From there, Pizarro and his men went on to capture and loot the Incan capital Cuzco, despite the heroic resistance led by the new *Inca*, Manco Copac. By 1535 the empire was, for all intents and purposes, under Spanish control.

How Could They Do It?

One question remains unresolved: How could a few hundred Spaniards conquer empires of millions? One reason would surely be the indomitable Spanish spirit forged in the crucible of Iberian culture, where for centuries men had symbolically pitted themselves against huge bulls and reveled in the seemingly impossible victory. It is difficult to explain all the reasons for the ease of the conquest, but authors such as Benjamin Keen note some of the following:

1. The Spaniards and Portuguese had honed their fighting and tactical skills in the 700-year reconquest of the Iberian peninsula from the Moors.
2. The Spaniards came outfitted as the soldiers of the great power of the time and enjoyed the latest in military armament and technology: steel swords and armor from foundries like those in Toledo, guns and cannons, horses, cavalries, and huge attack dogs. The Amero-Indian armies had neither steel nor guns and had never seen horses at all. Further, their notion of war was more limited, and their tactics were generally more ritualistic and emphasized advance warning of attack and capturing the enemy so as to increase the pool of sacrificial victims. The Europeans focused on swift, sure victory and dispensed with their enemies quickly.
3. As suggested earlier, the diseases that the Europeans brought wiped out whole native populations and greatly debilitated the native armies.
4. The Indian peoples often first saw the Spaniards as gods or demigods and were initially reluctant to destroy them.

5. The three most highly advanced indigenous civilizations had become quite sedentary over the years and would not think of fleeing their agricultural land to regroup elsewhere.
6. The hierarchical and often cruel nature of the political leadership in the native civilizations had accustomed the common people to authoritarian decision making and arbitrary acts from above and had conditioned the common people not to rebel against the current leaders or those who wielded power. The Spaniards were at least initially perceived as just one more ruling group that had taken over.

Early Colony

The conquest was a joint endeavor between the crown and private entrepreneurs. The conquistador leader was expected to equip his band with the necessary arms and supplies or find financial backers who would. In turn, he and his mates had a royal license to hunt treasure and native peoples who had not embraced Christianity, for their own profit. The only requirement was that they pay the royal fifth, or *quinto real* to the crown. Much of the nature of the early colony was dictated by the conditions of the conquest. The Spaniards came for gold, glory, and God and competed fiercely for the former. Many were poor noblemen or *hidalgos*, but most came from more humble origins. The wealth from looted native cities and civilizations was shared among the members of the conquering military bands. *Encomiendas* and titles were handed out later but usually just to the captains and leaders. Cortés, for instance, proved to be as successful in business as he was in conquest. He amassed a series of large and very profitable holdings in Mexico and proved very apt in his business dealings.

However, only a few of the *conquistadores* achieved the fortunes they desired, and many remained disappointed and bitter. After the initial years of the conquest, more and more Spaniards came in search of fortune at a time when there were few additional native civilizations to loot. In Peru, much of the early sixteenth century was spent in fighting, assassination, and intrigue among the conqueror Francisco Pizarro, his brother, and other Spaniards. Treachery and betrayal were common. The native peoples were often completely brutalized in the plundering of their societies and were at best seen by most as instruments of lucre and occasionally lust: slaves to capture and sell, laborers to exploit, owners of land or property to be seized, women to be used. The colonialists often rose in rebellion when reforms were attempted.

The Spaniards conquered an area forty times the size of Spain. They and the Portuguese had the power and the audacity to enslave the better part of the population on two continents. They did not come as equals but as forceful conquerors. It was their belief that they were morally superior, possessed of the true faith (which was to be imposed more than practiced), and presented with the opportunity of their lives for fame and wealth. The nature of the colony was foretold by Columbus's action on the island of Hispaniola during his second voyage. Anxious to prove the economic viability of the lands he had found, he began to force the natives to bring him a tribute of gold dust. When they refused and rebelled against their would-be masters, Columbus gave the orders to have large numbers of the locals captured and held. As a way of continuing to extract value from the natives, he sent several hundred to Europe as slaves. To placate the gold-starved settlers on the island, he distributed most of the remaining prisoners to them as a form of bounty. As was to be the case throughout the region, the original Americans would be enslaved outright or divided among the European settlers who took their land and then forced them to contribute their labor to the new European enterprise. The original inhabitants of Hispaniola declined rapidly because of disease and the harsh treatment handed out by the Europeans. Of the several hundred thousand inhabitants on Hispaniola at the time of Columbus's arrival, only some 29,000 were alive two decades later. By the mid-1500s, hardly any natives were left.

Ironically, the original *conquistadores* proved to be an endangered group as well. They were soon removed from power and replaced by direct representatives of the king whose loyalty to the crown was unquestioned. In this and other areas, European institutions began to replace the military structures and unbridled civilian power that marked the conquest. Thus, the Iberian colonial bureaucracy began to replace the arbitrary rapaciousness of the conquerors.

ESTABLISHING A NEW SOCIAL STRUCTURE: THE *CASTAS*

Spanish legislation created a complicated system of social classification consisting of the *castas*, defined by descent and color. On the top were the recently immigrated white Spaniards, the peninsular whites; below them were the descendants of the white colonists, called white *criollos*; after them came the brown people, the *pardos* or *mestizos*, who consisted of people with mixed ancestry. As time went on, the ranks of the lower and middle classes were bolstered by *mestizos, mulattos,* and *zambos.* The social pyramid that resulted from the conquest and the colonization consisted of a small group of powerful and usually wealthy Europeans or their descendants on top; a large number of natives and, soon, African slaves on the bottom; and a few Spanish artisans, soldiers, or small merchants as a wisp of a middle class.

The society that the Europeans brought with them from the Iberian peninsula was feudal in nature. Land tenure and many of the social institutions of the colony were more feudal than modern. The early colony still labored under the medieval philosophical doctrine of scholasticism. Thus, considerable time was spent debating the true nature of the Indian population and the comparability of their souls with those of the Europeans. Moral argument and ethical debate were, however, rarely a match for the immense influence of a powerful person in the New World. Like the *grand señor* in Spain or Portugal, he (rarely she) was the unchallenged master of his domain. His will could be imposed in high and low places. Judges would listen, and peons, his to use as he saw fit, had very few practical rights (as contrasted to often extensive but unrealized legal rights).

WOMEN AND POWER

Few European women came in the earliest years of the colony. Those who did were subject to the strict traditional mores of the Iberian peninsula. However, women unprotected by both class (upper) and race (white) might well be available to the person of power to *coger* (generally meaning "to grab or seize," although in parts of Latin America it came to mean "to have sexual relations"). Thus, lower-class women of color were often at the disposal of men of lighter caste and higher class.

In mostly Indian Bolivia, for instance, many *latifundistas,* or large landowners, were able to exercise the *derecho de pernada* (the sexual right to women on their estate) well into the twentieth century. Most upper-class women were strongly subordinated to male members of the family. There are, however, cases of a few women running large estates and even participating in colonial administration. There are more cases of women being the owners of record for huge amounts of land or other forms of wealth. Many of these inherited their wealth and prestige from a husband or father. In more general transgender terms, their power and strength were respected (although not necessarily liked or even accepted whenever an opportunity for non-compliance or rebellion presented itself). In that women were socialized to be meek, they were at a distinct disadvantage. Further, domination in many forms was omnipresent, and it colored the colony and subsequent social and political relations in Latin America in gender relations, politics, and many other areas.

LABOR

Persons of importance in Spain and Portugal did not engage in manual labor, in large part because they were nobles or aspired to be like them. This attitude was carried over into the American colonies and permeated the societies with a disdain for manual labor that is perhaps most poignantly manifest in the low wages and lack of respect such labor still engenders and the hesitancy to engage in it carried by most members of the upper class and many in the middle class. The initial abundance of free Indian labor heightened this characteristic, as did the subsequent importation of large numbers of African slaves. Over time these labor pools were augmented by the progeny of often illicit unions of Europeans and Amero-Indians (*mestizos*) and Europeans and Africans (*mulattos*).

Symbolic of the exploitative use of Amero-Indian labor and land was the *encomienda* (*sesmaria* in Brazil). The *encomienda* originated in a Spanish practice of granting jurisdiction over lands and peoples captured from the Moors to one of the warriors who led the reconquest. In Spanish and Portuguese America, it came to be the assignment of a group of native people to a conquistador or other colonist. He would oversee them and the land on which they lived and be responsible for their proper Christianization. They in turn were to serve him with their labor and by paying him tribute. This form of forced semi–slave labor was often supplemented with the labor of Indian slaves. The Dominicans and church officials like Bishop Bartolomé de Las Casas championed Indian rights and endeavored to stop some of the worst practices against the indigenous population. In 1512, the crown responded with the Laws of Burgos to outlaw some of the worst abuses of the Native Americans and make Indian slavery illegal. In 1549, the *encomendero's* right to demand labor from his *tributarios* was also outlawed. Both practices did, however, continue well beyond these dates in some areas.

After the decline of the *encomienda,* land, mine, and *obraje* (textile workshop) owners were forced to rely on the *repartimiento* for their free labor. The *repartimiento* was the practice of requiring the Indian population to provide a set amount of free labor to the landowners, the owners of the mines, the workshop or *obraje* operators, or the state for public works. In Peru, where the *repartimiento* was known by the old Incan term *mita,* as much as six months to a year of service could be required from each male every seven years. The Indians were often horribly exploited (thousands died at mines like Potosí, in what is now Bolivia), even though they did receive a token wage. As the historian Benjamin Keen observes, "the repartimiento like the encomienda was a disguised form of slavery." Indeed, there were harsh penalties for those who avoided service and for community leaders who could not provide the required quotas of laborers.

SLAVERY AND OTHER FORMS OF ORGANIZATION

As is the case in the United States, Latin America is still feeling the effects of slavery. It is not possible to understand society or working conditions in Brazil, Cuba, Haiti, the Dominican Republic, or the other Latin American societies without understanding the lasting effects of this institution. As suggested by the popularity of the Brazilian *telenovelas* (soap operas), Brazilian society is still reverberating from the adoration a rich Brazilian miner showered on Xica da Silva, the mulatto slave woman he called his "African queen." Yet, one of the worst aspects of the process of colonization was enslavement. The Eurocentrism and racism of the European colonizers initially allowed them to see the native peoples as non-Christian pagans who were inferior and, like the rest of what they found, there to be used by the colonizers. Slavery existed in Europe, North Africa, and the Middle East from long before the conquest. From here, the practice of enslaving native people spread to the Americas. Initially, raiding parties were sent out to find slaves to be used for forced labor and thus thousands of the original inhabitants of the Americas were enslaved in the first century of colonization. As the native population was rapidly depleted and as more laws to protect the indigenous population were passed and sometimes enforced by the crown, landowners needed to look elsewhere for exploitable labor. The outlawing of Indian slavery accelerated this process.

As in other areas, slavery was also an institution in Africa, but it was tied to specific functions. It was, for instance, a way of punishing incorrigible criminals in societies that had mores against drawing blood from their own clansmen. Slavery became a recognized institution in Middle Eastern Muslim societies. So it was that there was a growing slave trade in Arab lands and from northern African societies that were conquered by them. Slave traders were soon penetrating farther south into Africa from the area around the Sudan and elsewhere. The proximity of the market for African slaves in the Middle East and North Africa helped to establish the slave trade as an international activity.

In the process of seeking a route to the Far East that did not have to pass through the Muslim-controlled Middle East, the Portuguese began to penetrate farther and farther south along Africa's west coast. Spurred on by advances in navigation that were supported by Prince Henry the Navigator after 1450, they eventually circumnavigated the African continent to establish sea routes to the Indies. As they did this, Portuguese settlements were established all along the African coast and trade was begun. Soon, the Portuguese took over islands off the Atlantic coast (Madeira, Cape Verde Islands). Later, they colonized several of the areas where they had settlements (Angola, Guinea Bissau, and Mozambique).

Stimulated by the strong market for sugar in Europe, Arabs had begun the cultivation of sugarcane in North Africa. Slave labor was used to supply the intense labor needed in the cutting and milling process. When the Portuguese decided to cultivate sugarcane in their Atlantic islands, they copied the Arab use of slave labor. The Portuguese then began to use their outposts in western and southern Africa to capture or buy slaves. When the Portuguese took the cultivation of sugarcane to their colony in Brazil in the 1500s, they also installed a plantation system based on slave labor. As the Dutch, English, and French adopted this crop in their Caribbean possessions, they too relied on a system of slave labor. On arriving in the Americas, the European colonists were faced with tremendous expanses of land available to them. It soon became clear that they needed to find crops and the labor to cultivate them if they were to turn their new possessions into paying propositions. In northern Brazil and the Caribbean, native slavery failed, and the native peoples would not otherwise provide the abundant labor needed. The superutilization of native peoples and their understandable dislike for the European system combined with factors like their rapid depletion by European-borne diseases (particularly in the Caribbean) and their ability to flee farther into the interior of Brazil to minimize the number of available workers. This ensured that the Europeans' voracious appetite for cheap and easily exploitable labor could not be satisfied by the local supply in these areas. The use of indentured servants was also to become part of colonial life, but this source of cheap labor also proved insufficient for the demand. Nor did the well-to-do European landowning elite have any intention of farming the land themselves. They were much more prone to use the labor of others to accumulate their wealth and finance trips to London, Madrid, or Lisbon.

Slaves, then, had initially been acquired by Portuguese and Arab raiding parties and traders. Later, the Portuguese used their trade connections, outposts, and a series of slave forts to buy more and more slaves for the growing market in the Americas. During the first century of the colony, they enjoyed a monopoly on the importation of slaves in the Spanish colonies and Brazil. In this way, the transatlantic slave trade was begun. As the trade in humans grew, England and other countries also engaged in the lucrative business. The triangular trade took guns, rum, metal tools, and whiskey to Africa, where these were traded for slaves. Those who survived the horrendous Middle Passage were in turn sold in the slave markets in Havana and elsewhere and the ships were loaded with tobacco, rum, and indigo for the trip back to Europe. From here the journey began anew. More than 7 million souls were brought to the Portuguese and Spanish colonies in this way.

The African diaspora had a major demographic and cultural impact on all areas of Latin America and the Caribbean, from Mexico to the Bahamas, Martinique, Grenada, Guatemala, Cuba, and Brazil. The arrival of African slaves to the Americas started roughly in 1502. African slaves were imported to substitute for the rapidly diminishing indigenous population. These first groups of slaves came from the slave markets of Spain. The slave markets in Seville, while relatively small, were the most active in Europe during this time. With colonization of the Americas, the demand for slave labor increased dramatically. Europeans were looking to satisfy their labor demands in the New World. After 1519, slaves were taken directly from Africa by European slave ships. The transatlantic slave trade dates from 1519 to

1867; by 1530, the Spanish crown had authorized the spread of slavery to Puerto Rico, Cuba, and Jamaica.

Law and Slavery. Spanish law legitimized the practice and ownership of other persons in the Caribbean and Latin America. The foundation of Spanish jurisprudence acknowledged the legality of the institution of slavery even while declaring it contrary to natural law. These laws protected enslaved persons from serious abuse by their masters and gave them the right to marry, inherit property, and be manumitted. Spanish slave law was developed from Roman slave codes. The French had no slave laws on the books, so they eventually enacted the Code Noir, a 1685 compilation designed to regulate slavery in the French Caribbean. Like Spanish law, the Code Noir accorded the slaves basic rights such as marriage, manumission, and judicial recourse in the case of mistreatment. The British had no tradition of slavery in their land and had no elaborated slave codes to define relations between slave and master. This left the English slaveholders in the Caribbean to their own devices. They developed slave codes that essentially gave all the power to the slave masters.

Comparative Slave Thesis. In the areas of the New World where there were more carefully elaborated slave codes and laws, as in the Spanish colonies, one theory holds that the nature of slavery was more humane or less dehumanizing. The slave—according to the argument—had a legal personality and was recognized by the law. Thus, slaves could learn to read and even buy their freedom. Along with the process of *miscegenation*—the mixing of the races—some scholars believe that the Spanish slave codes created a far different life for slaves.

In contrast to the Spanish-speaking Caribbean, the English had no elaborated slave codes and had to make them up as they went along. Thus, in British slave codes, slaves were not recognized as persons but as property. They were accorded no rights: slaves were strictly forbidden to learn how to read or write and to own property. Moreover, miscegenation was less frequent.

Nonetheless, the massive degradation and exploitation of millions of human beings uprooted from their homes in Africa combined with the treatment of the Native American population imbued the Spanish and Portuguese colonies with a deep-seated racism, institutionalized callousness toward laborers (particularly when they were of color), and a proclivity toward (often brutal) exploitation that remains today.

Not all exploited the indigenous or African population with the same degree of harshness. The settlements that the Jesuits set up in Paraguay and elsewhere were notable exceptions, although they too enforced cultural assimilation of native peoples like the Guaraní. The Spanish and Portuguese crowns did not take kindly to the independent power of the Jesuits in these or other matters. Further, many of the powerful in the colonies resisted and sharply criticized the protective role progressive sectors in the Catholic Church played in regard to Indian rights. The *encomendero* turned priest and Indian advocate Bishop Bartolomé de Las Casas was repeatedly rebuked and threatened. Bishop Antonio Valdivieso was threatened and eventually assassinated for his pro-native stances in the area that is now Nicaragua. The Spanish crown did eventually decree minimal protection for indigenous peoples starting with the Law of Burgos (1512) and outlawed practices like Indian slavery. Compliance took much longer. Nor was the more humane treatment by the Jesuits always accepted. They were expelled from the colonies by the Portuguese in 1757 and the Spanish in 1767. African slavery continued into the nineteenth century in the remaining Spanish colonies in the Caribbean and until 1888 in Brazil. The status of enslaved or horribly exploited Africans did not attract the attention of enlightened Church officials. Even Las Casas recommended the use of African slave labor to free the indigenous people from slavery. Further, given the power and prerogative of local notables and their influence on local public officials, many of the worst practices toward the natives and former slaves continued on long after being outlawed. One could draw parallels between these practices and the way sectors of the old elite in the American South were able to exploit and deny fundamental rights to former slaves and their descendants in rural areas of Mississippi and Louisiana.

The Indian and African slaves and laborers were, it seemed, to be used and exploited (at times to the point of extinction) to achieve the production necessary to enrich the European owners and to funnel wealth and products back to the metropolitan centers of power and wealth in Europe. As pointed out by many observers, the conditions in the mines, workshops, and farms were often horrendous. They were reflective of the callousness of many of the powerful to the condition and suffering of those more lowly than they.

Production, Trade, and Extraction of Riches

The native gold and silver were quickly expropriated and sent back to Spain in fleets of galleons. The crown always got its *quinto real* (royal fifth–20 percent commission). After the existing riches in gold, silver, and gems were depleted by the first conquerors, the Spanish administration began to foster the establishment of durable production of mercantile goods and the introduction of trade in Indian societies that had not yet begun to exchange their products for money. Of primary interest to the mercantilist leadership were precious metals, such as gold and silver, pearls, and precious stones. Where these were not found, the colonial leadership sought to grow commercial goods such as dyes, sugar cane, tobacco, and cocoa. Soon after the conquest, they discovered rich silver mines in Mexico and in Potosí Mountain in the Andes in Upper Peru (Bolivia). The extraction of silver and gold in Mexico and Peru stimulated the colonizers' keen interest in the lands of the former Aztec and Incan empires. In the regions surroundings these centers, the production of food and other necessary supplies began to determine how the land was used. In Chile, the land was used to produce wheat for Spanish bread; in northern Argentina, the land was used to breed cattle, horses, and mules for work in the mines and for hides to make leather. The beef was dried and salted to make *charqui,* jerked meat.

Tremendous amounts of wealth were removed from the colonies in the form of preexisting gold and silver. Next, the conquerors turned to mining, often expending thousands of Indian lives each year to extract the precious metal (as suggested earlier, mining at Potosí is reputed to have consumed as many as 8 million native lives over three centuries). Between 1531 and 1600, over 14,969 meric tons (33 million pounds) of silver were exported back to Spain. By the last quarter of the sixteenth century, silver bullion accounted for about 90 percent of Latin American exports. Some three-fifths came from mines in what is now Peru and Bolivia. The silver mine at Potosí was legendary. The town attracted so many fortune seekers that it was the largest city in Latin America (population 160,000) at the beginning of the seventeenth century.

The silver was extracted by the miners and shipped to Spain in different ways. First, the crown took the *quinto real* of gross production. The other 80 percent stayed in the hands of the mine owners and was used to pay the workforce and for materials, animals for transportation, food, and luxury products for the rich miners. Here, the merchants who worked in the colony itself dominated, as did those who had the exclusive rights to export goods from Spain to the American possessions. This latter group principally resided in the center of Spanish colonial administration in Spain, Seville. Furthermore, the Spanish crown levied taxes on all imported goods. The capacity of the Spanish state to add more and higher taxes on colonial commerce was astonishing. The consequence was that the goods became very expensive because of the excessive taxation imposed by Spain's colonial monopoly.

As a way of ensuring increased consumption of such imported goods, the *repartimiento de mercancias* (distribution of goods) was introduced as a way to tax native Americans who were not or were only marginally incorporated in the market economy. Under this system, the *corregidor* or other local official was able to oblige each household in his charge to buy some Western merchandise at a substantial (and usually highly inflated) price. The colonial official became the monopoly supplier to a captive market.

The high taxes on all imported and exported goods caused considerable discontent among the *criollo* producers and merchants in the colonies, and they were soon ready to evade them by trading with unauthorized merchants from other countries. Their trade was principally with Dutch, British, and French *contrabandistas*. The whole of colonial history is characterized by the efforts of the Spanish authorities to eliminate smuggling by patrolling the coasts, controlling the accounts of the merchants, or forming monopolistic companies such as Guipuzcoana in Venezuela. These efforts never enjoyed much success because smuggled goods were much cheaper than those coming from Spain.

The Church

The Catholic Church was a major political institution in the colony and had responsibility for (Catholic) Christianization and education. In other words, it was in charge of the spiritual conquest of the Americas. It acted as an agent for the crown, incorporating native peoples into the European world and European economy through participation in and payment for baptism and other rites and the still popular street processions celebrating Church holy days and the lives of favorite saints and local madonnas. The Church's power was exercised in concert with the state and utilized to extend European control and influence. Its autonomy was mitigated by the fact that in 1508 Pope Julius II granted the Spanish monarch the *patronato real*—the right to nominate all church officials, collect tithes, and found churches and monasteries in the Spanish Americas. This allowed the state a great deal of control over the Church and helped to fuse the two. Nonetheless, the Church did engage in a variety of different activities, amassed considerable wealth, and was often the largest landowner in different regions of the colony.

The cultural and political evolution of Spanish America was also influenced by an instrument employed to purify the Catholic faith. The Spanish Inquisition persecuted alleged heretics (mostly Jewish and Muslim converts to Christianity) and was in large part responsible for the mass exodus of non-Christians from Spain in the late fifteenth and sixteenth centuries. In 1569, the institution of the Inquisition began in Latin America in Lima and Mexico City. It was charged with investigating signs of heresy. Later, it spread to other Spanish (but not Portuguese) possessions and became a license to search out any deviant or different thinking or innovation. Although indigenous people were exempted from the Inquisition after the 1570s and its victims were relatively few in number, it did have the effect of enforcing a certain heterodoxy in thought and suppressing an unfettered spirit of inquiry. Some have even seen it as the forerunner of the infamous secret police employed by Latin American dictatorships and military governments. Others speculate that the lax enforcement of the Inquisition in the Portuguese territories helps to account for the less constrained approach to thinking and social and business relations that developed in Brazil. The Museum of the Inquisition in downtown Lima attests to the chilling nature of the interrogation and brutality of the instruments of torture employed to induce confessions in Spanish America.

Colonial State Organization

Political power was highly concentrated in colonial governmental structures as well. A *virrey*, or viceking (viceroy), headed the colonial administration, ruling as the king's representative in his designated area. The region was first divided into the Spanish viceroyalties of Nueva España (Mexico, Central America, and the Caribbean), Lima (all the Andean countries, present-day Panama, Argentina, Paraguay, and Uruguay), and the Portuguese viceroyalty of Brazil. Later, the viceroyalties of New Granada (present-day Venezuela, Colombia, and Ecuador) and Río de la Plata (present-day Argentina, Uruguay, and Paraguay) were separated. Unlike the English colonies in North America, there were no representative assemblies in Latin America. Laws and decrees came from the Iberian monarchs or the Council of the Indies in Seville, Spain, and were implemented by colonial authorities from Spain and Portugal. Communication was slow, imprecise, and greatly filtered by the interests of the powerful. The colonists often felt that they were living under orders or laws imposed from afar that did not respond to their needs. This led to one of the most famous dictums during the colony—*Obedezco pero no cumplo;* "I obey but I do not comply." In other words, I will yield to your orders and authority, but you will be hard-pressed to make me carry them out. The colonial elite that emerged amassed considerable wealth and power. They were all too willing to employ both to frustrate laws or decrees they found objectionable or impractical. The large landowners in Brazil were perhaps the most independent, a tradition that continues to the present. In Spanish and Portuguese America, laws like those that protected the native peoples were often unenforceable because of the concerted power of local elites. There was also a fault line between the newly arrived colonists from Spain and Portugal, the *peninsulares*, and the sons and daughters of the earlier arrivals from the Iberian peninsula, the *criollos*. The *criollos* resented the fact that the best positions in the colonial administration and the Church went to the *peninsulares* even though they had just stepped off the boat and did not have the *criollos'* history, family, or wealth in the Americas.

Governmental Organization

The viceroy was indeed the king's representative and could truly rule. Executive, military, and some legislative powers were combined in such a way as to establish the cultural model of the all-powerful executive that has permeated Latin American political (and business) culture to the present day. Captains general were appointed to rule over smaller and usually more distant divisions of the viceroyalties and governed in much the same way. Thus, the captain general of Guatemala ruled Central America (excluding present-day Panama) from his headquarters in Guatemala City but was ostensibly subordinate to the viceroy of New Spain in Mexico City. The captains general in colonial Brazil were given even greater power over their domains and enjoyed greater autonomy from the crown and the viceroy.

The viceroyalties of New Spain and Peru were further subdivided into *audiencias*, or advisory councils, that were presided over by judge-presidents and composed of appointed judges, or *oidores*. They were established in Santo Domingo, Mexico City, Panama, Lima, Guatemala, Guadalajara, Santa Fe, La Plata, Buenos Aires, Quito, Santiago, Cuzco, and Caracas. Beneath the *audiencias* were the governors and at the local level, the notoriously corrupt *corregidores* and mayors (*alcaldes*). At the higher levels of government, the judicial, legislative, and executive functions were mixed, with the viceroys generally also in charge of the military. Functions and powers often overlapped in a system that was designed to encourage mutual suspicion, spying, checking a potential rival's power, and thus the supremacy of the power of the crown. The *cabildo*, or town council (*câmara* in Brazil), was one of the few political structures with any degree of popular participation or democracy. Many councils were all or partly elected and were truly representative of the population. Many others were dominated by powerful and often corrupt political appointees. Offices were, however, frequently sold, and corruption and intense exploitation of the native population were all too often the norm. The official who did not use his office to accumulate a fortune to take back to the Iberian Peninsula might well be considered the exception.

The Bourbon Reforms

Conditions did improve somewhat after the late eighteenth-century Bourbon reforms, but many of the worst practices had by then become ingrained and segments of the population were already chafing under the colonial yoke. This helped lead to the uprisings in the central Andes led by Túpac Amaru II (José Gabriel

Condorcanqui, a *mestizo* descendant of the last Inca, Túpac Amaru, who had also rebelled against Spanish rule) in 1780 and Túpac Katari in 1781, and the revolt of the *comuneros* in New Granada (1781). These uprisings helped set the stage for the independence movement.

Historical Time Line in the Americas

40,000 B.C.E.–8000 B.C.E.   Migration of Asian peoples to North America across the Bering Strait

1500 B.C.E.–1000 C.E.   Mayan civilization develops in the Yucatán Peninsula, Guatemala, and parts of Honduras and El Salvador

1150 B.C.E.–500 C.E.   Olmec culture flourishes in Mesoamerica

1000   Incan culture emerges in the Cuzco Valley of South America

1200   The Aztecs arrive in the central plateau of Mexico

1466   The Aztec emperor Moctezuma Xocoyotzín is born in Mexico

1492   Christopher Columbus arrives at what he called San Salvador Island in the Caribbean and encounters Native American culture

1494   Treaty of Tordesillas is signed by Spain and Portugal, establishing a line of demarcation from pole to pole 370 leagues west of the Cape Verde Islands; Spain receives the right to colonize all territory to the west of that line; Portugal colonizes lands to the east

1500   Pedro Alvares Cabral arrives in Brazil and claims it for Portugal

1508   In Hispaniola, the first sugar mill is constructed

1509   Pope Julius II authorizes the Spanish Catholic monarchs to propagate the Catholic Church in the Americas; *patronato real* gives power to the crown to appoint Church officials

1510   250 slaves are imported to the Americas to work in the gold mines in Hispaniola

1512   The Laws of Burgos are promulgated to protect the Native Americans from the worst ravages of Spanish conquest

1516   Bartolomé de Las Casas is named the official protector of the Indians

1519   Hernán Cortés marches into Tenochtitlán and takes Moctezuma prisoner

1521   Spaniards complete conquest of the Aztec Empire

1521   Conquistador Gil González de Avila converts 30,000 Indians to Christianity in the area called Nicaragua and sends some 500,000 as slaves to other parts of the Spanish Empire

1524   Council of the Indies is established by King Charles V (Holy Roman Emperor Charles V)

1532   Francisco Pizarro invades the Incan Empire, captures and executes Emperor Atahualpa, and conquers the Incas

1538   The first university in the Americas is established: Saint Thomas Aquinas in the city of Santo Domingo

1541   Francisco de Orellana discovers the headwaters of the Amazon River in what is now Ecuador

1542   The New Laws of the Indies are issued by Spain, officially eliminating the *encomienda*

1551 In Mexico and Lima, new universities are created

1554 Araucan Indian chief Caupolican, allied with Chief Lautaro, defeats Spaniards, kills Pedro de Valdivia, and defeats the forces of Francisco de Villagrá of Chile

1739–1780s Bourbon Reforms

1767 King Charles III expels the Jesuits from the Spanish Empire

1780 Incan descendant Túpac Amaru II leads a two-year rebellion against authorities on behalf of the Indians

1781 Túpac Katari leads rebellion in what is now Bolivia and besieges La Paz in 1781

1781 *Comunero* revolt in New Granada

Bibliography

Adelman, Jeremy. *Colonial Legacies: The Problem of Persistence in Latin American History*. New York: Routledge, 1999.

Bakewell, Peter. *A History of Latin American Empires and Sequels, 1450–1930*. Oxford: Blackwell Publishers, 1997.

Burkholder, Mark A., and Lyman L. Johnson. *Colonial Latin America*. 5th ed. New York: Oxford University Press, 2004.

Conniff, Michael, and Thomas Davis. *Africans in the Americas: A History of the Black Diaspora*. New York: St. Martin's Press, 1994.

Chasteen, John C. *Born in Blood and Fire: A Concise History of Latin America*. 2nd ed. New York: W.W. Norton, 2006.

Davis, Darien, ed. *Slavery and Beyond: The African Impact on Latin America and the Caribbean* (Jaguar Books on Latin America, 5). Wilmington, DE: Scholarly Resources, 1995.

Fagan, Brian. *Kingdoms of Gold, Kingdoms of Jade: The Americas Before Columbus*. London: Thames and Hudson, 1991.

Keen, Benjamin. *A History of Latin America*. 7th ed. Boston: Houghton Mifflin, 2004.

Kicza, John E., ed. *The Indian in Latin American History: Resistance, Resilience and Acculturation*. Wilmington, DE: Scholarly Resources, 1993.

Leon-Portilla, Miguel, ed. *The Broken Spears: The Aztec Account of the Conquest of Mexico*. Translated by Lysander Kemp. Boston: Beacon Press, 1992.

Newson, Linda. "The Latin American Colonial Experience." In *Latin American Development: Geographical Perspectives*, edited by David Preston, 2nd ed. Harlow, UK: Longman, 1996.

Ohaegbulam, Festus U. *Toward an Understanding of the African Experience from Historical and Contemporary Perspectives*. Lunham, MD: University Press of America, 1990.

Rosenberg, Mark B., A. Douglas Kincaid, and Kathleen Logan, eds. *Americas, An Anthology*. New York: Oxford University Press, 1992.

Schele, Linda, and David Freidel. *A Forest of Kings: The Untold Story of the Ancient Maya*. New York: William Morrow, 1990.

Smith, Carol. *Guatemalan Indians and the State: 1540 to 1988*. Austin: University of Texas Press, 1990.

Soustelle, Jacques. *Daily Life of the Aztecs, on the Eve of the Spanish Conquest*. Stanford, CA: Stanford University Press, 1970.

Stavig, Ward. *The World of Túpac Amaru: Conflict, Community, and Identity in Colonial Peru*. Lincoln: University of Nebraska Press, 1999.

FILMS AND VIDEOS

The Buried Mirror. Reflections of Spain in the New World. Part Two: The Conflict of the Gods. United States, 1991. Video version of Carlos Fuentes' insightful commentary on the indigenous world conquered by Spain and the transposition of the new belief system.

The Mission. United States, 1986. An excellent feature-length film starring Robert De Niro; graphically depicts the colonization process among indigenous peoples above the Iguassú Falls in southern Brazil.

Popol Vuh. United States, 1991. An animated video that portrays the creation myth of the Maya.

Prayer of Viracocha. United States. A beautifully animated indigenous lament to the Incan god Viracocha at the time of the conquest.

Quetzalcóatl. United States, 1951. A vision of the Mesoamerican winged serpent god.

The Spanish Conquest of Mexico. United States, 1999. Tells the story of how the Aztec empire was conquered.

Sword and Cross. United States, 1991. Tells the story of the conquest.

Xica. Brazil, 1976. The embellished story of Xica da Silva.

THREE

DEMOCRACY, DICTATORS, AND TÍO SAM

A Historical Overview from Independence to the Present Day

▨

Independence

The independence movements that created most of the nation-states that currently make up Latin America developed during the first twenty-five years of the nineteenth century as the result of events occurring in both Europe and Latin America. Haiti became an independent republic in 1804, and most of the other Latin American states achieved their independence by the early 1820s. The local elites succeeded in transferring political power into their own hands outside the control of Madrid or Lisbon. However, the underlying systems of social and economic power inherited from the colonial era remained largely intact. Further, the authoritarian tradition inherited from Spanish and Portuguese colonialism was very much in place and would plague Latin America into the twenty-first century. There was a continual and generally unresolved tension between authoritarian rule learned from years of heavy-handed, top-down colonial (and often precolonial) practice, on the one hand, and the democratic ideals and inspiration that the independence movements chose to rely on to explain and set up the state structures in the independent nations, on the other. Nonetheless, the end of direct colonialism did initiate a nation-building process that would eventually modernize governmental structures and bring Latin America closer to the world economic system. The political change also produced a legitimacy crisis that led to nearly a century of political struggle and the eventual hegemony of liberalism. These more profound changes for the Americas began in the last twenty-five years of the nineteenth century, when the region's long-standing social and economic structures were challenged by the arrival of the industrial revolution and market capitalism. These forces eventually weakened the traditional elites and laid the groundwork for the political struggles of the twentieth century.

To better understand the independence movements of the early nineteenth century in Latin America, it is necessary to look to Europe. By the beginning of the eighteenth century, the Spanish Empire was already well into a decline that proved to be permanent. However, as was suggested in the last chapter, the Bourbon monarchs of Spain, whose family had assumed the crown in 1713, had embarked on a series of political and economic reforms in their American colonies that they hoped would solidify that rule. In reality, these reforms contributed to the eventual triumph of the independence movements. Inspired by Enlightenment political and economic thought, the Bourbons sought to reform the existing overlapping systems of authority by centralizing political power. They created new administrative units in New Granada (1717) and Buenos Aires (1776). More importantly, Charles III, who ruled from 1759 to 1788, established a new administrative system that resulted in the appointment of local governors by the crown in Madrid. These rulers, called "intendants," were almost all Spanish-born rather than American *criollos*. This approach marginally solidified the hold of the monarchy over the colonies but brought the crown into more direct conflict with the local *criollo* elites, who had prospered under the previous system of less intrusive rule from Madrid. In one significant example, the monarchy sharply reduced *criollo* control of the administrative and court system, which it had originally established in the late seventeenth century by purchasing judgeships. Charles III also strengthened his hand by taking greater control of the Church. In his boldest move, he expelled the Jesuits from all Spanish colonies in 1767. Charles saw the Jesuits as an independent power base, so he removed them and profited from the sale of their lands. The Spanish crown also engaged in economic reform that freed the various ports of the empire to trade with other ports in Spanish America and in Spain itself. Illegal trade had long flourished on the forbidden routes, with most of the profits staying within the Americas; but now the Spanish crown was gaining a greater share of the wealth through the collection of customs duties. These economic reforms resulted in a more prosperous colonial economy, where new ports such as Buenos Aires flourished; but their most important long-term effect was the resentment generated among *criollos*, who saw the moves as a plot to undermine their status and power. This resentment, more than any other factor, fueled the independence movements of the early nineteenth century.

Ironically, another reform instituted by the Spanish crown unwittingly aided the cause of American independence. During the eighteenth century, the monarchy had authorized the creation of colonial militias as a protection against feared British and French invasions; by 1800, 80 percent of the soldiers serving in Spanish America were American-born. A military career was one of the few remaining avenues of advancement for socially ambitious *criollos*. These forces provided the core of the local forces that would later fight for independence.

THE FRENCH REVOLUTION, LOCAL UPRISINGS, AND INDEPENDENCE

Events in Europe determined the timing of the independence movement. The French Revolution of 1789 launched ideas of freedom and equality throughout the French Empire, and cries of *liberté*, *égalité*, and *fraternité* fell on receptive ears among the slave population in Haiti. In 1791, a slave uprising was led by Toussaint L'Ouverture, an extremely able, self-educated freed slave. After a series of successful battles against opposition forces that included a formidable contingent of Napoleon's army in 1802, the popular forces triumphed. Haiti gained its independence from France in 1804 and thus became the first independent Latin American nation. In other parts of Latin America, a few, like the Afro-Venezuelan José Leonardo Chirinos, even spoke of proclaiming a republic of the "law of the French" in 1795. Meanwhile, the Spanish monarchy had tried to save its Bourbon counterparts during the French Revolution in 1789; but having failed that, Spain allied itself with Napoleon Bonaparte in 1796. However, in 1808, Napoleon turned on his Spanish allies and occupied Madrid, placing his brother Joseph on the Spanish throne. This act by Napoleon was the catalyst for rebellion in Spain and the Americas that would eventually lead to independence for most of Spanish America. Some historians do argue, however, that the resistance of indigenous peoples in the latter part of the eighteenth century was the real catalyst. As noted in the last chapter, in 1780, Túpac Amaru II, claiming lineage from the ancient Incan Empire, led a revolt that mobilized more than 80,000 mostly indigenous fighters and lasted for two years in southern Peru and Bolivia before it was defeated by the Spanish army. The struggle was joined by Túpac Katari in Upper Peru (now Bolivia) in 1781. There was also a popular revolt of the *comuneros* in New Granada in 1781. These movements are important in the history of indigenous struggles and popular uprisings but may be better understood outside the context of the independence movements. With radical demands for land reform and indigenous rights, the political thrust of these movements was not supported by the *criollo* independence leaders of the early nineteenth century. In fact, the Peruvian rebellions and the later rebellion in Mexico led by Father Hidalgo in 1810 frightened the *criollos* into making common cause with the Spanish-born elites and delayed independence in both Mexico and Peru. It also meant that, outside of Haiti, rebellions against colonial rule by the masses (who were predominantly people of color) did not triumph.

The *criollos*, born in America, increasingly longed to wrest political power from the *peninsulares*. In the late eighteenth century, the *criollos* began to look outward for guidance, increasingly to France. As a result, the French Revolution had more impact than the American Revolution. As suggested earlier, the most dramatic example of the influence in Latin America was in Haiti. Of course, the majority of creoles were not Jacobin revolutionaries. They wanted to reform the local political systems to give themselves power, but they were in no way interested in revolution or in giving all the power to the common people. Napoleon's invasion of Spain in 1808 provided that opportunity.

In the wake of the Napoleonic invasion, the Spanish king, Ferdinand VII, was imprisoned and the Braganzas, Portugal's royal family, escaped to Rio de Janeiro. The Brazilians received their royal family warmly and celebrated their extended stay in Rio de Janeiro. In contrast, the initial instincts of Spanish Americans were to pledge loyalty to Ferdinand; but fairly quickly, the creole elites began to realize their own power, and by 1810 the creoles had moved from tentative autonomy to open declarations of independence. However, despite the fortuitous circumstances for independence, the events that followed did not easily lead to independence for most of Latin America during the ensuing twenty-five years. Nor did the newly formed United States Republic assist in the struggles for independence.

ARGENTINA, 1806–1810

One of the earliest examples of the capacity of resistance by the local population came in Buenos Aires. In 1806, the British occupied the city, forcing the viceroy to flee to Córdoba. The British, however, were driven out by a locally organized citizens' army, which also successfully defended against a counterattack in 1807. This local action independent of Madrid set a powerful example for future actions. The viceroyalty of Buenos Aires was also able to negotiate a better deal in the arena of free trade after the expulsion of the British forces. Ironically, it involved the desire of the local commercial elite to trade directly with the British, who provided the most promising market for their growing production of hides and salted beef. In 1809, Spain granted Buenos Aires limited freedom of trade with nations allied to Spain or neutral in the Napoleonic Wars. This agreement helped to strengthen the self-confidence of the local elites.

Early Drive for Independence in Hispanic America

The first phase of the Spanish American independence movements occurred between 1810 and 1814. In 1810, Napoleon's forces completed their victory over the Bourbons and established a liberal constitution for Spain; but in 1814, Ferdinand VII returned to the Spanish throne and annulled the liberal constitution of 1812. In 1810, Argentine local elites came together to create a provisional government of the provinces of the Río de la Plata. Prior to their declaration of independence of 1816, these local elites pledged their allegiance to Ferdinand VII; but the pattern of local initiative, first shown in the rebellions against the British, was institutionalized.

Venezuela was the scene of a movement similar to that in Buenos Aires. In Caracas, a local council expelled the Spanish governors and organized a new government under Ferdinand VII. The best-known of the leaders was Simón Bolívar. Born into a wealthy Caracas family and tutored by the great Latin American liberal thinker Simón Rodríguez, Bolívar was educated in Spain and came in contact with the ideas of the Enlightenment (especially Rousseau and romanticism). In 1805, he committed himself to the independence of his homeland. In 1811, the local Caracas authorities, under his influence, declared Venezuela's independence. After an initial series of military defeats, the exiled Bolívar returned to Venezuela and defeated the Spanish army in a series of exceptional military victories, earning him the title *El Libertador* (The Liberator).

In the provinces of New Spain (Mexico), this time period also saw exceptional developments. By 1810, a group of *criollos*, including a priest named Miguel Hidalgo, began plotting to seize authority in the name of Ferdinand. When the plot was discovered by the Spanish authorities, Hidalgo led a popular uprising centered in the village of Dolores, thus the famous *grito de Dolores*. A powerful response came not from the local elites but rather from the impoverished *mestizos* and indigenous people. Uniting under the banner of the long-adored dark-skinned Virgin of Guadalupe, they comprised a fighting force of 50,000. In a decision whose motivation has been debated ever since, Hidalgo turned away from a probable victory over the Spanish authorities in Mexico City and moved to the north. In 1811, his army was defeated near Guadalajara, leading to his capture and execution.

Following Hidalgo's death, leadership of the independence forces was taken by José María Morelos, another priest even more strongly committed to radical social reform, including the end of slavery. A republican, Morelos believed that the whole population should participate in political affairs. In 1813, the Congress of Chilpancingo declared Mexico's independence from Spain and decreed that slavery should be abolished. The congress's liberal constitution of 1814 created a system of indirect elections and a powerful legislature. However, it was never enacted because Morelos's guerrilla army did not control enough territory to seriously threaten Spanish authority.

In 1814, Napoleon's defeat restored Ferdinand VII to power in Spain. The colonial authorities used this fortuitous event—along with military reinforcements—to regain control in the face of the developing independence movements. Ferdinand annulled the liberal Spanish constitution of 1812 and reestablished himself as an absolute ruler. The king's return divided *criollo* leaders, with many concluding that there was no reason to continue their rebellions. By 1816, with the exception of Buenos Aires, Spanish rule had been reestablished throughout the empire. In Venezuela, even the victorious Bolívar saw his support significantly reduced; he was forced into exile on the English island of Jamaica. The independence movement in New Spain also suffered serious setbacks. In 1815, Morelos was captured,

Símon Bolívar, El Libertador, 1783–1830. *(The Art Archive)*

tried, and executed as the Spanish military commanders regained the upper hand and blocked implementation of the liberal constitution that had been enacted the previous year. Only the government in Río de la Plata survived the reconquest. It struggled to survive and had not yet become a full-blown independence movement.

The Spanish reconquest was short-lived. In 1816, Bolívar returned to Venezuela from his exile on Jamaica and launched a new campaign for the independence of his country. His new ally was José Antonio Páez, the leader of the *llaneros* (cowboys) who had fought alongside the royalists during the previous struggles. In 1819, Bolívar mounted an army of 4,000 and succeeded in defeating the Spanish and their royalist collaborators. Meanwhile in the south, José de San Martín initiated a significant military campaign. San Martín, the son of a Spanish military officer, entered the service at age eleven. In 1812, he offered his services to the junta in Buenos Aires. Over the next five years, he developed the rebel forces into an army and then led 5,000 soldiers across the Andes in a surprise attack on the loyalist forces in Chile. The Spaniards were defeated in the battle of Chacabuco, and San Martín entered Santiago triumphantly. San Martín's next target was the liberation of Peru; in 1820, he prepared for an attack on Lima, the capital of the viceroyalty. He faced a city where monarchist sentiment was quite strong. Both the *criollos* and the *peninsulares* favored the continuation of Ferdinand's rule. Wary of a defeat, San Martín withheld his attack. At that point, decisive events in Spain again intervened. Ferdinand reversed his political course and abruptly embraced the previously annulled Spanish liberal constitution of 1812. Monarchists throughout Spanish America were shocked by the turnabout, which abolished the Inquisition, thus unacceptably weakening the power of the Church. The changes in Spain suddenly altered the climate for independence in both Lima and Mexico City, where the monarchists held sway. The monarchists now viewed independence as a means of preserving the status quo, which would uphold traditional values and social codes. As a result of this sudden change of perspective, in 1821 the municipal council of Lima invited San Martín to enter the city; on July 28, he formally proclaimed the independence of Peru. Meanwhile in the north, Bolívar, after defeating the Spanish forces in New Granada, attempted to create a new state of Gran Colombia, uniting Venezuela, New Granada, and Ecuador under republican principles. This effort received little support, so Bolívar moved south, hoping to confront and defeat more of the royalist forces as he sought to achieve his vision of a united continent independent of colonial control and organized along republican principles.

Antonio José de Sucre was sent by Bolívar to liberate Ecuador. Sucre led the combined Ecuadorian, Colombian, and Venezuelan forces against the Spanish and finally defeated them in the battle of Pichincha in 1822. In Ecuador, Bolívar met with San Martín and declared that they were "the two greatest men in America." Personal and political differences, however, precluded the consummation of an alliance. Bolívar rejected San Martín's proposal for a monarchy in Peru and San Martín's offer for Bolívar to serve under his command. Further, Bolívar's plans for the union of Gran Colombia were rejected by San Martín. Disillusioned and unwilling to split the revolutionary forces, San Martín soon after resigned his post and retired to France, where he died in 1850. However, even San Martín's departure did not slow the independence movement. In late 1823, Bolívar's forces confronted the large Spanish force that had retreated inland from Lima; and a year later, the royalists were defeated decisively at the battle of Ayachucho, effectively ending three centuries of Spanish rule in the Americas. In 1825, Bolívar entered Upper Peru to press the idea that the two Perus should form a single nation. The leaders of Upper Peru, however, having already struck an independent course, declared their own republic and named it Bolivia in honor of Bolívar. Over the next five years Bolívar tried unsuccessfully to promote his idea of political union. His ideas were resisted by the local elites, including some of his own lieutenants, who feared the reinstatement of centralized control. In 1826, Bolívar tried to implement his vision of a united Spanish America by convening the Congress of Panama. His efforts were not successful, and in 1830, the Liberator died a bitter man who failed to achieve a united Latin America and saw many of his democratic dreams languish. Toward the end of his life he concluded that he and the other independence leaders "had plowed the sea."

Simultaneous to these events in South America, the conservative independence movement went forward in Mexico. The royal government was disintegrating; Agustín de Iturbide, the creole commander of the army in Mexico, seized the moment to declare Mexican independence with little bloodshed on September 28, 1821. Only the Spanish garrison in Veracruz held out against Iturbide's proclamation. It was a conservative revolt that even many Spaniards supported. The new regime was marked by three conservative principles: constitutional monarchy, official Catholicism, and equality of *peninsulares* and *criollos*. Iturbide had himself proclaimed emperor only when "no suitable European monarch could be found." Central America, with its traditional strong ties to Mexico, followed suit and declared its independence from Spain in 1821. In 1822, the Central American landowners, fearing liberal dominance in Spain, transferred their loyalty to royalist Mexico. However, the Mexican monarchy lasted only two years. In 1823, when Iturbide abdicated, the modern-day Central American states from Guatemala to Costa Rica became the Independent United Provinces of Central America. With the independence of Mexico and Central America, Spanish control in the Western Hemisphere was reduced to Cuba and Puerto Rico.

Brazilian Independence

Brazilian independence was achieved in a manner very different from that of Spanish America. The differences were rooted in the character of the Brazilian state and economy and in the special role played by Britain in the context of the Napoleonic Wars. When the Napoleonic army invaded Portugal in 1807, the entire royal family was able to flee to Brazil with the assistance of the British navy. The royal family ended Portugal's commercial monopoly by opening Brazil's ports. Soon after 1810, Britain gained privileged access to Brazil through low tariffs, a commitment to the gradual end of the African slave trade, and extraterritorial privileges for British citizens living in Brazil.

When Napoleon was decisively defeated, the Portuguese monarchy was free to return to Lisbon; initially, they did not, and instead Dom João proclaimed Brazil to be a coequal kingdom with the same rank as Portugal. Dom João, however, did eventually return to Lisbon and left his son Dom Pedro behind with the prerogative to declare Brazil independent. The new king declared independence on September 7, 1822, with the full support of the Brazilian elites and with only token resistance from a few Portuguese garrisons. In sharp contrast to much of Spanish America, independence was achieved in Brazil without significant bloodshed and without the development of a strong military caste. The nation also remained united despite some small-scale regional revolts. Furthermore, Brazil did not see a strong republican/monarchist split because the overwhelming majority of the local elite sided with monarchism. Brazilian sugar barons were dependent on the slave trade and thus on the monarchy, which lasted only a year beyond the abolition of slavery in 1888.

Early Years of Independence

Thus, the Latin American nations became independent of European rule. It was, however, a much longer struggle to liberate themselves from their inherited political and cultural traditions. Foremost among these was the authoritarian proclivity that was strongly ingrained in political culture. For instance, Bolívar, the great liberator, frustrated with regionalism and the assertion of political autonomy by various leaders in the Republic of Gran Colombia, often forsook formal democracy and reverted to dictatorial rule in order to hold the republic together. Much of the early history of the republics was filled with such local and national *caudillos*—by men on white horses. An even more telling example is that of Dr. Francia. Soon after independence in Paraguay, the then-leader of the country, Dr. José Gaspar Rodríguez de Francia, proclaimed himself dictator in perpetuity. His rule from 1816 to 1840 set a pattern for extended dictatorial rule that would continue to plague Paraguay until 1989. This and similar traditions of extended authoritarian rule continued to haunt many other Latin American countries through the nineteenth and twentieth centuries. Indeed, authoritarian rule would predominate in Paraguay, Bolivia, and Haiti through the nineteenth and twentieth centuries. The military-style leaders would dominate the period up until the 1850s in most countries, including Mexico, Argentina, and Peru. The seeds of democracy had been planted, but the early years of republican history seemed to justify Bolívar's previously noted conclusion that "we have plowed the sea."

The Aftermath of Independence and the Monroe Doctrine

The aftermath of independence was a difficult time for most of Latin America. The newly independent nations faced terrible obstacles as they sought to move forward economically, politically, and socially. The consolidation of national rule was even more difficult than in the United States, which in light of its defeat by Great Britain in the War of 1812, limited its initial contacts with Latin America and formulated the still controversial Monroe Doctrine in 1823. Enunciated by John Quincy Adams, it was primarily designed to preclude continued European interference in independent Latin America and stop any reimposition of colonial rule in the hemisphere.

Within the Latin American nations, it was a considerable struggle to establish national control and move beyond the regionalism that was so strong in most of the nations. Further, politics were generally dominated by the upper-class landowning elite, whose concept of democracy was quite limited. With the primary exception of Brazil, the new leaders took over power in the context of the physical devastation brought by the wars for independence. Devastation was particularly heavy in Mexico and Venezuela, but everywhere the burden of supporting the large armies of liberation was significant. Economic activity was also greatly affected by the continuous wars. Trade had almost ceased during the period. Trade with Spain ceased, of course; but inter-American trade was also adversely affected. Communication almost completely collapsed among the new countries. The economies of the newly independent countries also faced challenges related to their very nature. Based almost exclusively on mining and agriculture, the colonies had been marginally integrated into the world economy before independence; but they now faced new challenges not based on their previous colonial commitments. The failure to achieve political unity meant that each new country faced the challenge of creating its own national economy. There were also regional differences; Mexico had a fairly well-developed national economy, but most of the other countries did not. As countries sought to develop themselves, they often faced internal divisions as well as interference from outside political and economic influences. Most new regimes lacked the financial assets even to equip a national army, let alone embark on significant national economic development. Mechanisms for tax collection and other standard methods of revenue collection were simply not sophisticated enough to meet the new nations' considerable needs. As a result, many countries, including Mexico and Argentina, turned to loans from foreign banks as a way out of their crises. Foreign governments, especially Britain, eagerly provided money in hope of significant returns. These loans, made more than 150 years ago, began a dependence on external finance and external actors that has persisted to the present day.

The era of free trade was also launched during this time period, as Latin America slowly adapted itself to the world economy. Exports to the United States and Europe began to increase—nitrates from Chile, hides and salted beef from Argentina, sugar from Cuba, and sugar from Brazil. The growth in exports was also accompanied by a corresponding rise in manufactured imports, especially textiles. Latin American artisans and small producers were often driven out of business in the exchange. This time also saw the arrival of a small number of foreign merchants who took up key positions in the fields of shipping, insurance, and banking. The pattern of losing out to foreign competitors was primarily the result of the technological superiority of the Europeans, but the local elites exacerbated the problem with misguided political choices. The traditional landowning elites first ensured that their holdings were secure and then retreated to the security of their *haciendas* and *fazendas,* not particularly concerned about maximizing production or contributing to the economic modernization of their countries. Political power was left largely in the hands of military men who had become *caudillos,* among them Juan Manuel de Rosas, the governor of Buenos Aires province; Antonio López de Santa Anna, the president of Mexico; and a lieutenant of Bolívar, José Antonio Páez. These military governments, without significant streams of revenue, were vulnerable to being overthrown and incapable of sustaining local economic growth. Some leaders recognized the dangers inherent in a weak central state, so in many countries conflict developed between locally based power brokers and the centralizers. These struggles were to be the forerunners of later battles for political power between conservatives and liberals.

One group negatively affected by independence was the indigenous peoples. They had not been a consistent force for elite-led independence and therefore were not seen by the new governments as important allies. As a result, they lost whatever protections they may have had under colonial administrations. Their land became increasingly vulnerable to takeover and their condition even more impoverished.

Enter the United States

By the mid-nineteenth century the United States, often motivated by the doctrine of Manifest Destiny, began to expand its economic and political power into Latin America. Cornelius Vanderbilt established a transisthmus transportation route through Nicaragua. U.S. nationals flocked to the Mexican territory of Texas and soon pushed for independence from Mexico. Subsequent tensions with Mexico under Santa Anna's rule led to broader conflicts and the Mexican-American War of 1846–1848. Further, this conflict reestablished a pattern of foreign intervention in Latin America and cost Mexico nearly half its national territory.

1850–1880

The second stage of Latin America's integration into the world economy occurred between 1850 and 1880. National unification became the political theme as local *caudillo* rulers were slowly supplanted by national leaders, who began to construct the apparatus of the modern state. Liberal reform leaders like Benito Juárez in Mexico, Domingo Sarmiento in Argentina, and Justo Rufino Barrios in Guatemala appeared.

As Latin American nations were ever more integrated into the commercialized world economy, liberal political (and economic) reforms and modernization that began in the 1850s continued. The epic Argentine struggle between the rural *gaucho* and remaining Indians, on the one hand, and the Europeanized *porteño* (port) elite from Buenos Aires, on the other, was indicative of this trend. The 1853 defeat of the *gaucho* dictator Juan Manuel de Rosas by reformist forces ushered in a new regime that opted for the "civilizing" influence of the port city over the rural landowners, the *estanciaros*. The government and economy were modernized, and massive European immigration (mostly from Italy) began. European capital, science, and technology were injected into the development process. Liberal reforms set the stage for the emergence of other sectors in Argentine society. The meat-packing and grain-exporting industries gradually facilitated the emergence of an industrial proletariat and the beginning of a middle class. Argentina became ever more closely tied to England through the sale of its beef and the influx of British investment.

Meanwhile, peasants were beginning to feel the squeeze as their countries were further incorporated into the world market. Economic pressures and social upheaval

Benito Juárez, The Great Reformer, 1806–1872. *(Photo by Gianni Dagli Orti/The Art Archive)*

fomented political restructuring as well. As a result, the region began to witness the emergence of reformist parties like the Radical Civic Union in Argentina, which held sway for most of the second and third decades of the twentieth century.

Periods of democratic rule began to appear, and political participation and the franchise were slowly widened beyond the elite to include common people in most countries. The transformation was in part driven by the slow rise of Latin America's export trade and the need to have a national infrastructure to support such trade. This era saw the beginning of efforts by national governments to transform long-standing land tenure arrangements that were dominated by largely unproductive *latifundios* and government land. This was the era of liberal ascendency almost everywhere in Latin America. During this period, there were significant efforts to undermine Church authority and establish secular, public education. Liberal ideas also made their way into the prison system and even military organizations. All of these liberal reforms and this nation building occurred in the context of the penetration of North American and European capital.

To transport the region's coffee, sugar, nitrates, and other primary products to Europe and elsewhere, there was a strong need to replace the region's antiquated transportation system with new roads, canals, railroads, and docks. The traditional landowning elites had no need for infrastructure development to prosper, so they had not built it and were indifferent to its construction. The impetus for such development came primarily from abroad. European industrialization created a great thirst for everything from foodstuffs to fertilizers to metals. The developing European industries also sought out new markets for their manufactured goods. These twin European needs laid the groundwork for the next phase of Latin American development. Latin American countries willing to do business with Europe gained rising political power and wealth that challenged the traditional elites. However, the character of this economic arrangement—Latin American primary goods traded for European finished goods—established the pattern of Latin America's role in the world economy that persists to this day. The countries saw very little growth of domestic industry as European producers of machinery, weapons, and other light manufactured goods often blocked the development of indigenous industries. Competing with European entrepreneurs would have been difficult given their head start in technology; nor were Latin American governments of the time inclined to set up tariff barriers to spur local development. Generally, they were more than happy to welcome unrestricted foreign trade in return for their share of the profits. The era of 1850–1880 was one of laying the groundwork for even more dramatic changes that would occur in the last twenty years of the nineteenth century.

1880–1910

The needs of European industrialization that had been developing slowly throughout the nineteenth century came to a head after 1880. The demands for food by Europe's industrial workers and for raw materials to fuel factories were insatiable. Several key Latin American countries were transformed by these demands. Argentina became a great producer of beef, wool, and wheat. Brazil and El Salvador became the world's primary producers of coffee, satisfying Europe's newfound addiction, with Peru, Mexico, and Cuba supplying the sugar. Mexico provided Europe and North America with a variety of raw materials, including hemp, copper, and zinc. Thus, the pattern established in earlier decades of Latin American countries producing primary goods in exchange for European manufactured goods was deepened.

European countries also invested in Latin America. During this period Britain was by far the dominant investor, with almost two-thirds of the total investment by 1913. Railroads and mining were the two key sectors into which Europeans and North Americans placed their money. American investment also began to increase dramatically after 1900. Only modest amounts of Latin American capital went into these sectors, so the pattern of economic control by foreign powers became well established. Thus, Latin American prosperity became increasingly tied to the health of the European and North American economies. It also meant that most of the key decisions about the economic direction of Latin America were not being made in Rio de Janeiro or Buenos Aires but rather in New York, London, and Paris.

The new economic reality was justified and validated by the growing predominance of liberal ideology in most parts of Latin America. Free-trade political liberals who favored less centralized state rule formed liberal parties, while traditional agricultural interests and pro-Church conservatives formed conservative parties.

Local political leaders and their foreign counterparts extolled the virtues of free trade and open borders. It was viewed as simply "unnatural" to stand in the way of the economic and social progress that such arrangements were supposed to bring. Even the traditional landed elites in large measure cooperated in the modernization process, providing generous concessions to foreign companies while relying on traditional labor practices. To local governments it seemed only logical to collect some revenue from commercial trade, which during colonial times had flourished illegally outside their control. Of course, it was only a tiny slice (less than 5 percent) of the populations that benefited from these free-trade agreements. Local elites, who viewed the native populations as significantly inferior, excluded them systematically from national political life. Democracy developed slowly. Where elections were held in Latin America in the nineteenth century, less than 10 percent of the population was eligible to vote through most of these years. Most of the countries were organized as republics, but it was in form only. Political participation was limited to segments of the elite, democracy was weak, and popular participation was weaker.

Elitist domination of politics persisted through the end of the nineteenth century but in a different form. The dominance of the local *caudillo* was over. National governments were now dominant, epitomized in the Porfirio Díaz regime in Mexico (1876–1880 and 1884–1911). In some ways, leaders like Díaz were mirror images of the local *caudillo*. Usually military men, they were no longer doing the bidding of a local *hacienda* owner. Instead, they were representing the interests of commercial farmers and merchants whose economic success was predicated on foreign trade and a national infrastructure. To achieve the national power they needed, local authorities had to be put in line, a process that was consummated in Argentina and Mexico during this period. All such national regimes had a law-and-order focus designed to achieve political stability and therefore attract foreign investment.

The turn of the twentieth century saw the beginning of the consolidation of the modern nation-state in Latin America. As suggested earlier, this process had begun with liberal reforms in Mexico under Benito Júarez in the 1850s by Bartolomé Mitre and Domingo Faustino Sarmiento (1862–1874) in Argentina, and Justo Rufino Barrios (1871–1885) in Guatemala. In each country, the consolidation of power by newly emerging commercial elites was tied to increasing trade with the industrialized world. This movement of power away from more traditionally oriented elites would continue in the region through the 1940s.

Late-nineteenth-century Brazil and Mexico saw the strong influence of developmental thought associated with Auguste Comte's philosophical positivism. Indeed, it was positivism that inspired the modernization of the Brazilian state and the foundation of the Brazilian republic in 1889. Thus, the new elites in both of these countries began to rely on science and technology and tried to organize their societies to conform to the scientific law of progress. Following the advice of his positivist scientific advisors, or *científicos*, Díaz consolidated the commercial integration of Mexico into the world economy and was responsible for the massive foreign investment and improved infrastructure that characterized his rule. As with elite-run regimes in virtually all Latin American countries save Argentina, these new regimes did little to enfranchise the peasant and laboring masses economically (or politically). Indeed, the economic conditions of the common people had changed little since independence, and conditions that favored the emergence of a substantial middle class developed at a slow pace.

Early U.S. Involvement: *Tío* Sam and the Gringos

As a young republic suspicious of European ambitions for the region, the United States enunciated the Monroe Doctrine, mentioned earlier, in 1823 as a way to foreclose continuing intervention by the European powers in the hemisphere. From the earliest years, U.S.–Latin American relations were made more difficult by a commonly held view that U.S politicians and U.S. citizens were politically and economically, if not morally, more developed than the sister republics and their citizens to the south. Indeed, questions were at times raised as to Latin Americans' fitness for stable government. By the mid-nineteenth century, some in the United States had designs on parts of Latin America. In this context, the Mexican-American War (1846–1848) marked the beginning of a period of more direct U.S. involvement. Indeed, the term *gringo* is reputed to have been a by-product of the war. As the story goes, it resulted from a group of Mexicans overhearing the U.S. soldiers singing a song of the time that repeated the phrase "green grows." Thus, the Mexicans began to refer to the Americans as "green grows" or *gringos*. Needless to say, after losing the war and half their territory, the Mexicans did not always think well of their *gringo* neighbors. The way the term spread and the slightly pejorative connotation usually attached suggested that Latin Americans would not always value the involvement of their North American neighbor. However, *Tío* Sam maintained economic and political interest in the region. By the last decade of the century, the **Pan-American Union** was formed (1890) as a mechanism to facilitate commercial and other interactions between the United States and the Latin American states. The nineteenth century ended with U.S. involvement in Cuba (1898). The twentieth century would see increasing U.S. intervention in Latin American affairs as the United States aided the residents of Panama to become independent from Colombia in 1903 and then constructed a canal there. Although no longer interested in Nicaragua as the preferred location for a transoceanic canal, U.S. involvement continued with a Marine incursion in 1909. The Mexican Revolution prompted renewed involvement in Mexico, such as the naval bombardment of Vera Cruz in 1914. Theodore Roosevelt's **"big stick"** became legendary in the Caribbean basin, as did **"gunboat diplomacy."** As financial interests intensified, these more primitive instruments of U.S. policy were replaced by **"dollar diplomacy."** Nonetheless, numerous interventions and heavy-handed diplomacy became common. The Marines were not only in Nicaragua again (1912–1925 and 1926–1933) but also in Haiti (1916–1934) and the Dominican Republic (1916–1922).

The Good Neighbor Policy under Franklin Delano Roosevelt and the need for allies and bases during World War II made for more cordial relations and much less outright intervention until the early 1950s and the onset of the Cold War. Nonetheless, strong U.S. interest and occasional intervention would continue to be a factor in the domestic politics of most Latin American nations well into the twenty-first century.

Post-1910

By 1910, Latin America was being integrated ever more strongly into the world capitalist economy, assigned the role of peripheral producer of primary goods and consumer of industrialized goods from the developed nations at the center of the system. Further, there was increasing investment in plantations like those that grew sugar in Cuba or bananas in Central America and mines in countries like Mexico (silver), Chile (copper), and Bolivia (tin). Likewise, British and American financial capital sought even more investment opportunities in the expanding Latin American economies. The Great Depression temporarily halted the integration of Latin America into the international capitalist economic system, but the pace of integration continued and quickened in the second half of the century.

As we suggest in the chapter on economics (chapter 8), increased demand for the export commodities and increasing imports helped commercialize Latin American economies. Import substitution industrialization (ISI) further changed the face of Latin America, as did the subsequent phase of export-led growth and the growing production and export of manufactured goods. The 1970s saw Latin American countries borrow more and more capital from outside the region, greatly increasing their external debts in the process. Debt and debt repayment remained a poignant problem into the twenty-first century. The last decades of the twentieth century witnessed the transformation of the region from what at the beginning of the century was a rural area where wealthy landowners and poor peasants or rural laborers predominated to a modern, urbanized area where three-quarters of the people lived in cities. By the turn of the twenty-first century, the largest class in most countries was the urban working class, which included a growing informal sector. Likewise, a significant middle class had developed and cut its political teeth. As these new classes were joined by new segments of the upper class tied to industrialization and commercialization and the increased involvement of multinational corporations and foreign investors, new political forces were mobilized and new political coalitions developed.

THE MEXICAN REVOLUTION

These and other factors led to the development of the first great revolutionary movement of the twentieth century, the Mexican Revolution. The dominance of traditional landowners, the Church, and the Díaz dictatorship kept developing social and political forces in check for many years. However, the struggle for change finally erupted in 1910 and spread throughout society. The mostly rural masses soon mobilized with cries of *"pan y tierra"* (bread and land) and participated full force in the many revolutionary armies that fought for the next seven years under such generals as Pancho Villa and Emiliano Zapata. It was indeed a revolution won by *los de abajo*, those from below, to use Mariano Azuela's term. The radical constitution of 1917 manifested many of the new ideas of the revolutionaries, set the stage for the development of modern Mexico, and infected the rest of Latin America with new ideas and expectations. Hereafter, land reform, legislation protecting workers, secular education, reduction of the power of foreign investors, and the Church's power and influence—as well as the ability to break with overly European models in favor of those that recognized the culture, history, and ethnicity of the masses—began to filter through Latin America. They soon combined with ideas from the second great revolution of the twentieth century (in Russia in 1917) to stimulate the development of new, more progressive social movements and political parties that would endeavor to forge a very different Latin American reality. The rest of the twentieth century witnessed myriad struggles between the conservative political and economic forces and mobilized classes and coalitions advocating significant reformist or revolutionary change.

Forces favoring reform and revolution would hereafter battle conservative forces and those tied to the existent system. After the Russian Revolution and subsequent spread of more radical forms of socialism and Marxism, these struggles would often become more class-oriented and often quite bloody as the dominant classes fought tooth and nail to preserve their status and privilege.

Democratic Reformism in Uruguay

The modern reformist era arrived in Uruguay at the turn of the century. Like Argentina, Uruguay had an urban working class and the beginning of a middle class whose interests were quite different from those of the traditional landholders. The dynamic leader of the liberal Colorado Party, José Batlle y Ordóñez, chose his 1903 election as president to enact a series of extensive economic and political reforms that would turn Uruguay into a modern social democracy and welfare state by the 1920s. Further, in a fascinating experiment with less autocratic forms of rule, Uruguay was even governed by a *colegiado*, or collective presidency (where power was shared among members of a presidential council and the titular head of state rotated), from 1917 to 1933 and from 1951 to 1967. Thus, from 1903 until 1973, Uruguay was regarded as the Switzerland of Latin America and as an example of just how democracy and enlightened social democratic-style rule could triumph in a Latin American state.

Later, conditions changed in Uruguay, and the threat of even greater popular mobilizations and the threat to the domestic upper class and foreign capitalists posed by the often popular Tupamaro guerrillas mobilized conservative forces against further change. Thus, even in democratic Uruguay, the rising tide of bureaucratic authoritarian military governments in the 1970s undermined their hard-won democratic political culture and the working and middle-class benefits and liberties that had been achieved. This experiment with reformist democracy and a fully developed welfare state was cut short when the military staged a coup in 1973. The military controlled the country for the next twelve years. Full democratic rule was not restored until 1985; but the *colegiado* was no longer employed, and the working and middle classes were forced to accept government cutbacks and other structural adjustments. More recently, a progressive coalition, the *Frente Amplio*, has become a major power contender. Dr. Tabaré Vázquez led an even broader leftist electoral coalition, the Frente Amplio Encuentro Progresista Nueva Mayoria, to a first-round electoral victory in October 2004. The Tupamaro guerrilla group turned political party (Movimiento de Liberación Nacional-Tupamaros) was a member of the winning coalition, which also carried a legislative majority in both houses. The leftist victory is seen as a clear repudiation of neoliberal policies and an assertion of popular control. This leftist tact in Uruguan politics was further underlined by the 2009 presidential electoral victory of José Mujica. The former Tupamaro guerrilla headed the *Frente Amplio* slate, which also maintained a majority in both legilative houses.

DEMOCRACY AND DICTATORSHIP IN ARGENTINA

It was suggested earlier that in the nineteenth century Argentina evolved from the gaucho dictatorship of Juan Manuel de Rosas to the reformist civilian rule of presidents like Domingo Sarmiento. By the turn of the century, Argentine beef and wheat were flooding into Europe and British investment was pouring into Argentina. The South American nation was developing rapidly and had a higher per capita income than several European nations. It soon spawned a proletariat and a nascent middle class. These groups became the base for a newly formed, European-inspired Radical Party, which promised to bring enlightened democratic rule to Argentina. Before Argentina could experience sustained economic or political development, the Great Depression dashed hope for continued economic development, and the weakening of the Radical Party and a subsequent coup d'état in 1930 plunged the nation back into a military dictatorship.

After oligarchy-inspired conservative rule in most of the 1930s and early 1940s, a group of officers again intervened to take over the government in 1943. The junta they formed was eventually dominated by Colonel Juan Domingo Perón, who was later able to consolidate his power with the help of Eva Duarte and successfully ran for president in the 1946 elections. Peronism, as his political movement came to be called, became the dominant political party and political movement in Argentina. Peronism displaced the Socialist Party as the party of the masses and remained the largest political party for the rest of the twentieth century. Juan Perón was a dynamic, charismatic, and often dictatorial leader who was famous for his mass rallies and ties to the Argentine labor movement. Eva Perón became the darling of the masses and greatly bolstered the Peronist project. She died in 1952 and Juan Perón was ousted from power in 1955, yet their influence would linger: When again allowed to run for president in 1973, Juan Perón was reelected, with his then wife María Isabel Martínez Perón as his vice president. He died the next year, and Isabel Perón became the first female president in Latin America, only to be overthrown by a military coup in 1976.

From 1955 to 1966, Argentina was characterized by frequent alternation between military regimes and weak democratic governments. The country was industrializing and engaging in successful policies of import substitution, but it continued to be plagued by high inflation and a growing foreign debt. Strikes, labor actions, and guerrilla warfare challenged the oligarchy and the government. The military ruled outright from 1966 to 1973 and instituted a brutal "dirty war" against leftists and other political enemies from 1976 to 1983. After the military government initiated and lost the Falkland Islands War in 1982, elections brought a return to civilian government in 1983. Although initially threatened by barracks revolts and plagued by economic difficulties that allowed rightist Peronist President Carlos Menem to impose unpopular austerity measures, democracy continued through the rest of the century. His replacement, Fernando de la Rua, was forced from office because of an economic meltdown in 2001 and early 2002. Mass mobilizations, economic chaos, and massive street demonstrations continued until the third congressionally appointed president (Eduardo Duhalde) was able to stabilize the situation and hold presidential elections in 2003. Néstor Kirchner, a leftist Peronist who voiced strong opposition to the neoliberal policies advocated by the International Monetary Fund (IMF), won the presidency. Economic conditions had finally stabilized by 2005 as Kirchner developed policies that contested much of the advice of international financial institutions and neoliberal economists. With Venezuela's help, the Kirchner administration was able to cancel Argentina's debt with the International Monitary Fund and strengthen its independent, anti-neoliberal stance. In 2007 Kirchner's wife, Cristina Fernández, successfully ran for president to continue his policies. Her attempts to increase the export taxes on agricultural exports did, however, generate considerable opposition, which caused a drop in her popularity. The government's legislative coalition lost it majority in both houses in the 2009 elections.

Authoritarianism, Aprismo, Marxismo, and Democracy in Peru

Peru's defeat in the War of the Pacific (1879–1883) caused a national reexamination that began the consolidation of the modern nation-state and unleashed new social and political forces. Critical writers like Manuel González Prada spawned the radical reformist movements that eventually led to state centralization and consolidation under subsequent presidents and radical political movements like Victor Raúl Haya de la Torre's Alianza Popular Revolucionaria Americana (American Popular Revolutionary Alliance, APRA) and José Carlos Mariátegui's Peruvian Socialist Party (later the Peruvian Communist Party).

Haya de la Torre, heavily influenced by the Mexican as well as the Russian Revolution, came to believe in a necessary political, economic, and social restructuring of all of Latin America. He founded APRA while visiting Mexico in 1924 and began a lifelong struggle to found political movements that would enfranchise the masses, promote land reform, improve the treatment of indigenous Americans, and resist the dominance of the United States. This movement led to the formation of APRA in Peru (which was kept from power by conservative and then reformist military forces until Alan García's presidency in 1985) and similar political movements in other countries. These movements represented the aspirations of the toiling masses—particularly indigenous peoples—and many sectors of the emerging middle class. The groups were often characterized as national revolutionary parties even though they were generally more reformist than revolutionary by the time they came to power. They came to be dominant parties in Venezuela (Acción Democrática, founded by Rómulo Betancourt), Costa Rica (Liberación Nacional, founded by José Figueres), Bolivia (Movimiento Nacionalista Revolucionario [National Revolutionary Movement, MNR], founded by Víctor Paz Estenssoro), Puerto Rico (Popular Democratic Party [PDP], founded by Luis Muñoz Marín), and the Dominican Republic (Partido Revolucionario, founded by Juan Bosch).

Coming from a more modest background than the aristocratic Haya de la Torre and more specifically focused on the Indian peasants and rural laborers, miners, and the small urban proletariat, the self-educated Mariátegui was heavily influenced by his reading of Manuel González Prada and about the indigenist movement in Peru, Marxist literature, Lenin and the Russian Revolution, and the Mexican Revolution. He supported indigenous rights and the workers' movement in Peru and went on to found the Peruvian Socialist Party, which soon affiliated with the Communist International. In so doing he stimulated the development of a Marxist-Leninist movement in Peru and gave impetus to revolutionary struggle in Peru and elsewhere. Indeed, he argued for a Latin American socialism that was "neither copy nor imitation" of any other; but his early demise in 1930 and strong criticism from the Soviet-controlled Communist International limited his influence for many years. Marxists in Peru and elsewhere in Latin America rarely followed his independent stance, and communist parties were generally subordinate to European influences and Soviet control. Not until the last decades of the twentieth century was Mariátegui's open brand of Marxism fully appreciated by a broad spectrum of the Latin American left.

Substantial structural change did not come to Peru through a socialist movement or through APRA; rather, it arrived with a reformist military takeover in 1968 that maintained power until 1980. Thus, it was the military—not reformist or radical civilian politicians—that instituted a comprehensive system of land reform in Peru (although they did not set up sufficient financial mechanisms to empower poor peasants and agricultural workers who were the beneficiaries of this reform) and addressed the conditions of the workers. Previously, Peru's political history had been marked by dictators like Augusto Leguía (1919–1930) and Manuel Prado (1949 and 1956–1962) and by intermittent periods of democracy.

There was a return to democratically elected governments after 1980, but the struggle against severe economic conditions for the masses and the rise of the guerrilla group Sendero Luminoso stretched the democratic institutions beyond their limits. By the mid-1990s, events such as the 1992 *auto-glope* (self-coup) of elected president Alberto Fujimori had greatly diminished the practice of democracy. This trend was continued with the 2000 fraudulent reelection of Fujimori for a constitutionally prohibited third term, though he was forced from office in 2001 and new elections were held. By 2004, his elected successor, Alejandro Toledo, who was accused of favoritism and corruption, insisted on following neoliberal policies that became increasingly unpopular. His support was so small (measured in single digits in opinion polls) that some wondered if he would even be able to finish his term. Indeed, 2005 began with an armed uprising demanding his ouster. In 2006 former Aprista president Alan García was elected president in a run-off election against radical nationalist candidate Ollanta Humala. During his five-year term García continued more conservative policies informed by neoliberal economics and became more closely allied with the United States.

DEMOCRACY, SOCIALISM, INTERVENTION, AND DICTATORSHIP IN CHILE

Political reform came to Chile earlier. It began with the formation of a parliamentary republic (1891–1924) and came to include a proletariat and a nascent middle class. The predominance of copper mines owned by foreign corporations sparked the formation of a strong socialist-oriented union movement, and the large number of socialist immigrants helped create a socialist political movement in Chile. Like Mariátegui in Peru, the labor leader Luis Emilio Recabarren championed a Marxist party in Chile. Building on the newly developing political forces unleashed by a nitrate boom, the parliamentary republic, and the development of copper mining, Chile continued to evolve, experiencing a short-lived socialist republic under Marmaduke Grove in the early 1930s.

Along with more traditional parties, a substantial socialist movement developed. As its support grew among the miners and urban working class and sectors of the middle class, it was challenged by a strong, reformist Christian Democratic Party that had also created a union movement. The Christian Democrats headed off the leftist challenge, mobilized workers, and, with support from the United States and their Christian Democratic allies in Europe, won two important elections in the 1960s and went on to establish themselves as a major reformist party. Even greater structural change began when the Socialist Party, in coalition with the Communist and Radical parties, finally achieved power in 1970 with the election of Salvador Allende as president. This was a clear triumph of the popular classes.

Up to this point Chile, like Uruguay and Costa Rica after 1948, was considered a nation where the seeds of democracy had taken root and flowered. Indeed, many thought that the thoroughgoing socialist restructuring proposed by Allende might

Salvador Allende, Socialist President of Chile, 1908–1973. *(AP Images)*

actually be carried out by peaceful, constitutional means. Some significant progress was made during the first years of Allende's Popular Unity government from 1970 to 1973, but Chilean society became increasingly polarized. The United States and conservative sectors in Chile made every effort to destabilize the newly elected government. U.S. military aid to the Chilean military was, interestingly, continued, even though all other aid was cut. Finally, Chilean democracy was shattered by a brutal United States–supported and Central Intelligence Agency (CIA)-sponsored military coup in September 1973. The workers had lost. The coup displaced all progressive forces and instituted a repressive military regime run by Augusto Pinochet that lasted until 1990. Thousands were murdered by the state security forces. A return to free market economics was one of the primary goals of the military dictatorship. As the country came to terms with the brutality of the military dictatorship in the post-Pinochet period, five democratic elections were held. The CPD or Coalition of Opposition Parties or *Concertación* won the first four elections and a socialist once again became president in 2000. From 1990 on, civilian presidents helped to soften aspects of the rather austere neoliberal economic policies. On the whole, the country was considered to have developed a thriving economy based on neoliberal principles. Even so, many suffered from poor wages and living conditions. George W. Bush administration's plan to privatize Social Security was based on a similar plan implemented in Chile, where it became fraught with problems and many of the privatized pension funds left their participants with very little indeed. The election of former defense minister and Socialist Party member Michelle Bachelet as president in 2005 helped to institutionalize more progressive democratic rule in Chile and provide an independently minded woman president as a new political and personal role model. As democratic rule became more strongly re-institutionalized, January 2010 saw Chileans elect Sebastián Piñera, of the National Renewal Party in the centre-right Coalition for Change. He was the first rightist to be elected President of Chile after the Pinochet dictatorship.

U.S. Policy and the Cold War

The end of World War II set the stage for the Cold War, and Latin America became one of the theaters of operation. Fearing communist influence in Guatemala (and because of complaints by the United Fruit Company), the U.S. CIA planned and executed a coup that overthrew the constitutionally elected government in 1954. This became a model for often heavy-handed meddling in the internal politics of Latin American nations by the United States. The specter of world communism facilitated a retreat from the Good Neighbor Policy to one premised on the assumption that Latin American sovereignty could be subordinate to the fight against communism, if not U.S. policy interests generally. As will be detailed below, there were a series of subsequent interventions in sovereign Latin American states. Further, throughout the Cold War period, the U.S. military, the State Department, and other U.S. agencies also worked closely with Latin American militaries to train them in counterinsurgency and national security policy to resist Marxist guerrillas and other real and imagined threats from the left. More positive policy instruments such as the Alliance for Progress and U.S. aid were also used to try to remedy the economic and social conditions that might breed communism and instability.

Cuba, Colonialism, and Communism

Much of the inspiration for the democratic attempt at a constitutional socialist revolution in Chile was derived from the Cuban example as well as from Chile's own socialist and democratic tradition. Indeed, the event after the Mexican Revolution that inspired the most attempts at radical change in Latin America was the revolution that took place in Cuba in 1959. As it evolved toward a socialist path that eventually embraced Marxism-Leninism, Cuba became a model for radical change throughout the region.

Cuba, like Mexico, was an example of change delayed. Even independence had come late to Cuba; Cuban patriots lost the Ten Years' War (1868–1878), and slavery was not abolished until 1886. Spanish colonial rule endured until 1898, and independence was not achieved until 1902 (and then only under U.S. tutelage). The system that ensued was dominated by sugar plantations and sugar refineries (*centrales*) that were increasingly owned or controlled by U.S. businesses as American investment capital flooded into the island in the first decades of the twentieth century. A Cuban upper class centered in sugar production also developed, while the masses were generally relegated to positions as cane workers and *guajiros* (peasants). Poverty and seasonal unemployment characterized rural agricultural labor, as did de facto subordination of people of color. A monocrop economy and dependent nation par excellence, Cuba became closely tied to the United States for sugar sales and the importation of finished goods. Indeed, it was often suggested that the American ambassador to Havana was nothing less than a proconsul.

By the 1920s Cuba had already experienced its first dictatorship (Gerardo Machado, 1924–1933) which was only ended by military coup. A second coup was led by a noncommissioned officer, Sergeant Fulgencio Batista, in 1933. Batista maintained good relations with the United States and, promoted to colonel, was elected to the presidency in 1940 as a reformer. In 1952, he executed another coup and established what became a brutal and unpopular dictatorship, which was eventually overthrown by Fidel Castro's 26th of July Movement. Supported by peasants and agricultural workers, segments of the Cuban upper class, and many from the middle class that had emerged in Havana, the revolutionaries took power in 1959 and went about reforming the country, basing many of their ideas on the reformist constitution of 1940. The guerrilla war that put them in power became immortalized in fellow guerrilla leader Ernesto "Che" Guevara's manual on guerrilla fighting, *Guerrilla Warfare*.

The examples of the Cuban Revolution and of forming guerrilla groups to wrest power from dominant elites were of immediate interest to the Latin American left. The Cuban Revolution became Marxist after the United States organized the Bay of Pigs invasion in 1961 and, thus, became an example of the revolutionary transformation of a Latin American society. The notion of overthrowing the status quo with a band of guerrilla fighters and addressing the economic and social injustices and foreign control that had characterized the region was widely acclaimed by progressive forces. A variety of Fidelista guerrilla groups were organized throughout Latin America and set about emulating the Cuban example and fighting their way down from the hills into the corridors of power in the nations' capitals. Guerrilla

become radicalized as they struggled to break away from the stultifying economic and social structures that had condemned the vast majority of Latin Americans to poverty and suffering. U.S. policy toward Latin America in the 1960s was twofold: foment gradual change and restructuring through the Alliance for Progress and related activities (this would undermine the political base of more revolutionary movements) and support the development of counterinsurgency and the national security states to fight and defeat the radical guerrilla movements that did appear. To the latter end, military training in places like the School of the Americas in the Panama Canal Zone and aid to Latin American militaries were greatly increased. Soldiers and lower-level officers were trained in counterinsurgency tactics. Command officers were imbued with a version of the national security doctrine that suggested that the Latin American governments and especially the military were responsible for protecting the nation and state from the threat posed by guerrillas, leftist political movements, and communism. Since many Latin American military leaders already thought of themselves as guardians of the nation, this training—which was replicated and emphasized in national war colleges—served as a further impetus to intervene when there was danger of uncontrollable popular mobilization or unchecked guerrilla activity. In 1965, U.S. President Lyndon Johnson even enunciated the Johnson Doctrine (a corollary to the Monroe Doctrine) to explain the need of the United States to intervene in its sister republics to stop the spread of communism.

The shadow of the Cuban Revolution, peasant mobilization, worker militancy, and domestic radicals who might opt for violent revolution—all seen through the lens of national security doctrine—convinced the Brazilian military and conservative forces that they were facing a revolutionary situation. The United States had already expressed concern and was communicating with the military and sympathetic politicians. A military coup was staged in 1964, and a long period of authoritarian military rule was initiated.

The military regime that took power did not, however, stabilize the situation and then hold elections, as was often the case when military juntas took over. Rather, it usurped power from civilian politicians, closing congress, arresting some leftist leaders, banning traditional political parties, and generally arguing that the Brazilian military could develop the country much better than the civilian politicians could. The peasant mobilization and worker militancy that helped spark the popular movement were suppressed, as were radical groups. There would be no revolution in Brazil. Instead, a long period of military rule (lasting until 1985) was initiated, and the military took it upon itself to guide Brazil in achieving its *grandeza* (greatness) by developing along more conservative, state-directed capitalist lines. Large *fazendas* were continued, foreign capital was invited in, the government went into joint business ventures with multinational corporations, the Amazon was thrown open for development, and indigenous people were seen as expendable in the rapid developmental process that ensued. Growth and development were expected; socioeconomic restructuring and income redistribution were unacceptable. This long-term economically and politically involved military rule and the resultant national security state designed to stop political or social revolutions like that which occurred in Cuba came to be called *bureaucratic authoritarianism*. Brazil was the prototype for this extended military rule. After Brazil's return to democracy in 1985, new power contenders like the Workers' Party (PT) appeared. Although still dominated by more conservative forces until 2002, the Workers' Party finally managed to win the presidency in that year and again in 2006. By 2010 the Brazilian economy had grown substantially and the second administration of the Workers' Party President, Luiz Inácio Lula da Silva, popularly known as Lula, had consolidated its power after making peace with Brazil's economic elites. However, many felt that the impoverished sectors of the population were not benefiting fully from Brazil's economic growth and were still marginalized economically.

The Cold War and Change

THE DOMINICAN CASE

In early 1965, political instability and the possibility of the mobilization of the Dominican masses by Juan Bosch and his APRA-style Dominican Revolutionary Party raised the specter of a reformist party taking power but, as had happened with the 26th of July Movement in Cuba, then becoming radicalized as it endeavored to effect change in an economy heavy with U.S. investment. Red flags went up in the White House and the Pentagon, and in April 1965, 25,000 marines were dispatched to Santo Domingo to restore order and staunch any leftist threat. No more Cubas would be tolerated. Conservative rule was restored and continued into the 1980s. More progressive leaders such as Leonel Fernández (PLD, 1996–2000, 2004–2008, and 2008–2012) charted a new course in the 1990s and after. With the signing of the Central American Free Trade Agreement (CAFTA) and the inclusion of the Dominican Republic in that agreement, the island nation was drawn even more strongly into the U.S. sphere of influence.

CENTRAL AMERICA AND U.S. HEGEMONY

The quest for change in Central America came more slowly. American involvement in the region dated from William Walker's intervention in Nicaragua in the 1850s. American investment grew through the latter part of the nineteenth century and all during the twentieth.

The case of U.S.–Nicaraguan relations will be discussed below. Other attempts were also made to transform the traditional reality of Central America. For instance, from 1944 to 1954, reformist forces in Guatemala attempted to consolidate a modern nation-state and make economic and social reforms that would economically and politically empower the peasants, banana workers, and majority indigenous population for the first time. However, the new government soon found itself in a heated dispute with the Boston-based United Fruit Company, which had very strong ties to the U.S. government. Before the land reform program could be completed, the revolution of 1944 was overthrown by a CIA-organized military coup in 1954. A virtual civil war erupted in the 1960s as Cuba-inspired guerrillas tried unsuccessfully to overthrow the military and conservative forces. The struggle continued into the 1990s and claimed some 200,000 Guatemalan lives. A peace accord was finally negotiated with the help of the United Nations in 1996.

In El Salvador, a small oligarchy reigned as fourteen families ruled and used brutal repression to maintain their virtual monopoly on wealth and power (as in the Matanza of 1932). The families frequently used their military allies to maintain an unjust status quo. Military rule predominated in the 1960s and 1970s, and pressure for change grew by 1979. Rather than allow needed land and other reforms, the rulers once again opted for repression. This led to strong civilian opposition and the eventual formation of the Farabundo Martí Front for National Liberation (FMLN). A civil war developed in the 1980s as a coalition of reformers and revolutionaries battled the military and the U.S.-backed civilian government. More than 70,000 lives were lost in the civil war in El Salvador; the United States supplied more than $5 billion in military and economic aid to stop the revolution. Peace was finally negotiated in the 1990s, and the FMLN was transformed into a major political party, although the U.S-backed Alianza Republicana Nacionalista (ARENA, National Republican Alliance) consistently won the presidency and most though certainly not all other offices through 2007; the electoral fortunes of FMLN began to change in 2008 and FMLN candidate Mauricio Funes was elected president in early 2009. Breaking with right-wing rule in Guatemala, Alvaro Colom was elected president in 2007 as a reform candidate.

But El Salvador and Guatemala had not been able to escape the consequences of the lack of socioeconomic reform or the culture of violence that the brutal civil wars had engendered. Brutal gangs *(Maras)* developed. MS or MS-13 (the Mara Salvatrucha) and M-18 were reputed to have as many as 100,000 members in Central America by

M-18 gang photo of a *clica* (local gang group) in El Salvador. *(Photo by Kylla Hanson)*

2008 and could not be controlled by the governments in El Salvador, Guatemala, or Honduras. El Salvador and Guatemala were two of the most violent societies in the world. The homicide rate for El Salvador alone was 55 per 100,000 (as compared to 5.7 in the United States). There were 10 homicides a day in a total population of 6.8 million. By the beginning of 2008, the *Maras'* organizations extended through the three countries and reached back into the United States where gang members from Central America began to appear. Similarly, thousands of Central Americans were fleeing the Maras and the crime and violence in the region.

NOTES ON NICARAGUAN–U.S. RELATIONS: A CAUTIONARY TALE

As a way of understanding what many consider the hegemonic relations that the United States has with Latin America, a brief look at how relations between Nicaragua and the United States have developed is offered below.

Nicaragua has seen many manifestations of the hegemonic influence of the United States. The United States not only waged a massive covert action against the small Central American state for almost a decade but also intervened to influence the outcome of the 1990 election. More subtle forms of intervention have extended through the late 1990s and into the twenty-first century as neoliberalism and globalization were strongly advocated. Other forms of intervention began nearly 150 years ago when a group of Nicaraguan liberals mistakenly invited a band of U.S. mercenaries to aid them in their ongoing struggle with the conservatives. The result was unique among Latin American nations because a U.S. citizen (William Walker) was able to force his way into the presidential palace and the nation's presidency. Nicaragua had become a transit corridor for Americans wishing to take advantage of the gold rush boom on the west coast of the United States. It was seriously considered as a location for a canal to connect the Atlantic and Pacific oceans. Indeed, Nicaragua has been tied to U.S. power since the 1850s and is still struggling to assert its sovereign independence.

Nicaraguan and Central American relations with the United States were once more fraternal. Contacts between the United States and the region were at first sparse but sometimes based on the Jeffersonian concept of relations among equal, sister republics. Indeed, in the first half of the nineteenth century, the United States was still a struggling young republic that had not yet consolidated its power or position in the world. It fought and lost its last anticolonial war against the British in 1812. However, by the middle of the nineteenth century, the nature of international relations in the hemisphere began to change. American power was first projected south in the Mexican-American War of 1846–1848, which resulted in the annexation of half of Mexico's territory by the United States. Commercial penetration also increased. This projection of power from Washington was soon manifest in Nicaragua. Cornelius Vanderbilt developed financial interests when he set up a stagecoach and steamship line to carry passengers across the Central American isthmus after the California gold rush in 1849. Soon thereafter, the American filibuster William Walker took over Nicaragua in 1855 and even had himself declared president after he stipulated that English was to be the official language. Later, the post–Civil War industrialization and economic expansion of the United States began to redefine the economic interests of the northern state. It would no longer be primarily a producer and exporter of raw materials like its sister republics to the south.

Rather, it was becoming an industrialized creditor nation that started to search out new markets for its industrial products, additional sources of raw materials, and new locations to invest its growing capital. By the turn of the century, relations began to reflect the hegemonic position that the United States was establishing in the Caribbean basin, if not Latin America more generally. From 1903 through the 1990s, Central America witnessed a diverse variety of hegemonic initiatives by the United States: marine occupations, gunboat diplomacy, dollar diplomacy and financial penetration, Roosevelt's Good Neighbor Policy, anticommunism, the Alliance for Progress, covert intervention, and direct occupation by U.S. troops, as most recently occurred in Panama in 1989.

Nicaragua started to consolidate its power as a nation-state under the presidency of José Santos Zelaya (1893–1909). The liberal president soon introduced reforms that alarmed the conservative forces and threatened the interests of U.S. capital. As Zelaya faced increasing internal and external pressure, his rule became more dictatorial. The United States did not hesitate to show its displeasure and even went so far as to land marines in the Atlantic coast city of Bluefields in 1909. Zelaya was forced from power in that same year. U.S. intervention increased over the next years as marines were again landed in 1912 to prop up the U.S.-installed puppet regime of Adolfo Díaz. They stayed until 1925 and suppressed several nationalist uprisings, like that begun by nationalist hero Benjamín Zeledón in 1912.

In 1925, a new liberal uprising against a conservative coup and the U.S.-inspired reinstallation of Adolfo Díaz as president developed. The marines once again intervened. Sandinista namesake Augusto César Sandino returned from Mexico in 1926 to head one of the liberal bands and continue the struggle after the other liberal generals accepted a U.S.-brokered peace. The marines stayed on to fight the strongly nationalist movement headed by Sandino and based primarily on segments of the popular classes who grasped the nationalist, anti-imperialist nature of the struggle. The first Sandinistas fought the marines and a U.S.-organized Nicaraguan National Guard to a stalemate. The negotiated settlement of 1933 was, however, betrayed by the guard and its sycophant leader Anastasio Somoza García. Somoza parleyed his close ties to the United States and his position as leader of the National Guard to become the most powerful leader in the country and had himself elected president in 1936. He and his sons would rule Nicaragua until militarily defeated by the Frente Sandinista de Liberación Nacional (FSLN) in July 1979. Always a great friend of the United States, Somoza opened the country to U.S. investment and encouraged companies like United Fruit and Standard Fruit to increase their business operations in Nicaragua. The leadership in Washington became accustomed to what they perceived as a subservient government in Managua. Indeed, the training for the Bay of Pigs invasion of Cuba was done in Nicaragua. Thereafter, the Somozas were vociferous in their anticommunist declarations.

To understand the specifics of the Nicaraguan case, it is necessary to follow the development of the country since the Sandinista takeover in 1979. Under the Sandinistas, Nicaragua was one of the countries that insisted on maintaining its national sovereignty in economic and political matters and argued for a new international economic order. The Sandinistas endeavored to remove the nation from the hegemonic control of the United States. It became a member of the Nonaligned Movement and pursued a very independent foreign policy. Its ties to the nonaligned movements and its economic relations with a variety of countries including Cuba, the Soviet Union, and Eastern Europe allowed it a certain amount of economic flexibility. However, when Ronald Reagan was elected president of the United States in 1980, he began a policy of bringing pressure to bear on Nicaragua. This included an economic embargo and low-intensity warfare that utilized CIA-organized counterrevolutionaries who came to be called contras. Indeed, the Contra War cost some 30,000 Nicaraguan lives and devastated the Nicaraguan economy. In 1990, casualties and material damages inflicted by the contras, external pressure, Sandinista errors, and the dynamics of internal Nicaraguan politics combined to cause the electoral defeat of the Sandinistas and the election of Violeta Chamorro to the Nicaraguan presidency. Yet, the electoral victory of the anti-Somoza martyr Pedro Joaquín Chamorro's widow was in large part engineered by the United States, which in turn left the new government beholden to Washington and consequently with much less autonomy.

In Nicaragua, Guatemala, and El Salvador, the United States had mobilized considerable resources to make sure that the revolutionary forces would be defeated. Through U.S. military involvement and the Central American peace process championed by Costa Rican president Oscar Arias and other regional leaders, the struggle was moved from military to political and electoral means. By the early 1990s, the independent, radical thrust of political movements in all of these countries had been greatly reduced and no radicals were in control of their respective nations. Official relations were once again cordial with the United States, which expressed great satisfaction that (U.S.-style) democracy had been restored in Nicaragua and Central America. By the end of the 1990s, democratization was in full bloom and political struggle in these nations had been channeled into less violent avenues that were more easily influenced by the United States. Nicaragua's new subservience to U.S. policy suggested that it would vigorously implement neoliberal economic policies. As it did, its economy worsened even more; and by the end of the 1990s, it suffered massive unemployment and was the second poorest country in the hemisphere. Reacting to these conditions and governmental corruption, the Sandinistas began to increase their strength in local elections and were voted back in power in 2006, as Daniel Ortega once again assumed the presidency.

Events were different in Costa Rica. The victory of José Figueres and his National Liberation forces in the Costa Rican civil war of 1948 and the subsequent establishment of a modern social democratic state in the 1950s marked the only example of progressive change to endure in the region. Figueres's strong ties to the United States and his American wife helped facilitate the success of the Costa Rican experiment, which turned into a two-party dominant democracy that valued honest elections and electoral competition. The country opted for a European-style social democracy that achieved high levels of education, health care, and sanitation.

COUNTERINSURGENCY, HEGEMONY, AND U.S. INTERVENTION

As mentioned earlier, the Cold War and the socialist turn of the Cuban Revolution encouraged the United States to suppress progressive political movements throughout the second half of the twentieth century, lest they lead to communism or Cuba-like revolutions. This often buttressed the most conservative forces and the status quo at the expense of much-needed reforms. Indeed, it sometimes served to kill hope for those who tried to effect change. U.S. policy makers encouraged their military and civilian allies in Latin America to think in terms of the national

Farmers and ox cart in rural Costa Rica. *(Photo by Patrice Olsen)*

security state. Thus, the United States sponsored counterinsurgency training for Latin American militaries at the School of the Americas in the Panama Canal Zone and at U.S. military bases such as Fort Bragg, North Carolina. Since the U.S. intervention in Guatemala in 1954, there has been significant U.S. military or political involvement in Cuba (Bay of Pigs, 1961), the Dominican Republic (marines in Santo Domingo, 1965), Chile (destabilization and overthrow of Allende, 1973), Jamaica (destabilization of Manley government, 1980), El Salvador (continued political and military involvement, 1980–1992), Nicaragua (U.S.-inspired Contra War, 1981–1990), Grenada (military invasion, 1982), Panama (military invasion, 1989), and Colombia (aid and military advisors, 2000 on). Thus, reform, revolution, and change often had to be played against a backdrop of real or potential involvement by the United States. As civil wars and guerrilla movements wound down in the 1990s, the United States continued to exert strong pressure on the internal politics of Latin American countries. The end of the Cold War and the new international order, however, made for less violent—but no less forceful—forms of economically focused intervention.

THE POST-COLD WAR PERIOD AND U.S. HEGEMONY

The 1991 demise of the Soviet Union, the main socialist rival to the ascending hegemony of the United States, and the resultant difficulties for Cuba and the Cuban revolutionary model meant that neither communism nor Cuba was now perceived as an immediate threat in Latin America. This, in turn, relaxed the emphasis on the national security state and counterinsurgency in Latin America. Further, the end of bureaucratic authoritarian (military) regimes by the early 1990s signaled a return to greater formal democracy. The triumph of capitalism in Eastern Europe further stimulated the process of free-market capitalist globalization. In Latin America, nationalist economic policies that protected and promoted import substitution industrialization and the growth of national businesses were rapidly abandoned in favor of free markets, free trade, and the free flow of investment capital. Latin America now seemed to be a safe place for international capital to do business. By 2000, Colombia was the only country to have any significant radical groups contesting power through the use of force and challenging the new Pax Americana. Throughout the region, increasing pressure came from international financial institutions like the International Monetary Fund (IMF) to globalize and set aside policies that would directly transfer benefits, income, or wealth to the still-suffering masses of Latin Americans. The new focus was not on socioeconomic change, restructuring, or income redistribution; rather, it was on capitalist growth that would—Latin Americans were told—benefit all. Those suspicious of the continuing intervention of the United States believed that marine uniforms and guns may well have given way to business suits and IMF portfolios. Others felt that Latin American nations might now finally be able to compete in the international economic arena on more equal ground because the globalization of their economies would force them to modernize and become more competitive. By 2010, this latter view was not widely shared as neoliberal economic policies were discredited and the global economic crisis began to be felt across Latin America.

Venezuela: Dictatorship, Democracy, and the Post-Cold War Bolivarian Republic

The combination of neoliberal-inspired economic policy, continued impoverishment of the masses, and shoddy statesmanship created conditions that generated a movement led by a progressive army officer in the country where Simón Bolívar had started the struggle for independence in South America. In 1810, Bolívar and the junta in Caracas struggled to establish democracy in Caracas and the rest of what is now Venezuela and Colombia. Yet, the march toward democracy was not always easy in Bolívar's homeland. The Venezuelan nation saw its share of dictators in the remaining years of the nineteenth century and experienced a long period of dictatorial rule in the first part of the twentieth century. Indeed, the dictatorship of Juan Vicente Gómez (1908–1935) is one of the most notorious in Latin American history. Before Gómez, Venezuela almost experienced another wave of European intervention. At the turn of the century, several European states, led by Germany, wanted to take over the customs operations of the nation to get funds to repay debts owed by Venezuela. This plan was frustrated by the U.S. invocation of the Monroe Doctrine, but even so, Germany, England, and Italy did engage in a naval bombardment of Puerto Cabezas in 1903. These economic problems were resolved with the beginning of petroleum production under the Gómez dictatorship.

Modern democracy came to Venezuela with the APRA-inspired Acción Democrática takeover in 1945 and the election of civilian president Rómulo Gallegos in 1947. But he too was overthrown by another coup in 1948. From 1952 to 1958 Venezuela suffered the military dictatorship of Marcos Pérez Jiménez. Led by

Rómulo Betancourt, Acción Democrática instituted an open democracy, political competition (mostly with the Christian Democratic COPEI Party) that lasted until 1998. A founding member of the Organization of Petroleum Exporting Countries (OPEC), Venezuela was able to build a governmental and physical infrastructure from its increasing petroleum revenues. Although many lived well, the proceeds from petroleum production were concentrated in the middle and upper classes and a few well-paid unionized petroleum workers. The vast majority continued to live in poverty despite the petroleum bonanza. Strong civilian government and a stable two-party system did, however, develop. This system suffered its first challenge when major riots broke out after IMF-inspired austerity measures were met with massive rioting by the poor in Caracas in 1989. The inability of successive governments to govern and increasing corruption led to two serious coup attempts by reformist military officers in 1992 and the eventual emergence of one of the coup leaders as a challenger to the old political system. After serving two years in prison, Hugo Chávez assembled an opposition movement (Fifth Republic Movement) and successfully ran for the presidency in December 1998. He defeated the candidates fielded by the two main parties and swept many of his supporters into office throughout the nation. The two long-dominant parties lost legitimacy in the face of the traditional system's breakdown and Chávez's promises to confront neoliberalism and the conditions that were keeping the masses in poverty. Further, he charged the old political structures with corruption and of only benefiting the elite. He spoke of the need for structural change and made favorable references to the achievements of the Cuban Revolution and Fidel Castro after his visit to the island. In 2000, Chávez managed to have a much revised constitutional system passed in a national plebiscite and to again hold elections at all levels to legitimize his mandate. He won 60 percent of the vote. The newly restructured state was dubbed the "Bolivarian Republic of Venezuela." His power was threatened by a coup attempt in 2002 and a popular referendum to remove him from office in 2004. Neither was successful, and *Chavismo* was still solidly in control in 2010. Though Chávez was not able to initially secure a majority for all the constitutional reforms he championed, he did get most passed with a second referendum in 2010.

GROWTH, PERSISTENT POVERTY, AND IMMIGRATION TO THE UNITED STATES

As was the case in Venezuela, by 2005 most Latin American economies experienced some economic growth but maintained a wide gap between upper-class beneficiaries of globalization and the still-prevalent misery of the masses. In many cases, income distribution even widened. However, a few countries, such as Costa Rica and Chile after 1990, developed sufficient social welfare programs to at least soften the savage capitalism that globalization had unleashed in Latin America. It remains to be seen if this new direction in economic policy will engender sufficient benefits to satisfy the masses, if the people will mobilize behind new political leaders and political movements that challenge the status quo and promise greater economic equality, or if they will just leave if they can. By 2005, there was an upsurge in popular movements and leftist leaders had taken power in Argentina, Brazil, Uruguay, and Venezuela. Radical popular movements had displaced less progressive politics in Bolivia and Ecuador and leftist presidents were elected in both Andean nations. For a while a leftist was the leading candidate for the 2006 election in Mexico but was narrowly defeated at the polls. Alternatively, Latin American immigration into the United States was increasingly adopted by others as a survival strategy, and the number of legal and illegal immigrants crossing U.S. borders continued to surge. Indeed, remittances sent home by Latin Americans working in the United States became a major source of income in many countries like Mexico and the Dominican Republic. This also began to change the population dynamics and politics on both sides of the U.S. border. People and thus labor—like capital—became ever more fluid and able to flow past borders. Indeed, there were many dimensions to the globalization process in the twenty-first century in the Americas and fences, walls, or increased border patrols could not even begin to stop it. It should also be noted that there was increased migration within the region as well, especially to economic centers such as southern Brazil, Argentina, and Costa Rica. However, the economic

TABLE 3.   Remittances to Latin America and the Caribbean Countries, 2009

Country	Amount (millions of dollars)
Argentina	853
Belize	100
Bolivia	1,023
Brazil	4,746
Chile	756
Colombia	4,134
Costa Rica	535
Cuba	...
Dominican Republic	2,790
Ecuador	2,495
El Salvador	3,465
Guatemala	3,912
Guyana	356
Haiti	1,641
Honduras	2,483
Jamaica	1,798
Mexico	21,132
Nicaragua	915
Panama	291
Paraguay	691
Peru	2,665
Trinidad & Tobago	116
Uruguay	116
Venezuela	733

... = Data not available

Note: These figures represent total remittances rather than those only from the U.S., although the U.S. accounts for 75% of the total.

Source: Inter-American Development Bank (online: http://www.iadb.org/ mif/remesas_map.cfm?language=english&parid=5&item1d=2,2008).

TABLE 4.   Immigrants in the United States by Region and Country of Birth, 1996–2009

Region and Country of Birth	Legal Immigrants			Estimated Illegal Immigrants Residing in the U.S.	
	1996	2002	2009	1990	2007
North America	340,428	402,949	375,236	2,789,000	8,800,000
Mexico	163,556	218,822	164,920	2,040,000	7,030,000
Caribbean	X	93,914	134,744	X	X
Antigua-Barbuda	406	380	437	X	X
Bahamas	767	808	751	X	X
Barbados	1,041	813	603	4,000	5000^
Cuba	26,438	28,182	38,954	2,000	7000^
Dominica	797	148	484	3,000	4000^
Dominican Republic	39,599	22,515	49,414	91,000	91000^
Grenada	785	634	748	X	X
Haiti	18,383	20,213	24,280	67,000	76000^
Jamaica	19,084	14,835	21,783	37,000	41000^
Trinidad and Tobago	7,331	5,738	6,256	23,000	34000^
Central America	X	66,298	47,013	X	X
Belize	785	966	1,041	10,000	8000^
Costa Rica	1,502	1,591	2,384	5,000	17000^
El Salvador	17,902	31,060	19,909	298,000	570,000
Guatemala	8,762	16,178	12,187	118,000	430,000
Honduras	5,866	6,435	6,404	42,000	300,000
Nicaragua	6,901	10,659	4,137	50,000	21000^
Panama	2,559	1,680	1,806	7,000	11000^
South America	61,744	74,151	102,878	185,000	800,000
Argentina	2,450	3,661	5,780	7,000	15000^
Bolivia	1,913	1,664	2,837	8,000	13000^
Brazil	5,888	9,439	14,701	20,000	180,000
Chile	1,706	1,839	2,250	6,000	17000^
Colombia	14,275	18,758	27,849	51,000	141000^
Ecuador	8,319	10,561	12,128	37,000	170,000
Guyana	9,489	9,938	6,670	13,000	22000^
Paraguay	615	356	530	X	X
Peru	12,869	11,918	16,957	27,000	61000^
Suriname	211	247	227	X	X
Uruguay	539	536	1,775	2,000	2000^
Venezuela	3,465	5,228	11,154	10,000	34000^

X = Data not available. ^From the year 2000 instead of 2008; DHS does not provide a comprehensive breakdown of illegal immigration in 2008.

Source: 2009 Yearbook of Immigration Statistics, Table 2 and Table 3. Office of Immigration Statistics in the Department of Homeland Security.

Located on the internet at http://www.dhs.gov/ximgtn/statistics/publications/LPR08.shtm.

Estimates of the Unauthorized Immigrant Population Residing in the United States, August, 2008. Department of Homeland Security. Located on the internet at http://www.dhs.gov/files/statistics/immigration.shtm

crisis that began in 2008 not only discredited many neoliberal tenets and reduced immigration to the United States and better off countries in the hemisphere, it drastically reduced the amount of the remittances sent back to the poorer countries and even stimulated some reverse migration as jobs disappeared in the U.S.

Nineteenth-Century Time Line

1804 Following mass slave rebellion led by Toussaint L'Ouverture, Haiti becomes the first independent republic in Latin America

1807 Napoleon Bonaparte invades Spain and Portugal; Ferdinand VII imprisoned and forced from Spanish throne, and Napoleon names his brother as successor; in the Americas, creoles begin plotting the independence of their Spanish American countries; the Portuguese court escapes and, with the British navy's help, flees to Brazil

1810 Mexico declares independence from Spain under the leadership of Father Miguel Hidalgo

1811 Venezuela declares its independence by forming a junta that expels the Spanish governor

1813 Father José María Morelos revives the Mexican independence movement; José de San Martín and the Army of the Andes liberate Argentina

1816 The United Provinces of the Río de la Plata declare their independence

1817 Chile is liberated by Bernardo O'Higgins; Spain outlaws the slave trade in all of its provinces to the north of the equator

1819 The United States buys Florida for $5 million

1821 On July 28, San Martín proclaims Peru independent; Dom Pedro defies summons of Cortés by remaining in Brazil, creating the only durable monarchy in Latin American history; Stephen F. Austin and other settlers move into Texas; Mexico and Central America gain independence

1822 Agustín de Iturbide is crowned emperor of Mexico

1823 The Central American Federation is established; the Monroe Doctrine is announced by U.S. president James Monroe; Peru passes its constitution

1824 The defeat of the Spanish army in Ayachucho, Peru, marks the end of Spanish rule in the Americas

1825 Bolivia gains its independence

1825–1828 War between Brazil and United Provinces of the Río de la Plata (present-day Argentina); the peace treaty created the independent state of Uruguay

1826 Congress of American Republics held in Panama; independence leaders sign concordats with the Vatican making Catholicism the state religion

1830 In Chile, beginning of the Conservative Republic; the Conservative Party holds power for thirty years

1835 Texans revolt

1836 Texans declare independence from Mexico

1845 U.S. Congress annexes Texas

1846 War between the United States and Mexico begins

1848 The Treaty of Guadalupe Hidalgo brings end to war between United States and Mexico; the United States gains approximately half of Mexico's territory

1855 U.S. citizen William Walker and former troops from the Mexican-American War invade Nicaragua; Walker declares himself president and holds power until 1857

1857 In Mexico, the Laws of Reform are promulgated by Benito Juárez

1864 Maximilian given Mexican throne by Napoleon III

1867 President Juárez expels the French and marches into Mexico City

1868–1878 Ten Years' War; nationalist Cubans lose fight for independence from Spain

1871 Chilean constitution is changed, disallowing consecutive presidential terms; Brazil passes "law of the free womb"—all children born to Brazilian slaves are considered free; also in Brazil, ex-Liberal Party members found the Republican Party

1876–1880, 1884–1911 General Porfirio Díaz rules over Mexico

1879–1883 War of the Pacific between Chile, Peru, and Bolivia; Bolivia loses land access to sea

1886 Slavery ends in Cuba

1887 In Chile, the Democratic Party is founded

1888 Brazil passes "golden law," which frees all slaves without compensation

1889 On November 16, Brazil is declared a republic as Emperor Dom Pedro II and his family leave in exile

1890 Increasing commercial relations between United States and Latin America and formation of the Pan-American Union

Contemporary Time Line

1910–1917 Mexican Revolution

1911 Francisco Madero elected president of Mexico

1912 Universal male suffrage granted in Argentina; U.S. military intervenes in Nicaragua; U.S. troops stay until 1925

1913 Madero killed

1914 Panama Canal opens

1915–1934 United States occupies Haiti

1916–1922 U.S. Marines occupy Dominican Republic

1916 Hipólito Yrigoyen, leader of the Unión Cívica Radical (UCR, or Radicals), elected president of Argentina; workers' compensation laws passed in Chile

1917 Chile passes employer liability laws; Venustiano Carranza assumes presidency in Mexico; a new constitution is written; U.S. military intervenes in Cuba; Puerto Rico is legally annexed to the United States; Puerto Ricans given U.S. citizenship

1919 Chile passes retirement system for railway workers in the same year that 100,000 workers march past presidential palace; Emiliano Zapata murdered

1922 Communist Party formed in Brazil; oil found in Venezuela

1924 Military junta in Chile; Alianza Popular Revolucionaria Americana (APRA) formed by Victor Raúl Haya de la Torre

1926 Augusto César Sandino returns to Nicaragua to fight with liberals; begins guerrilla war against newly occupying U.S. forces

1926–1929 Mexican Church suspends worship, protesting state harassment; many priests and civilians killed in the Cristero rebellion

1926 Democratic Party founded in São Paulo, Brazil

1929 Ecuador is the first Latin American country to grant suffrage to women

1930 On September 6, the military of Argentina overthrows the Yrigoyen government; October coup in Brazil; Getúlio Vargas takes over government

1932 Brazil and Uruguay grant suffrage to women; Chaco War between Bolivia and Paraguay; Paraguay gains more territory; uprising in El Salvador is brutally repressed in la Matanza

1933 U.S. troops leave Nicaragua; Anastasio Somoza begins to take power; U.S. president Franklin Roosevelt announces Good Neighbor Policy

1934 Lázaro Cárdenas becomes president of Mexico; during his term he redistributes 17,806,168 hectares (44 million acres) of land to landless Mexicans; Sandino murdered in Nicaragua

1938 Mexican oil industry nationalized under Cárdenas

1939 El Salvador grants suffrage to women

1943 Juan Perón and other military officers take over in Argentina

1944 Democratic revolution in Guatemala

1945 Modern democratic era begins in Venezuela with takeover by APRA-inspired Acción Democrática, led by Rómulo Betancourt; Guatemala and Panama grant suffrage to women

1946 Juan Perón elected president of Argentina; Eva "Evita" Duarte Perón becomes first lady

1947 Argentina and Venezuela grant women suffrage

1948 José Figueres and APRA-inspired Liberación Nacional Party lead reformist revolution in Costa Rica and establish modern democratic social welfare state; Costa Rican army banned by its new constitution; *Bogotazo* in Colombia; *La Violencia* begins

1949 Chile and Costa Rica grant women suffrage

1952 Evita Perón dies of cancer; Fulgencio Batista takes direct power in Cuba; Puerto Rico becomes a commonwealth of the United States; Marcos Pérez Jiménez stages coup in Venezuela, initiating a dictatorship that lasts until 1958; Bolivia grants women suffrage; Bolivian revolution led by Movimiento Nacionalista Revolucionario (MNR) and Víctor Paz Estenssoro

1954 Alfredo Stroessner takes over as president of Paraguay and rules until 1989; in Guatemala, CIA-organized coup deposes constitutional president Jacobo Arbenz and begins three decades of often brutal military rule; United Fruit regains land nationalized in land reform program during 1944 revolution

1955 Juan Perón ousted from power by the military and goes into exile; Honduras, Nicaragua, and Peru grant women suffrage

1956 Juscelino Kubitschek de Oliveira inaugurated president of Brazil; construction of Brasília begins

1957 François "Papa Doc" Duvalier elected president of Haiti; Colombia grants women suffrage

1958 Dictator Pérez Jiménez ousted in Venezuela; Acción Démocratica's Rómulo Betancourt elected president, beginning modern democratic era

1959 Batista flees Cuba; Fidel Castro and the 26th of July Movement take power

1960 Construction of Brasília completed

1961 Paraguay is the last Latin American country to grant suffrage to women; the United States organizes unsuccessful Bay of Pigs invasion by Cuban exiles

1962–1965 The Second Vatican Council (Vatican II) commits the Church to work for human rights, justice, and freedom

1962 Peronists again allowed to run for office in Argentina; Cuban Missile Crisis; Jamaica gains independence from Britain

1963 Rural unionization legalized in Brazil; peasant leagues grow

1964 Eduardo Frei Montalva elected president of Chile; military coup in Brazil; bureaucratic authoritarian military stays in power until 1985

1965 U.S. marines invade the Dominican Republic

1966 Brazil's government unveils Operation Amazonia, a plan to develop the Amazon basin

1967 Ernesto "Che" Guevara dies in Bolivia

1968 October 2 student massacre in Tlatelolco, Mexico City; meeting of Latin American bishops in Medellín; Colombia adopts a "preferential option for the poor" under the influence of liberation theology; reformist military leaders take over in Peru under Juan Velasco Alvarado

1970 Salvador Allende elected president of Chile; he is the first freely elected Marxist president in Latin America; the Communist Party of Peru—Sendero Luminoso (PCP-SL)—emerges after an ideological split in Peru's Communist Party; origins of the group can be traced to a study group formed in the early 1960s by Professor Abimael Guzmán Reynoso at the University of San Cristóbal de Huamanga; Sendero Luminoso, the Shining Path, later takes the form of a revolutionary movement

1971 Haitian president "Papa Doc" Duvalier dies; his son, Jean-Claude "Baby Doc" Duvalier, takes control; U.S. Peace Corps accused of sterilizing Indian women without their knowledge, expelled from Bolivia

1973 Juan Perón reelected president of Argentina; his wife Isabel becomes vice president; Salvador Allende dies in a September 11 military coup in Chile; General Augusto Pinochet initiates a brutal military dictatorship that rules until 1990

1974 Juan Perón dies; Isabel Perón becomes first female president of a Latin American country

1975 UN Conference on Women held in Mexico City, kicking off the Decade for Women; Cuba passes law requiring men and women to share responsibilities for housework and childrearing

1976 Argentine military ousts Isabel Perón; General Jorge Rafael Videla takes power, and the "dirty war" begins; the Mothers of the Disappeared begin to hold weekly vigils challenging the military government's human rights abuses

1978 John Paul II becomes pope; the Catholic Church becomes more conservative; conservative Church leaders begin to attempt to eliminate liberation theology

1979 Somoza regime collapses; the Frente Sandinista de Liberación Nacional (FSLN), or Sandinista National Liberation Front, takes power

1980 Archbishop Oscar Romero of San Salvador assassinated; four American church women murdered by Salvadoran military; Farabundo Martí National Liberation Front (FMLN) formed in El Salvador

1981 United States inspires contras to war against Nicaraguan government; 30,000 die before 1990

1982 Falklands/Malvinas War begins between Argentina and Britain; Brazil elects first freely elected governors since 1965; General Efrain Rios Montt becomes Latin America's first evangelical dictator in Guatemala and embarks on a brutal counterinsurgency that often targets entire Indian communities

1983 U.S. marines land in Grenada

1985 Brazil elects Tancredo Neves as first freely elected president; the night of his inauguration he has surgery and never recovers; Vice President José Sarney becomes president

1986 "Baby Doc" Duvalier flees Haiti

1988 Amid well-documented charges of election fraud, Institutional Revolutionary Party (PRI) candidate Carlos Salinas defeats Cuauhtémoc Cárdenas and Party of the Democratic Revolution (PRD) to gain presidency of Mexico

1989 Carlos Menem elected president of Argentina; Patricio Aylwin elected president of Chile, the first elected president of Chile since Allende took power; Pinochet maintains his position as commander-in-chief of the Chilean armed forces and as senator for life; in Brazil, Fernando Collor de Mello elected president, defeating Workers' Party (PT) leader Luiz Inácio "Lula" da Silva; U.S. troops invade Panama to oust Manuel Noriega; six Jesuit priests assassinated in El Salvador by U.S.-trained troops after the FMLN overruns much of San Salvador; announcement of austerity package in Venezuela causes riots, in which 276 die

1990 Alberto Fujimori elected president of Peru; stays in office until 2001; President Salinas of Mexico announces his intention to negotiate the North American Free Trade Agreement (NAFTA) with the United States; Jean-Bertrand Aristide elected president of Haiti; a military coup prevents him from taking power; Violeta Barrios de Chamorro elected president of Nicaragua, defeating FSLN candidate Daniel Ortega

1991 Jorge Serrano of Guatemala becomes Latin America's first elected evangelical president

1992 In Brazil, Collor is impeached and Vice President Itamar Franco becomes president; Fujimori closes congress in an *auto-golpe,* or self-coup; leader of the Sendero Luminoso Abimael Guzmán captured; World Summit on the Environment and Development held in Rio de Janeiro; guerrilla war ends in El Salvador; two military coup attempts occur in Venezuela

1993 Eduardo Frei Ruiz-Tagle (son of the president 1964–1970) elected president of Chile; Carlos Andrés Pérez forced to step down in Venezuela

1994 Fernando Henrique Cardoso elected president of Brazil; NAFTA goes into effect on January 1; Zapatista National Liberation Army revolts in Chiapas; Ernesto Zedillo elected president of Mexico after first PRI candidate is assassinated; United States occupies Haiti; Aristide assumes presidency

1995 Menem reelected president of Argentina; Fujimori reelected president of Peru; new quota in Argentina making sure that one in four congresspeople are women; Mercosur, or Southern Cone Common Market is founded, including Argentina, Brazil, Uruguay, and Paraguay, later joined by Bolivia and Chile

1998   Pinochet loses post as commander-in-chief of Chilean armed forces; Cardoso reelected president of Brazil, once again defeating Lula; former coup leader Hugo Chávez elected president of Venezuela, ending domination by two traditional parties, Acción Democrática and the Social Christian Party (COPEI)

1999   Mireya Moscoso elected first female president of Panama; Plan Colombia initiated

2000   Socialist Ricardo Lagos elected president of Chile as the Concertación candidate; Confederation of Indigenous Nationalities of Ecuador (CONAIE) and military officers briefly take over congress in Ecuador; Fujimori reelected in Peru after forcing constitutional changes allowing him to run for a third term; opposition candidate Vicente Fox elected president of Mexico, breaking seven decades of presidential domination by the PRI; in Venezuela, president Hugo Chávez reelected for six-year term under new constitution

2001   Argentina experiences severe economic and political crisis; President Fernando de la Rua resigns; Alejandro Toledo elected president in Peru after Fujimori forced out of office

2002   Workers' Party candidate Luiz Inácio "Lula" da Silva elected to presidency of Brazil on fourth run; attempted coup in Venezuela reversed by massive street demonstration supporting President Hugo Chávez; hard-liner Alvaro Uribe elected president of Colombia

2003   Massive mobilization by *cocaleros*, indigenous peoples, unions, and others force Bolivian President Gonzalo Sánchez de Lozada from office; Argentina elects leftist Peronist Néstor Kirchner as president

2004   Dr. Tabaré Vázquez of leftist Broad Front wins presidency in Uruguay; Venezuelan president Hugo Chávez registers strong support in referendum on his rule

2005   Ecuadoran president Lucio Gutiérrez is forced from office by popular mobilizations; Bolivian president Carlos Mesa also forced to resign and former *cocalero* leader Evo Morales becomes first indigenous president of Bolivia later in the year

2006   Lula and Worker's Party government survive scandal to win second presidential term in Brazil; left-leaning Rafael Correa elected president of Ecuador; Alvaro Uribe continues hard-line on negotiating with guerrillas and is reelected president of Colombia; Sandinista leader and former president Daniel Ortega is again elected president in Nicaragua; in a hard-fought campaign in Mexico, PAN candidate Felipe Calderón wins presidential election by razor-thin margin; Leftist PRD candidate Miguel López Obrador contests vote and vows parallel government; Hugo Chávez reelected president of Venezuela with 62 percent of vote; Michelle Bachelet elected first female president of Chile

2007   Evo Morales continues reforms in Bolivia and asserts nation's right to own and control all natural gas; Hugo Chávez asserts socialist nature of Venezuelan regime and continues strong leadership style while confronting George Bush and increasingly hostile U.S. foreign policy; Nobel prize winner Rigoberta Menchú makes poor showing in Guatemalan presidential election, which is won by Alvaro Colom; Néstor Kirchner decides not to run for a second presidential term in Argentina in favor of his wife Cristina Fernández de Kirchner, who wins vote to become first woman elected to the presidency

2008   Leftist former Archbishop Fernando Lugo elected president of Paraguay; Fidel Castro resigns as president of Cuba and Raúl Castro is elected president by National Assembly; United Socialist Party advocated by Venezuelan government; relations between Venezuela and the United States become more tense. Evo Morales faces sucessionist movement in Bolivia

2009   Obama adminsitration takes more conciliatory tone with Venezuela and eases travel restrictions for Cuba, opening a dialogue with Raúl Castro and Cuban leadership; Hugo Chávez continues move toward United Socialist Party for Venezuela and finally wins referendum allowing elected officials to serve more than two terms; 2009 coup d'état against progressive Honduran President Manuel Zelaya met with street demonstrations and universal international condemnation (including that of Obama administration) and calls for the restitution of constitutional democratic government. Honduran leaders ignore international condemnation and hold presidential election, which is accepted by the United States amidst intense criticism from most Latin American states.

2010   U.S. negotiates base agreement with Colombia; former defense minister Juan Manuel Santos elected Colombian president. Center-right candidate Sebastián Piñera elected president in Chile. Former Tupamaro guerrilla José Mujíca elected president on Frente Amplio ticket in Uruguay. Evo Morales reelected President in Bolivia with 64 percent of the vote.

Bibliography

Azuela, Mariano. *The Underdogs (Los de abajo).* New York: Penguin, 1962.

Beezley, William H., and Judith Ewell, eds. *The Human Tradition in Latin America.* Wilmington, DE: Scholarly Resources, 1997.

Bethell, Leslie, ed. *The Cambridge History of Latin America.* Vols. 4 and 5. Cambridge, UK: Cambridge University Press, 1986.

Blum, William. *Killing Hope: U.S. Military and CIA Interventions since World War II.* Monroe, ME: Common Courage Press, 1995.

Bulmer-Thomas, Victor. *The Economic History of Latin America since Independence.* New York: Cambridge University Press, 1994.

Burns, E. Bradford. *Latin America, A Concise Interpretive History.* 6th ed. Englewood Cliffs, NJ: Prentice Hall, 1994.

Butler, Smedley D. *War is a Racket.* Los Angeles: Feral House, 2003.

Chasteen, John C. *Born in Blood and Fire: A Concise History of Latin Amrica.* 2nd ed. New York: W.W. Norton, 2006.

Cortés Conde, Roberto, and Shane J. Hunt, eds. *The Latin American Economies: Growth and the Export Sector, 1880–1930.* New York: Holmes and Meier, 1985.

Galeano, Eduardo. *Open Veins of Latin America: Five Centuries of the Pillage of a Continent.* New York: Monthly Review Press, 1997.

Galeano, Eduardo. *We Say No: Chronicles 1963–1991.* New York: W. W. Norton, 1992.

Keen, Benjamin. *A History of Latin America: Independence to the Present.* 7th ed. Boston: Houghton Mifflin, 2004.

LaFeber, Walter. *Inevitable Revolutions.* 2nd ed. New York: W. W. Norton, 1992.

Langley, Lester. *The Americas in the Age of Revolution 1750–1850.* New Haven, CT: Yale University Press, 1996.

Leo Grande, William. *Our Own Back Yard: The United States in Central America, 1977–1992*. Chapel Hill: University of North Carolina Press, 1998.

Lynch, John. *The Spanish-American Revolutions 1806–1826*. New York: W. W. Norton, 1986.

Macauley, Neil. *The Emergence of Latin America in the Nineteenth Century*. New York: Oxford University Press, 1988.

McSherry, J. Patrice. *Predatory States: Operation Condor and Covert War in Latin America*. Lanham, MD: Rowman and Littlefield, 2005.

Oliva Campos, Carlos, and Gary Prevost, eds. *The Bush Doctrine and Latin America*. New York: Palgrave, 2007.

Rodríquez, O. Jaime E. *The Independence of Spanish America*. Cambridge: Cambridge University Press, 1998.

Russell-Wood, A. J. R. *From Colony to Nation: Essays on the Independence of Brazil*. Baltimore, MD: Johns Hopkins University Press, 1975.

Schoultz, Lars. *Beneath the United States: A History of U.S. Policy Toward Latin America*. Cambridge, MA: Harvard University Press, 1998.

Skidmore, Thomas E., and Peter H. Smith. *Modern Latin America*. 6th ed. New York: Oxford University Press, 2005.

Smith, Peter H. *Talons of the Eagle: Dynamics of U.S.–Latin American Relations*. 2nd ed. New York: Oxford University Press, 2008.

Vanden, Harry E. "Nicaraguan Foreign Relations." In *Revolution and Counterrevolution in Nicaragua: 1979 Through 1989*, edited by Thomas Walker. Boulder, CO: Westview Press, 1991.

Vanden, Harry E. "State Policy and the Cult of Terror in Central America." In *Contemporary Research on Terrorism*, edited by Paul Wilkinson and A. M. Stewart. Aberdeen, UK: Aberdeen University Press, 1987.

Vanden, Harry E. "Terrorism, Law and State Policy in Central America: The Eighties." *New Political Science* 18/19 (fall/winter 1990): 55–73.

Vanden, Harry E., and Thomas Walker. "U.S.–Nicaraguan Relations." In *The Central American Crisis*, 2nd ed., edited by Kenneth M. Coleman and George C. Herring. Wilmington, DE: Scholarly Resources, 1991.

FILMS AND VIDEOS

The Battle of Chile. Chile, 1976.
Evita. United States, 1997.
Machuca. Chile 2004.
Missing. United States, 1982.
The Official Story. Argentina, 1985.
Que Viva Mexico. Russia/USSR, 1931.
Reed: Mexico Insurgente. Mexico, 1971.
Romero. United States, 1989.
State of Siege. France, 1973.

WEBSITES

www.presidencia.gov.bo/   Presidential website in Bolivia.
www.presidencia.gov.ve/   Presidential website in Venezuela.

FOUR

THE OTHER AMERICANS

Details of the Spanish and Portuguese colonization of Latin America were provided in earlier chapters in this volume. The purpose of this chapter is to explore the contemporary consequences of that conquest on the indigenous peoples of the Americas who lived in the region prior to 1492 and to examine the fate of the more than 10 million Africans who were brought to the Caribbean and Latin America as slaves.

In 1992, the 500th anniversary of the first voyage of Columbus provided renewed focus on the current conditions of those segments of Latin American society who have been often ignored and marginalized by governments and scholars alike. It is estimated that close to 70 million indigenous people are alive today. Indigenous people constitute a clear majority in Bolivia, close to half of the population in Peru and Guatemala, and a substantial minority in countries such as Ecuador, Mexico, Panama, and Nicaragua. In the 1980s, conflict and then negotiation between the revolutionary government of Nicaragua and the peoples of the Atlantic Coast focused international attention on the region's indigenous people. In recent years, indigenous people have become more politically active in both Latin America and worldwide. In 1990, a nationwide indigenous uprising paralyzed Ecuador. A decade later the national indigenous group, the Confederation of Indigenous Nationalities of Ecuador (CONAIE), was one of the primary political actors in a government takeover that forced out President Jamil Mahuad. In 1994, an indigenous-based guerrilla movement, the Zapatistas, drew international attention to the southern Mexican state of Chiapas. In the early 2000s, indigenous groups helped to bring down unpopular governments in Ecuador and Bolivia. In many countries, indigenous movements have been in the forefront of struggles over the control of natural resources and the environment and have begun to move from a position of marginalization to one of centrality in Latin American society. In 2005, the Bolivian people elected their first indigenous president, Evo Morales. Once in office Morales moved to bring the country's natural resources under government control.

In 1492, Spain turned westward in search of wealth and empire. That same year the Spanish monarchy had recovered Granada from the Moors, the culmination of a struggle that had lasted seven centuries. It was an era of reconquest for Spain, undertaken in the context of its Christian vision. Queen Isabella became the patroness of the Inquisition, which was designed to root out all alien religions (Judaism, Islam, and others) in Spain. Pope Alexander VI, who was Spanish, ordained Isabella the master of the New World. Three years after the discovery, Columbus directed a military campaign against the native population in Hispaniola. His cavalry decimated the native inhabitants, and more than 500 were shipped to Spain and sold as slaves. Most died within a few years. Throughout the conquest of the Americas, each military action began with the Indians being read a long narrative (in Spanish, without an interpreter) exhorting them to join the Catholic faith and threatening them with death or slavery if they did not comply. The brutality of the proselytization notwithstanding, in many ways the religious arguments were only a cover for the primarily commercial basis of the conquest.

The newly powerful Spanish government had decided to establish its own direct links to the east, hoping to bypass the independent traders who up until that time had monopolized the trade there for spices and tropical plants. The voyages also sought precious metals. All of Europe needed silver. The existing sources in central Europe had largely been exhausted. In the Renaissance era, gold and silver were becoming the basis of a new economic system, mercantilism. Those nations that had supplies of these precious metals could dominate the Western world. Despite that, most of the expeditions that came to the Americas in search of wealth were not sponsored by governments (Columbus and Magellan were the exceptions) but by the *conquistadores* themselves or by businessmen who backed them. The *conquistadores* did indeed find gold and silver in large quantities; but in order to mine it, they needed local labor. That drive for labor produced what Eduardo Galeano has called the "Antillean holocaust":

> The Carribean island populations were totally exterminated in the gold mines, in the deadly task of sifting auriferous sands with their bodies half submerged in water or in breaking up the ground beyond the point of exhaustion, doubled up over the heavy cultivating tools brought from Spain. Many natives of Haiti anticipated the fate imposed by their white oppressors: they killed their children and committed mass suicide.

The civilizations confronted by the Spaniards in Mexico and Peru were large and prosperous ones. The Aztec capital Tenochtitlán (present-day Mexico City), with 300,000 people, was then five times larger than Madrid and double the population of Seville, Spain's largest city. Tenochtitlán had an advanced sanitation system and engaged in sophisticated agricultural techniques in the marshland around the city. It was a majestic city dominated by the Templo Major, its most sacred site.

When the conqueror Pizarro arrived in South America, the Incan Empire was at its height, spreading over the area of what is now Peru, Bolivia, and Ecuador and including parts of Colombia and Chile. The third great civilization was that of the Maya, who inhabited the Yucatán peninsula of Mexico and south into Guatemala. The Maya were skilled astronomers and mathematicians who had developed the concept of the number zero.

Despite their high level of civic and scientific development, the indigenous people in the Americas were defeated by a variety of factors that favored the European invaders. The European military commanders were also quite skillful at exploiting divisions among the indigenous people. In Mexico, Cortés allied with the Tlaxcalans against Moctezuma and the Aztecs of Tenochtitlán. Pizarro also succeeded in exploiting family disputes among the Incas to foster his advantage in Peru.

The brutality of their conquest was unlimited. They took the gold and melted it into bars for shipment to Spain. Sacred temples and other public places were simply destroyed. Later, in Mexico City, the Spanish would build their metropolitan cathedral and government buildings on the foundations of the primary religious and political buildings of the old Aztec capital, as if to symbolize the total subjugation of the original inhabitants. Pizarro's forces in Peru did the same, sacking the Temple of the Sun in Cuzco, the capital of the Incan Empire.

The Europeans also brought with them diseases not found in the Americas— smallpox, tetanus, leprosy, and yellow fever. Smallpox, the first to appear, had devastating consequences. The indigenous people had no defenses against these plagues and died in overwhelming numbers. As much as half of the existing population may have died as a result of the first contact.

As suggested in Chapter 2, the scope of the genocide against the indigenous people of the Americas is staggering. There were probably upward of 70 million people living in the Americas when the Europeans arrived, between 30 and 40 million in Mexico alone. By the middle of the seventeenth century, that number had been reduced to 3.5 million. In some countries, such as Cuba, the native population had been completely exterminated, while in one region of Peru, where there had been more than 2 million people, only about 4,000 families survived. Over the course of three centuries, silver production at Potosí consumed 8 million lives.

In addition to such dramatic loss of life through forced labor, the mining system indirectly destroyed the farming system. Forced to work in the mines or as virtual slaves on crown lands, indigenous people were forced to neglect their own cultivated lands. In the Incan Empire, the Spanish conquest resulted in the abandonment of the large, sophisticated farms that had grown corn, peanuts, yucca, and sweet potato. The irrigation systems that had been built over centuries were neglected, and the land reverted to desert, a condition that persists today.

European Justification

While millions of indigenous people perished, Europeans engaged in marginalized debates over the legal status of their victims. The Spanish court in the sixteenth century acknowledged in principle their legal rights and entitlement to dignity. Various religious leaders spoke out against the inhumane treatment that the native people received, but these legal statements and religious proclamations ultimately had no meaning because the exploitation of indigenous labor was essential to the functioning of the colonial system. In 1601, Philip III formally banned forced labor in the mines but in a secret decree allowed it to go forward; his successors, Philip IV and Charles II, continued the exploitation.

The ideological justifications for the exploitation of the indigenous people were many and varied. Political and religious leaders often characterized the native people as "naturally wicked" and viewed their backbreaking work in the mines as retribution for prior transgressions. Many religious leaders offered the opinion that as a race indigenous people lacked a soul and therefore could not be "saved" by the Church in the traditional sense. Many Church leaders never accepted Pope Paul III's declaration of 1537 that the indigenous people were "true men." Others viewed them as natural beasts of burden, better suited for much of the region's manual labor than its four-legged creatures. The Spanish and Portuguese colonizers were not alone in consigning the indigenous to a subhuman status. Some European intellectuals of the Enlightenment, such as Voltaire and Montesquieu, refused to recognize them as equals.

The indigenous population of the Americas, though conquered and defeated by the Spanish and Portuguese during the sixteenth century, continued its resistance on an ongoing basis. Probably the most dramatic example of that resistance occurred in Peru near the end of the eighteenth century. At that time, Spanish pressures and demands on the Peruvian Indians increased considerably. In particular, under the *repartimiento de mercancias* the natives had to purchase goods from Spanish traders whether or not the items were useful. Locals were often unable to pay for these purchases and, as a result, were forced from their villages to earn money in mines or on *haciendas,* neglecting their own productive enterprises. During this time, the Spanish rulers also sought to dramatically increase silver production at Potosí and did so with harsh forced labor programs. These conditions fostered a strong desire among the indigenous population to return to the glories of the Incan Empire of three centuries earlier. Their aspirations led to the great revolt of 1780–1781. These dramatic events had many forerunners; 128 rebellions took place in the Andean area between 1730 and 1780. From 1742 to 1755, a native leader, Juan Santos, waged partisan warfare against the Spaniards. The memory of his exploits was still alive when the revolt of José Gabriel Condorcanqui erupted. A well-educated, wealthy *mestizo* descendant of Incan kings, Condorcanqui took the name of the last head of the neo-Incan state and became Túpac Amaru II. His actions began with an ambush of a hated local Spanish commander; by early 1781, the southern highlands of Peru were in full revolt. The objective of Amaru's revolt was the establishment of an independent Peruvian state that would be essentially European in its political and social organization. His vision was that caste distinctions would disappear and that the *criollos* would live in harmony with Indians, blacks, and *mestizos.* The Catholic Church was to remain the state church. However, the Indian peasantry who responded to his call for revolt had clearly more radical goals, no less than total inversion of the existing social order and a return to an idealized Incan Empire where the humble peasant would be dominant. The peasants exacted their revenge on all those viewed as European, including the Church hierarchy and its priests. These actions frustrated Amaru's strategy of forming a common proindependence front of all social and racial groups. Some Indian leaders, fearing the radical direction of the revolt, threw their support to the Spaniards. Despite some initial successes, the rebel movement soon suffered a complete rout. Amaru, members of his family, and his leading captains were captured and brutally executed in Cuzco. While the most spectacular indigenous rebellion of that era, it was not unique. The revolt of the *comuneros* in New Granada in 1781–1782 had its origin in intolerable economic conditions. Unlike the Peruvian upheaval, it was more clearly limited in its aims. Its organization and its effort to form a common front of all colonial groups with grievances against Spanish authority were advances over Amaru's rebellion. A central committee elected by thousands of peasants and artisans directed the insurrection, which carried out an assault on Bogotá. Negotiations followed the rebellion, and an apparent agreement reached in June 1781 satisfied virtually all of the rebels' demands. However, the Spanish commissioners secretly voided the deal and, following the demobilization of the rebel army, regained control by crushing the leadership of the *comuneros*.

The exploitation of the indigenous population did not end with Spanish and Portuguese colonial rule. The continuing oppression was never more graphic than in Bolivia, which always had one of the highest percentages of indigenous people. Well into the twentieth century, *pongos,* or domestic servants, were being offered for hire as virtual slaves. As they had in colonial times, the locals acted as beasts of burden for the equivalent of a few pennies. Throughout much of the continent, they continued to be marginalized, driven from the little good land they had been able to maintain during colonial times. In the latter part of the nineteenth century, and the early part of the twentieth century, the dramatic expansion of commercial farming fell heavily on those indigenous communities that had survived the earlier genocide of the mining operations.

TABLE 5.   How Many Native People?

	Estimated Population	% of Total Population
Mexico	33,363,537	30.0%
Peru	13,296,133	45.0%
Guatemala	5,390,266	40.6%
Bolivia	5,376,385	55.0%
United States	3,686,545	1.2%
Ecuador	3,643,275	25.0%
Brazil	1,788,653	0.9%
Argentina	1,227,408	3.0%
Chile	763,679	4.6%
Panama	672,095	20.0%
Canada	669,744	2.0%
Honduras	545,500	7.0%
Colombia	456,440	1.0%
Venezuela	402,223	1.5%
Nicaragua	294,600	5.0%
Paraguay	174,891	2.5%
El Salvador	71,852	1.0%
Guyana	70,279	9.1%
Belize	51,419	16.7%
Costa Rica	42,539	1.0%
Suriname	9,625	2.0%
Total	71,997,088	13.1%

Source: *CIA World Factbook*, https://www.cia.gov/library/publications/ the-world-factbook, 2009.

The Role of Sugar and Slavery

Gold and silver were the primary targets of the conquest, but on his second voyage Columbus brought sugar cane roots from the Canary Islands and planted them in what is now the Dominican Republic, where they grew quite rapidly. Sugar was already a prized product in Europe because it was grown and refined in only a few places (Sicily, Madeira, and the Cape Verde Islands). Over the next three centuries, it would become the most important agricultural product shipped from the Western Hemisphere to Europe. Cane was planted in northeast Brazil and then in most of the Caribbean colonies—Barbados, Jamaica, Haiti, Santo Domingo, Guadeloupe, Cuba, and Puerto Rico. In the places where it was developed, the sugar industry quickly became dependent on the importation of slaves from western Africa. This industry became central to the development of significant parts of Latin America and left a legacy of environmental destruction and racism that still influences the region.

This is not to say that all slave systems in the Caribbean and elsewhere were based on the sugar plantation. Also, not all black people in the Americas are descendants of slaves, and not all slaves worked on sugar plantations. An important exception is the role slaves played in the extraction of gold in Brazil, which will be discussed later. However, it was the development of the sugar plantations of Brazil and the Caribbean in the seventeenth century that provided the impetus for the massive importation of Africans throughout the Americas. A full-blown transatlantic slave trade began after 1518 when Charles I of Spain authorized the direct commercial transfer of Africans to his possessions in the New World. It took some time for slavery to develop as we would come to know it, but it is estimated that eventually the slave trade moved more than 10 million Africans into various parts of the Americas between 1518 and 1870. Of those 10 to 11 million, more than 4 million wound up in the Caribbean islands. Brazil was the only area of the Americas to receive more slaves than did the Caribbean, with more than 5 million. The North American colonies received fewer than 1 million. Brazil was the first place where a slave society was established in the Americas, and it was the last country in the Western Hemisphere to abolish slavery, doing so only in 1888, two years after it was ended in Cuba and twenty-three years after it came to an end in the United States.

The contemporary condition of northeast Brazil is a testament to the destructive power of the sugar industry. From the beginning of Portuguese colonization early in the sixteenth century, Brazil was the world's largest producer of sugar; initially in the Spanish colonies, it was only a secondary activity. Brazil would remain the largest producer of sugar for over 150 years; from early on, it required the importation of African slaves because of scarce local labor and the large-scale loss of life among the native population. The sugar industry was labor-intensive, needing thousands of workers to prepare the ground and plant, harvest, grind, and refine the cane. Ironically, although the Portuguese crown initiated the colonization of northeast Brazil, Dutch entrepreneurs actually dominated the sugar industry, including participation in the slave trade. In 1630, the Dutch West India Company conquered northeast Brazil and took direct control of sugar production. From there the sugar production facilities were exported to the British in Barbados. Eventually, sharp competition developed between the two regions, with the Caribbean island eventually winning out as the Brazilian land began to deteriorate. The land was left permanently scarred by the 150 years of sugar monoculture. It had been a vast and fertile area when the colonists arrived, but the agricultural methods used were not sustainable. Fire was used to clear the land, and as a result considerable flora and fauna were permanently destroyed. The conditions of life for the African slaves who worked on the plantations was horrendous. No food was grown; all had to be imported, along with luxury goods, by the owners of the plantations. In this way, the plantation workers were totally dependent on the landowners. The result was chronic malnutrition and misery for most of the population. The current legacy of the sugar monoculture is that northeast Brazil is one of the most underdeveloped regions of the Americas, inhabited by more than 30 million people who are primarily the descendants of African slaves brought there more than four centuries ago. Sugar remains an important crop for the region, but today less than 20 percent of the land is used for sugar production; much of the rest is simply unusable because of environmental degradation. Other regions of Brazil have gone on to produce more sugar. As a result, this once fertile region must import food from other parts of Brazil, and more than half the people in the region live below the poverty line.

Northeast Brazil is not the only region to be permanently scarred by the production of sugar and the slavery that accompanied it. The islands of the Caribbean have suffered much the same fate. The Spanish had originally grown sugar cane in Cuba and Santo Domingo but on a relatively small scale. Barbados under Dutch entrepreneurship became the first great sugar experiment in the Caribbean, beginning in 1641. In just twenty-five years, Barbados had 800 plantations and over 80,000 slaves. The island's previously diverse agricultural production was slowly destroyed as virtually all good land was given over to sugar production. However, before long, the island's ecology was destroyed and its sugar production was no longer competitive, leaving behind a destitute people. From Barbados, sugar production shifted northward to Jamaica, where by 1700 there were ten times as many slaves as white inhabitants; by the middle of the eighteenth century, its land had also become depleted. In the second half of the eighteenth century, sugar production shifted to Haiti, where more than 25,000 slaves per year were being imported to increase the size of the industry to meet growing European demand. Haiti soon ceased to be the center of Caribbean sugar production, not as the result of an ecological disaster but rather as the result of revolution.

Revolution erupted in Haiti in 1791, and over the course of the next twelve years the sugar economy of the island was devastated. The rebellious slaves eventually succeeded in driving out the French army in 1803 and establishing Haiti as an independent nation. However, independence had high costs, including an embargo by both the United States and France. Although Haiti eventually won its recognized independence from France in 1825, the island's economy was devastated by continual attacks by French expeditionary forces and because of a large cash indemnity paid upon recognition of independence. As a result, Haiti ceased to be at the center of sugar production; that focus shifted northward to Cuba.

After the Haitian rebellion and subsequent reduction in production, the price of sugar in Europe doubled; and after 1806, Cuba began to sharply increase its production. Sugar production had begun its shift toward Cuba in 1762 when the British briefly took control of Havana. To expand the sugar industry, the British dramatically increased the number of slaves brought into Cuba. During the eleven-month British occupation, Cuba's economy turned toward sugar. Previously vibrant Cuban production of fruit, beef, and light manufactured goods was largely set aside for the growth of the sugar industry. This period also saw the destruction of Cuba's forests and the beginning of the process of degrading the fertility of Cuban soil. Following the Haitian revolution, Cuban sugar production was also given a boost when Haitian sugar producers fled with their slaves to set up production in eastern Cuba. The doubling of the capacity of the Cuban sugar industry after 1806 also required the continued importation of slaves over the ensuing decades even as the slave trade was gaining more and more international condemnation. More than 1 million Africans were brought to Cuba as slaves and in the process transformed the face of Cuban society forever. Today, close to 50 percent of the Cuban population is of African heritage.

Resistance to Slavery

Similar to the long history of indigenous resistance to colonialism, Africans who survived the voyage and were sold into slavery did not willingly accept their fate. *Marronage* (flight from slavery) was a recorded fact almost from the first days that Africans were brought to the island of Hispaniola. Indigenous people and slaves fled into the inaccessible mountains of the interior, sustaining a condition of liberation and keeping alive a sense of independent identity. In 1514, on the island of Puerto Rico, two Taíno/Arawak chiefs and their people allied with Africans against the representatives of the Spanish crown. A second uprising occurred seventeen years later when the enslaved black population rose up against its oppressors. In 1522, an uprising in Santo Domingo began with the revolt of forty sugar mill workers. Although these uprisings were eventually defeated and no full-scale rebellion would succeed prior to 1803, *marronage* was common throughout the Americas where large numbers of African slaves were concentrated. As Michel Laguerre observed, "Wherever there were slaves, there were also maroons.... [L]iving in free camps or on the fringes of port cities, they were a model for the slaves to imitate, embodying the desires of most of the slaves. What the slaves used to say in Sotto Voce on the plantations, they were able to say aloud in the maroon settlements." These maroon communities were common through four centuries of slavery in the Americas. Known by a variety of names (*palenques*, *quilombos*, *mocombos*, *cumbes*, *ladeiras*, and *mambíses*), these communities ranged from tiny, ephemeral groupings to powerful states encompassing thousands of members and surviving for generations or even centuries. Such maroon communities were generally well organized. They had political and military organization and were not, as is sometimes said, groups of wild, runaway, disorganized blacks. Some of these maroon communities were so powerful that they were able to negotiate treaties with European powers. These free and independent communities forged autonomous societies and protected their freedom and liberty. They rejected any outside domination.

In some places throughout the Americas, these communities still exist, often maintaining their cultural heritage and bearing living witness to the earliest days of African presence in the Americas. One of the best examples of such a community are the maroons of the Cockpit Country of northwestern Jamaica, who trace their roots back to the sixteenth century and have survived as a community to the present day. Today, their early leaders are recognized as national heroes by the Jamaican government. The maroons of Jamaica are probably the best-known group in North America, but many other similar communities exist throughout the Americas. San Basilio de Palenque near Cartagena, Colombia, is a surviving example. There, the inhabitants of the ex-maroon community speak Palenquero, a dialect that fuses Spanish and elements of several West African languages. Most black people of the Pacific lowlands of Panama, Colombia, and Ecuador do not see themselves as so directly connected to Africa. They lay full claim to their own homeland—the coastal section of this tropical rain forest. They are similar in outlook to maroons in the interior of Suriname and French Guiana, who maintain their distinct cultural heritage.

In Brazil, fugitive slaves organized the black kingdom of Palmares in the northeast and throughout the seventeenth century successfully resisted military expeditions of both the Dutch and the Portuguese. The independent kingdom of Palmares was organized as a state, similar to many that existed in Africa in the seventeenth century. Encompassing an area one-third the size of Portugal, it boasted a diversified agriculture of corn, sweet potatoes, beans, bananas, and other foods. Land was held in common, and no money was circulated. The ruling chief was elected from the ranks of the tribe and organized a defense of the territory that successfully protected it for several decades. When the Portuguese finally conquered Palmares in 1690s, it required an army of several thousand, the largest colonial army of the time. Ten thousand former slaves fought to defend the kingdom in the final battle, but they were defeated by superior firepower.

The slave trade, which left its lasting legacy on the Americas, was driven in large measure by the profits it generated in Europe. Britain is probably the best example of that profiteering. Queen Elizabeth I was reportedly opposed to the slave trade on moral grounds when the first English slave traders landed in Britain, but she quickly changed her perspective when shown the financial benefits that could flow from the trade. Once its lucrative nature was clear, the British moved quickly to overcome the Dutch dominance of the early trade. A key factor in the success of the British was the concession of the trade monopoly granted to them by the weakened Spanish. The South Sea Company, with significant investment from Britain's most powerful families, including the royal court, was the chief beneficiary of the monopoly. The impact of the slave trade on Britain's economy was significant. Traffic in slaves made Bristol Britain's second most important city and helped make Liverpool the world's most important port. Ships left Britain for Africa with cargoes of weapons, cloth, rum, and glass, which served as payment for the slaves who were obtained in West Africa and then shipped to the Americas. The African chiefs who cooperated in the slave trade used the weapons and the liquor to embark on new slave-hunting expeditions. Conditions on the ships were horrific, and often as many as half of the people on board died during the voyage. Many died of disease, while others committed suicide by refusing to eat or throwing themselves overboard. Those who survived the voyage but were too weak to impress buyers were simply left on the docks to die. The healthy survivors were sold at public auction.

Despite the losses at sea, the trade was highly lucrative as the ships sailed back to Britain with rich cargoes of sugar, cotton, coffee, and cocoa. Liverpool slave merchants were making more than £1 million in profits per year, and there was considerable spinoff to the rest of the economy. Liverpool's dockyards were improved considerably to handle the increased commerce. Banks in Britain's largest cities prospered through the trade. Lloyd's of London became a dominant force in the insurance industry, covering slaves, ships, and plantations. Almost 200,000 textile workers labored in Manchester to provide needed products for the Americas, while workers in Birmingham and Sheffield made muskets and knives. Although initially dominated by the Portuguese, it was the slave trade that positioned Britain to be the dominant world power by the end of the eighteenth century. At the start of the nineteenth century, Britain turned against slavery, not primarily out of any newfound moral revulsion but through a calculation that its growing industrial production needed wage earners throughout the world to buy its products.

The British were by no means alone as a nation that participated in the slave trade. Equally important were the Portuguese, who supplied the millions of Africans necessary for the exploitation of their primary colony, Brazil. In addition to providing slaves for the sugar industry, the Portuguese developed gold extraction in Brazil using slave labor. From 1700 onward, the region of Minas Gerais in central Brazil was the focal point of the extraction. For more than a century, gold flowed out of the region, with Portuguese and British slave traders gaining massive profits. The region itself was left destitute, a condition that persists today for the descendants of those slaves who worked the mines. Subsistence farming replaced the mines and, as in northeast Brazil, became, in Galeano's words, "the Kingdom of *fazendas*."

Concept of Race

Race must be understood as a socially constructed, not biologically determined, concept. According to Michael Hanchard, race in Latin America determines status, class, and political power. In this respect, race relations are power relations. Being black in Brazil generally signifies having a lower standard of living and less access to health care and education than whites have, but in the minds of many it also signifies criminality, licentiousness, and other negative attributes considered to be related to African peoples. It follows, then, that the meaning and interpretation of racial categories are always subject to revision, change, and negotiation. Most importantly, racial constructs are dynamic and fluid insofar as racial groups are not categorized in isolation but in relation to other groups who have their own attendant values of class, status, and power. The concepts of blackness and race have long been controversial in Latin America, and only in recent years have scholars and political activists for black and indigenous rights begun to create a dialogue that can shed light on the issues. The term *black* is an adjective derived from Latin, meaning in a literal sense "sooted, smoked black from flame." In practical terms, in Latin America, it has been defined as being "not white" and as having a connection to Africa. As in North America, blackness can equally be the target of unrelenting racism or the basis of deeply held religious and aesthetic attachment to a heritage of struggle, survival, and achievement. The dominant, lighter-skinned ruling elites of Latin America historically have viewed the population of African descent with a mixture of fear and hatred. The blacks who lived free in isolated areas such as the Cauca Valley of Colombia have been the targets of campaigns of fear, labeling them as subhuman beasts who had brought a "primitive" culture with them from Africa. Such historical labeling meant that these groups in Colombia were marginalized from national political life.

The racism of the dominant classes of the Americas comes through in the historical treatment of the greatest of Latin America's heros, Simón Bolívar. In the wars of liberation led by Bolívar between 1813 and 1822, black troops from revolutionary Haiti helped overthrow colonial governments in the territory that became the Republic of Gran Colombia. The liberation of these territories helped foster an era of black consciousness among the indigenous black communities. It has often been speculated that Bolívar may have had black ancestors, but this idea has generally been rejected in Colombia and Venezuela by white and *mestizo* biographers who were clearly uneasy about the implications of such a possibility.

Race is a powerful ideological concept in contemporary times throughout the Americas. There are two competing concepts that vie for recognition. *Mestizaje* is the ideology of racial mixture and assimilation, which is the adopted perspective of most of the political elites of the region. *Negritude*, on the other hand, is a concept that celebrates the positive features of blackness. At the national government level only in Haiti is negritude the explicit national ideology. In most countries where there is a significant population of African heritage, the concept of negritude has been both the basis of societal discrimination and a symbol of racial pride for the oppressed. Of course, such pride is often seen by the dominant political culture to be a threat to the sovereignty and territoriality of the nation.

When reviewing their own history and social movements, black social activists and movement leaders in Latin America inevitably raise the comparison with the U.S. Civil Rights movement and state with deep regret that black Latin America never had an equivalent movement. However, black-based social movements over the years have gained momentum and are now challenging centuries of domination. For example, black social movements are gaining strength in Brazil, Colombia, Ecuador, Venezuela, Uruguay, Nicaragua, Costa Rica, Honduras, and other Latin American countries (see Dixon 1996). These movements are fighting for social inclusion and development, equality before the law, human rights protections, and democratic reform.

Black organizations in Brazil are some of the best organized and politically developed in the region. The black movements in Brazil are not monolithic and are quite diverse in scope, practice, and philosophy. Like all social movements, there are basic points of convergence and divergence. However, most of the progressive black movements agree that racism is an obstacle to Afro-Brazilian progress. One of the most powerful examples of a movement that has promoted black liberation is Brazil's black consciousness movement, a loosely linked network of nearly 600 organizations that has the goal of preserving ethnic heritage and fighting against the discrimination and poverty of contemporary Brazil. The groups are not

TABLE 6. How Many Afro-Latin Americans?

Country/Year	Estimated Population	% of Total Population
Brazil (2009)	88,836,453	44.7%
Venezuela (2009)	10,109,196	37.7%
Colombia (2009)	9,585,245	21.0%
Haiti (2009)	8,583,759	95.0%
Cuba (2002)	3,996,627	34.9%
Jamaica (2009)	2,752,454	97.4%
Mexico (2009)	1,112,118	1.0%
Dominican Republic (2009)	1,061,596	11.0%
Peru (2009)	886,409	3.0%
Trinidad and Tobago (2009)	713,372	58.0%
Nicaragua (2009)	530,208	9.0%
Panama (2009)	470,466	14.0%
Puerto Rico (2009)	448,725	11.3%
Ecuador (2009)	437,193	3.0%
Guyana (2009)	362,208	46.9%
Barbados (2009)	256,130	90.0%
Paraguay (2009)	244,848	3.5%
Suriname (2009)	197,319	41.0%
Bolivia (2009)	195,505	2.0%
Honduras (2009)	155,857	2.0%
Santa Lucia (2009)	151,292	94.4%
Uruguay (2009)	139,775	4.0%
Costa Rica (2009)	127,616	3.0%
Belize (2009)	125,315	40.7%
St. Vicente & The Grenadines (2009)	88,888	85.0%
Grenada (2009)	86,202	95.0%
Antigua & Barbuda (2009)	81,693	95.4%
St. Kitts & Nevis (2009)	39,168	97.6%

Note: Table accounts for both black and mixed race population.

Source: *CIA World Factbook*, https://www.cia.gov/library/publications/the-world-factbook/geos/br.html.

united by a single ideology, and they pursue their campaign against racism using a variety of methods. Some organizations focus almost exclusively on culture, believing that the rediscovery of African roots can transform the consciousness of Brazil's black population. Other groups, such as the São Paulo–based Unified Black Movement (MNU), are politically focused, arguing that racism must be combated through changes in political, social, and economic structures. The groups have demonstrated against police violence and have fought in the courts for the enforcement of existing laws against discrimination in the workplace. During the writing of Brazil's constitution in the 1980s, MNU was instrumental in convening the National Convention of Blacks for the Constitution. The grassroots debates of this initiative, together with the efforts of Carlos Alberto de Oliveira and Benedita da Silva, two black congresspeople elected in 1986, resulted in the inclusion of a constitutional amendment that outlawed racial discrimination. The activity of the black consciousness movement has also forced the traditional Brazilian political parties to react with statements against racism and to make commitments to include blacks among their lists of political candidates and appointments to public office. These efforts have borne some fruit with the appointment of a number of blacks to key positions by the centrist Brazilian Democratic Movement Party (PMDB), but there are only a handful of black deputies in the national legislature. Pressure on the political elites has helped break down the long-held elite-generated myth that Brazil is a "racial democracy."

However, the black movement is currently far from the mass political phenomenon that it aspires to be. Part of the limitation of the movement is its narrow social base. Black consciousness groups are composed primarily of professionals, intellectuals, and upwardly mobile students. The movement is relatively small in total numbers, with probably 25,000 sympathizers out of an Afro-Brazilian population of some 40 million. Despite these limitations, the movement does represent an important contribution to the cause of racial justice in the continent's largest country. The recent use of quotas to ensure adequate Afro-Brazilian admissions to universities was one gain achieved by the black movements. Afro-Colombians have also struggled for equality and have modestly succeeded in raising consciousness of their separateness from the majority of the Colombian nation.

Contemporary Struggle of the Indigenous People

The history of exploitation of the indigenous people at the time of the conquest and the century that followed is generally not disputed. Rather, it is the history that follows that is controversial. Even those who have sympathy and understanding for the oppression of the indigenous people have tended to avoid a systematic understanding of its contemporary reality. There has been a common perception that Native American cultures are primarily relics of the past, doomed to be abandoned as modernity spread to the deepest regions of rural Latin America. To the degree that indigenous cultures survived, it would be as rural, isolated communities clinging to traditional ways of life. Although such communities exist, they make up only a tiny fraction of the approximately 40 million native peoples who live in the Americas today. Because the stereotype of the isolated rural community is not actually the norm, our understanding of the issues and needs of this population must change.

The indigenous people who survived the conquest recovered their numbers slowly but steadily. Contrary to the predictions of assimilative policies, native peoples have remained demographically stable; bilingualism has increased without the disappearance of native languages. The native peoples have not been defeated or eliminated. Indigenous peoples still live in nearly all of the regions where they lived in the eighteenth century. They have expanded into new territories and established a presence in urban, industrialized society that challenges the stereotypical image of indigenous peasants. Indigenous squatters are prominent throughout the major cities of the continent.

ECUADOR

One of the strongest contemporary movements of indigenous peoples is CONAIE, a nationwide organization that has sought to represent the native peoples of Ecuador, who make up between 25 and 30 percent of the population—the fifth largest percentage of indigenous people in the hemisphere.

Provincial and regional indigenous organizations were created in the 1970s. In 1980, the Confederation of Indigenous Nationalities of the Ecuadorian Amazon (CONFENAIE) was founded to represent the indigenous population of the Oriente, an important step toward a national organization. In the highlands, indigenous organizations dated back to the founding of the Ecuadorian Indigenous Federation (FEI) in the 1940s. CONAIE was established in 1986 to form a single, national organization. In the 1970s and 1980s, the organizations tended to have a local focus; but in the 1990s, the movement adopted a broader agenda, the right to self-determination, the right to cultural identity and language, and the right to economic development within the framework of indigenous values and traditions. Land became the focal point for the indigenous movement in Ecuador. It has also been the issue on which it has connected most successfully with nonindigenous groups.

Indeed, land was the focal point of CONAIE's first national actions in 1990. After weeks of organizing and stagnated discussions with the national government, CONAIE orchestrated an uprising that paralyzed the country for a week. The protests ended when the government agreed to national-level negotiations with CONAIE. While not succeeding in most of its demands, CONAIE did win the right to name the national director of bilingual education programs and the granting of some significant tracts of land to indigenous organizations. These mobilizations laid the groundwork for the larger and more powerful actions of 1994. CONAIE reached greater prominence in June 1994, when it sponsored a strike that shut down the country for two weeks. The target of the protest was the Agrarian Development Law, approved by the Ecuadorian congress, which called for the elimination of communal lands in favor of agricultural enterprises. The 1994 protests in Ecuador also demonstrated the ability of the indigenous movement to link up successfully with other nonindigenous social and political movements. Commerce was brought to a halt throughout Ecuador when CONAIE set up roadblocks and boycotted marketplaces. Trade unions joined in the action by calling a general strike and stopped the delivery of goods into the cities. In parts of the Amazon, indigenous communities took over oil wells to protest the privatization of Petroecuador, the state-owned oil company.

CONAIE succeeded in getting a broad range of organizations to unite behind its own progressive agrarian reform proposal, which called for the modernization of communal agriculture but not through the government's plan of commercialization. Rather, CONAIE's proposal called for government support for sustainable, community-based projects that emphasized production for domestic consumption rather than foreign export. CONAIE also proposed the use of environmentally sound farming techniques. At the heart of their counterproposals was the idea that organized groups of civil society in the countryside would play a central role in implementing the new law.

The protests and counterproposal met stiff resistance from the government of Sixto Durán Ballen, which viewed the Agrarian Development Law to be at the center of its broader package of neoliberal reforms. The government declared a state of emergency and put the armed forces in charge of dealing with the protests. The

armed forces arrested protest leaders and violently suppressed street demonstrations. The army occupied many indigenous communities, destroying homes and
crops. However, the repression was not fully successful at stopping the protest
movement. The government was forced to negotiate with CONAIE and ultimately
to make modifications in the agrarian reform law that limited its potentially worst
features. However, probably the most important result of the 1994 protests was
the recognition that the indigenous movement is a significant actor in contemporary Ecuadorian politics. CONAIE and the indigenous people as a whole achieved
this position through their mobilizations, successful linking with nonindigenous
groups, and dynamic formation of political demands.

In January 2000, CONAIE organized several thousand indigenous people to
protest the government's handling of an economic crisis and to call on the president, Jamil Mahuad, to resign. Working with cooperative members of the military,
the protesters occupied the national parliament and declared a new government
headed by a three-person junta including indigenous leader Antonio Vargas.
However, their victory was short-lived. Under pressure from the United States and
the Organization of American States (OAS), the military withdrew from the junta
and conceded the presidency to Mahuad's vice president Gustavo Noboa. CONAIE
was defeated in the short term in its efforts at radical reform, but its considerable
power was made dramatically evident to the country's traditional rulers. In 2002,
support from CONAIE was crucial to the success of the presidential campaign of
populist Lucio Gutiérrez. Gutiérrez swept to victory promising to challenge the
neoliberal orthodoxy and appointing indigenous representatives to government
positions. However, by 2004, Gutiérrez had betrayed his promises and CONAIE
was back in the streets as a leading opposition force. In April 2005, CONAIE was
part of a broad coalition of opposition forces that drove Gutiérrez from office following an ill-fated scheme to overhaul the nation's court system to his benefit.
CONAIE has continued to press its agenda of indigenous rights in the era of Rafael
Correa, the progressive Ecuadorian president first elected in 2006 and reelected
in 2009. Given Correa's generally progressive stance CONAIE had some expectation for progress under Correa but have primarily found themselves at odds with
a president who has aimed his policies primarily at the urban poor and middle
classes who voted him into office. Correa has often upstaged CONAIE by backing
such CONAIE initiatives as the declaration of Ecuador to be a plurinational county.
The issue that has most separated Correa from CONAIE has been his advocacy of
large-scale mining. This strong difference of perspective led to demonstration of
thousands of indigenous in January 2009 opposing the new mining law by shut-
ting down the Pan American Highway for a brief period. Violent response from
the Correa government only served to alienate the two sides to an even greater
degree. At its most recent Congress in April 2009, CONAIE denounced Correa for
"governing from the right" and for setting up parallel indigenous organizations to
compete with CONAIE.

In spite of its strong confrontation with Correa and divisions within the indigenous movement CONAIE and its allied political party, Pachakutik, remain an
important political force in the province of Zamora Chinchipe in the southeast-
ern Amazon where its candidate Salvador Quishpe triumphed in the 2009 regional

The Confederation of Ecuadorean Indigenous Nationalities (CONAIE) in action. *(Photo by Dolores Ochoa/AP Images)*

election. This victory, in an area of the mining sector, gives CONAIE a continuing base from which to challenge the government in Quito.

BRAZIL

In Brazil, the issue that most marks the indigenous struggle is the contest for land. Land is the subsistence base of indigenous groups, whether they are hunters and gatherers in the Amazon or small farmers in the northeast. It is the issue that unites Brazil's 206 indigenous societies.

Brazil's indigenous people are only 0.2 percent of the national population, speaking 170 languages, with legal rights to about 11 percent of the national territory. Much of the indigenous land is rich in natural resources. Nearly 99 percent of indigenous land is in the Amazon region, occupying more than 18 percent of the region, but little more than half the indigenous population lives there. In the other densely populated parts of the country, almost half the indigenous population lives on less than 2 percent of the indigenous land.

The current struggle over land is not a new one. Expropriation of indigenous lands and decimation of the indigenous population have usually paralleled the drive by Europeans for a particular raw material, whether it be timber, gold, sugar, or rubber. A contemporary case of the devastation of an indigenous group occurred with the isolated Canoe and Mequens peoples in the Amazonian state of Rondônia. Fewer than fifteen people from these two groups have survived. Over the last decade, ranchers in the region may well have killed most of the two groups and destroyed their livelihood to make way for cattle pasture. There is evidence of some fifty-three still-isolated groups, probably small remnants of larger groups that moved in response to the Brazilian government's massive resettlement programs. The administration of President José Sarney (1985–1990) was especially aggressive in moving forward with Amazonian development projects. The army's Northern Tributaries Project, begun in 1987, had as its goals the reduction of indigenous land areas and the subsequent opening up of large new areas for both farming and mining. As a result, between 1987 and 1990 the Yanomami's 9.5-million-hectare (23.5-million-acre) territory was reduced by 70 percent and divided into nineteen different unconnected parcels of land. The Yanomami people were devastated by the activity of almost 50,000 freelance gold diggers. The gold diggers drove 9,000 Yanomami from their lands, and 15 percent of the population died from diseases introduced by the gold miners. Mercury contamination downriver and mercury vapors released into the atmosphere had serious environmental consequences. Protests at the 1992 Earth Summit led to the creation of land reserves by the governments of both Brazil and Venezuela. Despite the newly created reserves, conflict between the gold miners and the Yanomami continued. In 1993, many Yanomami were massacred in an attack by the miners and with no effective intervention by the Brazilian government. The 1988 Brazilian constitution contained progressive provisions for environmental protection and indigenous people's rights, but the reality was that they were generally not implemented. Powerful private economic interests moved forward with their projects, often buying off government officials with large bribes. The government itself moved forward with environmentally questionable projects such as the planned Paraná-Paraguay River seaway.

However, sole focus on these devastated and isolated groups would miss an important part of the story. In the last thirty years, the indigenous people have begun to change their situation through political organization. The demographic decline reached its low point in the mid-1970s, and the population has risen ever since. The first complete indigenous census, in 1990, counted about 235,000 indigenous people. By the year 2000, the number had grown to 300,000. Between 1990 and 1995, the area of indigenous land with complete legal documentation increased more than fourfold.

The most recent drive of the Brazilian government into the indigenous lands in the Amazon region was initiated in the 1940s but took on full force in the 1960s and 1970s. The military government that came to power in 1964 was motivated by an almost messianic desire to conquer these supposedly undeveloped lands so that Brazil could take its place among the world's most important countries. As a result, the Brazilian government conceived and executed the development of an infrastructure (roads, dams, and hydroelectric stations) that preceded the actual economic development of the region.

Because the concept of privately held land was largely nonexistent in the Amazon region, it was necessary for the government to step up mechanisms for the demarcation of land based on private ownership. Private investors were willing to enter the region only after such procedures had been established. From the beginning, the approach of the Brazilian government toward the indigenous groups was to limit their land ownership to relatively small areas so that their ambitious development plans could proceed on the rest. In 1967, the Brazilian government created the National Indian Foundation (FUNAI) as the agency responsible for indigenous people and their land. While it had not been the intent of the government to create a rallying point, FUNAI has become exactly that. For thirty years its headquarters in Brasília has been the focal point for indigenous groups rallying to register land claims and to forestall the projects of the developers. Using FUNAI as a target, indigenous groups developed their own organizations in the 1970s with the assistance of the wider society. The first organizations came from within the church community—the Indigenist Missionary Council (CIMI), the indigenous rights organization of the Catholic Church, and the Ecumenical Center for Documentation and Information (CEDI). Indigenous groups took a large step forward in 1978 with the formation of the first national organization, the Union of Indigenous Nations (UNI). The UNI was able to make important links both domestically and internationally. In the late 1970s and early 1980s, during the height of the movement against the military dictatorship, indigenous groups were able to make links with students and intellectuals. As a result, the issue of indigenous land rights made it to the agenda of the broad movement for the restoration of political democracy.

At the same time, the Brazilian indigenous movement also made important links in the international community, most especially with the environmental community. During the 1980s, there developed among environmentalists internationally a significant consciousness of the destruction of the Amazon rain forest. In developing international attention about the problem in Brazil, groups like Greenpeace and the World Wildlife Fund made common cause with Brazil's indigenous groups. Both sets of groups began to speak the same language—sustainable development. Both indigenous peoples and environmentalists argued that the rain forest was not a wilderness to simply be preserved but rather an area that was inhabited and contained important resources for the world that the people who currently lived there could provide—medicines, rubber, foodstuffs. The activists argued that the kind of development being projected and carried out by the Brazilian government— primarily slash-and-burn agriculture—was inappropriate for the fragile character of the land. They pointed to vast tracts of land that had been exploited in the 1960s and 1970s and were now worthless semidesert. Considerable international attention was also brought to the region by the work of Francisco "Chico" Alves Mendes, leader of the National Council of Rubber Tappers, who was assassinated in 1988 after his organization, the Alliance of the Peoples of the Forest, organized to block further dam construction and defend the environment. Internationally, consciousness has clearly developed on this and related environmental issues and has placed significant pressure on the Brazilian government since the mid-1980s. However, this has not stopped the government from moving forward with its development plans. Often, the government has successfully created a nationalist backlash against international pressure by characterizing it as a form of neocolonialism. However, in 2007 a potentially important development occurred when President Luiz Inacio da Silva announced an agreement with several indigenous groups acknowledging their autonomy and claim to resources.

MEXICO

On January 1, 1994, a rebellion led by the Zapatista National Liberation Army (EZLN) began in the state of Chiapas in southern Mexico. This rebellion, more than any other indigenous political action in the 1990s, captured the attention of scholars and political activists alike. On that day, within a few hours after the takeover of San Cristóbal de las Casas, computer screens around the world sparked with news of the uprising. The Zapatista uprising generated extensive online publicity as the EZLN communicated its cause directly and electronically. The indigenous explosion in Chiapas, in which several hundred people lost their lives in twelve days of fighting, was only the beginning. Fifteen years later, the government continued to renege on accords it had signed recognizing indigenous rights and culture and federal troops still occupied the indigenous parts of the state, though the rebels forged ahead with autonomous structures of local government.

The EZLN had its origins in indigenous and peasant organizing initiatives of the 1970s, which began to link up with leftist political organizers arriving in the Lacandón jungle of Chiapas from other parts of Mexico. A combination of growing repression and the impact of neoliberal policies in the early 1980s radicalized some of these groups, leading them to join in an armed movement initially known as the National Liberation Forces (FLN), the precursor of the EZLN, which burst on the scene as the North American Free Trade Agreement (NAFTA) went into effect. The roots of their rebellion ran very deep. The indigenous people of Chiapas, mostly Mayan, have labored under conditions of semislavery and servitude for centuries. The state is the principal source of the nation's coffee, and just over 100 people (0.16 percent of all coffee farmers) control 12 percent of all coffee lands. The large coffee farms have the best land, most of the credit, and the best infrastructure. Even more important are the cattle lands. Some 6,000 families hold more than 3 million hectares (7.4 million acres) of pastureland, equivalent to nearly half the territory of all Chiapas rural landholdings. Many of these vast cattle ranches were created through violent seizures of community and national land. The current struggles here date back to the early period of this century when the local oligarchs resisted any attempt at land reform. The program of the Institutional Revolutionary Party (PRI) president Lázaro Cárdenas, which distributed millions of acres of land elsewhere in Mexico in the 1930s, lagged in its implementation in Chiapas. In 1974, the local elites harshly repressed indigenous efforts at political organizing for land reform. The massive repression of the 1970s was followed by a more selective repression, consisting of the assassination of several peasant leaders. The peasants responded by creating networks of self-defense, but the authoritarian PRI governors responded with harsh tactics. The state repression was carried out by a combination of the federal army, state and local police forces, and so-called white guards—hired security forces at the service of the big landowners. PRI leaders deliberately provoked conflicts among peasants, between peasants and small proprietors, and between PRI village leaders and opponents of the regime. The local PRI leadership operated through a loose organization known as the "Chiapas Family." The family was made up primarily of big ranchers, owners of coffee farms, and lumber barons who controlled local elected offices. The control was enhanced by the cooption of local indigenous leaders, many of whom were bilingual teachers. Operating through PRI-dominated organizations like the National Peasant Confederation (CNC), the local leaders were given economic advantages that were passed on to their closest supporters in the communities. This divide-and-conquer strategy led to many violent confrontations in the period of the Zapatista uprising.

Despite the historic dominance of the region politically and economically by the PRI and its supporters, an independent civil society began to develop after 1975. Organizers from the outside participated, including liberation theology–inspired Catholic clergy and members of Mexican leftist parties. Two grassroots organizations formed in the 1970s exist today, the Regional Association of Collective Interest Union of Ejido Unions (ARIC-UU) and the Emiliano Zapata Peasant Organization (OCEZ). The organizations use a variety of tactics, including direct action, to press their grievances against the Mexican government. A new phase in the impact of civil society began on October 12, 1992, with a demonstration in San Cristóbal de las Casas to commemorate the 500th anniversary of indigenous resistance to the European conquest. Thousands of people from different ethnic groups took over the colonial capital and destroyed the statue of the conquistador Diego de Mazariegos. The event foreshadowed the EZLN uprising a little more than a year later.

A fundamental catalyst for the 1994 uprising was the reform of Article 27 of the Mexican constitution announced by President Carlos Salinas de Gortari in 1992. This reform, for the first time since the programs of Cárdenas, halted land redistribution and permitted the sale of communal lands that up until that time had been protected. For the peasants of Chiapas, this meant the end of agrarian reform, which up to that point had been slow and arbitrary but was now effectively dead. The peasants felt that they could no longer turn to the government as a mediator in land disputes. For the landowners, the reform was a green light to end once and for all peasant resistance to their plans for greater commercialization of agriculture in the region. Government troops first confronted a column of Zapatistas in May 1993, but the Salinas government, in the midst of an intense effort to win support for NAFTA, did not wish to tarnish its image by acknowledging the existence of a significant armed challenge within its borders. It was in that context of political change and resistance that the Zapatistas burst onto the scene.

From the beginning of their appearance, it was clear that the EZLN insurgency, made up of several thousand indigenous people and their "support base" communities throughout the highlands and the jungle, was a different kind of political movement from the traditional guerrilla armies that preceded them in Mexico and Central America. From the beginning they were a civil resistance organization seeking basic change using revolutionary tactics. The EZLN never claimed as a goal the overthrow of the Mexican state. Rather, it called for the immediate resignation of Salinas, subsequent fall elections, and the expansion of peaceful, popular political participation. From the beginning its actions were the catalyst for generalized civil resistance throughout Chiapas.

Within a month of the launching of the Zapatistas' war, the National Mediation Commission (CONAI) headed by Bishop Samuel Ruiz brokered a cease-fire between the warring parties and began negotiations that continued on and off until June 1998, when Bishop Ruiz resigned from CONAI and the commission dissolved, charging the government with pursuing a path of war rather than peace. The Mexican Congress formed the Commission for Concord and Pacification (COCOPA) in January 1995 to continue negotiations with the Zapatistas while a cease-fire was in place. The government broke the truce in February 1995 with an army offensive that unsuccessfully attempted to capture the Zapatista leaders. The 1995 offensive was made possible by a massive deployment of 60,000 Mexican soldiers into the region. The army, with U.S., Argentine, and Chilean advisors, employed counterinsurgency tactics honed during Latin America's guerrilla wars of the previous three decades. Between 1996 and 2007, the United States provided over $440 million in military and police aid to Mexico, including helicopters that can be used in counterinsurgency operations. The Mexican army cooperated on its southern border with the Guatemalan army, well trained in counterinsurgency warfare. During its February 1995 offensive, the army destroyed the basic resources of a number of villages suspected of collaborating with the Zapatistas. The offensive forced the EZLN to retreat into more remote areas, but the Mexican government was not able to destroy the EZLN, in part because of the presence of many international human rights observers in the area and the mounting of large demonstrations on behalf of the EZLN in Mexico City. Unable to destroy the EZLN militarily, the government returned to negotiations; and in February 1996, the government and the EZLN signed accords on the rights of indigenous communities. The San Andrés Accords included two key demands of the EZLN, official recognition of the rights of indigenous communities to choose their own leadership and to control the natural resources in their territory. However, in reality the Mexican government did not implement these measures. The primary point of conflict centered around the autonomous municipal councils created by the Zapatistas since 1994. The Zapatistas claimed the right to local self-governance under Article 39 of the Mexican Constitution, which gave people "the inalienable right to alter or modify the form of their government," and the International Labor Organization's Convention 169 (ratified by the Mexican government in 1991), which gave indigenous peoples control over their habitats. In scores of communities, local councils were elected only to be denied recognition by the Mexican government, which continued to recognize local government structures dominated by politicians from the major parties. As a result, many villages split into progovernment and pro-EZLN factions. Despite the lack of official recognition, these autonomous municipal councils no longer recognize the official judicial system and have established alternative methods of conflict resolution. They have also set up community development projects, such as community corn and coffee fields and vegetable gardens. These alternative institutions have gained some financial backing from international nongovernmental organizations in sympathy with the Zapatistas.

The end of the 1990s saw a dramatic increase in violence in the Chiapas region, much of it carried out by paramilitary organizations with links to the government. The most horrific incident occurred on December 22, 1997, when forty-five residents of the Tzotzil indigenous town of Acteal (including thirty-six women and children) were killed in an attack on their chapel by a heavily armed paramilitary gang. It has been reported that one group, the Anti-Zapatista Indigenous Revolutionary Movement (MIRA), received $1,250 a month from the PRI-led state government. From April through June 1998, the government launched a series of joint military and police invasions (often coordinated with paramilitaries) that dismantled the Zapatista autonomous municipalities of Ricardo Flores Magón, Tierra y Libertad, and San Juan de la Libertad and raids on Zapatista communities such as Unión Progreso, where eight indigenous residents were taken away by public security forces and their mutilated bodies later returned.

When this militarization provoked the dissolution of CONAI in 1998 and the collapse of negotiations, the Zapatistas launched a national "consultation" in which nearly 3 million Mexicans participated, expressing support for compromise legislation drafted by COCOPA to implement the San Andrés Accords on indigenous rights. Hopes for implementing legislation were briefly raised by the 2000 election of President Vicente Fox from the opposition National Action Party (PAN), who had boasted during the campaign that he would solve the Chiapas problem "in 15 minutes." Later that year, Pablo Salazar was elected state governor on an "Alliance for Chiapas" coalition ticket of anti-PRI parties, and the Zapatistas announced three conditions for resuming peace talks: (1) fulfillment of the San Andrés Accords approving the COCOPA law, (2) freeing all Zapatista prisoners, and (3) closing seven (out of 259) military bases in areas of major Zapatista influence. In response, the government closed four bases and released a few dozen out of about 100 prisoners and Fox presented an indigenous law to Congress but backpedaled from the COCOPA version. The Zapatistas then took their case directly to the public and to Congress, organizing a caravan from Chiapas to Mexico City in February-March 2001 that included twenty-three indigenous EZLN commanders plus Subcomandante Marcos. The caravan culminated in one of the largest gatherings in Mexico City's *zócalo* (main plaza) in modern history, and a historic address to the Congress by ski-masked Comandante Esther. However, after the Zapatistas returned to Chiapas, Congress passed an indigenous law that gutted the key provisions of the San Andrés Accords and the COCOPA law. The sham legislation was rejected by the congresses of all six Mexican states with the largest proportion of indigenous populations and denounced by indigenous and human rights organizations, which filed 329 constitutional challenges in the Supreme Court. Nevertheless, it was entered into law in August and upheld by the Supreme Court in September 2001.

The struggle for recognition of indigenous rights and for participatory democracy continued. On January 1, 2003, 20,000 indigenous people marched in San Cristóbal to demand revision of the indigenous rights law and the EZLN broke a two-year silence to condemn the three major parties for betraying the spirit of the San Andrés Accords. Meanwhile, in late 2002, government agencies and paramilitaries began a new escalation of violence against Zapatista support communities in the Montes Azules Biosphere Reserve near the Guatemalan border. This region was coveted by transnationals for its potential hydroelectric and biodiversity resources, in the wake of President Fox's multibillion-dollar Plan Puebla Panama (PPP), which would turn all of southern Mexico and Central America into a giant free-trade zone. Grassroots organizations in Chiapas joined their counterparts in Central America in cross-border networks to resist the PPP. Meanwhile, the Zapatistas continued their patient construction of autonomous government from the bottom up, announcing in July 2003 that their five *Aguascalientes* resistance centers in Chiapas would be renamed *Caracoles* and would be the seats of a new regional structure of "Good Governance Councils" (*Juntas de Buen Gobierno*). Each junta became a regional rebel government, incorporating rotating delegates from some thirty Zapatista rebel autonomous municipalities.

In June 2005, the EZLN issued the "Sixth Declaration of the Lacandón Jungle," inaugurating a national initiative called "The Other Campaign" to link progressive struggles across Mexico. Subcomandante Marcos headed the first phase of the campaign in early 2006 as "Delegate Zero." The tour was temporarily halted following massive government repression of some allied organizations in San Salvador Atenco (near Mexico City) in May 2006. After a disputed presidential election in July 2006 in which conservative PAN candidate Felipe Calderón claimed victory, the government appeared to shift to more militarized responses to social movements. Federal forces were deployed against protesters in Oaxaca in November 2006, and, in September 2007, the EZLN announced the suspension of the second phase of the Other Campaign (scheduled for south-central Mexico from October–December) due to escalating paramilitary attacks on Zapatista communities. In October 2007, a caravan carrying Marcos and other Zapatista leaders was detained at one of the growing number of roadblocks across Mexico as they traveled to an encounter of indigenous peoples in Vícam, Sonora, highlighting the escalating government threat against the movement. Some called this perspective "post liberation theology." Pope John Paul has passed from the scene but his successor, Benedict, while conservative theologically, has continued the Church's strong impetus for social justice. The new wave of center-left governments in the region over the last ten years resonate well with the Church's message of social justice and often work closely with Church leaders. Emblematic of this connection is Ecuadoran president Rafael Correa, whose progressive politics are firmly rooted in Catholic social teaching.

The long-standing connection between the Catholic Church hierarchy and military-oligarchic politics has been seriously undercut by the political developments of the last forty years. While a new and fully formed twenty-first-century vision of social justice from a religious perspective has yet to be fully articulated, the role of a generation of progressive religious thinking is clearly an important part of Latin America's transition to democracy and its current trend toward more progressive politics.

With or without official recognition from the state, the Zapatista movement continues to represent innovative forms of resistance to the dictates of global capital and oppressive government. As a result, the region is likely to remain a focal point of indigenous resistance that will be modeled elsewhere in the Western Hemisphere.

Conclusion

As Latin America enters the twenty-first century, its image as a continent populated only by Spanish- and Portuguese-speaking *mestizos* is gone forever. The indigenous peoples of the region and the descendants of the African slaves have clearly asserted their claim to a role in the future of the region. No longer forgotten and marginalized, these groups will likely grow in their political and social roles in the coming years.

Bibliography

Andrews, George Reid. *Afro-Latin America 1800–2000*. New York: Oxford University Press, 2004.

Applebaum, Nancy. *Race and Nation in Modern Latin America*. Chapel Hill: University of North Carolina Press, 2003.

Bailey, Stanley. *Legacies of Race: Identities, Attitudes, and Politics in Brazil*. Palo Alto, CA: Stanford University Press, 2009.

Becker, Marc. *Indians and Leftists in the Making of Ecuador's Modern Indigenous Movements*. Durham, NC: Duke University Press, 2008.

Benjamin, Thomas. *The Atlantic World: Europeans, Africans, Indians, and Their Shared History, 1400–1900*. New York: Cambridge University Press, 2009.

Conniff, Michael, and Thomas Davis. *Africans in the Americas: A History of the Black Diaspora*. New York: St. Martin's Press, 1994.

Cook, Noble David. *Born to Die: Disease and New World Conquest, 1492–1650*. Cambridge, UK: Cambridge University Press, 1998.

Davis, Darien, ed. *Slavery and Beyond: The African Impact on Latin America and the Caribbean*. Jaguar Books on Latin America, 5. Wilmington, DE: Scholarly Resources, 1995.

Dixon, Kwame. "Race, Class and National Identity in Ecuador: Afro-Ecuadoreans and the Struggle for Human Rights." Ph.D. diss., Clark Atlanta University, 1996.

French, Jan Hoffman. *Legalizing Identities: Becoming Black or Indian in Brazil's Northeast*. Chapel Hill: University of North Carolina Press, 2009.

Freyre, Gilberto. *The Masters and the Slaves, A Study in the Development of Brazilian Civilization*. Berkeley: University of California Press, 1986.

Gois Dantas, Beatrice. *Nago Grandma and White Papa: Candomble and the Creation of Afro-Brazilian Identity*. Chapel Hill: University of North Carolina Press, 2009.

Gotkowitz, Laura. *A Revolution for Our Rights: Indigenous Struggles for Land and Justice in Bolivia, 1880–1952*. Durham: Duke University Press, 2009.

Graham, Richard, ed. *The Idea of Race in Latin America, 1870–1940*. Austin: University of Texas Press, 1990.

Harvey, Neil. *The Chiapas Rebellion: The Struggle for Land and Democracy*. Durham, NC, and London: Duke University Press, 1998.

Hemming, John. *Amazon Frontier: The Defeat of the Brazilian Indians*. London: Macmillan, 1987.

Kicza, John E., ed. *The Indian in Latin American History: Resistance, Resilience and Acculturation*. Wilmington, DE: Scholarly Resources, 1993.

Klein, Herbert. *Slavery in Latin America and the Caribbean*. New York: Oxford University Press, 1986.

Mattiace, Shannon. *To See with Two Eyes: Peasant Activism and Indian Autonomy in Chiapas, Mexico*. Albuquerque: University of New Mexico Press, 2004.

Menchú, Rigoberta. *I Rigoberta Menchú: An Indian Woman in Guatemala*. Edited by Elizabeth Burgos-Debray. London: Verso, 1984.

Postero, Nancy Grey. *Now We Are Citizens: Indigenous Politics in Postmulticultural Bolivia*. Stanford, CA: Stanford University Press, 1998.

Postero, Nancy Grey, and Leon Zamosc, eds. *The Struggle for Indigenous Rights in Latin America*. Brighton, UK: Sussex Academic Press, 2004.

Price, Richard, ed. *Maroon Societies*. Baltimore: Johns Hopkins University Press, 1986.

Rus, Jan, Rosalva Aída Hernández Castillo, and Shannon L. Mattiace, Eds. *Mayan Lives, Mayan Utopias: The Indigenous Peoples of Chiapas and the Zapatista Rebellion*. Lanham, MD: Rowman and Littlefield Publishers, 2003.

Smith, Carol. *Guatemalan Indians and the State: 1540 to 1988*. Austin: University of Texas Press, 1990.

Speed, Shannon. *Rights in Rebellion: Indigenous Struggle and Human Rights in Chiapas*. Stanford, CA: Stanford University Press, 2008.

Twine, France. *Racism in a Racial Democracy: The Maintenance of White Supremacy in Brazil.* New Brunswick, NJ: Rutgers University Press, 1998.

Urban, Greg, and Joel Sherzer, eds. *Nation-States and Indians in Latin America.* Austin: University of Texas Press, 1991.

Van Cott, Donna Lee. *From Movements to Parties in Latin America: The Evolution of Ethnic Politics.* Cambridge, UK: Cambridge University Press, 2005.

Wade, Peter. *Blackness and Racial Mixture: The Dynamics of Racial Identity in Colombia.* Baltimore: Johns Hopkins University Press, 1993.

Wearne, Philip. *Return of the Indian: Conquest and Revival in the Americas.* London: Latin American Bureau, 1996.

Yashar, Deborah. *Contesting Citizenship in Latin America: The Rise of Indigenous Movements and the Postliberal Challenge.* Cambridge, UK: Cambridge University Press, 2005.

FILMS AND VIDEOS

Blood of the Condor. Bolivia, 1969.
How Tasty Was My Little Frenchman. Brazil, 1973.
Quilombo. Brazil, 1984.

FIVE

SOCIETY, FAMILY, AND GENDER

The social milieu in Latin America is a fascinating, complex, and often magical reality that frequently seems to defy description. Societies in the region were forged over five centuries from a multitude of diverse, dynamic influences. Foremost among these are the European values and social institutions the colonists brought with them. To these are added those of the preexisting native societies as well as those of the African cultures carried to the Americas by enslaved western and southern Africans. They have blended in different ways to form societal characteristics that have evolved over the centuries and are manifest in a fascinating array of different forms in each country. They have been molded and modified by land tenure, subsequent immigration, trade and commercialization, industrialization, intervention, the modern media, and, now, globalization. There are, however, some constants that will help us understand this reality.

To gain some insight into Latin American society, we can look at how competition among groups and individuals is carried out on the playing field. We need to see how the game is played. Sports are often an excellent reflection of culture—by understanding athletic interactions, we can often better understand other forms of societal relation.

Like politics, *futbol* (soccer) is an area of great passion in most Latin American countries. *Futbol* unifies regions, classes, racial groupings, and even gender in ways few other activities can. When the national team is competing for World Cup standing, it provides a focus, a commonality, and a sense of community much more strongly than most other activities, save a real or possible foreign military threat. World Cup victories are also used by governments to bolster their legitimacy.

Regional and team rivalries also exist. Fans show their spirit and team allegiance by wearing team colors, driving with team banners flowing, and engaging in rhythmic chants through the course of the game. Passions run so high that the field and the players are protected by high barbed wire fences and water-filled moats. In 1969, passions exploded after a game at a regional World Cup match between El

Salvador and Honduras; the event became the spark that ignited long-standing tensions to create the so-called Soccer War.

Like football and basketball in the United States, hockey in Canada, and soccer in Great Britain and continental Europe, *futbol* has provided a way out of slums and poverty. *Futbol* further offers one of the few ways to transcend classism and the omnipresent barriers to socioeconomic mobility. To carry the analogy further, it could be argued that the soccer field is one of the few places in society where one is not excluded from play or at least handicapped by class, color, or lack of connections to the powerful.

Traditionally, soccer was a male domain and there were few opportunities for young women to learn or play the game, although women were welcome to watch, cheer, and support the men who played. Only in recent years has the internationalization of women's sports begun to change this; the Brazilian women's soccer team made it to the 1999 World Cup semifinals before being defeated by the U.S. women's team and in 2007 reached the finals before falling to Germany.

These analogies are equally valid for baseball in those societies where the ongoing (usually military) presence of baseball-playing North American men has made the U.S. pastime the primary national sport: Cuba, Nicaragua, Panama, and the Dominican Republic. U.S. and Canadian oil technicians introduced baseball in Venezuela, where both baseball and *futbol* are played. The ease of baseball assimilation suggests not only the strong U.S. cultural influence but also the instant enthusiasm displayed by Latin Americans when they too could compete on a level playing field with occupying military forces or technologically sophisticated foreign workers. Their success is brought home by the presence of growing numbers of Latin American players in the U.S. major leagues. This was underscored when Dominican-born Sammy Sosa of the Chicago Cubs engaged in a dramatic duel for the home run record with Mark McGuire in the 1998 baseball season. Male success notwithstanding, at present women are not often invited to play baseball, nor are women's softball teams yet popular.

The popularity of ball games dates back to indigenous civilizations in Mexico and Central America, although the current version of soccer was brought from Europe. In these indigenous civilizations hotly contested matches were played for as long as days, and the winners could enjoy great success as bestowed by the wealthy and powerful. The losers were, however, often killed or sacrificed.

Like the losers of ball games in pre-Columbian times, those in Latin American society who cannot win the wealth-status-power game (the poor) suffer from powerlessness and repression and are frequently sacrificed to poverty, exploitation, humiliation, malnutrition, and occasionally torture and death. Their blood, it could be argued, flows to satisfy the new—now globalized—gods of the day. Why do the poor lose so often? Culture defines much of the playing field and most of the rules of the game. Latin American culture is quite distinct from that in the United States, Canada, Great Britain, or Australia. The sections that follow discuss some of the key aspects of Latin American culture.

From classical Mayan times to the present, the rules of the game have been dictated by those with power and wealth. This began with the Incan and Aztec emperors, Mayan kings, and aristocrats and priests—those who ruled. After the conquest, new hierarchies and dominant classes developed. Society in colonial times could be described as a sharply pointed upper-class pyramid seated on a broad base of indigenous and African peoples (see Figure 1). The small European elite enjoyed wealth, status, privilege, and power—they became the new ruling class. Even European artisans enjoyed a status well above virtually all of the indigenous masses. The exceptions to these classifications would be the *mestizo* sons and daughters of the Spanish and Portuguese elite and native women (who sometimes came from pre-Columbian royal families). Also in this category would be the mulatto children of Portuguese colonists and Africans in Brazil. However, the African and indigenous masses enjoyed neither wealth nor privilege and could exercise little power—they were the lower class. As the subaltern, those who were subjected to elite power, they most commonly led lives characterized by economic deprivation and exploitation.

This basic structure set the tone for Latin American society. A few continued to have it all, while the darker masses suffered the vicissitudes of poverty and powerlessness. With few exceptions, the elite upper class, or *oligarchy* as it is sometimes called, still makes the rules of the game and dominates the lives of the many. Lighter generally rules darker, and male typically dominates female. At the beginning of the twenty-first century, those living in poverty accounted for between 40 and 60 percent of the population in most Latin American countries. Even by the rather optimistic statistics used by the regions' governments, some 40 percent still lived in poverty as of the mid-1990s. Indeed, in 1999, the newly elected populist president of Venezuela, Hugo Chávez, spoke of the 80 percent of Venezuelans who lived in

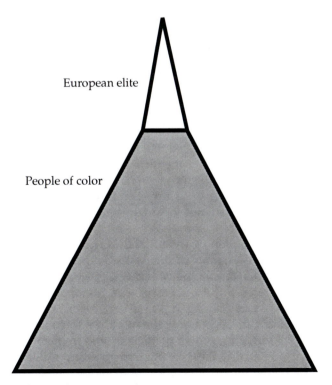

European elite

People of color

FIGURE 1.   Colonial Latin American society.

Venezuelan President Hugo Chávez playing the pitcher in a baseball game. *(Ministry of Information, Venezuela)*

poverty. Conversely, the wealthy and the superwealthy—the upper class—live very well indeed. For instance, it is estimated that the wealthiest 10 percent of the population receives close to 50 percent of the income, while the bottom half of society receives only about 4 percent of the income. The richest 20 percent of the Brazilian population receives an income that is thirty-two times the income received by the poorest 20 percent. Official statistics for urban households show much the same pattern (see Table 7).

The inequitable distribution of wealth and power continues to plague Latin American societies. In pre-Columbian times, it was the Aztec, Mayan, and Incan royalty and nobility and, later, the *conquistadores, viceroys, encomenderos,* and *latifundistas* who ran the game. Still later, power was monopolized by the rural landowners (the *hacendados, estanciaros,* and *fazendeiros*), *caudillos,* and Church leaders. By the twentieth century, it was not only the wealthy—the oligarchy—but also the military leaders, dictators, and civilian politicians who frequently shared and held absolute power on a recurring basis, using their political-military power to consolidate their place in the upper class. They were joined by emerging commercial,

TABLE 7.   Distribution of Income in Urban Households, by Quintile (Percentages)*

Country	Year	Quintile 1 (Poorest)		Quintile 2	Quintile 3	Quintile 4	Quintile 5 (Richest)	
		Decile 1	Decile 2	Quintile 2	Quintile 3	Quintile 4	Decile 9	Decile 10
Argentina	1990†	1.5	2.6	8.2	12.6	20.1	15.6	39.3
	1999§	1.2	2.3	7.3	11.7	19.1	15.6	42.9
	2006	1.2	2.4	7.9	12.5	19.7	15.5	40.8
Bolivia	1989	0.9	2.3	7.4	11.6	19.5	16.5	41.8
	1999	1.3	2.6	8.1	12.5	20.0	16.7	38.9
	2007	1.5	2.6	7.8	12.2	19.4	16.6	39.9
Brazil	1990	0.8	1.6	5.6	9.7	17.5	16.4	48.5
	1999	0.7	1.6	5.4	9.2	16.2	15.3	51.5
	2007	0.9	1.9	6.4	10.7	17.7	15.4	47.1
Chile	1990	1.3	2.4	7.2	11.2	18.4	15.9	43.7
	2000	1.2	2.3	7.0	10.9	17.7	15.3	45.7
	2006	1.5	2.6	7.8	11.8	18.8	15.6	41.9
Colombia	1991	1.6	2.9	8.6	12.8	20.2	16.0	38.0
	1999	0.8	1.8	5.9	9.5	15.9	14.1	51.9
	2005	0.9	1.9	6.2	10.0	16.9	14.9	49.2
Costa Rica	1990	1.4	3.3	10.1	15.4	22.8	16.4	30.6
	1999	1.5	3.0	9.0	14.0	22.3	17.1	33.2
	2007	1.6	2.9	8.6	12.9	20.7	16.3	37.0
Ecuador	1990	1.7	3.1	9.1	13.7	20.6	15.9	36.0
	1999	1.2	2.6	7.7	11.8	19.1	15.7	41.9
	2007	1.4	2.6	7.7	11.9	19.1	15.6	41.7
El Salvador	1995	1.6	3.1	9.2	13.6	20.4	15.3	36.8
	1999	1.5	2.9	8.9	13.8	21.5	16.6	34.8
	2004	1.5	3.0	9.1	14.1	21.6	16.4	34.2
Guatemala	1989	0.8	2.0	6.7	11.4	19.2	16.0	43.8
	1998	1.6	2.6	7.9	11.8	18.2	14.3	43.5
	2006	1.2	2.3	7.2	11.2	18.0	15.5	44.5
Honduras	1990	1.1	2.1	6.7	10.8	18.6	16.5	44.3
	1999	1.2	2.4	7.9	12.4	20.3	16.3	39.4
	2007	1.2	2.5	8.2	12.9	20.7	16.5	38.0
Mexico	1989	1.5	2.7	7.8	11.6	17.9	14.6	43.9
	1998	1.8	2.8	8.2	11.9	18.8	15.1	41.5
	2006	2.0	3.0	8.6	12.5	19.2	15.4	39.4
Nicaragua	1993	0.6	2.2	7.1	11.9	19.5	15.4	43.2
	1998	0.9	2.2	7.3	11.6	19.1	14.9	44.1
	2005	1.6	2.8	8.3	12.3	18.7	14.8	41.5
Panama	1991	0.8	2.1	7.0	11.5	20.1	16.9	41.6
	1999	1.2	2.4	7.6	12.4	20.5	17.1	38.9
	2007	1.5	2.8	8.7	13.5	20.9	16.3	36.3
Paraguay	1990	2.0	3.3	9.3	13.6	20.9	16.6	34.4
	2007	1.4	2.8	8.7	13.0	20.3	16.1	37.7
Peru	1997	1.7	3.0	8.7	12.9	19.9	15.8	38.1
	1999	1.6	2.8	8.2	12.2	18.3	15.0	42.0
	2003	1.8	3.2	9.1	13.4	20.1	15.7	36.7
Dominican	1997	1.4	2.6	8.2	12.4	19.3	15.3	40.7
Republic	2000	0.7	2.1	7.0	11.7	19.5	16.3	42.7

(Continued)

TABLE 7. Distribution of Income in Urban Households, by Quintile (Percentages)*
(*Continued*)

| Country | Year | Quintile 1 (Poorest) | | Quintile 2 | Quintile 3 | Quintile 4 | Quintile 5 (Richest) | |
		Decile 1	Decile 2				Decile 9	Decile 10
	2007	0.8	1.9	6.6	11.0	19.1	16.7	43.9
Uruguay	1990	1.9	3.2	9.4	13.7	20.0	15.0	36.9
	1999	1.8	3.1	9.6	14.3	21.5	16.2	33.5
	2007	1.9	3.0	8.9	13.7	21.3	16.5	34.8
Venezuela	1990	1.5	2.9	9.0	13.7	21.3	16.4	35.2
	1999**	1.1	2.5	8.2	13.1	20.7	16.6	37.8
	2007**	1.8	3.3	9.8	14.7	22.2	16.5	31.8

*Ordered according to per capita income.
**National total.
†Refers to metropolitan areas.
§Twenty-eight urban agglomerations.
Source: ECLAC/CEPAL, *Statistical Yearbook for Latin America and the Caribbean*. Santiago, Chile: United Nations, 2008, pp. 76–78.

financial, and industrialist elites and by multinational corporations and their foreign managers. Power, like wealth, remained concentrated—often absolutely. Indeed, some observers suggest that a requisite for belonging to the ruling class is to know, to have, and to exercise power. This was not only true with the hierarchical native civilizations but has been so since colonial times, when a small European elite allocated resources for larger societies whose majorities were made up of indigenous, African, *mestizo*, and mulatto majorities. For the sake of simplicity, one could argue that up to 1950 most of Latin America, outside of a few major cities like Buenos Aires, was comprised of an upper class including *hacienda-*, *fazenda-*, *plantation-*, or mine-owning *patrónes* and a lower class including peasant or rural laborer *peones*, or plantation or mine workers. Indeed, much of the basic socio-political structures of Latin America hearken back to the traditional large estate, plantation, or mine run by European or mostly European owners who commanded absolute or near absolute power over the masses of people of color toiling on their property. In this hierarchical, authoritarian system, the peasants, laborers, servants, and even overseers were strongly subordinated to the *patrón*. The difference in power, wealth, and status was extraordinary. The basic structure of the system was most often brutal for those on the bottom. Most struggled on in grinding poverty; a few fled to the interior like the runaway slaves (maroons); and occasionally there were local rebellions. In what became a classic part of Latin American society, some decided that they could best survive and maximize their lot by formalizing their position in a classic patron-client relationship. In this way, they made their well-being in large part a function of the paternalism of the *patrón* and his family. In return for their loyalty and support, the power and influence of the *patrón* would, they hoped, be employed to protect and promote them. Leaving the area and enlisting in reform or revolutionary movements were less frequently exercised options.

Yet, there have been changes. The advent of urbanization, industrialization, and the diffusion of advanced technology, as seen in the proliferation of televisions, cellular phones, computers, and cars, has stimulated the growth of new groups. There were hardly any members of the middle class through the nineteenth century in Latin America, yet their numbers have increased drastically in recent decades. They now account for as much as a quarter of the population in many countries and have lifestyles that are not totally unlike their North American or European counterparts. Further, the middle class has the added advantage of access to very affordable domestic help. Limited employment horizons for lower-class women and men, low wages, and a tradition of subordination make domestic help plentiful and affordable for most middle- and all upper-class households. Industrialization, *maquiladora*-style assembly plants, and a growing demand for services have burgeoned throughout the region, stimulating demand for middle-class positions in the clerical, supervisory, and technical fields. The social pyramid is now a little flatter and might look more like Figure 2.

As the new century begins, the vast majority of Latin Americans are urban workers of different types and peasants. As Latin America has industrialized in recent years, the number of industrial workers has skyrocketed and the number of peasants has fallen. Indeed, Karl Marx's vision of a large, brutally exploited, poorly treated proletariat driven from the land and unable to change its lot without total revolution could be coming to pass in Latin America in the twenty-first century. Unlike the nineteenth-century Europe of Marx, in most of Latin America, neither reformers nor the labor movement have been able to change the working conditions of most workers to any appreciable extent. Many still work for less than U.S.$5 a day (the minimum wage was less than $4 a day in Mexico in 2007), and few make more than $10. The boss is still very much the authoritarian figure; the workers are very much subordinate.

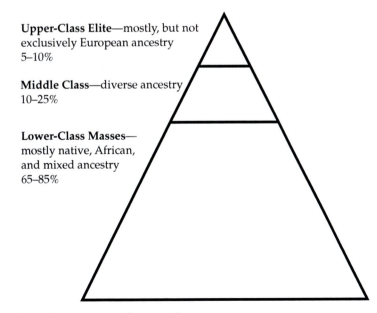

Upper-Class Elite—mostly, but not exclusively European ancestry 5–10%

Middle Class—diverse ancestry 10–25%

Lower-Class Masses— mostly native, African, and mixed ancestry 65–85%

FIGURE 2. Latin American social pyramid.

Soccer match between Argentina and Brazil, July 2009. *(AFP/Getty Images)*

This domination of the many by the few has not changed as more women enter the formal workforce. In Brazil, 56 percent of women are employed in the formal sector; in Mexico, the figure is 40 percent (see Table 8). If informal sectors (street vendors and in-home producers) are added, the figures would be 72 percent for Brazil and 62 percent for Mexico. Women are thought to be less apt to resist management decisions—or to strike—and more willing to work for lower wages. Further, the proclivity of predominantly male management to hire female workers in the *maquiladoras* has also helped reinforce authoritarian control systems and feminize some of the worst worker poverty. It has also exposed a new generation of younger Latin American women to new forms of patriarchy and sexual harassment that are outside of the protective familial and community contexts in which they were raised.

As the new millennium begins, the conditions in which most Latin Americans live are very difficult indeed. Although literacy rates have improved, educational levels are still low, and basic indicators like infant mortality reflect a great deal of suffering (see Table 1 in Chapter 1). Out of every 1,000 live births in Bolivia, 43 infants die in their first year of life. In Haiti, 47 of every 1,000 children die in their first year. Cuba, Costa Rica, and Chile are the only Spanish-, Portuguese-, or French-speaking countries in the hemisphere to have an infant mortality rate lower than 10 per 1,000 live births. Elsewhere in Latin America, thousands of children live on the streets and must struggle to survive each day. More than 7 million children live on the streets in Brazil alone. Large numbers die of neglect, disease, or outright murder each year; and many are eliminated as nuisances by merchant-paid death squads or off-duty police.

TABLE 8. Population and Social Conditions

	*Estimated Total Population (thousands) (2008)	*Annual Population Growth Rate (%) (2008)	*Life Expectancy at Birth (years) (2008)	**Population with Access to Drinking Water Services (%) (2006)	~Population with Access to Drinking Water Services (%) (Urban) (2006)	~Population with Access to Drinking Water Services (%) (Rural) (2006)	**Population with Access to Sewage Disposal Services (%) (2006)	>Female Economically Active Rate (%) (2007)
Argentina	39,934	1.0	75.5	96	98	80	91	50
Bolivia	9,694	1.7	65.9	86	96	69	43	66
Brazil	194,228	1.2	72.6	91	97	58	77	60
Chile	16,803	1.0	78.7	95	98	72	94	39
Colombia	46,741	1.2	73.1	99	77	64	78	64
Costa Rica	4,534	1.5	78.9	98	99	96	96	43
Cuba	11,265	0.0	78.4	91	95	78	98	45
Dominican Republic	9,904	1.4	72.4	95	97	91	79	57
Ecuador	13,481	1.1	75.2	95	98	91	84	52
El Salvador	6,953	1.3	72.1	84	94	68	86	47
Guatemala	13,686	2.5	70.5	95*	99	94	61*	45
Haiti	9,751	1.6	61.3	58	70	51	19	39
Honduras	7,246	1.9	70.4	84	95	74	66	37
Nicaragua	5,676	1.3	73.2	79	90	63	48	38
Panama	3,399	1.6	75.7	92	96	81	74	48
Paraguay	6,238	1.8	72.0	77	94	52	70	71
Peru	28,221	1.2	71.7	84	92	63	72	64
Puerto Rico	4,012	0.5	78.9	...	...	...	...	38
Uruguay	3,350	0.3	76.6	100	97	93	100	53
Venezuela	28,122	1.6	73.9	83*	...	...	68*	52

(Continued)

TABLE 8. Population and Social Conditions   (*Continued*)

	*Estimated Total Population (thousands) (2008)	*Annual Population Growth Rate (%) (2008)	*Life Expectancy at Birth (years) (2008)	**Population with Access to Drinking Water Services (%) (2006)	~Population with Access to Drinking Water Serivces (%) (Urban) (2006)	~Population with Access to Drinking Water Services (%) (Rural) (2006)	**Population with Access to Sewage Disposal Services (%) (2006)	>Female Economically Active Rate (%) (2007)
NAFTA countries								
Canada	33,170	0.9	80.8	100	...	...	100	63
Mexico	107,801	1.1	76.4	95	98	85	81	41
United States	308,798	1.0	78.4	99	...	...	100	59
				*2005			*2005	

Sources: *Pan-American Health Organization. Basic Indicators 2008, http://www.paho.org/English/SHA/coredata/tabulator/newTabulator.htm.

**Pan-American Health Organization, Health Analysis and Information Systems Area. Regional Core Health Data Initiative; Technical Health Information System. Washington DC, 2006.

http://www.paho.org/English/SHA/coredata/tabulator/newsqlTabulator.asp.

>Statistics and Indicators on women and men. U.N. Statistical Division. December 2008.

http://unstats.un.org/unsd/demographic/products/indwm/tab5a.htm.

~Statistical Yearbook for Latin America and the Caribbean 2008, pg. 73.

... Data not available.

As can be seen in Table 8, many who have dwellings do not even have water in their homes and fewer still have sewer services. Conditions are hard for the masses. Caloric intake and the availability of protein (see Table 9) are low among the many, and malnutrition is a severe problem for the poorer sectors in most Latin American countries. Cuba is one of the few countries to radically improve such conditions. Even there, as late as 1950, 30 to 40 percent of the general population and 60 percent of the rural population were undernourished. Twenty years after the revolution,

TABLE 9. Nutrition and Health Care

Country	*Availability of Calories Per Day (Kcal/day per capita) (2005)	***Availability of Protein per Person per Day (grams) (2003-2005)	*Physicians per 10,000 Population (2005)	**% of Births Attended by Trained Personnel (2006)	*Number of Deaths Due to AIDS (2005)	**Public Expenditure on Health as a Proportion of GDP (%)
Argentina	2992	93	32.1 (2004)	99.0%	4300	4.6 (2006)
Bolivia	2235	56	7.6 (2001)	67.0%	< 500	1.4 (2004)
Brazil	3049	84	20.6 (2001)	88.0%	14000	3.1 (2005)
Chile	2863	85	13 (1999)	100.0%	< 500	2.8 (2006)
Colombia	2585	61	12.7 (2003)	96.0%	8200	3.4 (2006)
Costa Rica	2876	70	11.5 (2000)	99.0%	< 100	6.0 (2007)
Cuba	3152	78	62.0 (2004)	100.0%	< 500	9.9 (2007)
Dominican Republic	2347	52	19 (1999)	96.0%	6700	2.1 (2007)
Ecuador	2754	56	16.4 (2001)	99.0%	1600	1.8 (1995)
El Salvador	2584	67	12.6 (2002)	92.0%	2500	4.1 (2007)
Guatemala	2219	57	9.5 (2003)	41.0%	2700	5.1 (2005)
Haiti	2086	42	2.5 (1999)	26.0%	16000	...
Honduras	2356	65	8.7 (1999)	67.0%	3700	3.1 (1995)
Nicaragua	2298	59	16.4 (2003)	67.0%	< 500	3.7 (2007)
Panama	2272	68	13.8 (2003)	93.0%	< 1000	3.5 (2007)
Paraguay	2565	68	6.3 (2004)	77.0%	< 500	3.0 (2006)
Peru	2571	70	11.7 (2000)	73.0%	5600	1.0 (2007)
Puerto Rico	...	...	17.5 (1999)	...	< 500	1.8 (2007)
Uruguay	2828	84	39.0 (2003)	100.0%	< 500	3.8 (2006)
Venezuela	2336	66	20.0 (2001)	95.0%	6100	1.6 (2004)
NAFTA Countries						
Canada	3589	105	18.9 (2002)	...	< 1000	...
Mexico	3145	92	15.6 (1999)	86.0%	6200	3.1 (2007)
United States	3774	116	22.5 (2002)	...	16000	...

Sources: *Pan-American Health Organization. Basic Indicators 2008. http://www.paho.org/English/dd/ais/BI_2008_ENG.pdf.
**Statistical yearbook of Latin America and the Caribbean, 2006. pg. 70.
***United Nations Food and Agriculture Organization (FAO). 2005-2006 FAO Statistical Yearbook. D.1 *Consumption*: http://www.fao.org/economic/ess/publications-studies/statistical-yearbook/fao-statistical-yearbook-2007-2008/d-consumption/en/
...data missing.

malnutrition had been lowered to 5 percent, although it began to grow again in the 1990s as a result of the decrease in Soviet and Eastern European trade and aid and the stiffening of the U.S. trade embargo to include food and medicines.

Health care for most Latin Americans is poor. The public hospitals that serve the great majority are generally of very low quality outside of a few countries such as Cuba and Costa Rica (see Table 9). Good health care is usually in short supply and rationed by wealth and power. The combination of lack of health care, poor sanitation, and malnutrition fed a major cholera epidemic that appeared in Peru in the early 1990s and then spread throughout the region. As with wealth, health care is also very poorly distributed in the region. The bulk of the best physicians and medical facilities are for the wealthy and the middle class and are concentrated in the capitals and largest cities. Many—particularly in rural areas—do not have access to modern health care at all and either simply suffer or die or seek relief from practitioners of folk or traditional medicine. Yet, the medical care provided for the upper classes in exclusive private clinics is often quite good, although many prefer to go to the United States for specialized treatment.

Conditions for the upper class rival or exceed upper-class lifestyles in industrialized, northern nations; conditions for the masses in areas like Brazil's northeast, Haiti, much of Bolivia, and Nicaragua rival those of the poor in less developed nations in Africa and parts of the Indian subcontinent. It could well be argued that this inequality of wealth and disparity of power and influence are Latin America's greatest curses and are at the root of many of the developmental, social, criminal, and thus political problems that continue to plague the region. Yet, if varied social strata have very different economic realities, cultural similarities and interconnecting social relations tie them together into national societies that share many characteristics, as well as a few differences. To fully understand the complexity of these relations, one needs to understand the nature and importance of the family and gender roles in Latin American society.

Family and Gender Roles

Throughout Latin America the family is of fundamental importance. The family and family ties are the basis of identity and orientation to the greater society and political system. Much of one's life revolves around the family, and young people (especially, but not exclusively, women) usually stay with the family at least until they marry, even if this does not occur until their late twenties or later. Unmarried daughters often stay in the family house and, according to some traditions—as depicted in the Mexican film *Like Water for Chocolate*—are to stay and care for their parents in their old age. Government and private pension systems are often unreliable in Latin America. Children, in fact, may be the main or only pension system that aging parents have.

Personal ties and relationships form the basis for much of Latin American society and politics, and these begin with the family. If the world outside the family unit is often perceived as hostile and dangerous, the world within is seen as safe and secure. It is a given that family members help and protect each other, and in Latin America the traditional family has been large. Most early social interaction occurs within the sphere of the extended family, which includes not only father, mother, and children but also grandparents, aunts, uncles, and first and second cousins on both sides. As beautifully depicted in novels like *One Hundred Years of Solitude* by Gabriel García Márquez and *House of the Spirits* by Isabel Allende, three or even four generations often live in the same household. Nor has the nuclear family been small. Families of eight to ten children were not uncommon in rural areas; now, three or four children are still common and double that number are still seen, although less so in urban areas. Treasured, doted upon, and highly valued, children generally receive special attention from all adults. Cultural values and the adamant stand of the Catholic Church against artificial means of contraception and abortion have combined with traditional practices of measuring women's and men's worth by how many children they have to maintain large families. Yet, as Latin America becomes increasingly urbanized (about 75 percent), financial pressures and the increasing need for a second income have begun to reduce family size but not necessarily the importance of the family unit.

Patriarchy is strong in Latin America and is even manifest in the old Roman term *patria potestas* (powerful patriarch). Frequently found in Latin American constitutions and legal codes, it means that the father is all-powerful in the family and in family matters. The term preceded *pater familias* in Roman times and originally meant that the father had unrivalled authority in the family and even held life-and-death power over other family members. Property for the family was most commonly held in the elder male's name (although there have been significant exceptions since colonial times), and women often had to go through fathers or brothers to exercise property-owning rights. Today, fathers and husbands enjoy a great deal of power in the Latin American family. Male prerogative often seems unbounded. While traditionally the woman is expected to come to the marriage pure and virgin and to protect the family honor by remaining above reproach, it is expected that the male has considerable sexual experience before marriage. Further, it has been the norm that any extramarital affairs he might have are considered by the general society to be something that men do and typically not sufficient to jeopardize the marriage or to besmirch the family's reputation or honor. Mistresses have been maintained, often openly, and the tradition of the *casa chica* (the little house or second household) continues. Wealthy and not so wealthy men often maintain an entire second family in a second household, acknowledge their children, and give them their name. Eva (Evita) Duarte Perón was the product of such a union. Even today one still hears of well-known public figures being seen with their mistresses, but the dual standard suggests a very different code of behavior for married women. For instance, in rural areas of Brazil and elsewhere in the region, a husband who comes upon his wife in bed with another man and shoots them dead may argue that his actions were necessary to protect family honor. Many a judge and jury have found this sufficient grounds for acquittal. In a similar vein, daughters are carefully guarded and protected by their fathers and brothers.

Men in general and male heads of household in particular have a great deal of power and prerogative in Latin American society. Most Latin Americans are socialized into households where a strong man ostensibly rules (strong women often head single-parent households or use indirect, yet no less effective, means of control in two-parent families). Thus, effective political action in the greater society is often equated with the strong, dominant, uncompromising ruling style that most Latin American patriarchs display. The traditional expectation for the Latin American politician, or *político*, is that he exhibit characteristics most often identified with the strong, dominant male—the *macho*. Strength and resolve are valued; weakness and an overly conciliatory orientation are not. Indeed, when a country is passing through a time of crisis, one can frequently hear the oft-repeated opinion that what is needed is a *mano dura*, a strong hand, and someone with the maleness to exercise it. Yet, in family and politics alike, the leader is expected to have a great deal of grace and style and not to be crude or coarse—at least until driven to it. Even so, the heavy-handed use of power may be grudgingly accepted if it is clear that the leader is intent on and competent enough to impose his will.

Gender roles are in the process of transition in Latin America, yet *machismo*, or maleness, is still very much a part of Latin American culture and clearly defines traditional male-female relations. In the 2000 presidential election in Mexico, the successful opposition candidate, Vicente Fox, frequently asserted his macho image in the campaign and even impugned the masculinity of his less forceful Institutional Revolutionary Party (PRI) opponent. In its worst forms, machismo rationalizes total male dominance and even domestic violence. In its less violent form, it frequently robs women of their confidence and independence by socializing them to believe they need a male to protect them, do things for them, provide for them economically, and guide them in their daily lives and development. From an early age, the socialization of male children is generally much different from that of female children. Males are taught to be assertive and their aggressiveness is tolerated, if not encouraged, while female children are most often taught to not cause a commotion, not challenge authority frontally, and at least appear to be submissive.

Traditional roles for women also coexist with modern feminist views. Of importance in traditional culture is *marianismo*, the glorification of the traditional female role. The term comes from the cult of the pure Virgin Mary (María)–like woman, who is expected to be the bastion of family honor, the submissive woman, and long-suffering family anchor. Yet, even in the traditional family, the woman often skillfully employs her role as mistress of her own home in childrearing, social engagements, and religion to guide and even manipulate the ostensibly dominant male.

It has further been suggested that Latin American women traditionally have been limited to the private space of the house and family while the public space outside the home was the sole preserve of the male. Traditionally, the woman's place was in the home with the children. She was to support her spouse in his endeavors in external public space. While this was generally true, it should be noted that Latin American women have sometimes used their traditional roles to penetrate public space. Thus, a very competent, ambitious Mexican noblewoman of the seventeenth century joined a convent and became Sor Juana Inés de la Cruz so that she could pursue her studies and be free to write some of the best (and most passionate) poetry and prose of the colonial era. Yet, the fact that she felt obliged to take this path suggests how limited the options were for education and public expression for women. Indeed, the Latin American universities started as seminaries and excluded women

President Cristina Fernández de Kirchner of Argentina. *(Latin Content/Getty Images)*

for many years. Only toward the middle of the twentieth century was it possible for women to pursue university education in large numbers, and most were concentrated in traditionally female fields like education, nursing, and social work. This has changed radically today, and one sees a large number of female students in traditional male bastions like engineering in most of Latin America.

Traditionally, women were controlled and inhibited. Courting—particularly for women of some status—was often supervised by the omnipresent chaperone in the form of a grandmother, aunt, or other female relative. Women were often expected to stay in the home and not work outside, while men were to go forth in the outside world to gain bread and fortune. Later, when it was more permissible for women to work outside the home, many occupations were closed and remuneration was markedly inferior to that of men. Nor has it been easy for women to occupy positions of authority or supervise large numbers of men. In the political sphere, those women who did aspire to public position often used their upper-class position or ties to a famous father or husband to gain access (as was the case for Violeta Chamorro in Nicaragua). Talented women like Eva Perón, President Mireya Moscoso of Panama, or President Cristina Fernández de Kirchner of Argentina sometimes traded on their husband's position to acquire visibility and power in their own right. Aside from a few such famous personages, competent *políticas* were, however, all too often assigned "female" posts, such as minister of education or minister of social welfare (see Table 10). However, with the election of Michelle Bachelet as president in Chile and Cristina Fernández de Kirchner to the same office in Argentina, it could be argued that women are taking a much more active role in national politics. The fact

Latin America

TABLE 10. Women Occupying Parliamentary Seats (Number)

Country	*Monocameral or Lower Chamber			**Upper Chamber
	1999	2004	2009	Last Election
Argentina	28	34	40	28
Bolivia	12	19	17	1
Brazil	6	9	9	10
Chile	11	13	15	2
Colombia	12	12	8	12
Costa Rica	19	35	37	N/A
Cuba	28	36	43	N/A
Dominican Republic	16	17	20	1
Ecuador	17	16	...	N/A
El Salvador	17	11	19	N/A
Guatemala	13	8	12	N/A
Haiti	4	4	4	...
Honduras	9	6	23	N/A
Mexico	17	23	23	23
Nicaragua	10	21	19	N/A
Panama	...	17	9	N/A
Paraguay	3	10	13	7
Peru	11	18	28	N/A
Uruguay	7	...	12	4
Venezuela	13	10	19	N/A

...Data not available.

Sources: *U.N. Statistics Division. Statistics and Indicators on Women and Men. June 2009. http://unstats.un.org/unsd/demographic/products/indwm/tab6a.htm.
**Inter-Parliamentary Union. Women in National Parliaments. Situation as of 31 May 2009. http://www.ipu.org/wmn-e/classif-arc.htm.

that Bachelet had been Latin America's first female minister of defense, was not married to the father of her third child, and was an agnostic suggested that women could be much less constrained by traditional roles—even when in public office.

Many have observed that some of the most assertive political actions by women have come from their traditional, private roles as mothers or wives. This was seen in the weekly protests begun by the Mothers of the Disappeared during the dirty war in Argentina in the late 1970s and early 1980s. The Madres de la Plaza de Mayo, as they came to be known, became politically active as they sought to find and, if possible, save their children and other family members. They marched every week in the Plaza de Mayo in the center of Buenos Aires, carrying pictures of their disappeared relatives. In Chile, women publicized the disappearance and murder of their family members by sewing together *arpilleras*—quilts that told the stories of their loved ones. When Violeta Chamorro emerged as a presidential candidate and then president in Nicaragua in 1990, she did so as the

Violeta Chamorro, campaigning in her successful bid for the Nicaraguan presidency in 1990. Note her white dress and hair and motherly outstretched arms. *(Photo by Bill Gentile/ CORBIS)*

wife of a martyred hero in the struggle against the dictator Anastasio Somoza and as the reconciling mother who could unite her politically divided children and the Nicaraguan nation itself. She arrived at her culminating political rally in Managua symbolically dressed all in white, white hair flowing, riding in the white "pope mobile" that John Paul II had used on his historic visit to Nicaragua a few years before.

The Nicaraguan figure of the Sandinista guerrilla Comandante Dora María Téllez, however, suggests the emergence of more independent and directly public roles for women. Women comprised some 33 percent of the Sandinista combatants, and women like Téllez and Mónica Baltodano were Sandinista *comandantes* in the struggle against the Somoza dictatorship. Many of their stories are told in *Sandino's Daughters* by Margaret Randal. The situation was similar among the insurgents in the civil war in El Salvador. As underlined by these examples, the emergence of other prominent female politicians such as 1998 Venezuelan presidential candidate and then governor Irene Saez, and statistics on the percent of economically active women (Table 8), the traditional role of the woman in Latin America is rapidly being redefined. This process is being moved forward by the following:

- Women who work outside the home.
- Women who exercise more independence by having their own apartments and entering into a relation with a *compañero*, exploring the full dimension of their sexuality.

- Revolutionary women like guerrilla *comandantes* in El Salvador and Nicaragua and the third of the Sandinista combatants who were women.
- The emerging figure of *La Presidenta*. With the election of Michelle Bachelet in Chile in 2006, Cristina Fernández de Kirchner in Argentina in 2007, and Mireya Moscoso in Panama in 1999, Latin America witnessed the election of four female presidents (Violeta Chamorro in Nicaragua was the first). Elected as vice president, Isabel Perón also served as president of Argentina for more than a year after husband Juan Perón died in office. Before this, three other Latin American women served as unelected chief executives in Bolivia, Haiti, and Ecuador for shorter periods.
- Radical feminists who challenge many vestiges of machismo and maintain a coherent line through their creative work, writing, magazines, journals, organizing, and personal example.
- Ever stronger national women's movements such as the Association of Nicaraguan Women Louisa Amanda Espinosa (AMNLAE) in Nicaragua.
- The new generation of young women who politely but persistently decide not to be bound by the same constraints that restricted the occupational and relational horizons of their mothers and grandmothers.

There is growing participation by women in education, the professions, government, and business (see Table 11). Gender roles are rapidly and radically being redefined. Feminism and women's movements have grown substantially in recent decades. There are a variety of women's organizations and feminist publications in Mexico, Argentina, Chile, Brazil, and the other larger countries. Strong women's movements can also be found in Nicaragua, Costa Rica, as well as Cuba. Women's groups are also active in the smaller countries and in cities and intellectual centers throughout the region. It should, however, be noted that feminism in Latin America is well rooted in Latin American culture and can be quite distinct from North American or European feminism. Thus, most Latin American feminists would define the female role as eventually including a role as spouse or *compañera* and mother. Attitudes on abortion—but not birth control—can also be quite divergent from those held by most feminists in the United States. Indeed, as the new century begins, Latin American women are seeking and gaining empowerment in a variety of ways that they define on their own terms.

Class, Gender, Race, and Mobility

Even though women are gaining power at an ever increasing rate, their mobility is still limited. Cuba is one of the Latin American countries with the highest degree of equality. Socialist Cuba legislated equality some years ago and even passed the Cuban Family Code in 1975. It requires men and women to share household tasks and childrearing equally. In a trend that is beginning to spread throughout the region, women can enter most career paths and most professions. Although conditions for women in Cuba are very good in comparison to most Latin American countries, their mobility is limited. Although thousands belong to the ruling Communist Party in Cuba, their representation is less than equal in the party congresses. As

TABLE 11. Women in High-Level and Decision-Making Occupations

Country	Legislators, Senior Officials, and Managers	Share of Women in the Adult Labor Force (%) (2007)
Argentina	23 (2006)	41
Bolivia	36 (2000)	45
Brazil	35 (2006)	43
Chile	23 (2007)	36
Colombia	38 (2000)	46
Costa Rica	27 (2007)	35
Cuba	31 (2007)	39
Dominican Republic	31 (2007)	44
Ecuador	28 (2006)	40
El Salvador	29 (2006)	39
Guatemala	...	37
Haiti	...	33
Honduras	41 (2005)	32
Mexico	31 (2007)	36
Nicaragua	41 (2006)	31
Panama	44 (2007)	37
Paraguay	35 (2007)	45
Peru	30 (2007)	44
Uruguay	40 (2007)	44
Venezuela	27 (2002)	39

... = No data.

Sources: http://unstats.un.org/unsd/Demographic/products/indwm/tab5d.htm
http://unstats.un.org/unsd/demographic/products/indwm/tab5a.htm.

one moves upward to the Central Committee and higher levels of government, the representation of women diminishes even further. Women generally experience greater equality at the lower levels: the higher women go in the political and party structure, the greater the barriers to their upward mobility. This is even more the case in most other Latin American countries. In countries where capitalism is dominant, women have generally found it very difficult to obtain management positions and even more so to rise to positions of power or prominence. Positions in the government bureaucracy or educational institutions have been easier to obtain. Not surprisingly, gender is frequently a barrier to upward mobility even in Cuba and Costa Rica (which has also passed progressive legislation guaranteeing legal equality), not to mention other more traditional areas of Latin America. Latin American nations are now beginning to pass legislation requiring a minimum percentage of women on party lists for the legislatures. But gender is not the only impediment to equality or upward mobility. Racism and a rigid class structure pose equally formidable barriers.

The class system in most of Latin America is fairly rigid, and it is very difficult for most to experience much upward mobility. As was suggested in the discussion of Amero-Indian and African peoples in Chapter 4, race has also remained a barrier to

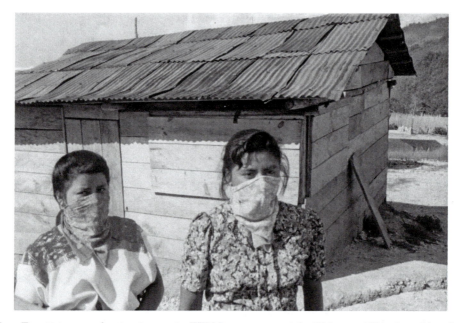

Two Zapatista guards at entrance to EZLN encampment in Chiapas, 1996. As with other mass and revolutionary organizations in Latin America, more and more women are participating in all aspects of activity. *(Photo by H. Vanden)*

acceptance and mobility. There have been examples of successful indigenous Latin Americans, such as Benito Juárez of Mexico, who ascended to the presidency of the republic without ever repudiating his native heritage. More commonly, native peoples have had to assimilate to some extent to occupy positions of responsibility outside their native communities. Even in countries like Guatemala and Bolivia, which are inhabited predominantly by native peoples, Hispanicizing family names, the predominant use of Spanish, and adoption of Western dress are generally necessary for upward mobility. Indeed, many native people feel obliged to pass as *mestizos* (*ladinos* in Guatemala). The election of Evo Morales as the first indigenous president in Bolivia (55 percent indigenous) is indicative of both the historic inclusion of indigenous people and the sea change that is underway. Yet, as suggested by the testimony of Domitila Barrios de Chungara (*Let Me Speak*) in Bolivia and Rigoberta Menchú (*I Rigoberta*) in Guatemala, indigenous peoples are still second-class citizens, particularly when they come from the working class. When they are also female, they suffer even more discrimination. When they are openly gay, their lives may be a living hell.

The lot of Afro-Latins has also been fraught with difficulty. Racial discrimination in Latin America was never as institutionalized as it was in the United States, but it nonetheless existed. Slavery continued in many countries until the second half of the nineteenth century. When it ended, black Latin Americans emerged from slavery into societies where official segregation was not legislated but was practiced in more subtle forms. Some observers have noted that most of the governments of Latin America have espoused a philosophy of racial democracy but have simultaneously instituted a social order that in large part excluded their African populations from many key aspects of national life. As suggested by the eloquent testimony of Brazilian congresswoman Benedita da Silva, in *Benedita da Silva,* lower-class origins and being female make the struggle of people of color even more difficult. Afro-Latin women have made a significant contribution to the women's movement in Latin America and have played a key role in social transformation. There is, however, a paucity of literature and research in this area.

Black women—like indigenous women—are at the bottom of the social pyramid in Latin America. Afro-Latin women have had to form their own organizations in order to address issues of specific concern. Indeed, many black women in Latin America complain that mainstream white organizations do not understand the intersection of race and gender. For many black women's organizations, this nexus provides a much-needed framework of understanding. Field research by Kwame Dixon suggests that in the human rights area, this framework allows researchers to see the racial and gender bases for many rights violations (personal communication, September 2000). For instance, as a result of the war in Colombia, displaced persons tend to be disproportionately female and Afro-Colombian or indigenous. This suggests the intersection of multiple forms of discrimination. There are also distinct forms of discrimination that occur against a person when gender and race or ethnicity intersect. That is, women who are black or indigenous are more apt to suffer discrimination than either a white woman or a black or indigenous man. Homosexuality compounds these factors if it is acknowledged.

As noted in Chapter 4, there is, however, growing black consciousness and movements in several countries to pass legislation prohibiting racial discrimination. Currently, black women's organizations are developing frameworks that incorporate race, class, and gender. Within the black community in Brazil, one finds several groups that also focus on gender inequality. Among these are the Geledés Instituto da Mulher Negra and the Centro de Referencia da Mulher Negra in Bahia.

Initial colonial society set up a rigid system in which classism, racism, patriarchy, and elitism in many forms were pervasive. Even today, one is still often judged by her or his birth and family name. Indeed, the Iberian tradition of using the maternal maiden name as well as the paternal name (paternal family name followed by maternal family name) is still in practice; for example, in Hispanic Latin America, José Sánchez López is the son of his father Sánchez and his mother, whose father's name is López (in Brazil both names may also be used, but the mother's family name appears first). Thus, mobility and entrance to social circles or employment opportunities are often defined more by who one is in terms of class, race, and gender and the circles in which one's family travels than by one's actual accomplishments and abilities. Indeed, it may take a generation or two for a family to gain access to social institutions like the Club Nacional in Peru, even if they have achieved economic or artistic success in their time. This process may take even longer in some countries if a person is primarily of indigenous or African ancestry. If they are openly gay, acceptance may never come. Some have even suggested that a process of whitening by wealth, great success (e.g., Pelé in Brazil), or substantial power (e.g., Batista in Cuba or Somoza in Nicaragua) must occur first. Indeed, many of the competent professionals who immigrate to the United States do so because they find that they have a much better chance of being hired or accepted for their actual accomplishments and demonstrated abilities rather than being prejudged by class, race, gender, or family. In this and other areas, cultural norms and mores strongly precondition perceptions.

CLASSISM CHALLENGED: MASS ORGANIZATIONS

Movements bubbled up in the nineteenth and twentieth centuries, such as those that resulted in major peasant uprisings in El Salvador in 1832 and—assisted by Farabundo Martí and the Salvadoran Communist Party—1932. Thus, there is a long and well-developed tradition of popular uprisings and resistance movements. In more recent times, these have coalesced in mass movements and nongovernmental organizations that take advantage of the increased political space that new regimes and democratization have provided to assert their strength and push for their objectives. Latin American women's and feminist movements are but one example of this. Likewise, there are urban slum-dweller movements such as those in Mexico City and movements of rural workers such as the Landless Movement (Sem Terra) in Brazil. The reemergence of indigenous people's movements, such as the Confederation of Indigenous Nationalities of Ecuador (CONAIE) in Ecuador, and the many indigenous movements in Bolivia are also of particular significance. Indeed, Alvarez, Dagnino, and Escobar argue that social movements are revitalizing civil society in their important *Cultures of Politics/Politics of Cultures: Revisioning of Latin American Social Movements.* (See section on social movements in Chapter 11.)

Homosexuality and Transgenderism

Another area that is undergoing challenge concerns traditional views about homosexuality. Although often not discussed openly, homosexuality has been part of Latin America since pre-Columbian times. Today, a growing awareness has allowed customs regarding gender, sexuality, and the family to be challenged by homosexuality and transgenderism. In this and other areas of Latin American culture and society, it is necessary to put aside preconceived notions and fixed labels coming from societies outside the region to understand the phenomena. Because most precolonial history was lost, destroyed, or interpreted through the eyes of the conquistadors, there are few accurate records of how indigenous societies prior to the conquest dealt with the issue. From the evidence that does exist, it appears that both Aztec and Mayan civilizations focused mostly on male-male sex acts and interpreted them through an honor-shame paradigm. In the systemization, there was a clear difference between the active and passive roles in intercourse: The active role stood for the masculine characteristics of strength and virility, whereas the passive role resembled the weakness and frailty of women. These discourses of penetration were frequently evoked in a number of ways to symbolize power and domination. Finally, in a slightly different understanding, sodomy signified the mentoring relationship involved in the transfer of knowledge and power through blood and semen from community elders to coming-of-age noble young. This understanding, called the *age-stratified model,* is similar to how ancient Greek civilization conceptualized sexuality. Indigenous groups in the Andean region conceptualized homosexuality and transgenderism quite differently. As opposed to focusing on the act of penetration as a means for domination, the Incans celebrated individuals, both male-bodied and female-bodied, who deviated from gender and sexual norms, often designating them as having a *third gender*. The term *two-spirited* has also recently been coined to explain these individuals, with its origin emanating from the belief that two-spirited persons did not just have one spirit living within them but two—a male and a female. Consequently, they were revered as enlightened and blessed individuals, often occupying very prestigious social roles within the tribes, such as chiefs and shamans.

The conquistadors from the Iberian Peninsula brought with them their own ideas about gender and sexual deviance, and much more is known about their thoughts on the subject compared to indigenous groups. Over time their ideas slowly overtook indigenous views and formed the basis of the social stigma and legal persecution that came to dominate the region for centuries. Two separate, and sometimes contradictory, strains of thought are of particular importance: the views of the Catholic Church and Mediterranean ideas of masculinity.

Catholicism was central to both the Spanish and Portuguese empires at the beginning of the 1500s and, as such, Church teachings played a significant role in how gender and sexual transgressions were considered. The official position of the Church was that sex for any purpose other than procreation was lustful, therefore violating the Sixth Commandment. Sodomy, or *pecado contra natura*, was a sin, whether man-man, woman-woman, or man-woman. Homosexuality was understood to be a behavior, rather than defining a person with a distinct gender identity.

Even though Church doctrine influenced the state's actions on homosexuality, the same gendered ideas of masculinity that form the basis of machismo also significantly influenced how colonial Latin American societies thought about gender and sexuality. Homosexuality was understood according to a *gender-stratified model*, whereby one's identity is strongly influenced by the "sexual function" one performs. The central characters of Manuel Puig's famous novel *Kiss of the Spider Woman*, about two prisoners locked away during the last military dictatorship in Argentina, epitomize this divide. Under this model, there was no homosexual group consciousness as no distinctive homosexual identity existed.

As Latin American countries achieved independence from Spain and Portugal, they fashioned their constitutions and laws after the Napoleonic code, removing most explicit prohibitions against sodomy. In Argentina, for example, Article 19 of the 1853 Constitution states: "Private activities that do not affect public order and morality and do not harm other people are reserved to the judgment of God and off-limits to the authority of magistrates." However, this does not mean that homosexuality was by any means more socially accepted. Similar to the social structuring in the United States at the time, inherent in this system was an implicit agreement that homosexuality would be tolerated in private as long as it was never openly discussed or visible in any way in public. Most countries had vague laws against vagrancy, public decency, and cross-dressing that were used at the discretion of police to enforce this public-private divide. This social and legal system came to dominate the region for centuries.

However, over the past few decades, globalization has helped bring along another paradigm shift in thinking about homosexuality in Latin America as the Western industrialized world's *gay-egalitarian model* is slowly replacing the gender-stratified model. Whereas before identity was based on the gendered notion of one's sexual role (*activo* or *pasivo*), this new understanding instead links one's identity to his or her object of sexual choice (male or female). The political implications of this are profound: both *activos* and *pasivos* now share a collective homosexual identity.

With this new understanding taking hold, modern homosexuality in Latin America has two characteristics that are of fundamental importance to how it has developed socially and politically. First, because attraction to members of the same sex is not necessarily an outwardly visible characteristic, gays and lesbians exert some power in controlling who knows. Strategically, this can be important, as homosexuals can hide their sexuality to avoid discrimination. Second, homosexuality is not a condition shared with members of one's core social group, the family, and therefore one can never be certain of their reaction on disclosure. Because the family plays such a fundamental role in social life in Latin America, it can be very dangerous for lesbians and gays to "come out" as they not only risk losing their primary social unit, but their economic base as well. This has led to what is understood as a public-private divide for most homosexuals, forcing them to live two separate lives: a public life revolving around their family and another private life where they engage in homosexual relationships. Also, because young adults typically live with their parents until they are married, it has prevented gay barrios from forming in most large Latin American cities, impeding the ability for gay communities to form. Homosexuality under this arrangement was tolerated as long as these boundaries stayed intact.

However, over the past several decades, two things have generally worn down this barrier. First, the emergence of AIDS (SIDA) in the 1980s forced a number of people to come out of the closet. Many people who formerly were able to compartmentalize their dual lives became visibly sick and could no longer hide it from their families. Also, as many gays and lesbians witnessed members of their private homosexual world begin to die en masse, it helped solidify group solidarity, as those affected sought ways to slow the spread of the epidemic and treat those who were sick. As organizations began to organize around issues like HIV, visibility became one of their primary political tactics.

Second, social movement organizations representing sexual and gender minorities began to appear in most Latin American countries starting in the 1970s. In South America, many groups began to form as repression eased with the end of the military dictatorships and the reemergence of democracy. In what was once a mostly underground phenomenon that was rarely discussed in public and not organized politically, this nascent movement has only recently begun publicly challenging social mores and entering public policy debates. This was all made possible because the new gay-egalitarian model created an identity from which to petition for rights and protections.

Many of the first organizations had very revolutionary philosophies, calling for radical social change. However, the Left in Latin America did not initially welcome them with open arms, following the doctrine of the Communist parties of the

Soviet Union and China that homosexuality was merely bourgeoisie decadence that went beyond the clearly demarcated lines of class. Because the gay rights movement was of multiclass composition, there was always the fear that its interests really did not align that clearly with the working class. Over time, leftist organizations continued to discriminate against homosexuals and transgender persons. Indeed, socialist Cuba after the revolution was repressive to homosexuals in the 1960s and 1970s as exemplified in the film *Before Night Falls*. In more recent years some parts of the left have changed their views. Homosexuals were allowed to play fairly active roles in the Sandinista revolution in Nicaragua, and recently the Cuban government has moderated its position significantly.

Over the past several decades, the homosexual and transgender movements that have appeared have not necessarily stayed together as cohesive units. In many countries, groups representing lesbians and transgender persons have splintered off from traditionally male-dominated organizations. Although gay men, lesbian women, and transgender persons all share stigma and repression from society at large, and are often the victims of violent acts, the problems they face are in many cases very different. Many of the political concerns for gay men, for instance, revolve around AIDS activism and sodomy laws. However, because HIV transmission sexually between two women is nearly nonexistent and most sodomy laws that do exist tend to punish only male-male sodomy, these are not the most pressing issues for lesbians. On the other hand, lesbians typically have felt more solidarity with the feminist movement and women's rights organizations. Their main concerns have typically focused on the same social restrictions and discrimination that heterosexual women also face. Finally, transgender persons have their own concerns. Typically, they are the demographic group hardest hit by HIV, but they also tend to face some of the greatest discrimination and violence as they are less able to hide their stigma than gays and lesbians.

Regardless of these fissures, homosexual and transgender organizations have made fairly steady progress in recent years. Political activism is growing: São Paulo, Brazil, is now home to the world's largest pride celebration, which in 2007 attracted more than 3.5 million people. Also, attitudes have warmed on the subject and the movements have secured some impressive legal victories thought impossible only a decade ago. Politically, a few issues have dominated the agendas of most gay rights organizations: decriminalizing sodomy/homosexuality, passing nondiscrimination protections, securing additional funding and protections for persons with HIV, and more recently getting the state to recognize same-sex partnerships.

Because rates of violence and other forms of discrimination against homosexuals and transgender persons are still high in most parts of Latin America, gay rights groups have also directed their attention to fight these problems. For example, even though Brazil has the reputation of being a country where "anything goes" because of its widely flamboyant Carnival, it is actually home to some of the most savage violence against homosexuals and lesbians. Rates of violence are also especially high in several Central American countries. As a result, many countries in South and Central America (some at the local and some at the national level) have enacted some types of ordinances making it a crime to discriminate based on sexual orientation, gender identity, or both. Finally, many gay and lesbian organizations have made HIV activism one of their top priorities. Brazil notably stands out, as it has provided HIV medication universally and free of charge since 1996 and has fought to obtain the rights to produce low-cost generic antiviral drugs to treat HIV.

Recently, same-sex partner recognition has become a new issue for many gay and lesbian organizations. Initially, lesbian and gay organizations began pushing for relationship recognition in a piecemeal fashion—first seeking health care benefits, inheritance rights, access to partner's pensions, and so on. Many groups throughout the regions have won significant concessions after long-fought battles in either legislatures or through the courts. More recently, however, LGBT groups have been pushing for broader social recognition in the form of state-sanctioned unions. The city legislature of Buenos Aires (an autonomous federal district) was the first to pass legislation recognizing these relationships in December 2002, quickly followed five days later by the southern province Rio Negro. Two years later the province of Rio Grande do Sul in Brazil followed suit recognizing same-sex "stable unions," but in this case did so because of a judicial ruling, not legislative action. In Mexico, Mexico City and the province of Coahuila became the next in 2006 and 2007. Uruguay has set many milestones becoming the first Latin American country to recognize civil unions nationwide in 2008 and went one step further granting adoption rights to same-sex couples in late 2009. As of this writing, most countries have yet to discuss giving full marriage rights to same-sex couples, with the exceptions of Argentina and Uruguay.

The main opposition today to homosexuality and transgenderism still comes from religious conservatives repeating many of the same arguments used centuries before. However, in some South American countries, the Catholic Church has lost some of its political effectiveness. In places such as Argentina and Chile, the Church's reputation was tarnished during the 1960s and 1970s as it was seen as being too complicit in human rights abuses at the hands of the military dictatorships. Because of this, it has had to carefully walk the fine line between arguing against homosexuality but not against human rights. In addition, clergy abuse scandals have also plagued the Church in some parts of Latin America, in some ways severely crippling their moral authority. However, the recent rise in Protestantism presents a unique challenge to gays and lesbians, as many of these denominations are more vehemently antihomosexual than Catholicism is today.

As Latin America becomes more urban and educated and as egalitarian values are championed by women, indigenous organizations, Afro-Latins, landless workers, neighborhood organizations, gays and lesbians, and many others, the nature and structure of Latin American society will continue to change, and many of the old barriers will be challenged, if not overcome.

Bibliography

Alvarez, Sonia E., Evelina Dagnino, and Arturo Escobar. *Cultures of Politics/Politics of Culture: Revisioning Latin American Social Movements.* Boulder, CO: Westview Press, 1998.
Balderston, Daniel, and Donna J. Guy. 1997. *Sex and Sexuality in Latin America.* New York: New York University Press.
Barrios de Chungara, Domitila, with Moema Viezzer. *Let Me Speak! Testimony of Domitila, a Woman of the Bolivian Mines.* New York: Monthly Review, 1978.

Bose, Christine E., and Edna Acosta-Belén, eds. *Women in the Latin American Development Process.* Philadelphia: Temple University Press, 1995.

Bouvard, Margarite Guzman. *Revolutionizing Motherhood: The Mothers of the Plaza de Mayo.* Wilmington, DE: Scholarly Resources, 1994.

Caipora Women's Group. *Women in Brazil.* New York: Monthly Review Press, 1993.

Craske, Nikki. *Women and Politics in Latin America.* Piscataway, NJ: Rutgers University Press, 1999.

Cubit, Tessa. *Latin American Society.* 2nd ed. Harlow, UK: Longman, 1995.

Dore, Elizabeth, ed. *Gender Politics in Latin America: Debate in Theory and Practice.* New York: Monthly Review Press, 1998.

Dore, Elizabeth, and Maxine Molyneux, eds. *Hidden Histories of Gender and the State in Latin America.* Durham, NC: Duke University Press, 2000.

Eckstein, Susan, ed. *Power and Protest: Latin American Social Movements.* Berkeley: University of California Press, 1989.

French, William, and Katherine Elaine Bliss, eds. *Gender, Sexuality and Power in Latin America Since Independence.* Lanham, MD: Rowman and Littlefield, 2006.

Grandin, Greg. *The Blood of Guatemala: A History of Race and Nation.* Durham, NC: Duke University Press, 2000.

Hanchard, Michael, ed. *Racial Politics in Contemporary Brazil.* Durham, NC: Duke University Press, 1999.

Hillman, Richard S., ed. *Understanding Contemporary Latin America.* Boulder, CO: Lynne Reinner, 1997.

Horswell, Michael J. *Decolonizing the Sodomite: Queer Tropes of Sexuality in Colonial Andean Culture.* Austin: University of Texas Press, 2005.

Imaz, José Luis de. *Los Que Mandan* [Those Who Rule]. Translated by Carlos A. Astiz. Albany: State University of New York Press, 1970.

Janvry, Alain de. *The Agrarian Question and Reformism in Latin America.* Baltimore: Johns Hopkins University Press, 1988.

Jesus, Carolina María de. *Britita's Diary: The Childhood Memories of Carolina María de Jesus.* Armonk, NY: M. E. Sharp, 1998.

Kampwirth, Karen. *Women and Guerrilla Movements.* State College, PA: Penn State University Press, 2002.

Kulick, Don. *Travesti: Sex, Gender, and Culture among Brazilian Transgendered Prostitutes.* Chicago: University of Chicago Press, 1998.

Kuppers, Gaby, ed. *Compañeras: Voices from the Latin American Women's Movement.* London: Latin American Bureau, 1994.

Levine, Daniel, ed. *Constructing Culture and Power in Latin America.* Ann Arbor: University of Michigan Press, 1993.

Minority Rights Group. *No Longer Invisible: Afro-Latins Today.* London: Minority Rights Group Publications, 1995.

Murray, Stephen O. *Latin American Male Homosexualities.* Albuquerque: University of New Mexico Press, 1995.

Randal, Margaret. *Sandino's Daughters.* New Brunswick, NJ: Rutgers University, 1995.

Sigal, Peter Herman. *Infamous Desire: Male Homosexuality in Colonial Latin America.* Chicago: University of Chicago Press, 2003.

Stahler-Sholk, Richard, Harry E. Vanden, and Glen Kuecker, eds., *Latin American Social Movements in the Twenty-first Century: Resistance, Power and Democracy.* Lanham, MD: Rowman and Littlefield, 2008.

Stephen, Lynn. *Women and Social Movements in Latin America.* Austin: University of Texas Press, 1997.

Thiesenhusen, William C. *Searching for Agrarian Reform in Latin America.* Boston: Unwin Hyman, 1989.

Trexler, Richard C. *Sex and Conquest: Gendered Violence, Political Order, and the European Conquest of the Americas.* Ithaca, NY: Cornell University Press, 1995.

Windance Twine, Francis. *Racism in a Racial Democracy: The Maintenance of White Supremacy in Brazil.* New Brunswick, NJ: Rutgers University Press, 1998.

FILMS AND VIDEOS

Before Night Falls. United States, 2000.
Black Orpheus. Brazil, 1958.

Blossoms of Fire. Mexico, 2000.
Buenos Días Compañeras/Women in Cuba. Cuba, 1974.
Burnt Money. Argentina, 2000.
Central Station. Brazil, 1998.
Details of a Duel: A Question of Honor. Chile/Cuba, 1988.
Doña Herlinda and Her Son. Mexico, 1985.
The Double Day. United States, 1975.
Eles ñao usam Black Tie. Brazil, 1980.
In Women's Hands (Americas Series). United States, 1993.
Like Water for Chocolate. Mexico, 1992.
Los Olvidados. Mexico, 1950.
Mexican Bus Ride. Mexico, 1951.
Mirrors of the Heart (Americas Series). United States, 1993.
Place without Limits. Mexico, 1978.
Portrait of Teresa. Cuba, 1979.
Shoot to Kill. Venezuela, 1990.
Strawberry and Chocolate. Cuba, 1994.
We're All Stars. Peru, 1993.

WEBSITES

www.casarosada.gov.ar/   President's office in Argentina.
www.presidencia.cl/   President's office in Chile.

SIX

RELIGION IN LATIN AMERICA

Treatments of contemporary Latin American politics often pay relatively little attention to the role of religion. Such an omission is a serious one because from the era of the great Meso-American civilizations to the present time spiritual factors have had a great impact on the political scene. This chapter will explore that evolution over time. The Roman Catholic Church will be a major focus but not to the exclusion of other religions, especially the rapid rise of evangelical Protestantism in the last twenty-five years.

The primary perception of the religious character of Latin America is Roman Catholic. For nearly five centuries the Catholic Church had a virtual monopoly on religious life. During that time, religious and political authorities were tightly bound together. The North American concept of separation of church and state was not known in Latin America until almost the twentieth century. Today's reality in Latin America is somewhat different, although close to 70 percent of the population still identify themselves as Roman Catholic. During the last twenty-five years, the most important development in Latin American religiosity has been the exponential growth of evangelical Protestantism. In 1970, only 2 to 3 percent of the population in most Latin American countries were evangelical; today, that number has reached close to 15 percent. The last forty years have also witnessed significant turmoil within the Catholic Church. Following the historic second Vatican Council in the early 1960s, the region's bishops began meeting regularly; in 1968, at a meeting in Medellín, Colombia, they issued a groundbreaking document that seemed to commit the Church to a much greater role in promoting social justice. If the Medellín document had been fully implemented, it would have marked a dramatic reversal of the historical role played by the Catholic Church as the ally of the wealthy and powerful. However, the promise of Medellín to stand with the poor brought resistance from the more conservative clergy in both Latin America and Rome, leaving a divided Church that has been vulnerable to inroads from Protestantism. It is also inaccurate to view the totality of Latin American religion as falling within the scope of Protestantism and Catholicism. A variety of spiritist religions and movements

TABLE 12.   Religious Affiliation in Latin America

Country	Roman Catholic	Protestant	Hindu	Muslim	Jewish	Other	Non-Believers/No Affiliation
Argentina	92.0%	2.0%			2.0%	4.0%	
Belize	49.6%	27.0%				14.0%	9.4%
Bolivia	95.0%	5.0%					
Brazil	73.6%	15.4%				3.6%	7.4%
Chile	70.0%	15.1%				6.7%	8.3%
Colombia	90.0%					10.0%	
Costa Rica	76.3%					20.5%	3.2%
Cuba	...	...	...	...	...	...	...
Dominican Republic	95.0%					5.0%	
Ecuador	95.0%					5.0%	
El Salvador	57.1%	21.2%				4.9%	16.8%
Guatemala	...	...	...	...	...	...	...
Haiti	80.0%	16.0%				3.0%	1.0%
Honduras	97.0%	3.0%					
Jamaica	2.6%	62.5%				14.2%	20.9%
Mexico	76.5%	6.3%				14.1%	3.1%
Nicaragua	58.5%					25.8%	15.7%
Panama	85.0%	15.0%					
Paraguay	89.6%	6.2%				3.1%	1.1%
Peru	81.3%					15.8%	2.9%
Suriname	22.8%	25.2%	27.4%	19.6%		5.0%	
Trinidad and Tobago	26.0%		22.5%	5.8%		43.8%	1.9%
Uruguay	47.1%				0.3%	35.4%	17.2%
Venezuela	96%	2.0%				2.0%	

... No data available.

Source: CIA World Factbook: https://www.cia.gov/library/publications/the-world-factbook/.

also continue to exist in the region, many with their roots in the large number of slaves brought to the Western Hemisphere from Africa in the sixteenth through the nineteenth centuries. In many cases, the indigenous peoples of the Americas have also maintained a spiritual identity independent of Western religions.

Historically, religion and politics have been deeply intertwined in Latin America. This interconnection began with the role the Roman Catholic Church played in the military conquests of the Spanish and Portuguese in the fifteenth and sixteenth centuries. Church authorities came ashore with the *conquistadores* in search of souls to convert and provided ideological justification for the military conquests and for monarchical rule. Ultimately, the Church was rewarded for this role with vast amounts of wealth and power. The Church set up parallel institutions to the royal administration. It was granted significant tracts of land from which it generated wealth and was given free rein to develop the region's educational system.

The relationship between religion and politics is a complex one. Strong religious communities help set the value structure of a society by stating what is important in life. In doing so, religious values help frame what the citizenry expects out of their lives and therefore, on one level, what they may expect from government authorities. For example, traditional Roman Catholic teaching, which emphasized the glories of eternal salvation rather than the material pleasures of one's current life, seemed to dampen the expectations of the citizenry and therefore reduce the pressure on the political authorities to provide a good life in the here and now. Catholic theology rooted in Thomas Aquinas also provided a direct justification for monarchy and elite rule. All humans were deemed to be born in original sin, and it was only through God's grace that some people were better suited to rule than others. The essence of politics was then to elevate such people to power so that they could be responsible to God's will, not to the will of the people. This reasoning was used to justify the Spanish and Portuguese monarchies. It was only in the eighteenth and nineteeth centuries that ideas began to develop in Church teaching that provide justification for democratic thinking. Religious authorities can also play a more direct role in politics by influencing their followers to support a particular political leader or party. In recent times, Argentina and Chile have shown contrasting examples of Church policy. In Argentina, the Catholic hierarchy actively supported the two military regimes that ruled between 1966 and 1983. Such support was important in a country where military rule had earlier been supplanted by constitutional democratic governance. In contrast, the Catholic hierarchy became an outspoken critic of the Chilean military regime during the 1980s. That opposition helped pave the way for the defeat of a military-sponsored referendum in 1988 and the return to civilian rule in 1990. Despite these contrasting examples, historically most interventions by the Church have been to support the status quo.

The question of separation of church and state has long been a contentious one, with the establishment of such a principle being slow to arrive in Latin America in comparison with the United States. As elsewhere, the impetus for such a separation came from those who sought independence in spiritual matters from an overbearing government that gave favors only to persons from a particular religion. In Latin America, the challenge to the tight relationship between church and state came from the Liberal political movements of the nineteenth century. In response, the Church closely allied itself with the Conservatives in an attempt to maintain its historically privileged position. When Liberal regimes came to power, the Church was usually *disestablished*, meaning that the hierarchy lost its direct control over political matters. The dates of disestablishment range from the initial case of Colombia in 1848 to Mexico in 1857 and Brazil in 1889. Unlike the liberal establishment in the United States, which granted freedom of religion and then largely stayed out of church affairs, the Latin American Liberals granted official freedom of worship but then sought to interfere in the affairs of the Church by attempting to compel priests to marry and reorganize diocesan boundaries. By 1910, virtually all Latin American countries, with the exception of Colombia, which reversed its disestablishment from 1886 until 1930, had granted formal religious liberty. As a result, the Catholic hierarchy ended its sole association with the Conservatives and broadened its relations to include the Liberal elites with whom they had fought so bitterly. The terms of their dealings with the state were now different, lacking the legal and financial privileges of the previous centuries.

In the early twentieth century, the Catholic Church also faced for the first time a significant thrust of Protestant missionary work into the region. However, Catholics retained a strong position based on their large following and the rootedness of their ideas in the popular culture. Also, as the fierce anticlericalism of the nineteenth century began to fade, the Church, without official representation in government, began to regain its political influence with the elites as newer, more powerful challenges from revolutionary movements united Liberal and Conservative elites. The Church concentrated its political efforts on protecting its own position in society by pushing for mandatory religious education and public funding of its organizations and projects. The new tactic of accommodating both Liberal and Conservative elites and even the populist leaders in Brazil and Argentina actually succeeded in winning back some privileges previously lost and in guaranteeing the Church a prominent societal position through education and public festivals.

Today, Roman Catholicism remains the dominant religion of Latin America, but it is facing increasing challenges from both evangelical Protestantism and the overall secularization of society. In several countries, Protestants may surpass Catholics in numbers of adherents if current trends continue. Phillip Berryman has observed that because of the relatively low percentage of Catholics attending mass regularly, the number of churchgoing Protestants may be roughly equal to that of Catholics. As Protestantism grows, the political implications of this development are unclear. Many of the evangelical movements are closely connected with right-wing political movements based in the United States, but overall the evangelical movement is quite pluralistic and represents a liberalizing trend in comparison to the most conservative forces within the Catholic Church. In this chapter, we analyze all the religious movements in greater depth, with an emphasis on their relationship to politics.

Indigenous Religious Practice

Any discussion of religion in Latin America must begin with a discussion of the spiritual practices of the indigenous peoples who lived in the Americas prior to the conquest. What are the traditional spirits of the indigenous people? Jean Schobinger argues that indigenous religious practice as it evolved to the time of the conquest was significantly different from that of European religious tradition. He argues that indigenous religion was intuitive, open to nature, and communitarian, and tended to see everything visible as a symbol of something greater on which the people depended. This religious tradition was seen as contrasting with the more individualistic thrust of European religion. Religious rites became more sophisticated over time, and practices were passed from one generation to the next and from one civilization to the next. Several high points are worth noting. The classic Mayan period from 300 to 900 C.E. in what is today southern Mexico and Guatemala was governed by a priestly elite who were inspired by deities. The civilization was sophisticated in that there was both an official religion of the upper classes and a popular spiritualism. This spiritual divergence may help us to understand the painful nature of the encounter between the two civilizations.

Anthropological research on the indigenous civilizations of the Americas demonstrates a broad evolution of religious and spiritual practices. Our knowledge of these activities comes primarily from wall art and carvings that survived to the twentieth century, when the majority of research was done. The pattern that can be observed is one of a growing religiosity of the lower classes. The spiritual life was constructed around both official ceremonies or feast days and series of myths and stories that framed a worldview.

Mayan religious life was centered around the magnificent stepped pyramids, which symbolically reached toward the cosmic world. Their worldview was embodied in the story of the Popol Vuh, the basic idea of which was that there had been four ages previous to the one in which they were living. Each previous one had been brought to a cataclysmic end by gods dissatisfied with the imperfections of humans. Life was focused on activities and rites designed to convince the gods not to bring their civilization to an abrupt end. The ceremonies were elaborate and preceded by strict fasts. Sacrifices played an important part, but in the classic Mayan period human sacrifice was not involved. That practice emerged only later; it originated in Mexico with the Toltecs and was then adopted by Mayans under their influence.

The arrival of the Spanish and Portuguese conquerors had a devastating impact on the spiritual life of the indigenous civilizations, especially the ones that were at the height of their development in the sixteenth century, the Aztecs and the Incas. The conquerors often destroyed the public religious buildings and, through the missionaries who accompanied them, forcibly converted the local population to Catholicism. Perhaps the most blatant example of this was in the capital of the Aztecs, Tenochtitlán, where the Spanish conquerors constructed the Catholic metropolitan cathedral on top of the foundations of the destroyed Templo Mayor of the Aztecs, destroying the official and public form of indigenous religion. Indigenous leaders were subjugated and, with them, the ability to conduct the festivals that had dominated their religious practice. This approach by the conquerors led to two parallel phenomena, the maintenance of indigenous religious beliefs through popular culture and the quiet practice of indigenous religions in former Mayan lands and Bolivia, and the adoption of European religious forms as a way to maintain traditional practices in the face of a superior power.

Colonial Catholic Church

From its first appearance in the New World, the Catholic Church was an essential element in the conquest and colonization of the native peoples by Spain and Portugal. From the beginning, it held a privileged position with considerable economic and political power. It provided ideological justification for the subjugation of the native peoples encountered by the conquerors. As a reward for its role, the Church was granted significant landholdings and a central role in the new colonial societies as the primary provider of education. The Church viewed the natives as people who could be converted to the faith, thus augmenting the Church's ranks worldwide. The Church had no respect whatsoever for the existing spiritual beliefs of the native peoples. For example, when the Spanish conquered Tenochtitlán, the capital of the Aztecs, they destroyed the chief temple and constructed the metropolitan cathedral of Mexico City directly on top of its foundations. This aggressive and intolerant Catholicism reflected that era when the Spanish monarchy defeated the Moors in southern Spain and expelled the Jews. The early sixteenth century was also marked by Catholicism's vigorous reaction to the Protestant Reformation. The Church's stature was further enhanced when Pope Alexander VI in 1494

adjudicated the division of the continent between Spain and Portugal and con-
ferred on their monarchies the right and duty of propagating the Catholic faith. The
model of social order the Iberian conquerors brought was that of "Christendom."
Ironically, this model arrived in Latin America just as it was beginning to unravel
in Europe. Berryman has called the Latin American form "colonial Christendom."
Under this system of patronage, the Spanish and Portuguese monarchs exercised
full administrative control over the churches in their territories. This set the stage
for struggles over church-state relations during the independence period when the
new leaders assumed that their governments would retain the administrative powers previously held by the monarchies.

In many ways, the role played by the Catholic Church in Latin America was
simply an extension of the role that it had played in Europe. After its first four
centuries of existence as a movement that struggled to survive in the face of hostile opponents, the Church succeeded in gaining recognition from the political and
economic elites who allowed it to carry out its spiritual mission without significant
interference from government authorities. It protected its position by endorsing
governments and social systems that were willing to further Catholic values and
protect Church interests. The Church always had an ambivalent view toward secular life. It tended to view the difficult human existence of the majority of the people
as a burden to be endured in the hope of a glorious afterlife. Secular authorities
were viewed with a skeptical eye, but as long as they permitted the Church authorities to carry out their pastoral mission, the Church leaders gave their backing to the
political and economic leaders.

The Latin American Catholic Church adopted this model and applied it
throughout the New World, but it is important to note that from the beginning of
the Church's presence in Latin America there were missionaries who protested the
cruelty of the conquest. The most famous is the Dominican priest Bartolomé de Las
Casas, who came to Hispaniola in 1502. Although he initially held Indian slaves,
Las Casas experienced a conversion and spent the remainder of his life arguing that
the indigenous people should be treated with respect and won over to Catholicism
with the power of the gospel rather than the force of arms. He wrote in *In Defense of
the Indians*, "With what swords and cannons did Christ arm his disciples when he
sent them to preach the gospel. Devastating provinces and exterminating natives
or putting them to flight, is this freely sharing the faith?" Many Dominican bishops
followed Las Casas in the defense of the Indians. The tradition continued in the late
twentieth century with Church leaders like Bishop Samuel Ruiz defending indigenous peasant interests in Chiapas. The primary motivation for such actions may
well be moral, but they are also aimed at preventing the government from interfer-
ing with the Church's efforts to increase the size of its ranks.

The Church in Modern Latin America

In the first twemty-five years of the nineteenth century, Latin America broke away
from Spain and Portugal. The independence movement and its aftermath created
a crisis for the Catholic Church. Most of the bishops sided with the Spanish crown,
and popes made pronouncements against independence in 1816 and 1823. Some

clerics, including the Mexican priests Miguel Hidalgo and José Morelos y Pavón, were leaders of the independence movement; but for the most part, the Church found itself on the losing side of the political change. The Vatican only began to recognize the new states in 1831, and in many countries the clergy left, leaving some dioceses vacant. Those clerics who remained in most cases allied themselves with the newly created conservative parties, who pledged to support the historic role of the Church in Latin American society. In societies where the Conservatives held sway, the Church was able to prosper, albeit in a more limited way. However, in those countries where the Liberals came to power, the Church faced new laws that enabled the government to confiscate their lands. In the eyes of the Liberals, the Church represented an obstacle to their vision of progress and development. The nineteenth century also saw the rise of Freemasonry in Latin America as a challenge to the dominance of the Church in secular matters. As a result of attacks from the Liberals and Freemasons, the Catholic Church was thrown into crisis in much of Latin America in the nineteenth century. The Church came to rely on a steady flow of priests from Europe as it could not recruit enough clergy from within the region. Even today Catholic clergy are primarily foreign in many Latin American countries, including Guatemala, Venezuela, and Bolivia.

The Catholic Church entered the twentieth century in considerable disarray, weakened by attacks from Liberal governments and facing an increasingly aggressive Protestant challenge. Protestant missionaries began arriving in the last decades of the nineteenth century and often received favorable treatment from the Liberal governments, which saw them as a useful tool in breaking the hold of the Catholic Church. Inroads in Catholic dominance did occur, but most Latin Americans continued to view themselves as Catholic. In the early twentieth century, the Catholic hierarchy initiated changes in response to the challenges it faced. The Church embraced new values as it sought to maintain its hold on a population that was also undergoing significant change. Religious freedom was embraced, and there was a limited recognition of the principle of separation of church and state. The latter was limited because Catholic schools continued to receive government subsidies and Catholic teaching was promoted in public schools. The Church also embraced the concept of social justice as it sought to relate the gospel to people's actual living circumstances on this earth as opposed to being concerned only with heavenly salvation. Church leaders also began to speak out on a variety of universal issues, such as freedom, equality, and women's rights. This era was marked by serious efforts to combat what the Church saw as alien influences on its traditional followers. The Church created organizations like Catholic Action to resist the influence of liberalism, Masonry, and Marxism. Catholic Action especially targeted university students and middle-class youth, who were seen as the likely future leaders.

The Vatican originally developed Catholic Action to combat socialism among working-class Europeans, but Pope Pius XI saw benefits in the Latin American incarnation. The organization was firmly rooted in such early social encyclicals as Rerum Novarum, but its success in Latin America was limited because the sectors to which it was targeted were so much smaller than in Western Europe. One exception to this pattern was in Chile, where the efforts of Catholic Action contributed to the formation of the Christian Democratic Party as a centrist alternative between the Conservatives and the Socialists and Communists.

The Church also organized competing unions or "workers' circles" to directly compete with socialist- and communist-led unions, which were gaining significant influence in the Latin American working class. Anthony Gill, an expert on the Roman Catholic Church in Latin America, points out that the turn to organizing workers did not represent a significant ideological shift for the Church because it was limited to those places and groups that were being seriously courted by socialist ideologies. In this period, the rural poor were largely ignored. In another break with tradition, the Church hierarchy also sanctioned a much greater role for laypeople. These changes occurred very slowly over the early decades of the century, but the pace of change accelerated in the 1950s and 1960s as the Latin American Church increasingly shaped its teaching and practice of Catholicism to the particular conditions of Latin America.

The first plenary meeting of the Latin American Bishops' Conference (CELAM) occurred in 1955 in Rio de Janeiro. This conference would become influential in shaping the direction of the Church over the remainder of the century. The Latin American Church had been moving closer to greater acceptance of a role in social change and social justice, but the Second Vatican Council in Rome (1962–1965) accelerated the process. The documents produced by the council committed the Church to oppose governments that restricted religious or political freedoms and to acknowledge the significance of working for social justice in a variety of settings. During the early 1960s, the Catholic Church became involved in various movements that sought agrarian reform, expanded voting rights, and greater government spending on health and education. The Church also became the direct vehicle for improving people's lives through health training, literacy programs, and production cooperatives. Such programs contributed to a wider movement for nonviolent, reformist-oriented change.

In addition to promoting social justice, Vatican II articulated a more collegial model for the bishops. Rather than simply being subordinates of the pope, bishops came to be seen as peers who needed to work together to address concerns in their particular geographical area. Although the Vatican Council was an important turning point, socially conscious activity by the Church predated it in some places. In Brazil in the late 1950s, the Catholic hierarchy united with the government of reformer Juscelino Kubitschek to oppose the country's landowning oligarchy. The Church was instrumental in the formation of a development agency for northeast Brazil. Kubitschek used the Christian language of social justice to justify his reforms. It was in this era that Paulo Freire, a Catholic educator in the northeast, developed a new method for teaching literacy. Catholic Action movements of students and workers organized in many places to promote a progressive agenda. The activities of Catholic Action led to discussion of the need for political action to change the basic structural inequalities that were limiting the effects of reform and social work. Before these discussions were fully consummated, the 1964 Brazilian military coup occurred, placing the Church and its activists in a more defensive mode and setting the stage for its next important contribution to Latin American political life. During the 1950s, bishops in Chile became involved in programs of land reform, literacy, and rural cooperatives. These efforts went beyond the Church's traditional social work and, as a result, brought the Church into conflict with the traditional elites.

A New Political Role

From the 1960s through the 1980s, the Catholic Church became a focal point in many areas of resistance to military rule. In Brazil after the military coup of 1964, the Catholic hierarchy broke from its traditional role of absolute defender of the status quo. This stance in Brazil contrasted with the role that the Catholic Church had played during the Cuban Revolution. The Church had stood with the Batista dictatorship to the end, and few Catholic activists had been involved in the revolutionary movement. After the 26th of July Movement took power, the Church became the focal point of resistance to the new government and suffered significant repression, including the expulsion of foreign priests, which further debilitated an already weak Cuban Church. As a result of the Cuban Revolution, the Latin American hierarchy saw the potential danger to the future of the Church in an uncompromising stand toward revolution and radical reform. In societies under dictatorial rule, like Brazil, the Church was just about the only institution that could provide a haven against the overwhelming power of the state. Aided by the Church's organizational and financial resources, local parishes were able to provide material and legal assistance for those who were repressed. Agencies established by the Church monitored human rights violations and provided lawyers for those accused of political crimes. The Church also set up programs that distributed food and clothing to the families of those who were imprisoned, and upon release from jail political prisoners received aid from the Church in the form of counseling and employment assistance.

In many countries, Catholic clerics and laypeople became part of nonviolent resistance movements that argued for the restoration of civilian rule. Catholic leaders not only criticized specific military governments but also rejected authoritarianism as a method of rule, a significant break from the past. In the context of that ferment, CELAM met in Medellín, Colombia, in 1968. The conference came on the heels of the historic Second Vatican Council, which had turned the Church to a social justice vision and encouraged the regional conferences of bishops to look more closely at the specific challenges of their areas. The Latin American bishops picked up this challenge and in the process produced a document that has influenced the Church's work ever since. In 1967, Pope Paul VI's encyclical On the Development of Peoples focused on Third-World development issues, containing a mild rebuke of the existing international economic order. Soon after the pope's encyclical, groups of bishops and priests began to lay out a program for Latin America in advance of the conference. A group of eighteen bishops, half from Brazil, went beyond the pope's statement while also drawing heavily upon it. They wrote approvingly of both revolution and socialism. In Argentina, Peru, Colombia, and Mexico, new groups of priests formed to press a progressive agenda as the gap between the rhetoric of the Vatican Council and the reality of everyday life in Latin America became more obvious. They raised fundamental questions about the wealth of the Church, its historic support for the status quo, and the need for political action to achieve change. These groups did not speak for anywhere near a majority of the clergy, but their ideas shook up the complacency of the Church and dominated the discussion leading into the conference.

The task of those at CELAM was to apply the work of the Second Vatican Council to Latin America, but they met at a particularly significant moment in the history of the struggle for social change. The year had been one of dramatic developments— students had occupied universities in the United States, factory workers and students had united in France, Mexican police had repressed student demonstrations, and the Soviet invasion of Czechoslovakia had ended the drive for reform in that country. Combined with the force of Pope Paul's encyclical, these events pushed the bishops to produce a philosophy and plan of action that would be more progressive than its conservative past and probably more radical than most were actually prepared to carry out in practice. The documents emerging from the conference were striking in that such topics as justice, peace, and education received greater attention than did the traditionally dominant topics of pastoral work and Church structures.

At the most basic level, the bishops called for Catholics to be involved in the transformation of society. "Institutionalized violence" in the form of poverty, repression, and underdevelopment was decried and categorized as "sin." Such a categorization represented a significant expansion of the concept beyond its traditional meaning of individual transgression. They called for "sweeping, bold, urgent, and profoundly renovating changes." Revolutionaries were presented in a very positive light and not tainted with an identification with violence. The Church made a number of commitments that included the defense of human rights and the sharing of the conditions of the poor. The conference also raised the idea of neighborhood-based, lay-led ecclesial communities that would soon begin springing up all over Latin America. The term *liberation* was used often and placed primarily in human rather than spiritual terms. However, the bishops stopped short of endorsing the right of the oppressed to fight for their rights. Some feared being labeled as condoning violence, while others remained committed in a principled way to nonviolence. The conference came to grips with the realization that a new Catholic theology needed to emerge from the Latin American condition. Theology was no longer viewed as universal and could not simply be imported from Europe or North America. A key figure in the development of liberation theology, as it came to be called, was the Peruvian theologian Gustavo Gutiérrez. Gutiérrez had first used the term *liberation theology* shortly before Medellín, and soon afterward Gutiérrez and the Brazilian theologian Hugo Assmann published full-length books on the subject. From the early 1960s, Catholic theologians had begun to discuss the necessity of developing a specific Latin American theology, but they were slow to break with the long-standing tradition of a universal theology. Ultimately, the pressure of events resulted in the breakthrough works of Gutiérrez and Assmann. For decades Catholicism had struggled to be relevant to the modern world, but with liberation theology it sought to find in Christianity guidance in the struggle for change. As Berryman states, "It is a critique of how social structures treat the poor and how Christians and the church itself operate."

As Gill points out, a key element of liberation theology is the reliance on Marxist methodology. The theologians based their understanding of Latin American poverty on dependence theory, a perspective that views poverty and oppression in the Third World as a direct consequence of the world capitalist economy dominated by Western Europe and the United States. Some theologians, such as Ernesto Cardenal of Nicaragua, also embraced the Marxist idea of class struggle and from that justified participation in revolutionary movements. In the wake of the 1968 conference, Catholic clergy and laypeople throughout Latin America increasingly took up the Church's call for greater attention to matters of social justice and political involvement. Thousands of Catholic nuns and priests moved out of traditional convents and religious houses and into poor neighborhoods, where they shared the difficult living conditions of the poor. Part of the motivation was to make the Church more relevant to its majority poor constituency. Traditionally, the Church had devoted a great proportion of its time and resources to the middle and upper classes and had sustained itself in significant measure through the tuition payments it received to educate the sons and daughters of the wealthy. The move to the poor neighborhoods was seen by those who did it as a means to better carry out their religious vocation. Although the moves did involve some personal hardship, the nuns and priests who engaged in this new form of pastoral work were freer than their counterparts who remained in traditional roles as parish priests and educators.

Most of the clergy who went into the poor neighborhoods adopted the educational approach of the Brazilian educator Paulo Freire, called *concientización* (consciousness-raising), detailed in his classic work *Pedagogy of the Oppressed.* Rather than imparting their wisdom to the people in the neighborhoods, the clergy saw their role as drawing out conclusions through group reflection. These discussions were often carried out in what became known as ecclesial base communities, meetings in homes to read and discuss the scriptures with the purpose of drawing conclusions about their relevance to everyday life. Those leading the discussions, religious or lay, urged people to search for the underlying causes of their poor situation. In rural areas, these discussions would often move from immediate problems to matters such as land ownership and class structures. Similar developments occurred in urban settings, where people would seek to understand the root cause of poor sanitation or poor public transportation in their neighborhoods. More often than not, the consciousness-raising led to the formation of groups that had a variety of purposes—soup kitchens, peasant associations, cooperatives, and so forth. Some were primarily self-helping in their focus, while others were oriented more toward political action. Self-help activities included programs to teach job skills or to serve as Alcoholics Anonymous centers. In Brazil, the groups formed an important core of the resistance to military rule at a time in the 1970s when few other outlets for political opposition existed. Political activities ranged from voter registration to serving as centers for revolutionary organizing in Nicaragua and El Salvador.

Impact of Liberation Theology

The impact of liberation theology and the work of nuns, priests, and laypeople in advancing an agenda for social change was considerable, but it never succeeded in fully transforming the historic role of the Church as a bastion of the status quo in Latin America. Within five years of the historic conference at Medellín, conservative Latin American bishops, especially in Brazil and Mexico, began a systematic counterattack against liberation theology. As the first step in their strategy, they took control of CELAM, the very organization that had initiated the progressive changes. Their counterattack was not initially a frontal assault. For example, no attempt was made to repeal the documents that were passed in Colombia. However, the conservatives were given a large lift with the ascension of Pope John Paul II in 1978. John Paul had been archbishop of Kraków, Poland, and a staunch anticommunist. It was natural that he would side strongly with those in the Latin American Church who saw themselves as working against the influences of Marxism within the Church. The papacy's assault on liberation theology proceeded on many fronts during the 1980s. In 1984, the Vatican issued a document that strongly criticized liberation theology; in the same time period, Rome was successful in marginalizing the influential Brazilian theologian Leonardo Boff. The revolutionary government in Nicaragua, which contained several priests sympathetic to liberation theology, was singled out for harsh criticism during a papal visit in 1983. Those priests in the Nicaraguan government were prevented from carrying out their religious duties. However, the papacy's strongest move against liberation theology may have been its appointment of new bishops who would hold steadfastly to Rome's conservative stance. Archbishop Helder Camera of Recife, Brazil, one of the region's harshest critics of military rule and a strong proponent of the strategy of working with the poor, was replaced by a conservative, who moved almost immediately to reverse the fruits of Camera's work. In Cuernavaca, Mexico, there was a high concentration of Christian base communities as a result of the work of Bishop Sergio Méndez Arceo; but when he retired in the late 1980s the Vatican appointed a conservative to replace him and the grassroots work suffered. Overall, the counterattack of the conservative forces in the Church was directly related to the growing strength of the left and the high stakes that were involved. In Brazil, the Workers' Party (PT) was on the verge of winning the national presidency in the late 1980s, and only a united front of all the conservative forces succeeded in defeating their candidate, Luiz Inacio da Silva, in the 1989 election. In Central America throughout the 1980s, revolutionary forces were on the upswing in Nicaragua, El Salvador, and Guatemala. The revolutionary shock waves were felt as far north as Mexico. In that context, the papacy weighed in on the side of the anticommunist forces, a decision that dovetailed with the foreign policy initiatives of the United States. Progressive Church forces came to be seen as part of a revolutionary upsurge that had to be suppressed.

The diminishing impact of liberation theology in the 1990s cannot be blamed exclusively on the counterattack by the Vatican. Part of the failure of liberation theology to fully transform the Church lies within the movement itself. Liberation theology never really succeeded in becoming a mass movement within the Church. Fewer than 10 percent of the nuns and priests actually moved into communities to work directly with the poor. CEBs did arise in significant numbers in some select places, such as in Brazil during the military government in the 1970s; but they never came close to their goal of transforming the manner in which the Church functioned. In Brazil, close to 100,000 CEBs developed by the mid-1980s, but that accounted for only about 2.5 percent of the Catholic population. Significant lay leadership was involved in the CEBs, but most remained dependent on the leadership of clergy, which limited the CEBs' ability to grow into a mass movement. However, one very positive result of the work of the CEBs was a significant increase in the proportion of women in leadership roles in comparison to the past. The CEBs also gave the Catholic Church a significant presence in working-class neighborhoods that had been previously ignored. The decline of liberation theology, acknowledged by Gutiérez in 1994, was also the result of a changing political climate. Born in the era of 1960s revolutionary idealism, liberation theology has declined with the assault on the progressive agenda marked by the collapse of Eastern European socialism and the defeat of the Sandinista revolutionary project in Nicaragua. These setbacks led many within the progressive Church community to scale back their short-term expectations for dramatic social change and to work for more reformist goals within the existing system. The restoration of democratic systems throughout the region in the 1980s facilitated this change in strategy.

The horizons of the reformers may have been limited by world events and their own shortcomings, but their political legacy has not been unimportant. In several key situations in the 1980s, progressive Roman Catholic bishops played an important political role as mediators. In El Salvador, Archbishop Arturo Rivera y Damas, who assumed the leadership of the Church after the military assassinated outspoken Archbishop Oscar Romero, made numerous attempts to bring an end to that country's devastating civil war. The military initially rejected such appeals as treason, but the archbishop's efforts eventually contributed to the 1992 peace agreement. The Guatemalan bishops played a similar role against the wishes of the military to help broker the eventual agreement in that country that ended a forty-year civil war in 1997. Chilean bishops were also instrumental in bringing about a negotiated end to the Pinochet regime. In the conflict in Chiapas in the 1990s, Bishop Samuel Ruiz played an important role as a mediator between the Mexican government and the Zapatistas. During the 1970s and 1980s, scores of human rights monitoring organizations were formed in the region, often with the protection and funding of the Church. Under different political circumstances, most of these organizations are now independent of the Church, but their work continues; they represent an important legacy of the movement for liberation theology.

Protestantism and Pentecostalism

The most important development in the Latin American religious sector in the last twenty years is the remarkable growth of Protestantism, especially Pentecostalism. Fewer than twenty years ago, these groups made up no more than 2 to 3 percent of the population, but today they have reached the significant level of 15 percent continentwide, with a much greater presence in countries such as Guatemala. It also should be pointed out that a focus on absolute numbers is misleading because in comparison to those who identify themselves as Catholic, the Evangelicals tend to be more active in church life. Pentecostal churches were founded mostly in the early part of the twentieth century. They are often connected to Charles Parham's spiritual revival in Topeka, Kansas, in 1901 and a subsequent revival in Los Angeles in 1906. From those revivals came churches such as the Assemblies of God, the Church of God, and the Church of God in Christ.

It is important to not place any single label on the Pentecostal churches, which are quite diverse in both their religious and political practices. Some, such as the Universal Church and the Deus e Amor Church, are not built around fixed church structures but instead draw followers to tents and warehouses where the emphasis is on singing and spiritual healing. Their services are dramatic, with considerable moaning, screaming, and crawling on hands and knees. The object of the services is to drive out the demons that have "infected" the members. These churches also have a considerable presence on the radio, with hundreds of hours of programming in countries such as Brazil. The Universal Church tends to draw a middle-class constituency, while the Deus e Amor Church followers are overwhelmingly poor. The largest single Pentecostal group in Latin America is the Assemblies of God, who have 8–12 million followers and 35,000 churches in Brazil alone. In contrast to lack of institutionalism in the previously discussed Evangelicals, the Assemblies of God, with their origins in North America, are highly organized and have considerable financial resources. Although the majority of their members are very poor, their relative wealth belies their North American ties.

Berryman has attributed the appeal of the Pentecostals to a simple message of love and prayer that provides community and a sense of self-respect. Another basis of the success of the movement among the region's poorest citizens is that most Evangelical ministers come from the same social class as their congregants. In contrast, most Catholic priests, even those who espouse liberation theology, come from middle- and upper-class backgrounds. It is also very difficult to characterize the political impact of the Evangelical movement. Unquestionably, some churches, such as the Word of God movement in Guatemala, have directly promoted right-wing politics through the born-again leader José Efraín Ríos Montt, who carried out massive repression in the early 1980s. Later Jorge Serrano based his Guatemalan presidential campaign on Evangelical votes, and Alberto Fujimori reached out to Evangelicals in his 1990 run for the presidency in Peru. Evangelical representatives are an important voting bloc in the Brazilian congress. However, beyond these examples, the Evangelicals have not really developed anything close to a clear, coherent political message. Not all Evangelicals are politically conservative. The Brazilian PT has many Evangelicals within its ranks, including one of its congressional leaders, Benedita da Silva, an active member of the Assemblies of God. Many Pentecostals consciously reject any significant involvement in politics.

African-Inspired Religions

After indigenous religion, Catholicism, and Protestantism, the fourth religious tradition in Latin America is that of African-inspired religion. This religious trend is present to some degree throughout the continent but is especially prevalent in countries such as Cuba, Haiti, and Brazil, where millions of slaves were imported from West Africa. The Africans brought their spiritual beliefs with them and have maintained them for more than three centuries in the face of efforts by both political and religious authorities to marginalize them. In some instances the well-developed Yoruba religion was transferred to the New World without significant modification (Santería in Cuba and Puerto Rico and Candomblé in Brazil). In other instances, the

African beliefs have commingled with Catholic and Protestant spirituality to form a hybrid. Generally speaking, those practicing these religious traditions believe that the dead continue to live and communicate with the world through a variety of means. They believe that these spirits influence the manner in which the living exist, sometimes for good and other times for evil. A series of deities or *Orishas* are also prominent in the Yoruba-based religions.

One of the strongest movements is the **Voodoo** of Haiti, which developed among the slave population and was influential in the abolitionist and independence movements at the end of the eighteenth century. It also would later become a tool of the Duvalier dictatorships from the 1950s to the 1980s. Voodoo spirits are called *loas*, and the objective of the religion is to connect the living with the *loas*. The spirits' help is sought to cure ailments and to provide advice for solving daily problems. Priests, called *hougans*, facilitate the connection between the spiritual world and the followers of voodoo. The priests have an authority that can be based on either their charisma or the patrimony of a local political or military leader.

Following an instrumental role in achieving Haitian independence in 1804, the voodoo movement was largely driven underground for the next 150 years at the behest of the country's mulatto and Catholic elite. However, a strong underground network of priests and their followers was constructed in Haiti's poorest communities, and the religious beliefs were passed on from generation to generation. Then, in the late 1950s, these local voodoo organizations became the power base for the political movement of François Duvalier, who won the 1957 elections and later established a harsh dictatorial rule that was eventually passed on to his son. The feared Tonton Macoute militias organized by Duvalier for use against his political foes came from his voodoo power base. The younger Duvalier was driven from power in the mid-1980s, but voodoo retains a strong spiritual following in contemporary Haiti without, however, the politicization that it had during the Duvalier period.

A less known but equally important African-based movement called **Santería** has a very important presence in contemporary Cuba and Puerto Rico and is part of the changes occurring in socialist Cuba. Like voodoo, Santería has its origins in the African slaves brought to Cuba to harvest sugar cane. Santería came from the Yoruba people of what is today Nigeria. Like voodoo, Santería provided a link to their African past and some respite from the brutality of slavery. As in Haiti, the bonds of the Santería communities helped pave the way for independence and abolitionist movements that developed in the latter part of the nineteenth century in Cuba. However, in contrast to voodoo, Santería, out of an instinct for survival in strongly Catholic Cuba, often linked its rituals and spirits to those of the Roman Catholic Church. The key figures of the Catholic Church, such as Jesus and various saints, were masked as Yoruba deities or *Orishas*. The *Santerístas* also timed their main festivals according to those of the Catholic Church, such as Easter and Christmas. Such accommodation simply reflected the relationship of forces that existed in Cuba and Puerto Rico during the long years of Spanish and Catholic rule. However, it was a very successful accommodation because it allowed the spiritual beliefs of the Afro-Cuban population to survive into the twentieth century. The movement went into decline with the advent of the revolutionary government in Cuba in 1959 but underwent a revival in the 1990s with the more tolerant

Shrine to the Black Virgin in Regla, outskirts of Havana. Type and placement of candles also suggest the shrine is worshipped by practitioners of Santería, who frequent the church along with the Catholic parishioners. *(Photo by Patrice Olsen)*

attitude toward religion by the government. The Cuban Catholic Church has even complained that the Santería movement is the favored religion of the current government. Santería is also practiced in the United States where there are heavy concentrations of Cubans and Puerto Ricans.

Brazil is another country where African-based religious movements have a significant following. There are two major variants in the country. **Umbanda** shares the practice with Santería of pairing its deities with those of the Catholic Church. Similar to voodoo and Santería, Umbanda's followers seek advice from the spirits on problems of everyday life. There are many Umbanda centers, especially in Rio de Janeiro, which holds full schedules of cultural activities alongside exercise programs and social services. The intermediaries between the people and the spirits, called *mediums,* often obtain a large personal following. Even more akin to Santería is **Candomblé**, also brought by slaves from the Yoruba region of West Africa. Like Santería, it sometimes links its deities or *Orishás* with those of

Practitioners of Santería. *(Photo by Jose Goitia/AP Images)*

the Catholic religion. **Candomblé** generally appeals more to the poor. The spirits are also less connected to practical advice and more to pageants of dancing and eating. The movements in Brazil have probably been less directly political than similar movements in Haiti and Cuba, but they can be credited with helping the poor maintain their cultural identity in the face of the dominant white and Catholic culture.

Judaism

Any discussion of religion in Latin America should make mention of the region's Jews. They are not large in number, probably under 500,000 in the region as a whole, with the largest communities in Argentina (240,000), Brazil (100,000), and Mexico (35,000). Most Jews who live in Latin America came as part of nineteenth- and twentieth-century immigration, but they have faced persistent anti-Semitism and marginalization that dates to the time of the conquest.

By the fifteenth century, Jews had lived in Spain for a thousand years. Always a minority, the Jews were often caught in the battle between Catholicism and Islam and manipulated by both. Over the 1,000 years, periods of great Jewish contribution to Spanish life alternated with periods of persecution and forced conversion. Their situation worsened after 1391 when pogroms broke out, first in Seville and then throughout Spain. In 1492, the Spanish crown expelled the Jews from Spain and soon established a series of laws that excluded all Jews, even those who had converted to Catholicism, from Spanish public life. Anyone who had any Jewish or

Moorish "blood" was excluded from positions in the professions, the Church, the military, and the government. This indelible labeling of those with Jewish ancestry, converted or not, led to the widespread labeling of Jews as a "race," a perspective that was imported to Latin America and continues to the present time.

The exclusion of Jews from Spain was extended to Spanish lands in the Americas. In her first instruction to the governor of Hispaniola, Queen Isabella forbade Jews and "new Christians" (as the converts were called) from settling in the Indies. This legal prohibition continued throughout Spanish rule into the nineteenth century. Many new Christians and some Jews did succeed in settling in the Indies by subverting the law. However, the local missionaries laid the groundwork for long-term anti-Semitism among the native population. Jews were singled out as the tormentors and killers of Christ. Primary among the charges leveled against Jews was subversion. Popular opinion blamed converted Jews for the Dutch defeat of the Portuguese in Brazil in 1630. It was alleged that the new Christians assisted the invaders because they hoped to reestablish Judaism under more tolerant Dutch rule. The stereotype of Jews as subversives persists in Argentina, the country with the largest Jewish population. The generals who carried out Argentina's dirty war in the 1970s attacked Jews as subversives and Marxists. Their most famous target was the Jewish journalist Jacobo Timmerman, but the campaign revived anti-Semitism in contemporary Latin America.

Conclusion

As the twenty-first century began in Latin America, the impact of religion on society was more complex than ever before. The absolute hold of Catholicism on the region is now part of history, and despite the Church's attempts to remake itself in the last thirty years, there will likely be no return to its former dominance. Protestantism has made great strides in recent years, especially with the rapid growth of Evangelical sects. However, it should be remembered that these groups claim the allegiance of fewer than one in five Latin Americans. The political impact of the rapid growth of Protestantism is difficult to measure. Some groups are avowedly conservative in their political thrust, but most discourage social activism in their theology. Although generally critical of liberation theology, the Evangelicals have largely failed to develop their own strategy for confronting the region's ongoing social ills. That failure may yet derail the long-term growth of the Evangelical movement.

It would seem that the work of liberation theology begun in the 1960s has run its course in the current dominant political climate in the region, but that does not mean that its future impact will be marginal. The Catholic Church's commitment to social justice seems to have been firmly established. Pope John Paul's visit to Mexico in early 1999 underscored this fact. Twenty years earlier, on his first visit to Mexico, he spoke harshly of liberation theology and emphasized his opposition to communism of any kind. That message inevitably bolstered the status quo and by implication was procapitalist. On the 1999 visit, the pope's message was strikingly different. In reference to the contemporary emphasis on neoliberalism and free markets, he said "The human race is facing forms of slavery which are new and more subtle than those of the past." The pope called on both governments and international organizations to carry out plans aimed at Third-World debt relief and wealth redistribution. Some called this perspective "post liberation theology." Pope John Paul has passed from the scene but his successor, Benedict, while conservative theologically, has continued the church's strong impetus for social justice. The new wave of center-left governments in the region over the last ten years resonate well with the Church's message of social justice and often work closely with Church leaders. Emblematic of this connection is the Ecuadoran president Rafael Correa, whose progressive politics are firmly rooted in Catholic social teaching.

The long-standing connection between the Catholic Church hierarchy and military-oligarchic politics has been seriously undercut by the political developments of the last forty years. While a new and fully formed twenty-first century vision of social justice from a religious perspective has yet to be fully articulated, the role of a generation of progressive religious thinking is clearly an important part of Latin America's transition to democracy and its current trend toward more progressive politics.

Bibliography

Berryman, Phillip. *Religion in the Megacity: Catholic and Protestant Portraits from Latin America*. Maryknoll, NY: Orbis Books, 1996.

Berryman, Phillip. *Stubborn Hope: Religion, Politics, and Revolution in Central America*. Maryknoll, NY: Orbis Books, 1994.

Betances, Emelio. *The Catholic Church and Power Politics in Latin America*. Lanham, MD: Rowman and Littlefield, 2007.

Cleary, Edward, and Hannah Stewart-Gambino. *Power, Politics, and Pentecostals in Latin America*. Boulder, CO: Westview Press, 1997.

Cleary, Edward, and Timothy Steigenga, eds. *Resurgent Voices in Latin America: Indigenous Peoples, Political Mobilization, and Religious Change*. Piscataway, NJ: Rutgers University Press: 2004.

Davis, Darien. *Beyond Slavery: The Multilayered Legacy of Africans in Latin America and the Caribbean*. Lanham, MD: Rowman and Littlefield, 2006.

Efunde, Agun. *Los Secretos de la Santería*. Miami, FL: Ediciones Cubamerica, 1983.

Fleet, Michael, and Brian Smith. *The Catholic Church and Democratization in Latin America: Twentieth-Century Chile and Peru*. Notre Dame, IN: University of Notre Dame Press, 1996.

Freire, Paulo. *Pedagogy of the Oppressed*. New York: Herder and Herder, 1970.

Gill, Anthony. *Rendering unto Caesar: The Catholic Church and the State in Latin America*. Chicago: University of Chicago Press, 1997.

Hess, David. *Samba in the Night: Spiritism in Brazil*. New York: Columbia University Press, 1994.

Languerre, Michael S. *Voodoo and Politics in Haiti*. New York: St. Martin's Press, 1989.

Levine, Daniel. *Popular Voices in Latin American Catholicism*. Princeton, NJ: Princeton University Press, 1992.

Martin, David. *Tongues of Fire: The Explosion of Protestantism in Latin America*. London: Blackwell, 1990.

Matibag, Eugenio. *Afro-Cuban Religious Experience: Cultural Reflections in Narrative*. Gainesville: University Press of Florida, 2004.

Peterson, Vasquez. *Christianity, Social Change, and Globalization in the Americas*. Piscataway, NJ: Rutgers University Press, 2001.

Selka, Stephen. *Religion and the Politics of Ethnic Identity in Bahia, Brazil*. Tallahassee: University Press of Florida, 2009.

Stevens-Arroyo, Anthony M., and Andrés I. Pérez y Mena. *Enigmatic Powers: Syncretism with African and Indigeneous Peoples' Religions among Latinos*. New York: Bildner Center for Western Hemispheric Studies, 1995.

FILMS AND VIDEOS

Americas 6, Miracles Are Not Enough. United States, 1993.
From Faith to Action in Brazil. United States, 1984.
Onward Christian Soldiers. United States, 1985.
Remembering Romero. United States, 1992.

SEVEN

LATIN AMERICAN CULTURE AND THOUGHT

Latin America is composed of twenty different Spanish-, Portuguese-, or French-speaking independent nations and one Spanish-speaking commonwealth (Puerto Rico). Although each has its unique features and specific history, there are many common threads. Seen as a region, Latin American has some literary and cultural commonalities that if understood help us better comprehend the region and those who live in it. Like many immigrant societies, Latin America is an amalgam of many peoples who have all made their contribution to the culture and thinking of each country and the region as a whole. Like the United States and Canada, the dominant culture has assimilated the richness of all its inhabitants and maintained a distinct and identifiable set of values and thought patterns that set it apart. Similar to Canada, Latin America nations, if not the region as a whole, still struggle to establish a clear identity that is fully cognizant of their diverse racial, cultural and intellectual roots. Latin America is European, Native American, African, Asian, Middle Eastern, scholastic, socialist, liberal, conservative, revolutionary, elitist, popular, and much more.

Latin American Thought

Brazil, the largest country in the region, is said to be the land of the future. Indeed, Latin America as a whole is a developing, vibrant part of the world that looks toward tomorrow and better days to come. In the words of a widely read thinker from neighboring Uruguay, José Enrique Rodó, "From generation to generation, humanity renews its active hope and anticipatory faith in an ideal even through the hard experience of the centuries." Like Don Quixote, Latin Americans frequently display a vibrant commitment to a better world, a more perfect society, particularly when they are young and idealistic and they do so despite the difficulties of every-day life. In unfinished societies things are still in the process of becoming, and of becoming better. Indeed, the unfinished, incomplete state of much that is Latin American suggests that a vision of a better world is often necessary to muddle through. Despite justifiable fits of pessimism and cynicism, there is a widespread faith in a better day, the benevolence of the gods, in newly arrived political leaders and sometimes movements, a belief that somehow individuals, groups, or nations of people will prosper despite the vicissitudes of the day. Salvation might be an act of grace or intervention by a favorite saint or local virgin, the Virgin Mary, Jesus, a favorite Orisha (a deity in African-based religions like Santería or Candomblé) or Pachamama (the earth mother in indigenous Andean religions). Miracles do happen and saints like the Virgen de Guadalupe in Mexico or the Virgen de Cobre in Cuba do answer prayers and can heal. As suggested by the burgeoning of magical realism in contemporary Latin American literature like the Nobel laureate Gabriel García Márquez' *Cien Años de Solidad* (*One Hundred Years of Solitude*), or the widely acclaimed author Isabel Allende's *Casa de los Espíritus* (*House of the Spirits*) magic can be part of daily life. Imagination soars and spirits rise. As Rodó suggests in his book *Ariel*, it is this blithe spirit of Ariel in Shakespeare's *Tempest* that best characterizes Latin Americans. In *Ariel* he lauds the cultural, creative, literary bent in Latin American culture and compares it unfavorably with the heavy materialistic, pragmatic, commercial inclination he believes characterizes U.S. culture and society. Indeed, from Rodó's Latin American perspective,

> In spite of [the United States'] titanic accomplishments...having drifted from the traditions that set their course, the peoples of this nation have not been able to replace the inspired idealism of the past with a high and selfless concept of the future. They live for immediate reality, for the present, and thereby subordinate all their activity to the egoism of personal and collective well being....
>
> The idealism of beauty does not fire the soul of a descendant of austere Puritans. Nor does the idealism of truth. He scorns as vain and unproductive any exercise of thought that does not yield an immediate result.

Another highly regarded Latin American essayist and *pensador* (thinker), José Carlos Mariátegui (1894–1930), was much taken by those Latin Americans who do dream of a new day populated by new men and new women in a new age. It was up to the new generation of Latin Americans to generate change through political, social, and esthetic revolution and renovation, to apply themselves to this task. A brilliant intellectual who rose from poverty and was arguably the most innovative of the Marxist thinkers in Latin America, he championed homegrown revolution and radical change. Committed to the "optimism of the ideal," when told that conditions would not allow for such a revolutionary change, he retorted that that was "so much the worse for reality." It was, then, the responsibility of those who had faith in the revolution to make it. To that end he and his fellow visionaries organized one of Latin America's great progressive magazines of literature, art, culture, and politics, *Amauta*, a workers' movement, a political party, and even a special culturally based newspaper for the workers and peasants, *Labor*. Mariátegui championed the indigenous masses and thought that their communalism and the socialism of the Incan Empire could serve as the basis for a homegrown, dynamic Indo-American socialism that would speak with its own voice—in its own language. His contemporary Victor Raúl Haya de la Torre even spoke of a Latin American revolution that

El *Amauta (wise teacher)* José Carlos Mariátegui.

would be unique because of the spatial-historical time in which it was developing (in Latin America in the post–Mexican and post–Russian revolutionary period of the 1920s and after).

As suggested by the above, Latin America has been struggling with its place in the world since the arrival of the Europeans. Before the invaders came, the Mayas, Aztecs, Incas, and many other of the original Americans had elaborate religious-mythical systems to explain their place in the historical cosmos. Their identity was clear and well rooted. They understood the cycles of time and, in the case of the Mayas, could directly tie them to the heavens through the astute use of astronomy. They were masters of their territory and subordinate only to the deities of their well-developed religious systems. Indeed both the Aztecs and Incas created empires that had subordinated other indigenous groups and established control over wide swaths of territory. Thus they considered themselves superior as did the separate Mayan city-states in what is now southern Mexico and northern Central America.

As the Europeans came, conquered, and subordinated, this changed. Indigenous religion, culture, and even language were decimated and Indian identity was denigrated. That which grounded the first Americans was battered and often lost. Thereafter the indigenous, the native was less than the European. To count in the European dominated world system that was imposed on what came to be called the Americas, one had to operate in a European framework and at least give the appearance of Europeanness. Thus recognition and repute would be given only to those who could master the European languages and literary and cultural forms. It would take some time for Latin Americans to again find their voice. Thus, for instance, much of the colonial plastic art in Latin America can be seen as poor imitations of the European work of the day, though the elaborate art and artisanship found in many colonial churches in indigenous areas clearly had its own grace and strength, owing in large part to the mostly indigenous craftsmen and the vision these artisans brought to the process of translating the European motifs into wood and stone.

Much later, as Latin American writers and intellectuals struggled to free themselves from this imposed identity a much more complex process emerged. In *The Latin American Mind*, Leopoldo Zea, one of Latin America's greatest thinkers and interpreters, argues that "the leaders of intellectual independence of Hispanic America sought a complete reformation of the Spanish and colonial heritage." The Latin American intellectual had to break with it definitively, but could not accept the obvious importance of this past as the first step to moving beyond it. "His history, his past, was considered as something which did not belong to him because it had not been his work. The past appeared to him as completely negative, as that which the Hispanic American ought not to be, even in the sense of having been it at one time." Caught in this conundrum of identity and emancipation, the process has been difficult indeed, and has proceeded in fits and starts. The following pages give a few instances in this agonistic struggle, but they do not pretend to cover all the important writers or thinkers that Latin America has produced.

Notes on Literature

One of the most highly regarded examples of colonial literature in Latin America is a work by the Inca Garcilaso de la Vega (Cuzco, Viceroyalty of Peru, 1539–1616). His writings were published as the *Comentarios Reales de los Incas* (literally as "Royal Commentaries of the Incas" but translated into English as *The Incas*). Based on his own research and stories that relatives of his mother (a descendent of the Inca royal family) told him as a youth, they chronicle Incan history, culture, and society. Although some suggest this is not a comprehensive overview of the Incan Empire and how it functioned, the work rescued elements of this society and precolonial time for posterity and allowed them to become part of Latin America's culture and rich past. In more recent times, the discovery of a more detailed manuscript with scores of detailed drawings of Incan times and the conquest by Guamán Poma (Felipe Guamán Poma de Ayala, c. 1535, 1616) provide greater detail and relate the greatness of the Incan Empire and the destruction and atrocities that caused its demise. An English translation was published in 2009 as *The First New Chronicle and Good Government* (*Nueva Crónica y Buen Gobierno*).

Of great importance in colonial literature was the writing of Sor Juana Inés de la Cruz (Nueva España, 1648–1695), an upper-class woman who decided to take vows and live in a convent so that she could be more free of the constraints colonial, conservative, patriarchal society placed on women. Considered one of the best, if not the best of the colonial writers, she wrote poems, prose, plays, and even carols. Her writings considered love, literature, and science, and expressed her well-argued views on the need for freedom and education for women. Her widely read poem "Hombres Necio" (Asinine or Witless Men) chronicles the sexism of Spanish colonial society and ridicules men who condemn prostitutes in public only to contract their favors in private:

Hombres necios que acusáis	Witless men who accuse
a la mujer sin razón,	women for no reason
sin ver que sois la ocasión	without seeing thou art the cause
de lo mismo que culpáis:	of that thou would condemn

Her prolific literary production was finally censured by a less enlightened archbishop, but her legacy lives on as she is celebrated in Mexico and throughout Latin America as a great feminist writer of astounding talent who transcended the narrowness of the times in which she wrote, and in the process helped to establish a Latin American and feminist literature in the Americas.

As Latin America began to struggle with the colonial shackles that bound her, new intellectuals emerged. Andrés Bello was arguably Latin America's first widely known humanist and person of letters par excellence. As such he set the standard for the encyclopedic culture and education that has marked Latin America's great thinkers, writers, and intellectuals. Born in Caracas in 1781, Andrés Bello was a teacher, scholar, and political leader who spread knowledge and enlightenment throughout the Americas. He taught Simón Bolívar for a brief time and later accompanied him to England as part of the insurgent Venezuelans' diplomatic representation, as they rebelled against Spanish colonial rule. He remained in England for twenty years and then moved to Chile where he wrote Chile's civil code, strengthened its culture and educational system, and founded educational institutions including the University of Chile, where he served as rector (president) for many years. Like Thomas Jefferson, he was erudite in many areas: literature, philosophy, political writings, and civil law. He was teacher, politician, and author of a highly regarded Spanish grammar. He even wrote one of the first treatments of international law in Spanish. Poet, philosopher, and legal scholar, he was the editor of the continentally acclaimed magazines *Biblioteca Americana* (1823) and *Repertorio Americano* (1826–1827), which widely disseminated scholarly research, creative works, criticism, and scientific and literary thought. He also edited his now famous *Silvas Americanas*, which introduced Latin America and its epic struggle for independence as a theme of importance in world literature. His breadth and brilliance were such that he is one of the first intellectuals to be acclaimed across the South American continent and in all of Latin America. Indeed, he is credited with giving life to the americanismo movement and encouraging Latin Americans to glory in the independence and freedom they acquired as they threw off the constraints of Spanish colonialism. He was instrumental in the development of post-independence thought in Latin America.

¡Salve, fecunda zona,...	Hail, fecund zone,...
¡Oh jóvenes naciones, que ceñida	Oh, young nations, who raise
alzáis sobre el atónito Occidente	above the astonished occident
de tempranos laurels la cabeza!	your heads girt with early laurels!
Honrad el campo, honrad la	Honor the field, honor the simple life
simple vida	
del labrador, y su frugal llaneza.	of the farmer and his frugal plainness.
Así tendrán en vos perpetuamente	Thus liberty will have in you
la libertad morada,	a perpetual dwelling,
y freno de ambición, y la ley templo.	ambition a restraint, and law a temple.
Las gentes a la senda	People on the path
de la inmortalidad, ardua y fragosa,	of immortality, arduous and rough,
se animarán, citando vuestro ejemplo.	will take heart, citing your example.
...	...

(From "Silva a la agricultura de la zona tórrida," by Andrés Bello,
translated by Donald Walsh)

Other thinkers added to the dynamic new thought that was beginning to emerge from the region. Simón Rodríguez was a thinker and educator who tutored Simón Bolívar and reinforced his belief in liberty and democracy. He accompanied the young Bolívar on a European trip and recorded the liberator of South America as he took his famous oath at Monte Sacro in Rome: "I swear before you, I swear by my parents and their God, by my honor and by my country, that I will not allow my arm to rest or my soul repose until the chains that the Spanish power wills to oppress us are broken." Yet as Bolívar began to implement much of what he had learned from his teacher, he began to realize the difficult road that lay ahead for governance in the countries he helped liberate. He noted in his Address to the Inauguration of the Second National Congress in Angostura in 1819, that "Liberty, says Rousseau, is a succulent morsel, but one difficult to digest." He concluded that constitutions and laws need to be adapted to the specific characteristics of each people, each land, and often suggested more authoritarian solutions for the Latin American republics. He did so because he felt they did not have the same democratic experiences as their North American and French counterparts on which the Latin American constitutions and republics were modeled.

It took time for Bolívar's dreams of democracy and some semblance of unity to take root. In fact, it was not until later in the nineteenth century that Latin Americans came to terms with their own reality. This was, in large part because political independence was, with the exception of Haiti where a slave revolt triumphed, achieved by *criollo* elites born almost exclusively of those who considered themselves culturally if not racially European. It took some years for Latin American political thought and literature to begin to come to terms with its popular identity, and the life and times of the lower classes. A bold step along this road was realized by the Peruvian writer Ricardo Palma, whose *Tradiciones* (1872) marked the beginning of a literature whose roots sprang from the rich popular reality in Latin America. As José Carlos Mariátegui notes in the "Literature on Trial" chapter of his seminal work *7 Ensayos* (translated into English as *Seven Interpretive Essays on Peruvian Reality*),

"The *Tradiciones* of Palma is politically and socially democratic; Palma interprets the common people. His ridicule, which reflects the mocking discontent of the criollo demos, undermines the prestige of the viceroyalty and its aristocracy."

A more critical approach could be found elsewhere in the Americas. More specific popular themes were explored in the Argentine classic (*El Gaucho*) *Martín Fierro*. Written by José Hernández and first published in 1872, the epic poem broke with the Europeanized focus of refined Buenos Aires to recount the saga of an honest gaucho mistreated by landowners and government bureaucrats and forced to become an outlaw who retreats to the interior and eventually lives with a group of Indians. It was written in part as a response to Domingo Faustino Sarmiento's depiction of a brutal, uncouth gaucho strongman, Facundo. It was a direct challenge to Sarmiento's famous dichotomy between the barbarism of the countryside versus the civilization of the city ("civilization and barbarity"). Immediately popular with the horsemen of the pampas, it took more educated readers, particularly the *porteños* from Buenos Aires, some time to warm to the gaucho virtues extolled in the tale. A major contribution to national identity, the work is now seen as Argentina's national classic.

Brazil too began to come to terms with the popular classes that inhabited its hinterlands as epitomized in the destitute interior of its famous *nordeste* (northeast). Euclydes da Cunha (1866–1909), a military engineer turned journalist for the daily *O Estado de São Paulo*, immortalized the backlanders' struggle against nature and the political struggle led by the strangely mystic Antônio O. Conseheiro. *Os Sertões* (*Rebellion in the Backlands*) chronicles the different military campaigns the nascent Brazilian republic launched in this desolate region to subdue the poor hardscrabble farmers and laborers who had become followers of the mystic and had created their own autonomous settlements like Canudos. *Os Sertões* notes the indigenous, African, as well as Portuguese, origin of the people, factually describes their culture and strength, and shows how little understood they were by the government functionaries and federal troops who so brutally suppressed them. This work and the discussions that followed helped the modern Brazilian nation realize its diverse origins and better appreciate its popular roots.

> The sertanejo, or man of the backlands, is above all else a strong individual....
>
> He is the man who is always tired. He displays this invincible sluggishness, this muscular atony, in everything he does....
>
> Yet all this apparent weariness is an illusion. Nothing is more surprising than to see the sertanejo's listlessness disappear all of a sudden. In this weakened organism complete transformations are effected in a few seconds. All that is needed is some incident that demands the release of slumbering energies. The figure is transfigured....Through an instantaneous discharge of nervous energy, he at once corrects all the faults that come from the habitual relaxation of his organs and the awkward rustic unexpectedly assumes the dominating aspect of a powerful, copper-hued Titan, an amazingly different being, capable of extraordinary feats of strength and agility....
>
> Now, nothing is more easily to be explained than this permanent state of contrast between extreme manifestations of strength and agility and the prolonged intervals of apathy. A perfect reflection of the physical forces at work about him....He goes

through life ambushed on all sides by sudden, incomprehensible surprises on the part of Nature, and he never knows a moment's respite. He is a combatant who all year round is weakened and exhausted, and all the year round is strong and daring, preparing himself always for an encounter in which he will not be victor, but in which he will not let himself be vanquished.

(from Latin American Social Thought,
translated by Harold Davis)

Elsewhere in the region, Cuba and Puerto Rico remained under Spanish rule long after the rest of the former Spanish colonies had been liberated. The independence struggle that the *mambises* (Cuban patriots) waged was closely followed in the rest of the Americas. One person in particular became the voice of political and intellectual emancipation. José Martí (1853–1895) was the apostle of Cuban independence and the multifaceted intellectual who spoke for all of Latin Americans in works like *Nuestra América*. Poet, writer, journalist, diplomat, and independence leader, he sought emancipation from the political and intellectual tyranny of colonial rulers and freedom of thought and action in his beloved island and the rest of the Americas.

"Liberty is the right of every man to be honest, to think and to speak without hypocrisy."

"It is preferable to die on one's feet than to live on one's knees." [A famous phrase reputed to have begun with Martí.]

Martí was also a renowned poet. Like his political writings, his highly celebrated lines of poetry reverberated through the Spanish-speaking republics and helped to loosen the grip of more traditional Spanish forms. In the process, he set the stage for the modernist movement in Spanish literature that would be headed by Rubén Dario.

Cultivo Una Rosa Blanca	**I Cultivate a White Rose**
Cultivo una rosa blanca	I cultivate a white rose
En julio como en enero,	In July as in January
Para el amigo sincero	For the sincere friend
Que me da su mano franca.	Who gives me his hand frankly.
Y para el cruel que me arranca	And for the cruel person who tears out
El corazon con que vivo,	the heart with which I live,
Cardo ni ortiga cultivo,	I cultivate neither nettles nor thorns:
Cultivo una rosa blanca.	I cultivate a white rose.

(by José Martí)

His famous essay, "Our America" ("Nuestra América") is a seminal statement of that which must define Latin America and a clarion call for honest, popular virtue and originality among the Latin American peoples.

To govern well, one must see things as they are....Government must originate in the country. The spirit of government must be that of the country. Its structure must conform to rules appropriate to the country. Good government is nothing more than the balance of the country's natural elements.

That is why in America the imported book has been conquered by the natural man. Natural men have conquered learned and artificial men. The native half-breed has conquered the exotic Creole. The struggle is not between civilization and barbarity, but between false erudition and Nature.

Martí was the champion of the common man and many socialist ideas and a stern critic of slavery (which existed until 1886 in Cuba) and racism. He championed the acceptance of Latin America's Indian and African heritage, and observed in "Nuestra America" that

> There is no racial hatred, because there are no races. Sickly, lamp-lit minds string together and rewarm the library-shelf races that the honest traveler and the cordial observer seek in vain in the justice of nature, where the universal identity of man leaps forth in victorious love and turbulent appetite. The soul, equal and eternal, emanates from bodies that are diverse in form and color. Anyone who promotes and disseminates opposition or hatred among races is committing a sin against humanity.

As the region began to undergo profound change, such thinking was incorporated in the new currents that later flowed from the Mexican revolutionary process. Writers like José Vasconcelos spoke of a new transcendent multiracial amalgam in the Americas—La Raza Cósmica (The Cosmic Race). At an earlier time these themes had been explored by the Puerto Rican writer, thinker, and educator Eugenio María de Hostos (1839–1903) in *El Cholo* (1870), written during his sojourn in Peru.

Like Bolívar, Martí worried about the power of the United States and how it would affect Latin Americans. As a journalist covering the first Pan American Congress held in Washington in 1889–1890, he observed that

> Never in America, from its independence to the present, has there been a matter requiring better judgment or more vigilance, or demanding a clearer and more thorough examination, than the invitation proposed by the powerful United States, glutted with unsalable merchandise and determined to extend its dominions in America, to invite the less powerful American nations to arrange an alliance against Europe and establish a trade ascendancy in the rest of the world. Spanish America knew how to save itself from the Spanish tyranny; and now, after viewing with wise eyes the antecedents, motives, and ingredients of the invitation, it is imperative to say, for it is true, that the time has come for Spanish America to declare its second independence.

As a new power was challenging the autonomy of the Latin American states and the grip of Spanish colonialism was slipping away, Latin America sought to break free of the formalism of traditional literary expression as well. Martí had argued for more sincere, authentic expression, suggesting a need to modernize literature. Alluding to the need to twist the neck of the swan as the symbol of overly formalistic traditional Spanish poetry, a young Nicaraguan burst on the literary scene. In his widely acclaimed verse and prose, Rubén Darío (1867–1916) launched a movement know as "modernismo" (because it was attempting to modernize Spanish expression) and in the process transformed poetry in the Spanish language.

In his ground breaking *Azul* (1888) and even more in *Prosas Profanas*, he uses the most exotic mixture of Parnassian prosody and verse to parody the formal romanticism that flowed from France and imitative writers in Spain. In his work he calls for a different kind of poetry, refined and exotic—a poetry of its own. Indeed, he went on to become one of the most celebrated poets of the Spanish language for all time.

Darío, who was influenced by Martí, was also wary of the expanding power of the United States as well. Many look to his "Ode to Roosevelt" (inspired by the U.S. intervention in the formation of Panama in 1903) as one of the most formidable reactions to U.S. hegemony and power politics as epitomized in Teddy Roosevelt's Big Stick.

A Roosevelt

Es con voz de la Biblia, o verso de Walt
   Whitman,
que habría que llegar hasta ti, Cazador!

Eres los Estados Unidos,
eres el futuro invasor
de la América ingenua que tiene sangre
   indígena,
que aún reza a Jesucristo y aún habla en
   español.

Eres soberbio y fuerte ejemplar de tu raza;
   eres culto, eres hábil; te opones a Tolstoy....

Crees que la vida es incendio,
que el progreso es erupción,
que donde pones la bala
el porvenir pones.

No.

Los Estados Unidos son potentes y
   grandes.
Cuando ellos se estremecen hay un hondo
   temblor
que pasa por las vértebras enormes de los
   Andes....

Mas la América nuestra, que tenía poetas
desde los viejos tiempos de Nezahualcóyotl,
que ha guardado las huellas de los pies del
   gran Baco,...

vive de luz, de fuego, de perfume, de amor,
la América del grande Moctezuma, del Inca,
la América fragante de Cristóbal Colón,

Ode to Roosevelt

The voice that would reach you, Hunter,
   must speak
In Biblical tones, or in the poetry of Walt
   Whitman....

You are the United States,
future invader of our naïve America
with its Indian blood, an America
that still prays to Christ and still speaks
   Spanish.

You are a strong, proud model of your race;
you are cultured and able; you oppose
   Tolstoy....

You think life is a fire, that progress is an
   eruption,
that the future is wherever
your bullet strikes.

No.

The United States are large and potent
When they shudder there is a deep quake
that passes through the enormous
   vertebrae that are the Andes...

But our America, that has had poets
Since the ancient times of Nezahualcóyotl,
That has guarded the footprints of great
   Bacchus,...

lives the light, the fire, the fragrance, the love,
the America of the great Moctezuma, of
   the Inca,
the fragrant America of Christopher Columbus,

la América católica, la América española	the Catholic America, the Spanish America
la América en que dijo el noble Cuauhtémoc:	the America where noble Cuauhtémoc said:
"Yo no estoy en un lecho de rosas"; esa América	"I am not on a bed of roses"; our America,
que tiembla de huracanes y que vive de amor,	trembling with hurricanes, trembling with love:
hombres de ojos sajones y alma bárbara, vive.	O men with Saxon eyes and barbarous souls,
Y sueña. Y ama, y vibra, y es la hija del Sol.	our America lives. And it dreams, and loves,
Tened cuidado. ¡Vive la América española!	and it is the daughter of the Sun.
	Be careful. Long live Spanish America!

The Aesthetics of the Mexican Revolution

And so we see that themes of a common Latin American heritage and identity reverberate more strongly through the various republics of the region by the end of the nineteenth century. The pressure for change and popular expression built up in fin-de-siècle Mexico and burst forth in 1910. The Mexican Revolution (1910–1920) would unleash a torrent of innovative thought, writing, and artistic expression. Mariano Azuela's widely read novel *Los de abajo* (literally Those on the Bottom, translated as *The Underdogs*) would provide a vision of the century's first great revolution from the perspective of the common men and women who fought in it. Led by Diego Rivera, one of the famed Mexican muralists (Rivera, José Orozco, and David Siqueiros), would visually rediscover native and mestizo themes. The pallid white of the Europeans would now be contrasted by the rich earthen browns of Mexico's mestizo and indigenous masses. Indigenous themes would be further developed by artists like José Sabogal of Peru.

As suggested above, José Vasconcelos would write of a new cosmic race composed of all the rich genetic material in the Americas and argue that a new culture that incorporated what each group had contributed, with special emphasis on the contributions of the mestizo masses and popular culture they created, and on Mexico's proud indigenous past culture was necessary. As the revolution progressed under a new regime, he was made minister of education to ensure that this new Americanist perspective was implemented. Writing on civilization and culture, he noted that

Civilization and Culture

Culture is the poetry of conduct and the music of the spirit.... All our antecedents incline us toward preferring the cultural act to the action which is merely civilizing. The century of imitation of the Nordic, the century of anguish due to the acquisition of a reflected civilization, is liquidating itself. To the prejudice concerning the inferiority of the Indian and the mestizo, the undeniable pith of our population, there succeeds today, in view of the failure of the North, the conviction that the secret of cultures lies in making adequate use of each temperament in its skill and aptitude....

The advantage of our fertile, unpopulated lands place us under obligation. All humanity expects of us not merely a greater civilization, but a culture freer, broader, and more equitable. It would be treason to the hope of the world for anyone to obstruct our vigorous growth. Honor imposes upon us the obligation to create and consolidate an authentic and indigenous culture.

(from *Bolivarismo y Monroismo*)

The Ongoing Struggle for Identity and Voice

As suggested above, José Enrique Rodó (1872–1917) further defined spiritual Latin America and contrasted it with the heavy, overly material North America. His assertion of Latin American virtue and the suggestion that it was in ways superior to the progress of the United States was indicative of a growing confidence and the emergence of a clear Latin American identity and a distinctive voice. As these congealed, the world witnessed the emergence of a torrent of Latin American writers and intellectuals who were unafraid to seek their own nuanced expression and to write from and about Latin America. Although conversant with European literature and culture and indeed world literature, they began to write in and for their culture and people, and to do so as part of what we would later be called the global south. Rubén Darío had exerted a tremendous influence on Spanish-language literature; the Mexican Revolution had rocked the world. Latin America was beginning to come of age. This process was aided greatly by a series of extremely talented writers. The Peruvian poet César Vallejo (1892–1938) developed a poetry of the avantgarde in work like his *Los Heroldos Negros*, whose famous lines are oft quoted: "Hay golpes en la vida, tan fuertes.... ¡Yo no sé!" / "There are such hard blows in life.... I don't know!"

A Louder Feminine Voice

Gabriela Mistral (1889–1957) of Chile interjected feminine if not proto-feminist lyricism into Latin American literature. She wrote of love, death, and faith in such lyrical verse that she was, after the publication of her first major work, *Desolación* (1922), soon a favorite across Latin America. Her fame spread to Europe and the United States where many of her works were published in translation. Her stays there also helped North America and Europe become familiar with her work and persona. She was awarded the Nobel Prize for Literature in 1945 in recognition of her work (and implicitly that of a whole host of other Latin American writers who had burst on the world stage).

La Liana	The Liana
En el secreto de la noche	In the secret of the night
mi oración sube como las lianas,	My prayer climbs like the liana,
así cayendo y levantando,	Gropes like a blind man
y a tanteos como el ciego,	Sees more than an owl.
pero viendo más que el búho.	Up the stalk of night
Por el tallo de la noche	That you loved, that I love,
que tú amabas y que yo amo,	Creeps my torn prayer,
ella sube despedazada y rehecha,	rent and mended, uncertain and sure
insegura y cierta.	Here the path breaks it,
Aquí la rompe una derrota,	Here breezes lift it,
más allá un aire la endereza.	Wind flurries toss it,

Una camada de aire la aúpa,
un no sé qué me la derriba.

And something I don't know
Hurls it to earth again.

O ya trepa como la liana
y el géiser a cada salto
recibidos y devueltos....

Now it creeps like the liana,
Now geysers up, at every thrust
Received and returned....

En esta noche, tú recoge
mi llamado, tómalo y tenlo;
duerme, mi amor, y por ella
hazme bajar mi propio sueño,
y como era sobre la tierra,
así amor mío, así quedemos.

Gather up my prayer tonight.
Take it and hold it.
Sleep, my love, let me sleep
Fall to me in prayer,
As we were on earth,
So do we remain.

(by Gabriela Mistral, from *Lagar* II, a posthumous compilation published in 1991, translated by Doris Dana as cited in Rodríguez Monegal, vol. 1)

Pablo Neruda. *(Fulton Archive/Getty Images)*

Other Voices

Foremost among the other writers were Mistral's compatriot Pablo Neruda and the Guatemalan novelist Miguel Angel Asturias. Neruda (1904–1973) is acclaimed as one of Latin America's greatest poets, some would say the greatest of the twentieth century. He evolved from his passionate *Twenty Love Poems* (1924) through *Residencia en la Tierra* (*Residence on Earth*, 1933) to his masterwork *Canto General* (1950), an epic poem (with influences of Walt Whitman) that tells the story of Latin America from precolonial times into the twentieth century. He was awarded the Nobel Prize in Literature in 1971. Like much of his poetry, *Canto General* clearly shows the Marxist perspective that many Latin American intellectuals adopted from the 1920s on. Neruda was a longtime member of the Chilean Communist Party and had an unwavering political commitment that had been forged during his stay in Spain during the Spanish Civil War. Like the Marxism of the Chilean Communist leader Luis Emilio Recabarren and the Peruvian Marxist José Carlos Mariátegui, Neruda's Marxism was forged from within Latin America. *Canto General* is, then, also well rooted in Latin American reality as suggested by the section "Heights of Machu Picchu" that was inspired after the poet visited the site. More political is the oft-quoted "The United Fruit."

La United Fruit Co.

Cuando sonó la trompeta, estuvo
todo preparado en la tierra,
y Jehová repartió el mundo
a Coca-Cola Inc., Anaconda,
Ford Motors, y otras entidades:
la Compañía Frutera Inc.
se reservó lo más jugoso,
la costa central de mi tierra,
la dulce cintura de América.
Bautizó de nuevo sus tierras
como "Repúblicas Bananas,"
    y sobre los muertos dormidos,
sobre los héroes inquietos
que conquistaron la grandeza,
la libertad y las banderas,
estableció la ópera bufa:
enajenó los albedríos,
regaló coronas de César,
desenvainó la envidia, atrajo
la dictadora de las moscas,
moscas Trujillo, moscas Tachos,
moscas Carías, moscas Martínez,
moscas Ubico, moscas húmedas...

Mientras tanto, por los abismos
azucaradas de los puertos,

The United Fruit Co.

When the trumpet sounded, it was
all prepared on the earth,
and Jehovah parceled out the earth
to Coca-Cola, Inc., Anaconda,
Ford Motors, and other entities:
The Fruit Company, Inc.
reserved for itself the most succulent,
the central coast of my own land,
the delicate waist of America.
It rechristened its territories
as the "Banana Republics"
and over the sleeping dead,
over the restless heroes
who brought about the greatness,
the liberty and the flags,
it established the comic opera:
abolished the independencies,
presented crowns of Caesar,
unsheathed envy, attracted
the dictatorship of the flies,
Trujillo flies, Tacho flies,
Carias flies, Martínez flies,
Ubico flies, damp flies...

Meanwhile Indians are falling
into the sugared chasms

caían indios sepultados	of the harbors, wrapped
en el vapor de la mañana:	for burial in the mist of the dawn:
un cuerpo rueda, una cosa	a body rolls, a thing
sin nombre, un número caído,	that has no name, a fallen cipher,
un racimo de fruta muerta	a cluster of dead fruit
derramada en el pudridero.	thrown down on the dump.

(by Pablo Neruda, translated from the Spanish by Robert Bly)

Voices in Brazilian Portuguese

Many writers in Latin America have less overt political orientations. In Brazil, writers like Mário Andrade (1893–1945) strengthened literary vanguardism and developed the modernist movement in Brazilian letters. A poet and gifted writer, his interest in anthropological studies and folklore enabled him to pen his masterful novel *Macunaíma* (1928). Writing from a deeply rooted Brazilian perspective, the now classic novel is a magical and mythical tale of a man born in the jungle who must travel to the modern city of São Paulo to retrieve the amulet his lover has given him before she ascended into the heavens to be a constellation. It is replete with indigenous Tupi vocabulary and African folklore and deities (Orishas), and popular speech patterns. Andrade forms whole mythological systems as part of the plot line. In language and popular culture it strives to be a pan Brazilian novel. The mixture of linguistic and cultural elements and focus on Afro-Brazilian culture at first caused some difficulty for the critics, but over time it became a beloved novel that is widely read as a treasure of Brazilianness.

After Andrade other writers developed their own style. Of particular note was Jorge Amado (1912–2001) whose earlier work was heavily influenced by Marxist ideology. He became a communist and even wrote a biography of the longtime head of the Brazilian Communist Party and leader of the Tenentes revolt, Luiz Carlos Prestes (*The Knight of Hope*, 1945). Later works describe the life of popular, mostly Afro-Brazilians in the northeast. He beautifully describes Brazil's own national dramas in works like *Dona Flor and Her Two Husbands* (1976) and his novel about a delightful, enchanting woman from the popular classes, *Gabriela of Clove and Cinnamon* (1958).

Born on the way to Brazil to Ukranian parents, Amado's friend and contemporary, Clarice Lispector (1920–1977) became one of Brazil's best known writers. Her fifth novel, *The Passion According to G.H.* (1964) is highly acclaimed. In it the reader sees how Lispector's feminist existentialism evokes the daily misery many must endure: "The time of living is so hellishly inexpressive that it is nothingness. What I called 'nothing' was nevertheless so inseparable from me that to me it was...I myself? and therefore it was becoming invisible as I was invisible to myself, it was becoming nothingness."

Other Voices

Another writer who, like Neruda, had well defined leftist politics was the renowned Guatemalan novelist Miguel Angel Asturias (1899–1974). He, like José

Carlos Mariátegui and many twentieth-century Latin American writers, discovered their Latin American voice while sojourning in Europe and found avantgarde artists and intellectuals who were quick to value that which they had not yet learned to love fully—their Latin America. As Rodríguez Monegal suggests, Asturias was to rediscover Guatemala and Mayan civilization and culture while in Paris. Thereafter, he had his feet firmly planted in Latin American reality. While still in Paris he published a translation of the *Popol Vuh*, the sacred book of Maya mythology, in 1930. His best known novel, *El Señor Presidente* (1946), is the quintessential tale of a Latin American dictator, modeled after Guatemala's brutal longtime dictator Estrada Cabrera. His second novel, *Man of Maize* delves even further into the Latin American past, and is composed of a series of tales about land and the indigenous people who are connected to it, in which the ancient Mayan myths were alive and seen as contemporary social and political conflicts. The work was an important contribution to the Latin American narrative that Jorge Luis Borges, Alejo Carpentier, and others were developing at that time. Subsequently he wrote more politicized works on the United Fruit Company, the banana industry, and how the United States resisted the nationalist revolutionary transformation in Guatemala and finally overthrew it with a CIA-sponsored coup in 1954. These included *Strong Wind* (1950), *The Green Pope* (1954), and *Week-End in Guatemala* (1956), which dealt with the actual coup. The later works were part of a growing climate of political and intellectual resistance to the perceived imperial power of the United States and made Asturias very popular among Latin American intellectuals and nationalists. In recognition of the brilliance of his work and its rootedness in the Mayan, Guatemalan, and Latin American reality, Asturias received the Nobel Prize in Literature in 1967. Hereafter, the native, indigenous, and that uniquely Latin American quality would be valued for itself and as a legitimate if not necessary form of expression that could not be neglected.

Latin American thought and politics were also evolving. The Cuban revolution established a socialist state in Latin America and gave the world Fidel Castro (1926–) and Enersto "Che" Guevara (1926–1967), and the socialism that spread through Latin America in the sixties, seventies, and eighties. Fidel was the statesman and revolutionary leader, but Che, the Argentine-born revolutionary, came to epitomize heroic struggle and selfless socialism. Indeed, his example has continued to inspire the young and revolutionary throughout Latin America and beyond. His short piece *Socialism and Man* is considered one of the most impassioned socialist tracts ever written.

> At the risk of seeming ridiculous, let me say that the true revolutionary is guided by a great feeling of love. It is impossible to think of a genuine revolutionary lacking this quality....Our vanguard revolutionaries must idealize this love of the people, the most sacred of cause, and make it one and indivisible....
>
> In these circumstances one must have a great deal of humanity and a strong sense of justice and truth in order not to fall into extreme dogmatism and cold scholasticism, into an isolation from the masses. We must strive every day so that this love of living humanity will be transformed into actual deeds, into acts that serve as examples, as a moving force.

The Boom

As the Cuban revolution marched on and Che's fame spread through the world, the tremendous outpouring of Latin American literature in the 1960s and 1970s and its acceptance on the world stage made for what came to be called the "boom" in Latin America literature. The success of the 1959 revolution in Cuba and the radical transformation it eventually engendered in thinking, identity, and resistance in Latin American and the global south and its importance in the anticolonial struggle (and in anticolonial studies), challenged the view of Latin America as a backwater. As Frantz Fanon (1925–1961), a writer from French Latin America (the French colony of Martinique) who was heavily influenced by the brilliant Antilian poet and anticolonialist Aimé Césaire (1913–2008), suggested in the essay on culture in his widely read *Wretched of the Earth* (*Les damnes de la terre.* Paris, 1961), it may be necessary to resist European culture as part of the process of liberation and the construction of national culture, but at a later date the native culture can then meet European culture as an equal on the world stage, shedding any sense of inferiority.

In Latin America, as the Latin American writers criticized United States political hegemony and the unenlightened rule of dictators and Amero-European sycophants, and separated themselves from Eurocentric views and traditional literary forms, they rediscovered their own Latin America and found their own, often very individually unique, voice.

It is often argued that the work of Jorge Luis Borges of Argentina (1899–1986) presaged the boom novelists because of his brilliant and unique form of expression, very personal literary description, and ability to spin whole worlds in his stories (he did not write novels). Borges became widely acclaimed later in his life as he developed his own descriptive style and unique voice incorporating other texts (intertextuality) in his work. His short stories were exquisite, full of vivid fantasy and even magic, and became highly influential for later writers. Although enthusiastically read by many Latin Americans, his international fame was not consolidated until after 1961, when he received the first International Publishers' Prize, the *Prix Formentor*, which he shared with Samuel Beckett. Soon many in Europe and elsewhere were scrambling to read the relatively unknown Argentine author who had shared the prize with the well-known Beckett. Thus the fame and recognition that Neruda and Asturias has received earlier came to Borges later in life. He lost his sight in his last decades, but continued to produce and became well known internationally. Yet, he died in 1986 without ever receiving the Nobel Prize that so many thought he merited.

But the dam had burst and the Latin Americans were now acknowledged; they strode on the world stage as equals if not the innovators of the day. Rather than inferior colonials, they were more often seen as the best and brightest of the writers and thinkers. When the well-respected Cuban writer Alejo Carpentier (1904–2008) used the term "lo real maravilloso" (the marvelous real), in the prologue to his 1949 novel *The Kingdom of This World*, he underlined a concept that is often used to characterize many of the boom and post-boom writers. By interjecting the magical and fantastic as a normal part of everyday reality, the Latin American writers were suggesting something very different from that found in an overly ordinary, uninspired, and unimaginative world in North America and Europe and the fiction from there. Though difficult for many English-language readers and others from the global north, the writers were showing a world where saints intervened, myth defined reality, time was cyclical, witches worked, and things flew around the room or disappeared in a whirlwind. They were using a view of the world that was common to many Latin Americans, was transmitted through their oral tradition, and was full of spirit and imagination. Later this particular take on events became know as magical realism. Novelists from several nations participated in the boom; their ranks included Julio Cortázar of Argentina (1914–1984), Carlos Fuentes (1928–) and Octavio Paz (1914–1998) of Mexico, and Mario Vargas Llosa of Peru (1936–), whose politics and political militancy could best be characterized as conservative, if not rightist.

Gabriel García Márquez (Colombia, 1928–) is perhaps the best known of these and a popularizer of the use of magical realism. His novel *One Hundred Years of Solitude* (*Cien Años de Soledad*), published in 1967, is a masterful story of the mythical town of Macondo and multiple generations of a Colombian family (the Buen Días) whose triumphs and vicissitudes indirectly tell the story of Colombian—and Latin American—history and society from the end of the nineteenth century to the second half of the twentieth. The tale encompasses the full complement of Latin American reality—magical and ordinary—from *coronels* to banana workers to

Gabriel García Márquez. *(Time & Life Pictures/Getty Images)*

prostitutes to healers to magicians. The masterpiece is considered a defining classic of twentieth-century literature. But Gabo, as Márquez is affectionately called, wrote many novels and stories steeped in the Latin American Reality from *Autumn of the Patriarch* (1975), a classic on the rumination of a dictator who ruled for 100 years, to *Love in a Time of Cholera*, published in 1985. Like Neruda and Asturias, he developed well-defined leftist political views and became a personal friend of Fidel Castro. In 1982 he was made a Nobel Laureate in Literature "for his novels and short stories, in which the fantastic and the realistic are combined in a richly composed world of imagination, reflecting a continent's life and conflicts." After a bout with cancer, Márquez recovered and has continued to write; in 2007 he published a partial memoir, *Memories of My Melancholy Whores*.

Post Boom and Writing from Exile

After the Latin American boom comes what has been called the post-boom. Here excellent feminist writers take the lead. Isabel Allende (1942–) is a well-known contemporary Chilean writer who achieved fame with her saga *La Casa de los Espíritus* (*The House of the Spirits*), which traces a family through four generations of women who are unafraid to define themselves on their own terms or struggle for their liberation. The internal politics of family and home that define many women's political perspectives in Latin America (as suggested by the "Mothers of the Plaza de Mayo"

Isabel Allende. *(Photo by Santiago Llanquin/AP Images)*

in Argentina) become the basis for understanding the passionate politics that rage on the national stage and eventually tear the country apart. Set in her native Chile, the niece of President Salvador Allende artfully weaves politics and history into the story through family. Pablo Neruda is "the poet," Salvador Allende is "the President"; toward the end of the novel, these and most of the then-living family members are caught up in the 1973 coup and its brutal aftermath. Allende further examined post-coup politics in Chile in *Of Love and Shadows*, but went on to write a variety of other works, including *Eva Luna, Paula*, a letter to her dying daughter, and *My Invented Country* (2003), which describes her recollections of Chile while in exile and after she settled in the United States.

> Clara continued to stare at the sky long after her uncle had become invisible. She thought she saw him ten minutes later, but it was only a migrating sparrow. After three days the initial euphoria that had accompanied the first airplane flight in the country died down and no one gave the episode another thought, except for Clara, who continued to peer at the horizon.
>
> After a week with no word from the flying uncle, people began to speculate that he had gone so high that he had disappeared into outer space, and the ignorant suggested he would reach the moon. With a mixture of sadness and relief, Severo decided that his brother-in-law and his machine must have fallen into some hidden crevice of the *cordillera*, where they would never be found. Nivea wept disconsolately and lit candles to San Antonio, patron of lost objects. Severo opposed the idea of having masses said, because he did not believe in them as a way of getting into heaven, much less of returning to earth, and he maintained that masses and religious vows, like the selling of indulgences, images, and scapulars, were a dishonest business. Because of his attitude, Nivea and Nana had the children say the rosary behind their father's back for nine days. Meanwhile, groups of volunteer explorers and mountain climbers tirelessly searched peaks and passes, combing every accessible stretch of land until they finally returned in triumph to hand the family the mortal remains of the deceased in a sealed black coffin. The intrepid traveler was laid to rest in a grandiose funeral. His death made him a hero and his name was on the front page of all the papers for several days. The same multitude that had gathered to see him off the day he flew away in his bird paraded past his coffin. The entire family wept as befit the occasion, except for Clara, who continued to watch the sky with the patience of an astronomer. One week after he had been buried, Uncle Marcos, a bright smile playing behind his pirate's mustache, appeared in person in the doorway of Nivea and Severo del Valle's house. Thanks to the surreptitious prayers of the women and children, as he himself admitted, he was alive and well and in full possession of his faculties, including his sense of humor. Despite the noble lineage of his aerial maps, the flight had been a failure. He had lost his airplane and had to return on foot, but he had not broken any bones and his adventurous spirit was intact. This confirmed the family's eternal devotion to San Antonio, but was not taken as a warning by future generations, who also tried to fly, although by different means. Legally, however, Marcos was a corpse. Severo del Valle was obliged to use all his legal ingenuity to bring his brother-in-law back to life and the full rights of citizenship. When the coffin was pried open in the presence of the appropriate authorities, it was found to contain a bag of sand. This discovery ruined the reputation, up till then untarnished, of the volunteer explorers and mountain climbers, who from that day on were considered little better than a pack of bandits.
>
> From *The House of the Spirits*

Suggesting a cyclical view, the novel begins and ends with the same sentence, "Barbaras came to us by sea." Allende is clear in her progressive political views and ardent feminism, but allows each character their own voice, thus the novel describes each character's particular piece of the Latin American mosaic and suggests the multifaceted nature of contemporary Latin American reality.

Today, we see a variety of new writers appearing and note that national frontiers and even language-imposed borders are often transcended. Julia Alvarez, born in New York City in 1950, who went back and forth to the Dominican Republic as her parents evaded the Trujillo dictatorship, and Francisco Goldman from Guatemala, tell their countries' stories but write in English. Their perspective, then, is mixed as a consequence of being writers within the Latin American diaspora (that was occasioned by flight from repression, economic hardship, and a multitude of other factors that stimulate them or their families to emigration), who reside in the United States, Europe, or even other Latin American countries. Alvarez is best know for her novel *In the Time of the Butterflies*, which tells the story of the four Mirabal sisters who used the code name Butterflies in the underground movement against the Dominican dictator Rafael Trujillo. Three are eventually brutally murdered by the dictatorship and became symbols of resistance and brutality toward women. The novel was widely read and subsequently made into a film produced by Salma Hayek. Securing her use of English in her novels, Alvarez was appointed as writer in residence at Middlebury College.

Francisco Goldman (1954–) is a novelist and journalist born in Boston, Massachusetts, to a Guatemalan mother and Jewish-American father. His first, highly acclaimed novel, *The Long Night of White Chickens* (1992), treats the selling of Guatemalan children for foreign adoption. Likewise, his second novel *The Ordinary Seaman* (1997), received excellent reviews. Goldman's latest work, *The Art of Political Murder: Who Killed the Bishop?*, is a nonfiction account of the assassination of the Guatemalan Catholic bishop Juan José Gerardi in 1996, days after his office released a human rights report attributing the vast majority of the murders in Guatemala's civil war to the Guatemalan military.

Nor has Haiti lacked voices for the transnational experience so many of her people have endured. Edwidge Danticat was born in Port-au-Prince. Escaping the poverty of the island, her parents emigrated to New York and she followed a few years later at age twelve. Like other diaspora writers, her novels alternate between the perspective of an immigrant in a Haitian community in Brooklyn and a Haitian national. She writes of the immigrant experience and her native Haiti in works such as *Breath, Eyes, Memory* (1994), *Krik? Krak!* (1996), and *The Farming of Bones* (1998).

And there are also exile writers who chronicle the unofficial histories of Latin America's brutal dictatorships of the 1970s and 1980s. Cristina Peri Rossi (Uruguay, 1941–) and Dialmela Eltit (Chile, 1949–) brought a strong feminist critique of the brutal Southern Cone dictatorial regimes. Rossi fled to Barcelona, Spain, in 1972 as the military dictatorship was descending on her native Uruguay. There she began her activity against the brutal military rule that followed. Writing in the pages of the mythic magazine *Triunfo*, she was again forced to flee (to Paris) until after the demise of the Franco dictatorship. She soon returned and obtained Spanish nationality and has lived in Catalan-speaking Barcelona ever since. From there she has written prolifically, attacking dictatorship, and advocating for feminism and homosexual rights. Her works have been translated into more than fifteen languages, and she is considered one the most important contemporary writers in the Spanish language. Her work includes poetry, short stories, novels, essays, articles, radio commentary and newspaper columns. See, for instance, *La nave de los locos* (The Ship of Fools) (1984) which is generally regarded by critics as her most important work. More recent novels include *Solitario de amor* (Solitaire of Love, 1989), *La última noche de Dostoievski* (Dostoevsky's Last Night, 1992), and *El amor es una droga dura* (Love Is a Hard Drug, 1999).

Speaking Truth to Power: Voices in Rebellion

With the advent of the Cuban revolution in the 1960s, dictatorships were challenged by guerrilla movements inspired by Cuban-style socialism. Different guerrilla groups proliferated throughout the Americas and had particularly strong influence in small countries like Nicaragua where the Sandinista National Liberation Front triumphed over the Somoza dictatorship in July 1979 and Guatemala, where brutal warfare raged from the 1960s until the peace accords in 1996. Now that the fighting is long over in Nicaragua, Guatemala, and El Salvador, those who struggled for change are now writing of the experience. Gioconda Belli (1948–) and Sergio Ramírez (1943–) were part of the Sandinista struggle in Nicaragua and went on to be its best chroniclers as well. Belli is best known for her poetry and her account of the guerrilla war in Guatemala, *The Country Under My Skin: A Memoir of Love and War* (2001): "With each shot I fired my body shuddered, the impact reverberating through every last joint, leaving an unbearable ringing in my head, sharp and disturbing...."

Ramírez, who is prolific, is well known for his memoir *Adiós Muchachos: Memoria de la revolución sandinista* (Goodbye Lads, A Memoir of the Sandinista Revolution, 1999). Similarly, the former Guatemalan guerrilla and acclaimed writer Mario Roberto Morales (1947–) provides a tightly narrated account of his experience as a guerrilla in *Los que se Fueron por la Libre* (Those Who Took Off on Their Own, 2008).

Ariel Dorfman (Chile, 1942–) also writes of the violence and the degradation that characterized dictatorship in his native land (see, for instance, his drama *Death and the Maiden* (1991), but has addressed broader themes as well. As a young writer, he gained some notoriety when he and colleagues published *Para Leer Pato Donald* in 1971. Published in English as *How to Read Donald Duck: Imperialist Ideology in the Disney Comic*, it is a biting statement on cultural imperialism in Disney comics. Since the end of the Pinochet dictatorship and the restoration of democracy in Chile in 1990, he divides his time between Santiago and the United States, where he teaches at Duke University.

Beyond Magical Realism

Finally, we should note that Latin American writers are still committed to their realities but they are not just "believers" in saints who will solve the problems of their societies. For instance, "realismo mágico" is being critically confronted by a new generation of writers who call themselves "The McOndo group" (from McDonald's globalized world as contrasted to García Márquez' Macondo, the fictional town in *One Hundred Years of Solitude* that is replete with magical realism) and whose leader is Alberto Fuguet (Chile, 1964–). They reject the need to employ magical realism as a sine qua non for a Latin American novel, believing this formula much too constraining. They question the folklorismo, the naïveté, and the spontaneous humor that was predominant before, and use irony, intertextuality, pastiche, and the grotesque to intervene in real scenes of everyday life in order to establish more critical distance. After others won the right to write within the historic Latin American context, they seek the freedom to transcend it. This being the case, and being fully cognizant that Allende and Márquez remain as prolific as ever, we can but conclude that Latin Americans continue to find renewed voice for and from their changing realities, and that their writers and thinkers remain vibrant, relevant, and influential.

Bibliography

Allende, Isabel. *The House of the Spirits (La Casa de los Espíritus)*. Translated by Magda Bogin. New York: Knopf, 1993.

_____. *My Imagined Country: A Nostalgic Stroll Through Chile (Mi País Inventado: Un Paseo Nostálgico por Chile)*. Translated by Margaret Sayers Peden. New York: Harper Collins, 2003.

_____. *Of Love and Shadows (De Amor y de Sombra)*. Translated by Margaret Sayers Peden. New York: Knopf, 1987.

_____. *Paula*. Translated by Margaret Sayers Peden. New York: HarperCollins, 1995.

Alvarez, Julia. *How the Garcia Girls Lost Their Accents*. New York: Plume, 1992.

_____. *In the Time of the Butterflies*. Chapel Hill, NC: Algonquin Books, 1994.

Amado, Jorge. *Dona Flor and Her Two Husbands: A Moral and Amorphous Tale (Dona Flor e seus dos maridos, historia moral e de amor)*. Translated by Harriet de Onís. New York: Knopf, 1969.

_____. *Gabriela of Clove and Cinnamon (Gabriela, clavo e canela)*. Translated by James L. Taylor and William L. Grossman. London: Chatto & Windus, 1963.

Andrade, Mario de. *Macunaíma (Macunaíma: o, Heroi sem Nenhum Carater)*. Translated by E. A. Goodland. New York: Random House, 1984.

Asturias, Miguel Angel. *Man of Corn (Hombre de Maize)*. Translated by Gerald Martin. Madrid: Alianza Editorial, 1975.

_____. *Mr. President (El Señor Presidente)*. Translated by Frances Partridge. New York: Atheneum, 1963.

Azuela, Mariano. *The Underdogs (Los de abajo)*. Translated by Frederick H. Fornoff. Pittsburgh, PA: University of Pittsburgh Press, 1992.

Belli, Gioconda, *The Country Under My Skin: A Memoir of Love and War*. Translated by Kristina Cordero with the author. New York: Knopf, 2002.

Bello, Andrés. *Selected Writings of Andrés Bello*. Translated by Frances M. Lopez-Morillas; edited with an introduction and notes by Iván Jaksić. New York: Oxford University Press, 1997.

Bolívar, Simón. *Selected Writings*. Compiled by Vicente Lecuna, edited by Harold A. Bierck, translated by Lewis Bertrand. Published by Banco de Venezuela. 2 vols. New York: The Colonial Press, Inc., 1951.

Borges, Jorge Luis. *The Aleph and Other Stories*. Translated by Norman Thomas di Giovanni and the author. New York: E.P. Dutton, 1970.

Carpentier, Alejo. *The Lost Steps*. Translated by Harriet de Onis. New York: Noonday Press, 1989.

Césaire, Aimé. *Discourse on Colonialism*. New York: Monthly Review Press, 1972.

Chang-Rodriguez, Raquel, and Malva E. Filer, eds. *Voces de Hispanoamérica, Antología Literaria*. 3rd ed. Boston: Thompson/Heinle, 2004.

Córtazer, Julio. *Hopscotch*. Translated by Gregory Rabassa. New York: Pantheon, 1966.

Cruz, Juana Inés de la. *A Sor Juana Anthology*. Translated by Alan S. Trueblood; foreword by Octavio Paz. Cambridge: Harvard University Press, 1988.

Da Cunha, Euclydes. *Rebellion in the Backlands (Os Sertões)*. Translated by Samuel Putnam. Chicago: University of Chicago Press, 1944.

Danticat, Edwidge. *Breath, Eyes, Memory*. New York: Vintage Books, 1998.

_____. *The Farming of Bones*. New York: Soho Press, 1998.

Davis, Harold Eugene. *Latin American Social Thought: the History of Its Development Since Independence, with Selected Readings*. 2nd ed. Washington, DC: University Press of Washington, 1966.

_____. *Latin American Thought: A Historical Introduction*. Baton Rouge: Louisiana State University Press, 1972.

Darío, Rubén. *Azul*. Madrid: Espasa-Calpe, 1968.

_____. *Prosas Profanas*. Madrid, Espasa-Calpe, 1967.

_____. *Rubén Darío: Selection from the Prose and Poetry*. Edited with introduction, notes, and vocabulary by George W. Umphrey and Carlos García Prada. New York: Macmillan, 1928.

Dorfman, Ariel. *Death and the Maiden*. New York: Penguin, 1992.

_____. *Windows*. New York: Pantheon, 1983.

Dorfman, Ariel, Armand Mattelart, and David Kunzle, *How to Read Donald Duck: Imperialist Ideology in the Disney Comic (Para leer Pato Donald)*. Translated by David Kunzle. New York: International General, 1984.

Fanon, Frantz. *The Wretched of the Earth (Les damnés de la terre)*. New York: Grove Press, 1963.

Fuentes, Carlos. *The Death of Artemio Cruz (La muerte de Artemio Cruz)*. New York: Noonday Press, 1991.

Fuguet, Alberto. *Mala Honda*. Santiago, Chile: Aguilar Chilena de Ediciones, 2003.

_____. *The Movies of My Life (Las Peliulas de mi vida: Una novela)*. Translated by Ezra E. Fitz. New York: Rayo, 2003.

_____. *Short Stories*. Translated by Ezra E. Fitz. New York: Rayo, 2005.

García Márquez, Gabriel. *Autumn of the Patriarch (Otoño del Patriarca)*. Translated by Gregory Rabassa. New York: Avon Books, 1976.

_____. *Love in a Time of Cholera (Amor en los Tiempos del Cólera)*. Translated by Edith Grossman. New York: Knopf, 1988.

_____. *One Hundred Years of Solitude (Cien Años de Solidad)*. Translated by Gregory Rabassa. New York: Harper & Row, 1970.

Goldman, Francisco. *The Art of Political Murder: Who Killed the Bishop?* New York: Grove Press, 2007.

_____. *The Long Night of the White Chickens*. New York: Atlantic Monthly Press, 1992.

_____. *The Ordinary Seaman*. New York: Atlantic Monthly Press, 1997.

Guamán Poma de Ayala, Felipe. *The First New Chronicle and Good Government*. Abridged, selected, translated, and annotated by David Frye. Indianapolis, IN: Hackett, 2006.

_____. *The First New Chronicle and Good Government: On the History of the World and the Incas up to 1615*. Translated and edited by Roland Hamilton. Austin: University of Texas Press, 2009.

Guevara, Ernesto "Che." *Che: Selected Works of Ernesto Guevara*. Cambridge, Massachusetts: MIT Press, 1969.

_____. *Socialism and Man*. New York: Pathfinder Press, 1971.

Hernández, José. *El Gaucho Martín Fierro*. Translated by Walter Owen. Buenos Aires: Editorial Pampa, 1964.

Hostos, Eugenio María de. *Obras completas* (Collected Works). Rio Piedras, PR: Editorial del Instituto de Cultura Puertoriqueño, 1988.

Lispector, Clarice. *The Passion According to G.H. (A Paixão segundo G.H)*. Translated by Ronald W. Sousa. Minneapolis: University of Minnesota Press, 1988.

Mariátegui, José Carlos. *Ideología y política*. Vol.13 of *Obras Completas*. 19th ed. Lima: Editorial Amauta, 1990.

_____. *Seven Interpretive Essays on Peruvian Reality (Siete ensayos de interpretación de la realidad peruana)*. Translated by Marjorie Urquidi. Austin: University of Texas Press, 1971.

Martí, José. *Nuestra América (Our America)*. Caracas: Biblioteca Ayacucho, 1977.

Mistral, Gabriela. *Lagar II*. Santiago: Dirección de Bibliotecas Archivos y Museso, 1991.

_____. *Selected Poems of Gabriela Mistral*. Edited by V. B. Price and Ursula Kroeber Le Guin. Albuquerque: University of New Mexico Press, 2003.

Morales, Mario Roberto. *Los que fueron por la libre. Una historia personal de la lucha armada y la guerra popular (Those Who Took Off on their Own, A Personal History of the Armed Struggle and People's War)*. Guatemala City: Consucultura, 2008.

Neruda, Pablo. *Canto General*. Translated by Jack Schmitt. Berkeley: University of California Press, 1991.

_____. *Residence on Earth (Residencia en la tierra)*. Translated by Donald Walsh. New York: New Directions, 1973.

_____. *Twenty Love Poems and a Song of Despair (Veinte Poemas de amor y una Canción Desesperada)*. Translated by W. S. Merwin. New York: Penguin, 2004.

Palma, Ricardo. *Tradiciones Peruanas*. Madrid: Calpe, 1923.

Paz, Octavio. *Labyrinth of Solitude: Life and Thought in Mexico (El laberinto de la soledad)*. Translated by Lysander Kemp, Yara Milos, and Rachael Phillips Belushi. New York: Grove Press, 1985.

Peri Rossi, Cristina. *Dostoevsky's Last Night (Ultima Noche de Dostoievski)*. Translated by Laura C. Dail. New York: Picador, 1994.

_____. *A Forbidden Passion: Stories*. Translated by Mary Jane Treacy. Pittsburgh, PA: Cleis Press, 1993.

_____. *Ship of Fools: A Novel (La nave de los locos)*. Translated by Psiche Hughes. Columbia, LA.: Readers International, 1989.

Rimiréz, Sergio. *Adiós Muchachos: Memoria de la Revolución Sandinista*. Mexico City and Madrid: El País/ Aguilar, 1999.

Rodó, José Enrique. *Ariel*. Translation, reader's reference, and annotated bibliography by Margaret Sayers Peden. Austin: University of Texas Press, 1988.

Rumazo Gonzalez, Alfonso. *Simón Rodríguez, the Liberator's Teacher (Simón Rodríguez, Maestro del Libertador)*. Bogotá: Intermedio, 2006.

Vallejo, César. *The Black Heralds (Los Heraldos Negros)*. Translated by Barry Fogden. Lewes, UK: Allardyce, Barnett, 1995.

Vargas Llosa, Mario. *Conversation in the Cathedral (Conversación en la Catedral)*. Translated by Gregory Rabassa. New York: Harper and Row, 1975.

_____. *The Feast of the Goat (La fiesta del chivo)*. Translated by Edith Grossman. New York: Farrar, Straus, and Giroux, 2001.

Vasconcelos, José. *De Bolivarismo y Monroeismo* (Santiago de Chile, 1935). In *Latin American Social Thought*, 2nd ed., edited and translated by Harold Eugene David. Washington, DC: University Press of Washington, 1966.

_____. *The Cosmic Race (La Raza Cósmica)*. Translated with an introduction by Helen Lane. Baltimore: Johns Hopkins University Press, 1979.

Vega, Garcilaso de la. *Royal Commentaries of the Incas, and General History of Peru (Comentarios Reales de los Incas)*. Translated with an introduction by Harold V. Livermore. Foreword by Arnold J. Toynbee. Austin: University of Texas Press, 1966.

Zea, Leopoldo. *The Latin American Mind (Dos etaps del pensamiento en Hispanoamérica)*. Translated by James H. Abbott and Lowell Dunham. Norman: University of Oklahoma Press, 1963.

EIGHT

The Political Economy of Latin America

On Economics and Political Economy

In Latin America, one cannot fully understand the political game without understanding its economic underpinnings. The initial encounter between the Old World and the Americas resulted from Iberian desire for the economic advantage gained from new trade routes to the East Indies. From the onset, the Americas were an economic enterprise for European colonizers; subsequently, local elites have used the region for their gain. Since the conquest, the economic good of the masses has frequently been sacrificed for the enrichment of foreign and domestic interests. Political power and economic power have generally reinforced each other in Latin America. Those with the wealth have written the political rules. Thus, an understanding of the economics of the region enriches our understanding of its politics and vice versa.

We note that the discipline of economics studies the allocation of scarce resources—how goods and services are produced, distributed, and consumed. It has its immediate origins in the eighteenth century in works such as Adam Smith's *An Inquiry into the Nature and Causes of the Wealth of Nations* (1776). In more recent times, economists—like political scientists—often have tried to separate the study of politics and economics. Yet, this was not the original intent of Smith, his fellow political economist David Ricardo, or a subsequent student of political economy, Karl Marx. Indeed, if we go back to the original writings of Adam Smith and David Ricardo, we find that they preferred the concept of "political economy" because such an approach took into account the complexity and unity of political and economic phenomena.

Modern students of political economy thus believe that an approach that encompasses both politics and economics is much more effective in studying how scarce resources are allocated and how political values and political power affect that allocation. Given the considerable concentration and interconnection of economic and political power in Latin America, a more comprehensive approach would seem in order.

When Adam Smith was writing in the late 1700s, the dominant economic system for Great Britain, Spain, Portugal, and the American colonies was *mercantilism*, in which the state implemented a policy of increasing exports and acquiring bullion and raw materials through carefully restricted commerce. This was a politically directed policy that used state control of trade and colonization. The government exercised considerable control by regulating production, directing foreign trade and tariffs, and exploiting commerce, particularly with a European nation's colonies. Thus, Smith and Ricardo realized the fundamental role of the state and the political power that defined the policy-making process. Indeed, they hoped to induce the state to exert less control over economic interactions. As the discipline of economics evolved over the years, the difficulty in understanding economic phenomena led some commentators to refer to economics as the "dismal science." Yet, by looking at economics and politics jointly and taking into consideration historical context and sociological factors, a more comprehensive approach to understanding resource and power allocation in different nations can be achieved. This is very much the case in Latin America. Such an approach will be employed in this text.

The Latin American Economy

As in the rest of the world, economies in the Americas began as small, local spheres that were isolated from events outside their valley, village, or small region. As time and productive forces progressed, this initial isolation slowly began to break down in many regions. Civilizations such as the Olmec in eastern Mexico (1500–400 B.C.E.), the early Maya (1500 B.C.E.–900 C.E.), and the Mochica (400–1000 C.E.) in northern Peru appeared and began to tie the hitherto isolated population clusters together. As the Aztec and Incan empires grew, trade and commerce over much wider regions developed. Such economic intercourse was, however, limited to regions and did not extend far beyond the actual political entities. Latin America's integration into the world economy only began when the Europeans arrived. However, even after centuries, one could still find isolated villages and valleys that were only marginally integrated into the world economy. During colonial times and well into the twentieth century, haciendas were often near self-contained economic units with minimal contact with the outside, save the sale of one or two cash crops for national consumption or export to Europe or North America. Indeed, a few native Amazonian groups such as the Yanomami were only being integrated into the world economy as the twentieth century ended.

A substantial sector of agriculture made up of Native American and other subsistence farmers who used the bulk of their production to feed themselves and their families was only slowly integrated into the international system. These farmers' growing need for goods that they could not produce themselves led to their gradual integration into the national and international economy as they sold small amounts of a cash crop, handicraft, or their labor to landowners, plantations, or tourist enterprises. Yet, as the sad history of the Yanomami in recent times suggests, integration into the international economic system did not necessarily benefit those who were losing their isolation. Indeed, as their consumption and nutritional patterns changed, they were more likely to suffer from malnutrition.

Latin America was integrated into the world economy after 1500. Due to improvements in navigation and seafaring, Portugal and Spain established world trade routes that circumnavigated Africa and eventually came to include the Americas. From Columbus's second voyage on, the Americas were used to extract wealth for European powers—beginning with gold and silver bullion and slaves. As suggested previously, a pattern was soon established whereby land, people, and resources were used to benefit nations outside the region and for the advantage of the local European or mostly European elite, rather than the native masses. As gold and silver stocks were eventually depleted, new crops and minerals were found to export to Europe and other industrializing areas such as the United States. Indigo, cacao, brazilwood, and sugar were exported in colonial times, as were rubber, nitrates, copper, and tin in the nineteenth century and coffee, grains, beef, bananas, and petroleum in the twentieth century.

As time passed, Western and Western-trained economists came to believe in the economic doctrine of *comparative advantage*, whereby a country that is especially well endowed by climate, resources, soil, or labor can produce a product comparatively better and more efficiently than any other. Coffee exports from Colombia are an example. By specializing in the production of that product and trading it in the international market for products that other countries could produce better and more cheaply because of their comparative advantage, the producing country can maximize revenues in world trade. That is, Colombia currently produces coffee cheaply and uses the money from the sales of the coffee to buy, for example, computers and stereos from Japan, where these products are produced best and most cheaply. This view holds that it would be expensive, inefficient, and all but impossible for Japan to produce coffee and difficult and costly for Colombia to produce stereos and computers. Both countries, it is argued, gain when they specialize in the production of one or a few products that they are best able to produce. After World War II, the Latin American experience with international trade and the pioneering work of the Economic Commission for Latin America (ECLA) challenged this view. However, before this view is explored, a more thorough explanation of the production and export of commodities will be offered.

After 1500, Latin America became tied to the Western economic system that had become the basis for the international economic system in two distinct ways: first, products were exported according to the demands of the market and development in Europe and, second, the region became an outlet for European products. Much like the old South in the United States, most of the local economy revolved around the production of one crop and most of the infrastructure was geared to getting that commodity to ports where it could be loaded on boats and shipped (see Table 13). As cotton was king in the antebellum South, so sugar was king in northern Brazil, Cuba, the Dominican Republic, Haiti, and much of the rest of the Caribbean. Coffee and bananas became the prime export crop in Central America and Colombia. Economies also revolved around the extraction and export of minerals: copper in Chile, tin in Bolivia, and oil in Venezuela. Luxury goods for the landowning elite or for mine owners came from the advanced industrialized areas, as did the tools and most of the finished products that could not be made by the local blacksmith or carpenter. There are even tales of Brazilian planters sending their shirts to Europe for proper cleaning and pressing. During colonial times, manufacturing was often outlawed (in 1785 all manufacturing was prohibited in Brazil) and was usually discouraged. Thus, most of the finished products came from outside. Indeed, such practice was consistent with the free trade concepts of specialization and comparative advantage. There was very little industry in Latin America until well into the twentieth century—after World War II in most countries—and very little interregional trade existed within countries or among them, given the external orientation of the infrastructure.

TABLE 13.   Major Exports of Latin American Nations, 2003–2007 (More Than Two Commodities When Closely Ranked)

		% of Total Exports				
Country	Commodity	2003	2004	2005	2006	2007
Argentina	oil seed cake and meal and other vegetable oil residues	11.2	10.7	9.7	9.6	10.5
	petroleum products	7.3	7.7	6.9	7.9	7.5
	soya beans	6.2	5	5.7	3.8	6.2
	soya bean oil	7	6.8	5.6	6.0	7.9
	crude petroleum	7.7	6.5	6.2	5.2	...
Bolivia	natural gas	23.3	27.5	37.1	39.5	40.6
	oil seed cake and meal and other vegetable oil residues	13.1	11.8	7.5	5.2	5.0
	ores and concentrates of zinc	7.4	6.7	6.9	13.0	14.3
	crude petroleum	5.7	7.6	10.7	8.2	5.5
Brazil	iron ore and concentrates	4.7	4.9	6.2	6.5	6.6
	soya beans	5.9	5.6	4.5	4.1	4.2
	petroleum products	3.8	3.3	4.1	4.4	4.4
Chile	refined copper including remelted	22.3	27.1	26.3	30.5	31.1
	ores and concentrates of copper	12	16	15.7	20.5	20.5
Colombia	crude petroleum	18.9	17.8	19	18.6	18.5
	coal	10.6	10.5	11.5	11.5	11.1
Costa Rica	thermionic valves and tubes, transistors, etc.	...	4.5	12.2	16.9	16.4
	parts of office machinery	23.7	15.1	10.2	8.7	11.4
	medical instruments	8	8	7.5	8.1	7.3
	fresh bananas including plantains	9.7	9.3	7.3	8.9	7.7
Cuba	cigars and cheroots	...	8.7	9.7	18.6	18.1
	medicaments	...	6.0	9.3	19.2	15.9
Dominican Republic	...	...	...	...	...	...
Ecuador	crude petroleum	38.1	50.3	53.4	54.5	53.8
	fresh bananas including plantains	17.7	13.2	10.7	9.5	9.4
El Salvador	coffee, green or roasted	8.4	8.4	9.9	9.9	8.6
	medicaments	4.7	4.8	4.8	4.8	4.5
	articles of artificial plastic materials	3.2	3.6	4.6	4.4	5.0
	raw sugar, beet and cane	3.7	2.5	4	3.8	3.3
Guatemala	coffee, green or roasted	11.4	11.2	13.8	14.5	12.8
	fresh bananas including plantains	9	8.5	7.7	7.3	7.2
	raw sugar, beet, and cane	8.1	6.4	7	9.3	7.9
Haiti	...		...	...	...	...	...

(Continued)

TABLE 13. Major Exports of Latin American Nations, 2003–2007 (More Than Two Commodities When Closely Ranked)   (*Continued*)

Country	Commodity	2003	2004	2005	2006	2007
		\% of Total Exports				
Mexico	crude petroleum	10.2	11.3	13.2	13.9	13.8
	passenger motor cars, other than buses	7.2	6.3	6.3	7.0	6.9
Nicaragua	coffee, green or roasted	14.2	17.4	15.1	26.6	15.9
	meat of bovine animals, fresh, chilled, salted, dried	13.9	15.2	14.4	10.4	15.0
	crustacea and mollusks, fresh, chilled, salted, dried	12.1	8.2	7	9.5	6.4
Panama	fish, fresh, chilled or frozen	35.9	35.5	32.3	24.4	24.4
	other fresh fruit	6	8	12.3	14.5	18.1
	fresh bananas including plantains	13.2	12.2	10	9.5	10.0
	crustacea and mollusks, fresh, chilled, salted, dried	9	8.4	9.4	6.2	10.1
Paraguay	soya beans	41.6	35.6	31.3	23.0	...
	meat of bovine animals, fresh, chilled, salted, dried	4.8	9.7	16	21.5	...
	oil seed cake and meal and other vegetable oil residues	10.4	10.8	7.6	7.2	...
Peru	gold, non-monetary, unwrought, semi-manufactured or dust	23.1	18.6	17.1	16.2	14.0
	refined copper including remelted	9.1	10.5	10.7	13.0	8.8
	ores and concentrates of copper	4.8	9.1	8.4	12.6	17.2
Uruguay	meat of bovine animals, fresh, chilled, salted, dried	16.3	20.5	21.6	23.5	17.8
	leather of other bovine cattle and equine leather	10.1	8	7.1	7.4	6.6
Venezuela	crude petroleum	81	57.6	64.6	68.9	...
	petroleum products	...	23.9	20.7	18.6	...

...Data not available.

Source: Statistical Yearbook for Latin America and the Caribbean, 2008. pp. 196–218. located at: http://www.eclac.cl/publicaciones/xml/7/35437/LCG2399B_2.pdf.

A new group of merchants sprung up as part of these trade patterns. The *comprador class* made their living from selling finished goods that were imported from the outside. From importer to wholesaler to distributor to merchant, each made a considerable markup on each product sold. This tendency toward high markup was also passed on to the local merchants and was even greater among those who transported the products to remote areas where choice was very limited. The idea of mass retailing to reduce unit cost came slowly and late to Latin America. The state also charged high import taxes on imported goods, particularly if they were classified as luxuries. Monopoly was not uncommon, and personal and political ties helped secure import licenses, exclusive rights, and favorable terms. The little manufacturing that existed was usually protected by power and privilege and was not forced to compete directly with foreign products. The quality of products was often well below that of similar products on the world market.

Agrarian Production

Until the second half of the twentieth century, most of Latin America was agrarian. Traditional landed estates (*latifundios, haciendas, fazendas*) produced crops such as cotton, cattle, sugar, or coffee. Their feudal-like origins in the Iberian Peninsula often meant very traditional forms of production as well as social relations. Workers were subordinated to the *patrón* (landlord) and his family, paid poorly, generally treated miserably, and often held in debt peonage through the monopolistic sale of necessary goods at high prices at the estate store. Armed guards and control over the roads into and out of the estate were—and sometimes still are—used to further control the labor force. The original landed estates were not overly efficient, relying principally on abundant land and inexpensive labor. The earnings from the sale of cash crops were generally used more to support the upper-class lifestyle of the family than for capital improvements on the estate. The owners often spent a considerable amount of their time in their city home in the regional or national capital or in Europe and thus were absentee landowners. The more abundant small farmers, or *minifundistas*, had very little land and thus had to use very labor-intensive forms of cultivation. Nor did they have capital or credit to invest in their land. The abundance of land (often left fallow or otherwise unused) in the hands of the landed elite and the paucity of land for the *campesinos* (farmers or tenant farmers) and rural landless laborers have perpetuated the disparity of income derived from the original distribution of land and power. Of equal importance, these inequities fueled demands for land reform, economic restructuring, and occasionally revolution. In more recent times, small farmers had to increasingly turn to paid labor outside their own land (usually for large landowners or commercial farms or plantations) to survive. Pressured by debt and intense poverty, they often sell what little land they have, become rural laborers, or move to urban areas.

As the national economies developed, regions and often whole nations became what is referred to as *monoculture* or *monocrop economies*—dedicated to the production of one crop or commodity (see Table 11). As late as 1985, more than 50 percent of Colombia's official export earnings were derived from the sale of coffee on the international market. In El Salvador, the focus on coffee was even greater—67 percent. Mexico also derived some 67 percent of its export earnings from the sale of one commodity—petroleum. In Venezuela, that figure was more than 84 percent for the same product. Chile derived 46 percent of its export earnings from the sale of copper. Reliance on one export commodity was even higher in previous decades. For instance, in 1958, the Bolivian economy centered around the production of tin; 58 percent of its export earnings derived from the sale of that commodity. Since the latter part of the nineteenth century, coffee and bananas have been big in Central America. By the middle of the twentieth century in Honduras, more than 50 percent of export earnings were derived from bananas (31 percent) and coffee (23 percent). Nor do radical political transformations necessarily change the basic production of a nation. In the last 100 years, Cuba has changed from a Spanish colony to a capitalist country closely linked to and dependent on the U.S. economy to a socialist state closely tied to the economies of the Soviet Union and its Eastern European allies to a socialist state going it alone. Only in the 1990s did Cuba's dependence on sugar change dramatically. In the 1920s, roughly 75 percent of Cuba's exports were sugar. That number had grown to 83 percent in 1958 on the eve of the revolution. Thirty years of a revolutionary government that sought to diversify the country's economy saw a decline to only 79 percent as Cuba assumed the role of sugar producer to the Eastern European socialist countries at above-world-market prices. Only in the 1990s with the collapse of the Soviet Union has Cuba's dependence on sugar decreased dramatically. By 1997, sugar fell to just 47 percent of Cuba's export earnings. The dramatic drop was brought about by sharply reduced sugar production and prices and the marked increase in the role of tourism in the Cuban economy. However, the impact of centuries of monocrop dependence on sugar production places great burdens on the Cuban government as it is forced to close sugar production facilities and retrain workers for other occupations.

Foreign Investment and Enclave Production

Mining and sugar and banana plantations have often been dominated by foreign investment as they are much more capital-intensive and strongly employ U.S. and Canadian concepts of business efficiency. Initially, these foreign corporations created types of *enclaves*, where the company, upper-level management, and even middle-level management were all foreign and often lived in a special compound fenced off from local inhabitants. Tools, explosives, fertilizers, and other elements in the productive process were shipped into the country and taken directly to the mine or plantation. Products were shipped directly out of the country—often on foreign-owned railroads—and profits were sent back to corporate headquarters in New York, Boston, or London. More local people and products were eventually incorporated into local production, but ownership, upper-level management, and the end source for profit remission (the countries where the profits ended up) remained foreign. An example would be a company known to much of North America, Chiquita Banana. United Brands (formerly United Fruit Company) started as a Boston-based company founded by a New England sea captain in the 1880s. It grew to become a huge producer and exporter of bananas and one of the largest multinational corporations (MNCs) operating in Central America. It conducted operations in Guatemala, Honduras, Nicaragua, Costa Rica, and Panama and came to exercise considerable power over local governments, particularly in Honduras and Guatemala. Union movements sometimes challenged United's treatment of the workers, and bitter strikes and repression often ensued, as was the case in Guatemala and Costa Rica in the 1930s. The Central Intelligence Agency (CIA)–organized coup against the constitutional government in Guatemala in 1954 was directly related to United Fruit's pressure on the U.S. government to stop the expropriation of its unused land by the reformist Jacobo Arbenz government.

Dependency and Underdevelopment

The problems with monocrop or near monocrop are twofold. By making the entire economy dependent on one primary product, the nation's economic health becomes heavily tied to the fortunes of that product in the international market. Boom periods are often followed by devastating busts. Coffee trees planted during a time of high coffee prices often mature a few years later when the coffee price is depressed. When their beans are sold on the international market, the excess supply only depresses coffee prices further. A dip of a few cents in the international price for coffee—or sugar or copper—can mean a recession or worse in the national economy. For instance, copper prices fell to 5 cents a pound during the Great Depression and rose steadily in the 1940s, only to fall 4 cents a pound in 1950. When this occurs, the resultant worsening economic conditions often stimulate unrest and have contributed to the downfall of many presidents and other political leaders in Latin America.

THE CROP THAT COULD

Since Latin America was brought into the international system as a producer of primary products, the region has sought a product that could demand a good price on the world market and that its farmers could produce using traditional methods without making huge investments. In this way, small and large farmers could easily grow the crop and earn a good living from its sale. They needed a crop that would hold its value in the markets in the north and could be turned into a finished product in the south with minimal investments in equipment and technology. To date, the only major crop to fill that bill has been coca. Unlike any other commodity, cocaine's manufacture, transport, and distribution in the north is controlled by Latin America–based business organizations (cartels) that bring most of the profits back to their home countries. Further, the coca leaves from which cocaine is made have been part of traditional indigenous culture for more than 1,000 years and are thought to have special spiritual and medicinal qualities by large parts of the populations of Peru, Bolivia, and Ecuador. In these Andean nations, chewing the coca leaf is legal and common among indigenous peoples in the highlands. The leaves are also used to make tea or moistened and applied directly to heal sore or swollen eyes. Thus, it is difficult for the local population to conceive of many of the pernicious effects of the highly refined extract of the coca leaves—cocaine.

It is estimated by the U.S. Drug Enforcement Agency (DEA) that drug trafficking in the United States is more than a $200 billion business each year. A great deal of this figure results from the sale of powdered or crack cocaine. South America exports some 600 metric tons of cocaine each year. As with other products from the region, the primary markets are the United States, Canada, and Western Europe. Using a minimal U.S. street value price of $14,500 per kilo (per 2.2 pounds), this would mean that sales of South American cocaine earn $8.7 billion a year. A great deal of this goes back to Latin America. For instance, it is estimated that Colombia alone exports 555 metric tons (612 tons) of cocaine each year (165 metric tons made from 101,000 metric tons of Colombian coca leaves, 390 metric tons made from Peruvian and Bolivian leaves). Using the street value price, this would mean that cocaine exports for Colombia account for some $8.05 billion per year. If only half of that amount stayed in the country, that would be more than $4 billion. The official figure for all goods and services exported from Colombia was $18.0 billion in 2003 (drug sales are not reported and thus not part of official figures). About half of this resulted from the sale of coffee. Using these figures, one could deduce that the revenue for the export sale of cocaine could be as much as half that for the sale of Colombian coffee.

Unlike the production of most other Latin American products, all who work in production are relatively well paid, from the peasant who grows the leaves to the pilot who flies it into the United States. It is only as the finished product begins to be consumed in the producing countries that the full extent of the hazard becomes known. Nor do many in the producing countries see the negative effect on tourism and investment or the damage done to legitimate businesses that are crowded out of the market by enterprises that sell on a very low or negative profit margin to launder huge amounts of money.

Efforts by the U.S. government to eradicate Latin America's most lucrative export commodity have been less than successful for the above reasons and because many local and national police officers usually make less than $200 per month and are hard put to make ends meet. One way to increase income has been to accept payments for not reporting traffic or other violations or for simply looking the other way. Commanders and military officers make relatively modest salaries, as do most judges. Governmental officials and politicians seem particularly susceptible to bribes and campaign donations. Even former Colombian president Ernesto Samper was accused of taking a large campaign donation from a drug cartel. The corruption has also spread into transshipment points in Central America, the Caribbean, and especially Mexico. In that country, drug-induced corruption has spread widely. Many police officers, upper-level officials, military officers, and governmental officials have been indicted for accepting bribes. In 1988, Mexico's drug czar was removed from office and indicted for being on a Mexican cartel's payroll. Throughout these countries, the amounts of money available to bribe or otherwise induce local and national officials to ignore certain activities or give intelligence on impending government actions is many times more than most officials make in a year, if not a lifetime. The temptation is too great for many; and for those who will not be bought, there are always other ways. Indeed, many police and other public officials are given a choice: *plata o plomo* (money or lead). Others are assassinated outright.

Attempts to organize producers into international cartels or producers' associations have generally had only the most minimal effect on the stabilization or maintenance of commodity prices. Attempts have been made to organize international associations of coffee producers to maintain the price of coffee. In the early 1960s, the International Coffee Agreement was signed and, later, the International Coffee Organization was established. Production quotas were assigned to all producing members in an effort to control the supply of coffee and thus the price. However, in part because of the resistance of African nations, who preferred to set their own production quotas, these efforts failed; and coffee continues to be subject to market fluctuations. The Organization of Petroleum Exporting Countries (OPEC), of which Venezuela was a founding member, was for many years the only producers' association that was able to influence the price of its product. Yet, by the late 1990s, petroleum prices had fallen significantly. These falling prices helped put considerable strain on the long-dominant Democratic Action and Independent Political Electoral Organizing Committee (COPEI) parties in Venezuela. As Venezuelan petroleum prices fell to a low of less than $10 per barrel at the end of 1998 (from a high of $35 a barrel in the early 1980s), the presidential election campaigns of candidates from these parties wilted in the face of the newly organized Patriotic Pole coalition formed to back Hugo Chávez. Both parties even abandoned their candidates in the last two weeks of the electoral campaign to back the candidate of the newly formed Project Venezuela movement. However, the opposition candidate and political outsider could not be stopped. Former coup leader Chávez won with 57 percent of the vote. Fortunately for his administration, prices for oil again rose to $30 a barrel by the second half of 2000, a result of the new OPEC agreement. However, it is not yet clear how long the OPEC agreement can sustain higher prices. Since 2001, driven in part by increased global demand, especially from China, world oil prices have soared, reaching $50 per barrel in 2005 and over $100 per barrel in 2008. This provided an economic base for many domestic and international programs launched by President Hugo Chávez.

Many national leaders and thinkers have wondered why Latin America has remained less developed than its neighbor to the north, the United States. Most Latin American nations have abundant resources and sufficient land. Gradually, national leaders and scholars have learned the same bitter lessons that U.S., Canadian, and many European farmers have found to be all too true: If unprotected by government price controls, prices for primary products fluctuate greatly and rise very slowly. Like the farmers, Latin Americans have produced more and more at ever greater efficiency but have received comparatively less and less for it—while paying increasing prices for cars, machinery, and other finished goods from industrial, more developed national and international centers.

Raúl Prebisch and the ECLA

Such an economic understanding by the Latin Americans was stimulated greatly by the pioneering work of ECLA and its director, Raúl Prebisch. Prebisch, an Argentine-born and -educated economist, had previously held high-level economic positions in the Argentine government. In the late 1940s, he gathered a team of Latin American economists at the Santiago, Chile, headquarters of ECLA. He and his fellow economists made extensive studies of the prices for primary products exported by Latin America and compared them to those of the finished goods that were imported. Their studies indicated that the relationship between these product prices, or the terms of trade, were unfavorable to Latin America. Posited as the now-famous *Prebisch thesis*, the theory argued that there is a structural tendency for Latin American terms of trade to deteriorate over time because of the concentration of exports in primary commodities. As suggested by Figure 3, over time the price for finished goods rises much faster than the price for primary goods.

These findings, which were initially considered controversial by Western economists from industrialized nations, called into question the argument for specialization in the production of any one primary product in the international market. Interestingly, later studies by the Economic Commission for Africa of the United Nations Economic and Social Council found that the terms of trade for African primary exports vis-à-vis finished imports from Europe and the United States were also unfavorable to Africa. ECLA's findings were one of the principal reasons that the organization so strongly advocated import substitution industrialization (ISI) for Latin America.

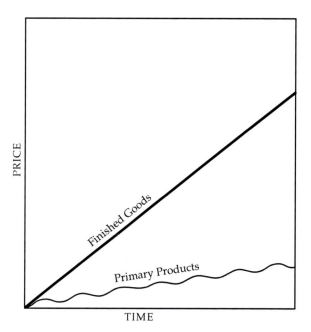

FIGURE 3.   Finished goods and primary products graph.

Dependency Theory

ECLA's work and the Prebisch thesis were fascinating examples of how Latin American economists working from a perspective grounded in their own reality could see how their relationship with the industrialized center (Europe and United States) was less than satisfactory. This gave great impetus not only to new economic policy direction in the Latin American nations but also to the development of a whole new way to view Latin American development—*dependency theory*. The ECLA studies were symbolic of the post–World War II decolonization process and the subsequent willingness to assign negative consequences to the relations imposed by actual or formal colonial masters on the development of native peoples. This also represented a significant break with metropolitan theorists and economists who saw underdevelopment as inherent to Latin America and other Third-World nations and caused primarily by economic, social, or cultural patterns that had developed within those societies.

The late 1940s also provided alternative explanations for the lack of development in Latin America, Africa, and Asia. Basing their understanding in large part on V. I. Lenin's classic Marxist work *Imperialism, the Highest Stage of Capitalism* (1916), scholars familiar with this Marxist analysis argued that the colonies were used as places to invest surplus capital and sell goods from the colonizing countries and as sources of cheap raw materials and cheap labor. Indeed, according to this view, the high return on investment and low prices paid for raw materials and labor meant that value was extracted from the colonized countries and exported to the developed countries, where it further fueled their development. It was further argued that such surplus value was the difference between what was paid and what it would have cost if fair value had been paid at the industrial center. As with the initial taking of gold bullion in the colonial era, this extracted wealth helped continue the impoverishment of the colonized country and made the colonial country rich.

This thesis was updated by the African leader and intellectual Kwame Nkrumah. The first president of Ghana and intellectual author of Pan-Africanism argued that imperialism had taken on a new but equally pernicious form—neocolonialism. In his work *Neocolonialism, the Last Stage of Imperialism* (1965), Nkrumah argued that former colonizers now controlled their former colonies and other former colonies by less direct means. They established economic spheres of influence, pound or franc areas where the former colonial currency and its financial sector dominated; dominated the area by investment and a foreign economic presence; and bought the same raw materials at the same prices and sold the same finished goods. Further, the former colonizers were aided in this endeavor by native politicians and pro-Western elements of the native bourgeoisie, who often did the bidding of the former colonial masters and generally helped maintain their neocolonial dominance in the face of any radical reformers or revolutionaries who attempted to change the subordinate nature of this relationship. The Latin American intellectual Eduardo Galeano labeled this group "the Commission bourgeoisie." Foreign aid and missionaries were but more subtle means of continuing neocolonial control. Political and economic control was exercised in a more indirect way than under direct colonialism, but the effect was very similar for the native people. The title of a book by the Guyanese intellectual Walter Rodney is most evocative of this view, *How Europe Underdeveloped Africa*. Such views clearly helped shape the intellectual climate in the Americas. Also of note was Paul Baran's seminal work, *The Political Economy of Growth*.

Other advocates of dependency theory argued that Latin America was maintained in a neocolonial state under the tutelage of the United States and European powers. Given that the Latin American nations had been independent much longer than the African states, the mechanisms of control were different and often more subtle. Thus, one finds more discussion of cultural imperialism in Latin America. It is often asserted that economic relations, foreign aid and diplomacy, and the media and other forms of control were employed to keep Latin America subordinate. Neocolonialism was thus manifest throughout Latin American society, as could be seen in U.S. movies, television series, religious evangelization, the spread of Western consumption patterns, the canonization of Mickey Mouse and Donald Duck, and the mass pilgrimage to Miami and Florida's Disney World by Latin America's elites and many from the middle class.

Andre Gunder Frank's *Capitalism and Underdevelopment in Latin America* brought dependency theory to the fore. As suggested earlier, Frank and other dependency theorists argued that the relationship between the developing area (satellite or periphery) and the developed area (center or metropol) was one of dependence. Thus, the *dependentistas* argued that underdevelopment in Latin America resulted from the region being brought into the capitalist system to satisfy the economic needs of the metropolitan powers. Decisions as to when and where to develop mines, plantations, or infrastructure were made according to the requirements of the metropolitan powers, not the Latin American nations. From colonial times on, economic decisions responded more to the needs of the industrializing center than to the needs of the agrarian periphery. Over time, the national economic systems in Latin America thus became dependent on the production and export of primary products to Europe and the United States (the industrialized center or metropol). The economic and political elites that emerged also became tied to this system and dependent on it for their well-being. Although they did not accumulate as much wealth per product unit as did their counterparts in the metropolitan nations, they were able to exploit the native labor force and take advantage of the abundant access to cheap land and minerals to accumulate their wealth. As more foreign corporations arrived to exploit these factors of production themselves, the national upper class often worked with or for them and became even more closely tied to the economic interests of the center.

It is argued, then, that the economic development and even the political autonomy of Latin American nations became dependent on the outside forces of the metropolitan powers. They did not possess full independence and, hence, were dependent on and subordinate to outside forces. Latin American underdevelopment was thus a result of the exploitation and control of forces outside the region. As Latin America had been incorporated into the international capitalist system, it had lost its wealth and autonomy. The plundering of the gold and silver of the region was symbolic of how the capitalist system had served the interests of the Latin American nations. Indeed, capitalism and economic penetration by the metropolitan capitalist powers were responsible for a great deal of Latin American underdevelopment. Frank and others argued that even the feudalistic *latifundios* had been incorporated into the international system and were part of the worldwide spread of capitalism. Latin America's problems thus resulted from the nature of capitalism itself and the way it subordinated classes in nations and even developing nations themselves. Some further expanded this concept to argue that the capital cities in the region acted as metropolitan areas that extracted value from the peripheral countryside.

The dependency perspective also contradicted what had become a common view about Latin American economies. The *dual-economy* view held that the economies were divided into two sectors. One was comprised of near-feudal social and economic relations on the *latifundio* and in landowner-sharecropper relations and subsistence agriculture; the other was centered in the modern export sector that tended to employ modern capitalist practices. Each national economy was divided in two, one traditional and feudal-like and the other modern and capitalist. The dependistas saw only one economy well integrated into the world capitalist system. Frank and the early dependency writers thus focused on external linkages and the international capitalist system in particular to explain Latin underdevelopment.

There were, however, later dependency writers who enriched this perspective by also looking more closely at the specific historical, social, and economic configurations of nations such as Brazil and Argentina. They examined such internal factors as class and intraclass competition to further explain the complex phenomenon of development in the region. Foremost among these was the Brazilian social scientist Fernando Henrique Cardoso, who, together with Chilean sociologist Enzo Faletto, wrote *Dependency and Development in Latin America* in 1971. The more subtle analysis of internal class formations and historical development patterns and the role of multinational corporations made this one of the most useful analyses of the Latin American reality.

Import Substitution Industrialization

As these new perspectives stimulated a rethinking of how development should be pursued, policies began to change more rapidly. ECLA recommended ISI as a way to reduce the importation of finished goods. From the 1930s on, several of the larger nations had begun to focus on what became known as *inward-looking development*, reasoning that the path to development was through developing internal economic capacity, including industrial capacity, while continuing to export primary products. ECLA now recommended strongly that internal industrialization be pursued. This would mean that less of the foreign exchange earned through the sale of primary products would be expended on finished goods and more capital would stay in the country. In this way, the negative effects of the terms of trade would be minimized. Latin American domestic manufacturing was officially and continually encouraged. A growing number of new industries began to produce for the domestic market. Sporadic industrialization had occurred in some of the large countries, such as Mexico, Argentina, and Brazil—particularly during World Wars I and II and even the Great Depression, when Latin America was cut off from its external supplies of finished goods. This time, however, ISI became official policy and was pursued vigorously through increasing domestic manufacturing. Domestic entrepreneurs were encouraged to set up new industries and expand old ones, and MNCs were invited to set up plants to supply the domestic market. Even car companies set up assembly plants, as was the case with Volkswagen in Mexico and Brazil and Fiat in Argentina. Chrysler also began assembling cars in Latin America and was joined by Toyota in the 1970s. Panasonic, Motorola, and other electronics companies began to manufacture in Latin America, as did most of the major pharmaceutical companies and even food processors like Nabisco and Nestlé.

Attempts were made to control the national content of the components used in the finished product, the percent of nationals in middle- and upper-level management, and the amount of profit that could be remitted to the home office of the MNC each year. These attempts to assert national sovereignty met with varying success and were often skillfully circumvented by sophisticated multinationals. From the late 1940s on, Mexico required that 51 percent of all companies doing business in Mexico be owned by Mexican nationals or Mexican corporations (the dropping of this provision after the North American Free Trade Agreement [NAFTA] caused some controversy in Mexico). There was some nationalization of foreign corporations by Latin American governments (Bolivian tin mines after 1954, foreign assets in Cuba after 1960, copper mines in Chile in the 1960s and 1970s, and the International Petroleum Company in Peru in 1968), but the general trend was for more and more foreign investment to flock to the region. This wave of investment was particularly strong after military coups in Brazil in 1964 and Chile in 1973. Manufacturing and MNCs became part of the economic panorama in Latin America. Smaller and relatively less developed nations such as Guatemala, El Salvador, Costa Rica, and even Honduras experienced increases in manufacturing and the arrival of MNCs that produced finished products. The formation of the Central American Common Market in 1959 attracted new manufacturing plants, as was the case with Firestone in Costa Rica and Van Heusen shirts in Honduras. The trend was also encouraged by U.S. government policies beginning with the Alliance for Progress programs after 1961.

A modern textile factory in Latin America. *(Glow Images/Alamy Images RF)*

Export Orientation

Industrial production was initially destined for internal national markets or those of neighboring nations who had entered into an agreement such as the Central American Common Market (1960), the Latin American Free Trade Association (1960), or the Andean Pact (1967). This was a great stimulus for the industrialization of Latin America; for example, Mexico and Brazil further developed their own steel and automobile industries. The nature of production also changed. Domestic manufactured products became more similar to those manufactured for Western consumer taste. Gradually, as the domestic demand for manufactures faltered, Latin American nations began to take on an externally oriented perspective. Hereafter, manufacturing and crop diversification would be done with an eye toward external sales as well as the domestic market.

The influx of international capital, more sophisticated technology, and the opening up of internal markets made for more and better manufactured goods. The entrance of the MNCs drove some local producers out of business, and others were forced to upgrade the quality of their products. Of those local producers who survived, many soon realized that they too could enter the global market with their more sophisticated products. Nor were the products limited to those produced by sophisticated MNCs and high-technology national producers. Other domestic industries also grew: weaving and handcraft in Guatemala, wine in Chile, shoes in Brazil. Indeed, the Brazilian shoe industry eventually became one of the largest producers of footwear on the world market. As another way of gaining more foreign exchange, many countries encouraged the production of nontraditional exports, not only producing more finished goods that could be exported but also diversifying production of primary products. Such was the case in Colombia, where a vigorous export industry in flowers developed. As this process occurred over the 1960s, 1970s, and 1980s, Latin America became more integrated into the international economic system, primarily through ties to industrialized capitalist nations—the United States, Western Europe, and later Japan.

The transformation of Latin American economies can be seen in the following:

- More extensive use of capital-intensive technology.
- Increased training in manufacturing-related engineering and for those who employed and replicated technology in capital-intensive techniques used in advanced industrial nations. Many engineering students were sent to the United States or Europe and brought back advanced capital-intensive technology with them.
- Lack of development of appropriate technology that could take advantage of Latin America's abundant and inexpensive labor supply.
- The spread of Western-style consumerism to the upper, middle, and lower classes.
- State intervention to encourage and protect export-oriented domestic industries and sometimes to nationalize them or, as in the case of Brazil, to set up key industries such as aircraft production.

- The growth of middle sectors who worked in management and technologically sophisticated aspects of production (e.g., engineers, skilled technicians, accountants).
- The growth of an industrial proletariat.

Increasing Foreign Debt and the Debt Crisis

Newer plants created in Latin America were often copies or near copies of standard plants from a particular MNC, although often using the less advanced technology and relatively outdated standards that operated in the developed world, where capital was plentiful and labor was expensive. The employment created for such plants was modest, but the investment in new machinery and patented processes was not. This type of production used up local sources of capital quickly. Thus, even as there were more goods to export, it became necessary to borrow money from abroad to satisfy these capital needs. The growing demand for Western consumer goods also meant that more and more products were being imported to keep consumers satisfied. This also used up scarce foreign exchange. These two processes and the acquisition of expensive military hardware by countries like Peru, Chile, Brazil, and Argentina meant that more external borrowing was necessary to compensate for the net outflows of funds. This caused what came to be called "debt-led growth." The result of this outward-directed orientation and debt-led growth was that the external indebtedness of Latin American nations began to grow. Brazil is a prime example of this.

Prior to 1970, most of the Latin American external debt was owed to individual states or to multilateral lending institutions such as the Inter-American Development Bank. Interest rates were minimal. The petroleum crisis of 1973–1974 changed this. First, it meant that those Latin American nations that were net importers of petroleum were forced to use more of their foreign exchange to pay for the hydrocarbons they imported. Second, it meant that petroleum-producing countries began to amass significant foreign exchange surpluses and needed to find places to invest these funds. Most of these petrodollars ended up in Western banks, which soon had more than ample funds for lending but, because of the stagnation in developed countries, could not find borrowers in those countries. Large banks like Chase Manhattan and Bank of America began to make large loans readily available to private and public borrowers in Latin America. These factors combined to radically increase the external debt in Latin America, which jumped from less than $30 billion in 1970 to more than $230 billion in 1980. By the beginning of the 1980s, debt service payments alone were some $18 billion per year. Drops in commodity prices and world recessions in the 1980s did not improve this picture. Economic growth slowed in most countries and shrank in a few. Indeed, the 1980s were referred to as the "lost decade" because growth rates were so abysmal in most of Latin America, for many countries only 1 or 2 percent per year. A few countries even experienced negative growth rates.

Mexico and Brazil experienced high levels of economic growth in the 1960s and 1970s; each had periods of economic growth during this time that were referred to as economic "miracles." Both, however, continued to borrow from abroad. This situation was aggravated by OPEC-induced increases in petroleum prices in the 1970s and early

1980s. The Latin American nations' indebtedness grew, and both Mexico and Brazil acquired external debts in excess of $110 billion (see Table 14). By 1982, Mexico declared that it could not meet all the loan payments that were due. This caused considerable concern in the international investment community. Large banks in the United States were particularly concerned and sought relief from the Reagan administration. After some discussion, the U.S. government tendered an emergency loan package to Mexico to stop it from defaulting. Other countries came close to defaulting as well; Peru, under the Alan García presidency, even declared a moratorium on repaying its external debt. The prospect of widespread default created near panic among many large banks in the United States and Europe since many of them had made very high percentages of their loans (mostly unsecured) to Latin American public and private institutions. Since a large portion of their capital had been loaned out and could not be called back, they were, in bankers' language, "overexposed." There was also talk of the Latin American nations joining together and negotiating terms of debt repayment or even refusing to pay altogether. Despite official encouragement from Cuba and Fidel Castro, this movement never materialized. Instead, Western nations and international financial institutions such as the International Monetary Fund (IMF) and the World Bank were instrumental in renegotiating more favorable repayment packages, reducing interest

TABLE 14.   Total Disbursed External Debt 2001, 2003, 2005, 2007

Country	Amount (year-end balance in millions of dollars)			
	2001	2003	2005	2007
Argentina	140,214	145,583	113,518	123,196
Bolivia	4,412	5,042	4,942	5,360
Brazil	226,067	235,415	169,450	193,219
Chile	38,032	41,179	45,014	54,146
Colombia	39,109	38,193	38,350	44,746
Costa Rica	3,243	3,753	3,626	8,348
Cuba	10,893	11,000	5,898	8,908
Dominican Republic	4,177	5,899	6,756	7,566
Ecuador	14,376	16,586	17,237	17,538
El Salvador	3,148	4,687	4,976	9,059
Guatemala	4,100	4,548	3,723	4,226
Guyana	1,193	1,048	1,094	718
Haiti	1,189	1,287	1,345	1,628
Honduras	4,757	5,122	5,082	3,036
Jamaica	4,146	4,192	5,372	6,122
Mexico	144,527	140,555	127,089	124,580
Nicaragua	6,374	6,596	5,348	3,384
Panama	6,263	6,502	7,580	8,275
Paraguay	2,652	2,871	2,761	3,087
Peru	27,195	29,708	28,605	31,360
Trinidad and Tobago	1,638	1,526	1,281	1,278
Uruguay	5,855	8,626	11,441	12,218
Venezuela	35,398	38,043	47,233	52,949

Source: Statistical Yearbook of Latin America. located at: http://www.eclac.org/cgi-bin/getProd.asp?xml=/
deype/agrupadores_xml/aes250.xml&xsl=/agrupadores_xml/agrupa_listado-i.xsl&base=/tpl-i/top-bottom.xsl.

rates, and even formulating debt-for-nature agreements, where debt is forgiven if environmental protection is guaranteed for parts of the national territory.

As the Latin American nations became even more dependent on external sources to solve their financial problems, the role of international financial institutions such as the IMF, the World Bank, and the Inter-American Development Bank became ever stronger. This was also true for the role of the Agency for International Development (AID) of the U.S. Department of State. In addition to the growing importance of AID, the United States and its Western capitalist allies were able to exercise a tremendous amount of control over decision making in these international bodies. Further, pursuant to the victory of the conservative economic policy embodied in Thatcherism in the United Kingdom and the Reagan revolution in the United States, the policies advocated by AID and the international financial institutions became ever more conservative. Indeed, the free market free trade ideas of Milton Friedman and the Chicago School soon began to appear as policy recommendations.

Structural Adjustment and the Move to Neoliberalism

As conditions for continued borrowing, international financial institutions began to first suggest and then insist on economic structural adjustments to the national economies. Indeed, more and more of the loans were conditional on such adjustments. It was argued that the Latin American nations must take the bitter pill of austerity through these structural adjustments. Government costs and inflation had to be reduced through such measures as fiscal reform, monetary restraint, cutting back jobs and services in the public sector, and stopping government subsidies for basic goods or petroleum. Likewise, wages were to be held down as a way of checking inflation and keeping wage costs at bay in the ever more important export industries. Orthodox economic thought became more widely accepted, and the ISI advocated by ECLA fell from favor.

As Eastern European socialism weakened and then began to disappear in the late 1980s and as the Soviet Union's breakup moved the world from the Cold War and a strong bipolar system to one dominated by Western capitalism and the United States, economic policy recommendations became ever more dominated by the orthodox capitalist economic thinking advocated by the conservative governments in power in the United States and United Kingdom. Keynesian economics and its advocacy of state intervention in the market economy and deficit spending to stimulate business activity was no longer in favor. Rather, the free market and free trade ideas championed by economists like Milton Friedman became popular. Indeed, the conservative economic thought of opponents of state intervention and planning, such as Friederich A. von Hayek, became influential. By the early 1990s, such thought was dominant in the IMF, the World Bank, the Inter-American Development Bank, and AID. Since the headquarters of all of these organizations are located in Washington, D.C., this thinking became referred to as the "Washington Consensus."

Neoliberalism

In Latin America, this type of economic policy was characterized as "neoliberalism" because it seemed to be a new version of the classical eighteenth-century economic liberalism of Adam Smith and other earlier economic liberals. Classical economic liberals believe that the magic hand of the market, not government control or trade barriers, should regulate the economy. Indeed, political liberalism in nineteenth-century Latin America included a belief in increasing commerce through free trade.

KEY COMPONENTS OF NEOLIBERALISM AND THE WASHINGTON CONSENSUS

1. Radically reducing government size and spending by cutting back on government jobs and programs—especially social programs.
2. Fiscal and monetary reform.
3. Minimizing government regulation in economic matters (deregulation).
4. Liberalizing commerce through the reduction and eventual elimination of all tariff barriers and trade restrictions.
5. Opening up the national economy to foreign investment and allowing the free flow of capital.
6. Privatization of government-owned corporations, industries, agencies, and utilities.
7. Eliminating government subsidies for essential consumer goods, such as bread or tortillas and petroleum products.

Globalization

Other factors were at work as well. The success that a variety of MNCs, such as Nike, had with moving all or part of their production to plants they established in Asia became widely known. More and more assembly plants, or *maquiladoras*, were established first just across the U.S. border in northern Mexico, then spread throughout the Caribbean basin and into some South American countries, such as Ecuador. Electronic components, the unsewn pieces of cloth that make up clothing, and other unassembled parts in other industries were manufactured in the United States, Japan, Western Europe, and even Taiwan and assembled in Latin America in an ever growing number of *maquiladoras*. Regular manufacturing for export production was also encouraged, and multinationals came to Latin America in increasing numbers to take advantage of low wages, lax labor and environmental protection, minimal regulation and taxation, and generally sympathetic governments. Free trade zones were also set up, where companies could be completely free of any governmental regulation. The process of neoliberal globalization, it was argued, would be beneficial for all; thus, all were expected to expedite its implementation.

As the world became increasingly subject to economic globalization, capital and production plants became ever more fluid, moving freely from one country to another according to who offered the most favorable terms. The new wisdom was for each nation to produce everything it could as efficiently as possible and to export as much of it as possible to maximize export earnings. This allowed the nation to keep up with external debt payments, pay for an expanding number and amount of imports, and hopefully have some foreign exchange earnings left over to add to foreign exchange reserves. The national borders were to be open to imports so that national consumers could get the lowest prices on the goods they consumed. If some national industries could not compete with the increased number and variety of imported goods then so be it. They should be closed and capital and labor should be shifted to those industries that could compete and export their goods.

Privatization and Neoliberalism

The new mantra was Globalize, Globalize, Globalize; and in Latin America it was combined with the specifically neoliberal mantra of Privatize, Privatize, Privatize. As suggested earlier, mines had been nationalized in Bolivia and Chile, and considerable state-owned industry existed in Brazil and elsewhere. Most of the states owned all or part of the national telephone and telecommunication companies, and many had autonomous state-owned agencies, such as the Peruvian national fishing company PescaPeru. In Mexico, all aspects of petroleum production had been nationalized since 1936; the resulting state-owned enterprise, Pemex, is one of the largest national companies. It was also thought that it might be possible to privatize some governmental infrastructure, such as new highways. Thus, much new superhighway construction in countries like Brazil and Mexico was financed by private capital and/or run by private companies through their direct administration of the roadways and collection of tolls.

The movement toward privatization was especially strong in Latin America because state-owned entities had generally been little more efficient than the government bureaucracies themselves. Often, they had been subject to cronyism, bloated employment practices to accommodate payback for political or personal support, and corruption. Thus, one could easily wait up to two years for the installation of a phone line (unless phone company employees were "motivated" through monetary inducements) or suffer frequent loss of electricity or water service.

As Latin American nations returned to international lending agencies (the IMF in particular) for additional short- and long-term loans, they found that the imposed neoliberal conditions (conditionality) included the privatization of major public enterprises, such as the telephone companies. They were to be sold or auctioned off, and a substantial part of the proceeds were to be used to pay off part of the external debt. This led to increasing pressure on the political leaders to sell off these enterprises (usually to foreign corporations or consortia) to meet the conditions of the loans. However, utility rates were generally very low for consumers, and thousands of jobs were at stake. Not surprisingly, there were substantial popular and political mobilizations, union strikes, and job actions to resist the sales. The mobilization to protest the privatization of the water company in Cochabamba, Bolivia was one of the most notable. Nonetheless, many of these entities were partially or wholly sold off, frequently at bargain prices. The lucrative entities that made good profits attracted considerable investment interest and sold rapidly, whereas those that lost money and were government liabilities went begging for buyers. This in turn led to the perception on the part of some that decisions were once again being made because of foreign influence and for the benefit of foreign corporations, not the national populace. As will be discussed later, these and other factors led to growing political discontent and new political mobilizations. Latin America soon became a place where MNCs could go to reduce their production costs. By the early twenty-first century, more and more manufacturing jobs from the United States were moving to Latin America.

Regional Integration, NAFTA, and the Globalization Process

In 1826, Simón Bolívar convened the Congress of Panama to foster the uniting of Spanish America into one political and economic entity. He dreamed of a united Latin America to rival the growing power of the United States in North America, but his proposal failed. Others had visions of unity in Central America. From 1824 to 1840, the Central American states that were part of the Captaincy General of Guatemala in colonial times (Guatemala, El Salvador, Honduras, Nicaragua, and Costa Rica) were united in the Central American Federation. However, the Central Americans could not remain united. Their shattered dreams of unity lay dormant until after the Europeans began a process of regional economic integration out of the ashes of World War II. The beginnings of a united Europe and the creation of the European Common Market in 1957 proved to be a catalyst for Latin American efforts at economic integration.

Encouraged by the ECLA and the United States, the Central American Common Market was formed in 1960. Its common tariff walls were to encourage import substitution and internally oriented economic growth within the region. Promoted more by Latin American initiative, the Latin American Free Trade Association was also founded in 1960, and the Andean Pact (1967) was forged with the same expectations. However, internal political pressure and vested national economic interests made it difficult to reduce tariffs among the respective member nations. None of these pacts had any appreciable success. The next stage in regional integration was not forged until the era of globalization.

In 1989, President George H. Bush launched the Enterprise for the Americas Initiative. This plan envisioned a common area of economic cooperation for the Americas extending from the frozen north in Canada to Tierra del Fuego in southern South America. All the Americas would move toward one gigantic economic zone that could easily rival a united Europe. Unlike the European Union, however, no attempt would be made to gradually integrate while ensuring that all member states had similar costs of production and approximately the same labor and political rights. Under this plan, Canada and the United States would combine with their less powerful sister republics in the south on the assumption that free trade and increased commerce could cure all ills and benefit all member nations. The first concrete action in this process developed among the United States, Mexico, and

Canada. **NAFTA** was signed in 1992 and went into effect on January 1, 1994, follow-ing ratification by the legislatures of the three governments. Building on a bilateral U.S.–Canadian agreement initiated in 1989, NAFTA created one of the two largest trading blocs in the world, with a population of 370 million and a combined eco-nomic production of $6 trillion, a worthy rival to the European Union. NAFTA also removed most restrictions on cross-border investment and allowed the free flow of goods and services. All tariffs on goods traded among the three were to be elimi-nated by 2005. The agreement was vigorously pursued by the Salinas administra-tion in Mexico in the hope that increased investment in Mexico and a greater North American market for its products would stimulate the Mexican economy and cre-ate jobs for the millions of unemployed and underemployed Mexicans. In contrast, the U.S. labor movement feared that thousands of jobs would head south, where wage rates were approximately one-tenth of what they were in the United States and labor rights and safety regulations were minimal. The movement convinced presidential candidate Bill Clinton to oppose the agreement in the 1992 election campaign. However, once in office, President Clinton bowed to pressure from large U.S. corporations that wanted to set up more factories and retail stores in Mexico and investment firms and business interests that saw lucrative investment oppor-tunities. Clinton led a difficult but successful battle for ratification of the agreement that had been negotiated by President Bush. After the agreement went into effect, many more U.S. firms moved their plants to Mexico to set up regular factories and *maquiladoras*. They took thousands of jobs with them, although some new jobs were created in the United States to supply the now open Mexican market. There was, however, a net loss of U.S. jobs. Ford, General Motors, and Chrysler set up factories in Mexico to manufacture cars for Mexico, the United States, and Canada that were not only put together locally but also made mostly from parts manufactured in Mexico, including the engines and transmissions.

In Mexico, many small- and medium-size industries and businesses were not able to compete with their larger U.S. or Canadian counterparts and went bank-rupt. Mexican agriculture in general and corn farmers, more specifically, were especially hard hit as they were unable to compete with heavily subsidized U.S. agriculture. These and related events caused considerable political turmoil in all three countries. In Mexico, they led to charges that the Mexican elite was selling out the country to U.S. corporate interests, especially since most of the jobs created were at or around the minimum wage of less than U.S. $4 per day. Many in both Canada and the United States feared that their political leaders entered into an agreement that will be more a net exporter of jobs than a bonanza for the common people. As with the general process of globalization and the implementation of neoliberal reforms elsewhere, the benefits of growth have been distributed very unevenly (see Table 15). As labor, political groups, and mass organizations have mobilized against the negative effects of many of these changes in a variety of countries, including Venezuela, Ecuador, Costa Rica, Nicaragua, Argentina, and Brazil, political leaders have felt internal pressure against neoliberal changes while still being pressured by the international financial institutions and the United States to make them.

Buoyed by the successful implementation of NAFTA at the beginning of 1994, the Clinton administration promoted and hosted the Summit of the Americas in Miami in

TABLE 15. U.S. Income Inequality: Household Shares of Aggregate Income by Fifths of the Income Distribution: 1967–2006

Year	Lowest	Second	Middle	Fourth	Highest	Top 5 Percent
2006	3.4	8.6	14.5	22.9	50.5	22.3
2005	3.4	8.6	14.6	23.0	50.4	22.2
2004	3.4	8.7	14.7	23.2	50.1	21.8
2003	3.4	8.7	14.8	23.4	49.8	21.4
2002	3.5	8.8	14.8	23.3	49.7	21.7
2001	3.5	8.7	14.6	23.0	50.1	22.4
2000*	3.6	8.9	14.8	23.0	49.8	22.1
1999	3.6	8.9	14.9	23.2	49.4	21.5
1998	3.6	9.0	15.0	23.2	49.2	21.4
1997	3.6	8.9	15.0	23.2	49.4	21.7
1996	3.6	9.0	15.1	23.3	49.0	21.4
1995	3.7	9.1	15.2	23.3	48.7	21.0
1994	3.6	8.9	15.0	23.4	49.1	21.2
1993	3.6	9.0	15.1	23.5	48.9	21.0
1992	3.8	9.4	15.8	24.2	46.9	18.6
1991	3.8	9.6	15.9	24.2	46.5	18.1
1990	3.8	9.6	15.9	24.0	46.6	18.5
1989	3.8	9.5	15.8	24.0	46.8	18.9
1988	3.8	9.6	16.0	24.2	46.3	18.3
1987	3.8	9.6	16.1	24.3	46.2	18.2
1986	3.8	9.7	16.2	24.3	46.1	18.0
1985	3.9	9.8	16.2	24.4	45.6	17.6
1984	4.0	9.9	16.3	24.6	45.2	17.1
1983	4.0	9.9	16.4	24.6	45.1	17.0
1982	4.0	10.0	16.5	24.5	45.0	17.0
1981	4.1	10.1	16.7	24.8	44.3	16.5
1980	4.2	10.2	16.8	24.7	44.1	16.5
1979	4.1	10.2	16.8	24.6	44.2	16.9
1978	4.2	10.2	16.8	24.7	44.1	16.8
1977	4.2	10.2	16.9	24.7	44.0	16.8
1976	4.3	10.3	17.0	24.7	43.7	16.6
1975	4.3	10.4	17.0	24.7	43.6	16.5
1974	4.3	10.6	17.0	24.6	43.5	16.5
1973	4.2	10.4	17.0	24.5	43.9	16.9
1972	4.1	10.4	17.0	24.5	43.9	17.0
1971	4.1	10.6	17.3	24.5	43.5	16.7
1970	4.1	10.8	17.4	24.5	43.3	16.6
1969	4.1	10.9	17.5	24.5	43.0	16.6
1968	4.2	11.1	17.6	24.5	42.6	16.3
1967	4.0	10.8	17.3	24.2	43.6	17.2

*after the implementation of a 28,000-household sample question.

Source: U.S. Census Bureau, Selected Measures of Income Dispersion: 1967–2006. http://www.census.gov/hhes/www/income/histinc/h02ar.html.

December 1994. Attended by thirty-four heads of state, with the conspicuous absence of Fidel Castro, it was the first such hemispheric gathering since 1967. The 1994 meeting represented an assurance from the United States to Latin America that it would not be neglected in the twenty-first century. The primary achievement of the meeting was to create a framework of negotiations for the creation of a hemisphere-wide customs union, the Free Trade Area of the Americas (**FTAA**) by 2005.

Clinton's statement that the gathering was "a watershed in the history of the continent" was overblown. As a first step, Chile was to be integrated quickly into NAFTA, then Clinton—with renewed "fast-track" negotiating authority from the U.S. Congress—would lay the groundwork for the FTAA. In the years since the Miami summit, the prospects for hemispheric economic integration have dimmed. President Clinton failed to get renewed negotiating authority. As a result, Chile's entry into NAFTA was not secured. It should also be noted that the same type of concentration of income in the hands of the economic elite that has characterized Latin America also began to be noticed in the United States (see Table 15).

Difficulties for the FTAA project and the expansion of NAFTA began at the end of 1994. At that time, the Mexican peso had to be sharply devalued and was rescued from disaster only by a multibillion-dollar bailout from the IMF spearheaded by the United States. The bailout stabilized NAFTA, but it undercut political support within the U.S. Congress for making new trade agreements and potential commitments for further financial bailouts. As a result, an anti-FTAA coalition developed in the U.S. Congress with support in both major parties; this coalition succeeded in both 1997 and 1998 in blocking attempts by FTAA supporters to grant renewed fast-track negotiating authority to the president. Without such authority, foreign governments became unwilling to negotiate agreements with the United States for fear that they will be significantly altered by the U.S. Congress. Until a U.S. president regained this authority, progress toward the FTAA was unlikely. In 2001, President George W. Bush recommitted to the FTAA project and began the process of lobbying Congress for the renewed fast-track authority. Bush, aided by the events of September 11, 2001, regained fast-track authority in 2002. 2003 was to be the breakthrough year for completing the treaty along the line of the U.S. vision. However, renewed Latin American skepticism, fueled by the election of Lula in Brazil in 2002 and Néstor Kirchner in Argentina in 2003, derailed U.S. plans. Meeting in the Argentine capital in October 2003, the two leaders formulated the Buenos Aires Consensus as an alternative to the Washington Consensus. This Argentine-Brazilian skepticism about the FTAA as projected by the United States doomed the project to failure. The November 2003 FTAA meeting in Miami went ahead as scheduled, and countries meeting there did not officially end the idea, but rather talked of a scaled-back treaty, a so-called FTAA Lite. In reality, no further FTAA meetings have been held and efforts at regional integration have moved along several parallel lines, reflecting the political differences in the hemisphere.

Following the defeat of the FTAA, the United States moved to implement an alternative strategy based on the Central American Free Trade Agreement (**CAFTA**) and selected bilateral agreements with willing Latin American countries. Since 2003 that U.S. strategy has seen some success. Negotiations for CAFTA were completed in late 2003, and the pact was eventually approved by most Central American governments and the U.S. Congress in 2006. The final piece of the CAFTA puzzle came into place in October 2007 with its approval by a narrow margin in a Costa Rican referendum. Thus Costa Rica joined Nicaragua, Guatemala, and El Salvador in the pact. In theory, the agreement will boost trade and investment among the countries involved, including more access to U.S. markets for the Central American countries and CAFTA's other member, the Dominican Republic. Its critics are skeptical, pointing out that NAFTA, structured along similar lines as CAFTA, has hurt the Latin American side, especially farmers. CAFTA was signed by the Central American countries without any significant reductions in U.S. agricultural subsidies, a key sticking point for Argentina and Brazil in the FTAA negotiations. Ultimately, the Central American countries, long more dependent on the United States in comparison to the larger countries of South America, felt compelled to sign on, hoping that less foreign investment might be shifted to Asia than would have been the case without CAFTA.

The United States also aggressively pursued bilateral agreements with sympathetic neoliberal governments in Peru, Ecuador, Colombia, and Panama. With all but Ecuador, the United States succeeded in crafting agreements along the lines of the 2004 U.S.-Chile agreement. Negotiations with Ecuador broke down when the neoliberal Lucio Gutiérrez was forced from office by mass demonstrations in 2005 and eventually replaced by Rafael Correa, a clear anti-neoliberal. The other three agreements were stalled in the U.S. Congress following the Democratic takeover after the 2006 midterm elections. However, the U.S. neoliberal trade agenda scored an important victory when the U.S.-Peru agreement was passed in late 2007, following the inclusion of significant labor and environmental clauses. The fate of the agreements with Panama and Colombia were uncertain in 2009. The strategy of the United States to pursue neoliberal trade deals remains largely intact with bipartisan support in the United States, but the main factor in the new century has been a growing reluctance in Latin America to accept the U.S.-driven plans.

As the FTAA was going down to defeat, the pace of Latin American efforts at regional integration independent of the United States began to take different forms, primarily under the leadership of Hugo Chávez, the Venezuelan president. Of course, **Mercosur**, the Common Market of the South, formed in 1994 by Argentina, Brazil, Paraguay, and Uruguay (Bolivia and Chile became associate members), has always been the most vibrant project, built around the two largest economies of Latin America and formed at the time of neoliberal optimism. It remains an important project that has expanded trade and investment in a modest way among its members over its nearly twenty-year existence. Venezuela requested membership in 2006 and Chávez has spoken of the need to reform its neoliberal character, but at this point little has changed and ongoing trade issues between Brazil and Argentina challenge its future. In addition, the smaller countries of Uruguay and Paraguay have complained that the agreement does not work well for them and have explored the possibilities of bilateral agreements with the United States, steps that have been sharply criticized by Argentina and Brazil. In any case, a dynamic future for Mercosur is uncertain.

Bolstered by its strong oil and gas revenues in recent years, the Venezuelan government has embarked on a bold path of challenging U.S. dominance in the region through government-to-government direct financial aid and through its support for two multilateral projects, the **Bank of the South** and the Bolivarian Alliance for the People of Our America (**ALBA**). In 2007 alone, Venezuela pledged close to $10 billion in aid to Latin American governments, three times the amount given by the United States. These are unprecedented amounts for a Latin American country and have the potential to fundamentally change the dynamic of political influence in the region. The most dramatic example of Venezuelan assistance has been to Argentina. Saddled with billions of debt to the IMF and wishing to free itself from the neoliberal constraints of the fund's conditionality programs, Argentina and president Néstor Kirchner turned to Chávez for help and Venezuela responded by purchasing more than $5 billion of Argentina's IMF debt, allowing them to repay the IMF and walk away from the IMF-imposed neoliberal policies. The independence from the IMF has proven to be a boon to the Argentinean economy and to the recovery of its social indicators. Other significant government-to-government aid has gone to Bolivia, Ecuador, and Nicaragua following the election of progressive presidents in those countries in 2005 and 2006.

Venezuela has also taken the lead in the creation in late 2007 of the Bank of the South, a project designed to sideline the role in Latin America of the U.S.-dominated Inter-American Development Bank, World Bank, and IMF. With seven initial members (Argentina, Brazil, Bolivia, Ecuador, Paraguay, Uruguay, and Venezuela) the bank has an initial capital base of $7 billion and is designed to give member states access to loans for emergency situations and to develop programs for social services. The bank, with its headquarters in Caracas, began functioning in November 2007 and represents another potential challenge to U.S. hegemony in the region.

A very different project under Venezuelan and Cuban leadership is ALBA. Launched in 2005 as The Bolivarian Alternative, initially as a project of bilateral cooperation between Cuba and Venezuela, it has now been broadened to include Bolivia, Ecuador, Honduras, Nicaragua and three Caribbean Island nations following the change of the political landscape in those countries. Presenting itself as an alternative to the neoliberal model of the FTAA, ALBA involves the exchange of services, primarily in the fields of education and health care. Cuba contributes its human resources, cultivated over the long years of the Cuban revolution in the form of teachers and medical personnel who do extended service in the other member countries of ALBA. In return, energy-poor Cuba receives oil and gas from the energy-rich members of the group, Venezuela and Bolivia. The current economic value of the exchange is dwarfed by the size of Venezuela's other aid programs but it has the potential to change the social dynamics in the impoverished countries that are participating. The exchange is especially important for Venezuela as Chávez seeks to deliver on his promises to improve the daily life of poor Venezuelans.

Economic Legacy

Neoliberalism, the structural adjustments of the 1990s, and the globalization process generally did have a considerable effect on the Latin American economies. They generally recovered from the lost decade of the 1980s and began to experience growth in the early and mid-1990s, although growth did begin to slow in many economies by decade's end. Another clear area of success was the reduction of inflation to single-digit figures in most of Latin America. This was particularly noteworthy in Brazil and Argentina, which had both experienced inflation in excess of 1,000 percent per year in past decades (see Table 16). Real wage rates for the vast majority of workers did not, however, improve. Unemployment remained a severe problem in most countries, and growing numbers of workers were forced to go into the informal sector to survive. Indeed, the number of those selling all manner of fruits, vegetables, clothing, household products, and auto products on the streets and at traffic lights in larger cities all over Latin America increased exponentially. A new type of dual economy may be developing where the working class is forced to buy its necessities in the markets and on the streets, where quality and prices are lower, while the upper and upper middle classes go to supermarkets, specialty shops, and the growing number of malls to make their purchases. The lower segments of the middle class may frequent all of these places depending on their precise need, income that month, and interest in being seen in the right place. More consumer goods of better quality are available at better prices, but many cannot begin to afford them. Poverty and misery continue and have increased in some countries. Income and wealth have become even more concentrated in the hands of the wealthy few, although the spread continues to the middle class. Many argue that the social costs of this form of development are too high. This consensus is spreading as far as the international financial institutions themselves, as suggested by the title of a recent book by the Inter-American Development Bank, *Facing Up to Inequality in Latin America: Economic and Social Progress in Latin America, 1998–99 Report.* Even the World Bank has begun to insist that loan packages contain programs specifically designed to improve living conditions for the masses and mitigate some of the worst aspects of the reforms. It remains to be seen, however, if such concerns are sufficient to prompt a reevaluation of the neoliberal model by the international financial institutions that are advocating it.

The economic scene is changing radically in Latin America. One sees major stock exchanges in São Paulo, Mexico City, Lima, Santiago, and Buenos Aires; more and more manufactured goods or key components are being made in the region; and modern aspects of Western consumption such as computers, cable TV, mass retail stores, and the omnipresent auto are inundating national societies. Brazil is already the ninth largest economy in the world, and more and more products on the world market come from Brazil and other countries in the region. Although conditions for the masses in Mexico are still bleak, Mexico is generating more and more millionaires and now counts some of the wealthiest people in the world among its population. On an international scale, Brazilian managers are among the very best paid. Yet, globalization and the neoliberal reforms imposed on Latin America have only added to the highly inequitable distribution of wealth and income that have historically characterized the region.

Twenty-First-Century Prospects

Fueled in part by higher commodity prices for the region's primary exports (beef, oil, corn, soybeans, coffee, etc.) the major economies have generally been growing

TABLE 16. Latin American Inflation (Average Annual Change in Consumer Price Index)

	1900s	1910s	1920s	1930s	1940s	1950s	1960s	1970s	1980s	1990–95	1996	1997	1998	1999	2000	2001	2002	2003	2004	2005	2006	2007	2008
Argentina	3.0	7.0	-3.0	0.0	36.0	31.0	21.0	142.0	437.6	43.0	0.2	0.5	0.7	-1.2	-0.9	-1.1	25.9	13.4	4.4	9.6	10.9	8.8	8.6
Bolivia		7.0	3.0	2.0	17.0	69.0	6.0	20.0	22.7	12.0	12.6	4.7	7.9	2.2	4.6	1.6	1.7	3.3	4.4	5.4	4.3	8.7	14.0
Brazil	-2.0		3.0	2.0	13.0	21.0	45.0	37.0	330.2	1270.0	15.4	6.1	3.7	4.9	6.2	6.8	8.5	14.7	6.6	6.9	4.2	3.6	5.7
Chile	8.0	6.0	2.0	7.0	18.0	38.0	27.0	175.0	20.3	19.0	7.6	5.9	5.1	3.3	3.8	3.6	2.5	2.8	1.1	3.1	3.4	4.4	8.7
Colombia	20.0	12.0	2.0	4.0	13.0	7.0	12.0	21.0	23.7	25.0	20.8	18.5	18.7	10.9	9.2	8.0	6.3	7.1	5.9	4.9	4.4	5.5	7.0
Costa Rica					10.0	2.0	2.0	11.0	25.6	19.0	17.5	13.3	11.6	10.0	11.0	11.3	9.2	9.4	12.3	13.8	11.5	9.4	13.4
Cuba	2.0	4.0	-2.0	-1.0	10.0	1.0	N/A	N/A	N/A	N/A													
Dominican Republic					10.0	1.0	2.0	11.0	26.0	16.0	5.4	8.3	4.8	6.5	7.8	8.8	5.3	27.5	51.5	4.2	7.6	6.1	10.6
Ecuador					15.0	2.0	4.0	13.0	36.4	40.0	24.4	30.6	40.8	52.2	96.1	37.7	12.5	7.9	2.8	2.1	3.3	2.3	8.4
El Salvador					10.0	3.0	1.0	11.0	19.0	13.0	9.8	4.5	2.5	0.5	2.3	3.8	1.8	2.1	4.4	4.7	3.9	4.6	7.3
Guatemala					11.0	1.0	1.0	10.0	13.9	16.0	11.1	9.2	6.6	5.2	6.0	7.3	8.1	5.6	7.6	9.1	6.6	6.8	11.4
Haiti						0.0	3.0	12.0	6.7	19.0	18.3	16.4	10.6	8.7	13.7	14.2	9.9	39.3	22.8	15.1	13.2	8.4	15.5
Honduras					6.0	2.0	2.0	8.0	7.8	21.0	23.8	20.2	13.7	11.6	11.1	9.7	7.7	7.7	8.1	8.8	5.6	6.9	11.4
Mexico	7.0	62.0	-2.0	2.0	11.0	8.0	3.0	17.0	65.1	12.0	34.4	20.6	15.9	16.6	9.5	6.4	5.1	4.5	4.7	4.0	3.6	4.0	5.1
Nicaragua					15.0	5.0	4.0	14.0	618.8	749.0	11.6	9.2	13.0	11.2	11.6	7.4	4.0	5.1	8.4	9.4	10.0	10.7	19.6
Panama					6.0	1.0	1.0	7.0	1.8	1.0	1.3	1.2	0.6	1.3	1.4	0.3	1.1	1.4	1.6	2.9	2.5	4.2	8.8
Paraguay					25.0	33.0	3.0	13.0	21.7	17.0	9.8	7.0	11.6	6.8	9.0	7.3	10.5	14.2	4.3	6.8	9.6	8.1	10.1
Peru		11.0	-2.0	1.0	15.0	8.0	9.0	32.0	332.1	113.0	11.5	8.5	7.3	3.5	3.8	2.0	0.2	2.3	3.7	1.6	2.0	1.8	5.8
Uruguay					5.0	17.0	48.0	59.0	60.6	62.0	28.3	19.8	10.8	2.6	4.8	4.4	13.9	19.4	9.2	4.7	6.4	8.1	7.9
Venezuela	3.0	7.0	-4.0	-3.0	8.0	2.0	1.0	9.0	23.3	45.0	99.9	50.1	35.7	23.6	15.7	12.5	22.4	31.1	21.7	16.0	12.6	18.7	31.4

Source: Statistical Yearbook of Latin America, 2008. pg. 294. located at http:/www.eclac.org/publicaciones/xml/7/35437/LCG2399B_2.pdf.

in the early years of the new century with annual growth rates between 5 and 10 percent. This newfound macroeconomic economic prosperity, coming in the wake of almost two decades of economic stagnation, finds democratic governments in power throughout the hemisphere and their historically influential militaries largely consigned to the barracks. With the exception of a few countries such as Colombia and Peru, left of center governments are in power, having been placed there by electorates who grew weary of the unfulfilled promises of Latin America's neoliberal governments in the 1990s (headed by Carlos Menem in Argentina and Fernando Henrique Cardoso in Brazil). This new political leadership, headed by Kirchner in Argentina and Lula in Brazil, stopped the U.S.-inspired FTAA dead in its tracks by 2003. That reversal was stunning as it had been unamiously endorsed by the Latin American presidents present at the 1994 Miami summit.

The FTAA is dead as a comprehensive U.S.-driven political and economic strategy for Latin Ameica but as discussed earlier in the chapter a comprehensive alternative strategy has not emerged. Chávez offers a socialist vision backed up by currently high oil and gas prices, but as his December 2007 referendum defeat showed, universal endorsement of his radical vision is not always present, even in his home country of Venezuela. Other political visions emanating from Brazil and Argentina seem to fall back toward older models of protectionism, akin to ISI. Although politically popular at home, especially in Argentina, they do not resonate well in the global economy of the twenty-first century. The reality is that the economics of Latin America face major challenges from their industrial competitors in Asia, who are generally better positioned in manufacturing in the new century. Brazil and Argentina have signed long-term trade deals to provide agricultural commodities to China. These agreements can be lucrative in the short term but over the long haul they may only serve to place Latin America even longer where it has been for centuries, the relatively impoverished region providing the more developed world, now including China, with its needed raw materials and food-stuffs. In the process Latin America will remain vulnerable to the inevitable swings of commodity prices, as dependent as ever, and without long-term solutions to its deep-seated history of poverty and inequality. To avoid that fate, Latin American governments must craft policies that use the current positive position in the world economy to diversify their own economies beyond commodity production while systematically working to reduce absolute poverty and make significant investments in health care and education.

Bibliography

Baran, Paul A. *The Political Economy of Growth*. New York: Monthly Review Press, 1957.

Berry, Albert, ed. *Poverty, Economic Reform, and Income Distribution in Latin America*. London: Lynne Reinner, 1998.

Blumer-Thomas, Victor. *The Economic History of Latin America since Independence*. Cambridge, UK: Cambridge University Press, 1994.

Cardoso, Eliana, and Ann Helweg. *Latin America's Economy: Diversity, Trends, and Conflicts*. Cambridge, MA: MIT Press, 1995.

Cardoso, Fernando Henrique, and Enzo Faletto. *Dependency and Development in Latin America*. Berkeley: University of California Press, 1979. First published as *Dependencia y Desarrollo en América Latina*, 1971.

Chilcote, Ronald. *Development in Theory and Practice: Latin American Perspectives*. Lanham, MD: Rowman and Littlefield, 2003.

ECLA. *Study of Inter-American Trade*. New York: United Nations, 1956.

ECLA. *Towards a Dynamic Development Policy for Latin America*. New York: United Nations, 1963.

Frank, Andre Gunder. *Capitalism and Underdevelopment in Latin America*. New York: Monthly Review Press, 1967.

Franko, Patrice. *The Puzzle of Latin American Economic Development*, 3rd ed. Lanham, MD: Rowman and Littlefield, 2007.

Handelman, Howard, and Werner Baer. *Paying the Costs of Austerity in Latin America*. Boulder, CO: Westview Press, 1989.

Inter-American Development Bank. *Beyond Facts: Understanding Quality of Life, Development in the Americas 2009*. Cambridge: David Rockefeller Center, 2009.

Jameson, Kenneth P., and Charles Wilber, eds. *The Political Economy of Development and Underdevelopment*. 6th ed. New York: McGraw-Hill, 1996.

Lenin, V. I. *Imperialism, The Highest Stage of Capitalism*. New York: International Publishers, 1979.

Miller, Shawn William. *An Environmental History of Latin America*. New York: Cambridge University Press, 2009.

Nkrumah, Kwame. *Neo-Colonialism, The Last Stage of Imperialism*. London: Nelson, 1965.

Rodney, Walter. *How Europe Underdeveloped Africa*. Washington, DC: Howard University Press, 1981.

Salvucci, Richard J. *Latin America and the World Economy, Dependency and Beyond*. Lexington, MA: D.C. Heath, 1996.

Sanchez-Ancochea, Diego, and Iwan Morgan, eds. *The Political Economy of the Public Budget in the Americas*. London, Institute for the Study of the Americas, 2009.

Smith, William C., and Roberto Patricio Korzeniewicz, eds. *Politics, Social Change, and Economic Restructuring in Latin America*. Miami, FL: North-South Center Press, 1997.

Tucker, Richard. *Insatiable Appetite: The United States and the Ecological Destruction of the Tropical World*. Lanham, MD: Rowman and Littlefield, 2007.

United Nations Human Development Program. *Human Development, 1999*. New York: Oxford University Press, 1999.

United States Drug Enforcement Agency. Data supplied by DEA Statistical Unit, Dr. Mark M. Eiler, Director, and *Major Coca & Opium Producing Nations, Cultivation and Production Estimates, 1994–98*. Washington, DC: Inter-Agency Narcotics Control Reports, 1999.

Veltmeyer, Henry, James Petras, and Steve Vieux. *Neoliberalism and Class Conflict in Latin America: A Comparative Perspective on the Political Economy of Structural Adjustment*. New York: St. Martin's Press, 1997.

FILMS AND VIDEOS

Unless otherwise noted, all films are available from the Filmmakers Library, New York.

Amazonia: The Road to the End of the Forest. Canada, 1990.

The Battle of the Titans. Denmark, 1993.

Coffee: A Sack Full of Power. United States, 1991.

Deadly Embrace, Nicaragua, the World Bank and the International Monetary Fund. United States, 1996. (Available through Ashley Eames, Wentworth, NH, 03282.)

The Debt Crisis. United States, 1989.

Lines of Blood—The Drug War in Colombia. United States, 1992.

Mama Coca. United States, 1991.

Traffic. United States, 2000.

WEBSITE

www.eclac.org.cl/   Economic Commission for Latin America. The Political Economy of Latin America.

NINE

DEMOCRACY AND AUTHORITARIANISM

Latin American Political Culture

In June 2009 Manuel Zelaya was rousted from his bed by a group of soldiers with their rifles trained on him. He was told he was being deposed as president of Honduras, then taken to a plane while still in his pajamas and flown our of the country. Honduras and Latin America had experienced their most recent coup d'etat. Even more remarkably, many members of the congress, judges on the supreme court, and many members of the public thought this was the right thing to do. They were following a long tradition of forcing a president from office when he had engaged in political action that powerful interests—including the military—did not like. He had recently doubled the minimum wage and was organizing a referendum to see if the voting public wanted to change the consitution. The economic threat to the business class was too great and others feared he would use any constitutional revision to extend his stay in office beyond the current one-term limit. So powerful interests in Honduras connived to use the military to oust the constitutional president from office and replace him with their appointee. He had, after all, threatened the interests of the powerful. Such actions would be met with universal condemnation if they occurred in Great Britain, Canada, Australia, or the United States and it is very doubtful indeed that many members of the military could be convinced to engage in such an action. Yet, this coup, or *golpe de estado*, scenario had been played out hundreds of times before in Latin America, often with the support of a significant section of the population, and usually with the support of a substantial part of the upper class and most if not virtually all of the military officers. One might rightly conclude that political values and attitudes about changing the president and government were quite different in Latin America.

To better understand the very unique context in which politics are conducted in Latin America, it is necessary to understand not only general aspects of Latin American society, economics, and culture but also those specific beliefs and views that affect how Latin Americans see, judge, and participate in politics. In the study of comparative politics, a term was developed to describe the associated values, attitudes and orientations toward politics that individuals have in a specific area or group. The term that was developed, *political culture*, has proven very useful in studying the way politics are conceived and practiced in different countries and regions. This conglomerate of attitudes and beliefs about politics or *political culture*, develops in a society over a period of time. The concept helps us focus on the political beliefs and values that are embedded in a particular national society, or in a specific group. As developed through the study of politics in different nations, *political culture* is defined as those attitudes and beliefs that affect the way we think about, engage in, and evaluate politics and political events. There have been several major studies of political culture dating back to the 1960s. Perhaps the most famous were *The Civic Culture* (Gabriel Almond and Sidney Verba, 1965) and the *Civic Culture Revisited* (Almond and Verba, eds, 1980). These studies, used (not always perfect) survey research to examine the ways in which the civic, or, as they conceived it, Western democratic culture, was manifest in five different democracies: the United States, Great Britain, Germany, Italy, and Mexico. Not surprisingly, the values, beliefs, and practices regarding democracy were quite different in the five democratic nations in regard to fundamental dimensions like political participation and respect for and expectations of government and its actions.

As suggested above, these values can differ sharply between countries, within countries or from one group to another in a particular nation or region. Thus, coups d'etat, strong-man rule, and authoritarian decision making that are common in Latin America might be totally unacceptable in Great Britain, Canada, or the United States, where moderation, compromise, and consensus are more highly valued. Conversely, the political vacillation for which U.S. President Bill Clinton became famous would be little tolerated in a Latin American president, even though his personal indiscretions might. Further, it can be argued that if indeed there is a political culture of authoritarianism in Latin America, as manifest in dictatorial rulers and their support, there is another that values democracy and constitutional rule and is seen in practitioners of open democracy in Costa Rica and those who insist on honest, transparent elections and the rule of law in recently reformed and reinvigorated democracies in Uruguay, Brazil, Venezuela, Bolivia, El Salvador, Ecuador, Paraguay and post-2000 Mexico.

The nature of politics in Latin America developed over many centuries, with the most remote origins in the pre-Columbian hierarchical and authoritarian rule that characterized the governing process among the Aztecs, Mayans, Incas, and other highly structured indigenous groups. There were, however, more participatory practices among less centralized indigenous groups and at lower levels in the far-flung Incan Empire. The communally based *ayllu* would be an example of the latter and one that has recently helped to engender community-based participatory politics in indigenous Andean areas where this kindship unit existed from Incan if not preIncan times. To this was added the authoritarian, hierarchical, and often dictatorial forms of governing that were brought from the Iberian Peninsula and developed in the colonial and early republican eras. Of particular note is the *absolutist tradition* (from the absolute monarchies in the Iberian Peninsula) that became manifest in the Americas in the unchecked power of the viceroy and other governmental leaders in the colonies and the fusion of political and military power in the hands of the viceroy or captain general. Similarly, the seignorial large landowner or *latifundista* enjoyed almost virtually unchecked power on his estate, if not in the area in which it was located. All these factors combined to make for a tradition and thus a political culture that was generally far from democratic in all too many instances.

Authoritarian Legacy and Weak Democratic Tradition

THE CAUDILLO TRADITION

Many believe that this authoritarian, dictatorial cluster of values that is commonly found throughout Latin America and which is an integral part of Latin America political culture is most clearly manifest in the person of the *caudillo* or strong, usually dictatorial, leader. The term originally meant a local or regional strong man, but was widened to describe national leaders who ruled in the same authoritarian, dictatorial manner as a local strong man. Thus the local Argentine gaucho leaders Juan Manuel de Rosas came to be a national caudillo as he and his gaucho bands took over the province of Buenos Aires in 1829 and later established a Latin American dictatorship in Argentina that lasted until 1852. Swinging toward democracy Argentina established a viable democratic tradition after Rosas' military defeat and expulsion. It lasted until the Great Depression of 1929. Dictatorship returned in 1930 and the 1940s saw the emergence of one of the most renowned of the Latin American caudillos—Juan Domingo Perón. Nor was he alone in this part of Latin America. The neighboring state of Brazil had seen the emergence of an extrordinary politician, Getulio Vargas. He began his rule as a caudillo from the state of Rio Grande do Sul who took over the national government and used his strongman rule to begin the consolidation of the modern Brazilian state. He dominated Brazilian politics from 1930 till his suicide in the presidential palace in 1954. Argentina's other northern neighbor, Paraguay, fell under the strong man rule of Alfredo Stroessner through a coup in 1954. He ruled over Paraguay with a strong hand until he was finally removed from office by another coup in 1989. In more recent times many have described Peru's president Alberto Fujimore (1990–2001) as a caudillo, particularly, after he suspended the constitution and dismissed congress and the supreme court with the help of the military in 1992. Others suggest now president Daniel Ortega of Nicaragua is a caudilllo because of the way he ruled the country from 1979 to 1990 and his heavy-handed methods in his own Sandinista party during this time and thereafter.

For the vast majority of Latin American countries that gained their independence in the early nineteenth century, this authoritarian tradition weighed heavily and was further strengthened by the dictatorial practices of the leaders of the independence movement as they took the reigns of power in the newly independent nations and by the less statesmanlike dictators who all too often followed. One is here reminded of authoritarian *libertadores* like Simón Bolívar and dictators like the above-mentioned Juan Manuel de Rosas in Argentina and Antonio López de Santa Anna in Mexico.

In *Authoritarian Regimes in Latin America: Dictators, Despots, and Tyrants*, Paul H. Lewis describes what he calls "the undemocratic or authoritarian culture" that predominated in Latin America. Although he does not examine the precolonial origins of this political culture, he argues that it has several roots: first, the hierarchical, autocratic, and crusading character of Spanish and Portuguese society found in the Iberian Peninsula; second, the nature of colonial society based on the conquest and later the explotation of slaves; and thirdly, the independence movement itself which left behind anarchy and banditry that required a strong hand on the part of those who governed in order to assert control and maintian order in the nacent republics. In a section on *"caudillo* power," he further chronicles the many caudillos who emerged as national leaders in the first decades of Latin American independence.

DEMOCRATIC DEFICIT

As Latin America developed, there was little experience with democracy during the colonial period. There were no legislatures or popular representative bodies where the people could make their views known or participate in governing, above the municipal level. This level was the exception. For instance, in many areas, the town council, or *cabildo,* did allow some degree of participation and democracy in many—but not all—municipalities. Many indigenous villages also exercised some degree of democracy in decision-making practices. But the general lack of experience with democracy led one astute student of Latin America, Mario Hernández Sánchez-Barba, to observe that the democratic constitutions patterned on the United States and France that were enacted in Latin America during the early nineteenth-century independence struggles were attempts to impose a democratic framework on a very authoritarian reality. Although the new Latin American nations were launched as democracies with constitutional structures similar to those of the United States and the French Republic, democratic experience and a democratic political culture lagged far behind. It was perhaps a little like introducing cricket and cricket rules to players who have never seen the game and have been playing soccer all their lives. Although some countries took to the new game faster than others, all underwent a long period of assimilation that included periods of play much more like the old game. Some even suggest that in times of crisis the players still revert to the old (authoritarian) patterns of play. As was suggested in Chapter 3, nineteenth- and twentieth-century Latin American history saw ongoing pendulum swings between periods of democracy and authoritarian rule. Indeed, it might be argued that Latin American political culture in most countries was characterized by a nominal commitment to the practice of democracy and a deep-seated reverence for authoritarian rulers with the strength to govern effectively. As noted above some have also suggested that two political cultures existed in these countries, one authoritarian and one nominally democratic, with diffferent groups favoring each at different times in the national history (and often according to their calculation of maximum benefit).

DEMOCRACY GROWS

The defeat of fascism during World War II and the wartime alliance all the Latin American states save Argentina had with the United States during the war set the stage for a deeper strengthening of democracy. The United States said it was fighting the Axis powers to save democracy. This had a certain resonance in Latin America, particularly after the Allied victory. Thus there were several attempts to break with the authoritarian tradition and initate a new democratic wave. There was an unsuccessful attempt to rid Nicaragua of the Somoza dictatorship in 1944. The democratic revolutions of 1944 and 1945 strengthened internal democratic trends elsewhere in Central America and other parts of Latin America. After the 1944 revolution in Guatemala a progressive democratic regime emerged. Costa Rica underwent a revolution in 1948 that established a democratic regime characterized by open and honest elections, respect for political rights and an adversion to authoritarian tendencies and military involvement in politics (the Costa Ricans even abolished their military). Thereafter Costa Rica has not experienced any subsequent coups or other unconstitutional changes of power, and has been characterized by its democratic elections and competitive two-party dominant political system. The democratic revolution in Venezuela launched a new democratic movement centered around the Acción Democrática party and put the Venezuelan novelist Romulo Gallegos in power as the president (1945–1948). Although there was a temporary reversion to authoritarian military rule under the dictatorship of Pérez Jiménez (1948–1958), constitutional democracy continued to develop in Venezuela thereafter. Jorge Gaitán and progressive forces in the Liberal Party started a movement to strengthen popular democracy in Colombia in 1946. The truncation of this process that occurred when Gaitan was assassinated in 1948 sparked the Bogotazo and the subsequent Violencia, but even here, elements of democratic political culture lived on. Uruguay also developed a strong democratic tradition that was sustained until it too succumbed to the wave of military coups that swept through Latin America in the 1960s and 1970s. Chile also developed strong democratic practices and had even had a parliamentary form of government in the 1890s. It had a well seated democratic tradition and a vibrant multiparty system by the 1960s. It was in this democratic tradition that Salvador Allende hoped to organize a democratic socialist revolution when he was elected president in 1970. He and his coalition of socialists, and members of the Radical and Communist parties were able to do so for three years until the military intervened with strong assistance and support from the U.S. government. The coup d'état and subsequent military dictatorship of Augusto Pinochet did, however, halt the practice of democracy from the date of the coup on September 11, 1973, to the return to democratic rule in 1990.

The 1950s and 1960s, then, had seen the intermittent growth of democracy in these countries and elsewhere in Latin America as well, although dictatorship and authoritarian rule were also common. As they had done in the nineteenth century, these periods of democratic rule from the 1940s on helped to strengthen democratic values and began to strengthen democratic political culture in Latin America.

MILITARY RULE AND BUREAUCRATIC AUTHORITARIANISM

While Costa Rica and Uruguay, and to a lesser degree, Venezuela, Chile, and Colombia saw the commitment to democracy and democratic means become much more pervasive from the 1950s on, the authoritarian dimension of Latin American political culture was to rear its head in a different way as authoritarian tendencies reemerged. Causes for a return to such authoritarian rule included the Cold War and the strong anticommunism that the United States (and many Latin American economic and political elites) had pushed throughout the hemisphere and the inculcation of the national security doctrine and counterinsurgency that U.S. diplomats, military trainers and the U.S. Army School of the Americas had taught Latin American politicians and military personnel. These ideas and U.S.-sponsored training and diplomacy mixed with class interests, the threat from left-wing guerrillas, and the authoritarian and autocratic tendencies that characterized the military and many sectors of the ruling economic and political groups. The result was the reversion to long periods of dictatorial military rule dubbed "bureaucratic authoritarianism" by the Argentine political scientist Guillermo O'Donnell. The term was coined to describe the institutional military dictatorships that arose in the 1960s and the 1970s and remained in power for as long as twenty years, as was the case in Brazil (1964–1984). The initial analysis stems from O'Donnell's work *Modernization and Authoritarianism* (1972 in Spanish) and was expanded later in *Bureaucratic Authoritarianism: Argentina, 1966–1973, in Comparative Perspective.* This long period of institutionalized military rule was to include not only Brazil and Argentina, but Bolivia, Uruguay, Chile, Peru, Panama, Guatemala, El Salvador, and Honduras. All these regimes challenged civilian rule, existent politics and political parties and many fundamental tenets of democracy itself. The United States accepted and even supported these military regimes (save that of Peru and Panama which had elements of leftist populism) in varying degrees and saw them as a bulwark against Communism and Marxism. Democracy was eroded significantly and many horrendous abuses of human rights became common. Indeed, the United States soon became seen not as an advocate of democracy but as a supporter of brutal right-wing dictatorships (as in Chile, Argentina, and Brazil) and an enemy of rooted democracy. Many of the worst human rights abuses were denounced by some sectors of the U.S. government under the Administration of Jimmy Carter, but the Reagan administration reversed the human rights policy of the Carter administration and embarked on a strong anti-communist policy that often embraced some of the worst regimes in Latin America and formed and supported the murderous *contras* as a means of destabilizing and trying to overthrow the leftist Sandinista government in Nicaragua in the eighties. But U.S. policy was to change with the demise of Eastern European Socialism after 1989. The United States and its Western European allies no longer believed they needed to guard against leftist insurgencies and radical political movements that would challenge U.S. interests and ally themselves with Cuba and the Soviet Bloc.

Democratization

Democratization has grown slowly in most of Latin America. Although the process has accelerated dramatically since the end of military rule in the 1980s and 1990s, it started in the early nineteenth century with elitist or aristocratic democracies where power was held in few hands. Gradually, it evolved and incorporated more participants as literacy levels rose, property requirements were abolished, slavery ended, women were afforded the franchise, and lower-class groups mobilized. And democratic ideals continue to inspire and suggest how the republics should function. The persistence of such ideals has helped to shape political culture. In *Democracy in Developing Countries: Latin America*, Larry Diamond notes that elitist democracies helped to get important players involved and invested in democracy, which in turn allowed for participation, to which others could aspire. The elitist model of democracy was gradually popularized as new groups began to participate effectively in the political systems. Diamond further argues that the constitutional, liberal, and democratic idea delegitimized the authoritarian use of power but ultimately did not radically change the elitist proclivity of the system. Discussing elite politics and the roots of democracy in *Building Democracy in Latin America*, John Peeler observes that the royal absolutism that so heavily influenced the authoritarian tradition became dominant only in the fifteenth century and that it was resisted at the elite level by the medieval tradition of the *fueros*, or special privileges extended to religious personnel and the nobility. Thus, the idea of special rights and privileges for favored groups

Luiz Inácio Lula da Silva, Brazil. *(Photo by Paulo Fridman/WPN/Photoshot)*

and their ability to resist even the strong control of the state became entrenched in Latin America as well. The local elite often displayed and used its own autonomy to resist state authority, as suggested by the oft-quoted phrase "obedezco pero no cumplo" (I obey but do not comply). This has continued to the present day and helps to explain why civilian and military elites are often loath to submit to governmental rule. Indeed, they often see themselves as immune from jurisdiction—not controlled by the law. Impunity in such situations is common.

In his seminal work, *Democracy in Latin America*, George Philip is clear as to the persistence of the authoritarian as well as democratic beliefs. He acknowledges the variation in the region but sees predemocratic patterns of political behavior surviving democratization. Nor does he see the broad institutional changes that have usually preceded democratization and democratic consolidation taking place in most of Latin America. There is positive institutional change in some countries, but, as suggested by the above Honduran case, throughout the region authoritarian legacies have survived even the most recent transition to democracy in the 1980s and 1990s. Even more critically, Philip observes that the bureaucracy remains patrimonialist, law enforcement is weak, and public opinion is often ready to support open law breaking by political leaders. Thus, the conflicting values that leaders and the public have about democracy versus authoritarian rule have not allowed for the consolidation of democracy in most of Latin America. Earlier in the work he cites a respected poll taken in Chile in 2001 to the effect that only 45 percent of those sampled thought democracy was preferable to any other kind of government, while 11 percent agreed that in "certain circumstances an authoritarian government can be preferable to a democratic one." Other polls have shown similar results elsewhere in Latin America.

Politicians and the public have often shown themselves quite willing to support extra-constitutional uses and assumptions of power at critical times. Venezuela developed one of the strongest democratic traditions in Latin America. But, even in democratic Venezuela, there was considerable support for the 1992 coup attempt by Hugo Chávez to overthrow the widely discredited Carlos Andrés Pérez government. The polarization of attitudes that transpired after Chávez was elected president and began to transform the state was also very strong. Indeed, the partisanship became so intense that there was also significant support for the short-lived coup that temporarily displaced President Chávez from power in 2002. Nor were most Chávez supporters overly concerned with the leader's tendency to concentrate more power in the presidency or his attempts to extend the presidential term in office.

Beginning with the administrations of Ronald Reagan in the United States and Margaret Thatcher in Great Britain, the free market liberal capitalist economic model championed by Milton Friedman and the free market, free trade Chicago School became a tenet of U.S. policy. As liberal free market economics were strongly advocated by U.S. policy makers and offered as the only means to develop for Latin America and other nations, liberal, Western style representative democracy was advocated as a means of achieving an environment in which such free markets could flourish. Dominant political and economic elites and U.S. and Western sycophants in Latin America soon picked up the new mantras and advocated for Western, free market capitalism and Western style representative democracy. Thus the new political mantras became the "transition to democracy" and then "democratization." For those who had always controlled politics in most of the Latin America nations, different skills became necessary. Military interventions, coups and different forms of brutal repression would be set aside. Gross electoral fraud and election manipulation would be called into question and increasingly open to scrutiny and denunciation from national electoral commissions, international electoral observation teams or even the United States government. The ability to manipulate and control politics through public relations and the media and orchestrated campaigns soon was championed as the most effective means of controlling the masses, and the brutal mechanisms of repression were no longer seen as necessary. As had been the case with military aid and the national security and counterinsurgency doctrines, the United States would be the primary supplier of doctrine, training and guidance, though homegrown national suppliers would also emerge.

Political consultants and pollsters were enrolled in the new democratization project in Latin America as new mechanisms of control and guidance were developed. For instance, negative campaigning, fear mongering and scare tactics were propagated through well orchestrated media campaigns. They would replace security concerns and counterinsurgencies as the preferred means to control the masses and ensure that they did not enroll in any leftist political movements or parties like the guerrilla-based FMLN party in El Salvador, or even the Sandinistas in Nicaragua. Leftist movements tried to adapt to the new game plan with varying degrees of success, but lacked the requisite resources and ties to the U.S. government, or even to many private concerns in the U.S. One of the early successes of this program was the electoral defeat of the Sandinistas in Nicaragua in 1990. Having been unable to defeat the Sandinista military with the U.S. trained and directed *contras* (counterrevolutionaries), the United States helped to organize an electoral coalition of fourteen opposition parties, pushed very strongly to pick Violeta Chamorro as their presidential candidate and funneled millions of dollars and other forms of support to the opposition. Indeed, the U.S. Congress had formed the National Endowment for Democracy to facilitate precisely this type of initiative. The Endowment invested 9 million dollars in the opposition in the 1990 election. Although the Sandinistas also organized a slick campaign and a rock star type image for Sandinista president Daniel Ortega, Nicaragua became "democratized" as the Sandinista lost and Violeta Chamorro and her UNO coalition triumphed. Try though they might, the Sandinistas could not regain power for sixteen years and then only after they had connived with a very corrupt political boss and former president (Arnaldo Alemán) to change the electoral rules to allow a presidential candidate to triumph with a plurality of the vote (an absolute majority would no longer required).

Recent events in Mexico provide another case study. By the 1980s the one party domination of the Mexican political system by the Institutional Revolutionary Party (PRI) was losing support and legitimacy. The leftist Revolutionary Democratic Party (PRD) and the rightist Party of National Action (PAN) began to receive increasing support and to win local elections. The situation came to a head in the 1988 national election. The PRD in all likelihood won the presidential election in that year, but was frustrated by what most independent observers saw as massive electoral fraud. Nor was the party successful in its attempts to take the presidency in 1994, or 2000 when a rightist party (PAN) did manage to unseat the long dominant PRI. The

2006 election was symbolic of the new forces in play. The PRD candidate for the presidency Andrés Manuel López Obrador had been a popular mayor of Mexico City and started the campaign with a substantial lead over PAN candidate Felipe Calderón. Intense negative media campaigning, support from conservative forces in the United States, and accusations of aid and support from Cuba and Venezuela had erased his lead by the time of the election. Amid some accusation of electoral fraud the government, business, and Bush administration candidate Calderón managed a razor thin electoral victory of less than 1 percent. López Obrador contested the election and held massive rallies for his parallel government for months after the election, but was shut out of power. The conservative leadership had been sustained in the United States' NAFTA partner. Yet, the upsurge in popular protest suggested that the masses would no longer be so easily manipulated.

As democratization developed, brutal repression declined radically and the citizenry was encouraged to participate in the political process, an interesting thing happened along the way. Popular forces that had been frustrated in their

TABLE 17.   Democracy Versus Authoritarianism

Which of the Following Statements Do You Agree with Most?										
	"Democracy is preferable to any other type of government"					"In certain circumstances an authoritarian government can be preferable to a democratic one"				
	1996	2001	2008	2009	change since 2008	1996	2001	2008	2009	change since 2008
El Salvador	56	25	50	68	+18	12	10	27	12	−15
Honduras	42	57	44	53	+9	14	8	15	12	−3
Brazil	50	30	47	55	+8	24	18	19	18	−1
Chile	54	45	51	59	+8	19	19	14	11	−3
Guatemala	50	33	34	41	+7	21	21	27	30	+3
Panama	75	34	56	64	+8	10	23	15	13	−2
Costa Rica	80	71	67	74	+7	7	8	14	9	−5
Peru	63	62	45	52	+7	13	12	20	16	−4
Argentina	71	58	60	64	+4	15	21	19	19	0
Bolivia	64	54	68	71	+3	17	17	10	13	+3
Uruguay	80	79	79	81	+2	9	10	6	8	+2
Venezuela	62	57	82	85	+3	19	20	9	7	−2
Mexico	53	46	43	42	−1	23	35	15	14	−1
Nicaragua	59	43	58	55	−3	14	22	8	10	+2
Dominican Rep.	N/A	N/A	73	67	−6	N/A	N/A	15	24	+9
Paraguay	59	35	53	45	−8	26	43	29	31	+2
Colombia	60	36	62	49	−13	20	16	9	14	+5
Ecuador	52	40	56	43	−13	18	24	16	25	+9
Latin America	61	47	57	59	+2	17	19	16	16	0

Source: Latinobarómetro 2009.

attempts at thorough-going change soon found that there was a lot of repression free political space in which they could mobilize. New movements began to appear. One sees early manifestations of this in Venezuela, where a democratic political culture that included fair elections had been developing since the 1940s. The free market policies advocated by the United States and international financial institutions like the IMF had made for a major uprising in 1989 (the Caracazo) and helped to spawn two unsuccessful military uprisings in 1992. This in turn engendered a new political movement that rejected the free market, neoliberal economic policies and the two mainstream parties that had implemented it. Hugo Chávez was able to mobilize his newly formed Fifth Republic Movement to take advantage of the democratic political and hemispheric movement toward democratization to win the 1998 presidential election in Venezuela. As he transformed the constitution and held additional elections, the Venezuelan masses found a framework in which the traditional political elites and their U.S. supporters no longer set the rules of the game or dominated politics. It is, however, less clear whether Chávez was carrying forth other aspects of authoritarianism with his strong presidential rule. But citizenship was being expanded and the masses were participating in a political process where they began to see palpable benefits reach them. Elsewhere, new political and social movements sprung up and had even more of a grassroots, popular base. The Zapatistas burst on the scene in January 1994 to graphically demonstrate that insurgencies would soon turn to popular movements that would be nourished by grass roots mobilization and participation and that original Americans and other nontraditional citizens and political actors would no longer be marginalized. The indigenous masses in Ecuador increased their participation in politics, formed the National Confederation of Indigenous Nationalities of Ecuador (CONAIE) and began local and national mobilizations that would depose traditional politicians and even take the national congress for one day in 2000. They went on to secure the election of Lucio Gutiérrez and then Rafael Correa as president. In Bolivia, another indigenous movement composed of peasants, *cocaleros*, miners, and neighborhood residents from Cochabamba and El Alto forced the pro-U.S. neoliberal president Gonzalo Sánchez de Lozado out of office and later elected the Aymara *cocalero* leader Evo Morales as president. The nontraditional leftist Workers' Party (PT) in Brazil would finally capture the presidency in 2002 amid calls for reform, land redistribution, and economic and social restructuring. Liberal Uruguay saw former guerrillas, communists, and other progressives forming the *Frente Amplio* coalition that would eventually elect two progressive presidents and take control of the national congress. And in Paraguay, the most traditional and authoritarian of Latin American countries, a former bishop and advocate of liberation theology would mobilize enough of those wanting fundamental change to win the presidency in 2008. Democratization, then, was unleashing new political forces and beginning to enfranchise the formally disenfranchised. Democracy, representative and participatory, was truly being practiced on a massive scale. Latin American political culture was undergoing root change.

But Latin American political culture is more than an admixture of democratic and authoritarian values. It carries many other attributes from the past. These include the following charasteristics and value clusters:

INDIVIDUALISM

Individualism is strong in Latin American political culture. The individual does not like to be subordinated by government or other powerful political forces and often will only accept such control when there is sufficient power to sustain it. When power weakens or countervailing power can be invoked, rebellion often follows and the will of another group or individual may become dominant. Political leaders have also sometimes individualized their rule. Power is used by the individual ruler and oftentimes for the individual benefit of the ruler or by or for the group to which the ruler belongs. Equally, power is wielded by small groups, such as the fourteen families in El Salvador or socioeconomic or political elites, and monopolized for their benefit. A commonly held view among many is that, like the colonial rulers, those who hold power will use it in ways that will directly benefit them or their political or socioeconomic group and that this will be done at the expense of the general population. This may result in special projects for home regions or political or business friends or, at times, outright corruption and individual enrichment. Nor do such actions buttress the belief that government benefits all the people equally or that special interests or elites do not rule.

CONFLICTUAL ATTITUDES

Societies and the proponents of political systems in nations like Great Britain often pride themselves on the high degree of consensus on fundamental values and the rules of the game. Others, like politicians in Lebanon and the former Yugoslavia, are divided into factions that have very different views of what the society—or even the nation—is or should be and held widely divergent ideas of how to achieve their political objectives in that national political system. There is also a willingness to resolve these issues through the concerted use of organized violence and forms of warfare and to engage in human rights violations of those who challenge their power.

As Latin America developed, different historical epochs added new terms of conflict. Thus, to the struggles of the nineteenth-century Liberals and Conservatives was added the conflict between those advocating radical restructuring on the lines of the Mexican Revolution, such as Alianza Popular Revolucionaria Americana (APRA) in Peru, or total, comprehensive revolution based on the Cuban process that began in 1959. After 1960 and the radicalization of the Cuban revolution, leftists and leftist insurgencies challenged mainstream parties in charge of governments and right-wing military groups. Thus, ideological values were often polarized between those advocating a political agenda inspired by socialism or leftist nationalism and those advocating a political agenda based on different conservative ideologies or U.S.-style anticommunism and the national security state. The wide gap between these positions and the lack of consensus on common objectives (and sometimes the rules of the game) made for a political culture that in most instances was not consensual (Costa Rica since 1948 is one notable exception). As suggested by the title of Kalman Silvert's well-respected work *The Conflict Society*, Latin American society and political culture have strong conflictual elements. Indeed, conflict is often taken to the extreme. Like a high-stakes poker game, there is a willingness on the part of many to take their political struggle to the wall. Politics is seen as a winner-take-all game, and losing often means losing power and thus being forced to fold and cash in one's chips. Players gamble with the power chips they have to win the game. The pot is not to be split. There are winners and losers. Power is to be used to the maximum. In the last hands of the game, push may come to shove—and that means one plays all one's power chips. This may mean buying votes, closing polling places where the opposition is strong, mobilizing friendly army garrisons, or executing a full-blown coup d'état. In such situations, there is frequently a resort to violence or the threat of violence. The willingness at times to take the political struggle to such intense and passionate levels means that violence is regularly employed through intimidation, repression, assassination, rebellion, guerrilla warfare, coups, or even civil war. The authoritarian military regimes in Chile and Argentina were even willing to engage in massive torture, murder, and other human rights violations to make sure that leftist groups would be kept from power. Alternatively, the Shining Path guerrillas in Peru executed a brutal campaign to overthrow the Peruvian government in the late 1980s and early 1990s that included frequent assassination and massive car and truck bombs. Much of the political conflict in Colombia has been played out in violent confrontations between Liberal and Conservative bands in the late 1940s and 1950s (*La Violencia*) and between guerrilla groups such as the Fuerzas Armadas Revolucionarias de Colombia (FARC) and the Ejército de Liberación Nacional (ELN) and the government from the early 1960s to the present day. The last few years have seen the interjection of extremely violent paramilitaries begun by wealthy landowners or businessmen and sometimes tied to elements of the Colombian military. They operate extralegally and are notable for their brutality and human rights violations.

ELITISM AND PACTED DEMOCRACY

Elites have dominated Latin America since the Mayan monarch and nobles ran the Mayan states in preclassical times. As suggested earlier, there have been a variety of economic, political, and social elites. Early democratization after independence was also controlled by these same elites. Similarly, there are intellectual elites, cultural elites, and even elites that dominate leftist parties and guerrilla movements. The conscious or unconscious belief that an elite should lead, decide, dictate, or otherwise rule has greatly buttressed authoritarian practices in politics and many other areas of society. From time to time the political and economic elites of a nation even get together to form a formal pact as a way of consolidating their rule, minimizing conflict and sharing power. This was done between the Conservatives and Liberals in the Pact of Benidorm in Colombia in 1958 and by the political leaders of Acción Democrática and COPEI in Venezuela in their Punto Fijo agreement also in 1958. In more recent times, mass mobilization and broad based social movements in countries like Bolivia and Ecuador have challenged such elitist political perspectives and the parties and power structures that perpetuate them.

PERSONALISM

As suggested in Chapter 5, personal relations are fundamental in Latin America. In societies where trust comes hard, one only wants to deal with those with whom one has *"confianza"*—trust. Further, since the time of the early *hidalgos* (less-well-off noblemen) and upper-class representatives of the crown, a charming personal veneer has been deemed necessary for successful civil relations. A charismatic manner and personal warmth are thus highly valued commodities that are pre-requisites for higher-level positions. Men physically embrace each other if they are friends or close business associates (the *abrazo/abraço*), and opposite-sex and female-female greetings in the same circles include a kiss on one cheek (Hispanic America) or both cheeks (most of Brazil and French Latin America). For new introductions and less-well-known acquaintances, one *always* shakes hands when one is intro-duced or enters a room and when one departs. The more grace and charm a person displays, the higher his or her presumed social status.

Such is equally the case in politics. *Personalismo* is a valued commodity among politicians. Much of their popularity and following may well be based on their personal charm and warmth. A leader is expected to be able to inspire a personal commitment from his or her following, and this is done in large part through his or her *personalismo*. In this context, the term takes on a meaning closer to *charisma* and has defined some of the region's most successful political leaders: Victor Raúl Haya de la Torre of Peru's APRA, Juan Domingo Perón of Argentina, or Fidel Castro of Cuba. Each of these leaders was capable of exuding an immense personal charm in virtually all social contacts, be it a private meeting with an

Juan Peron., Argentina *(Time & Life Pictures/Getty Images)*

individual or small group or a speech to an assembled throng of thousands. Fidel Castro became known for his ability to hold an audience's attention in speeches that lasted hours.

STRONG-MAN RULE: *CAUDILLO, CACIQUE,* AND *CORONEL*

We have established that political leadership in Latin America has often tended to be authoritarian, with the political leader exercising a great deal of power and control. Military dictators who can employ the force and power to maintain their position are tolerated or at least endured until time passes or they can be overthrown. But brutal rulers such as Augusto Pinochet (the military dictator in Chile from 1973 until 1990) have not always had the *personalismo* of most civilian politicians. Pinochet simply relied on overwhelming force. Since before the conquest, the tradition of the strong local leader became well established. The *cacique* came to mean a local indigenous leader who could be best described as a political boss. In his local community and among his own people, his power base was strong, but it diminished rapidly as he moved away from it. After colonial rule was put in place, other strong men developed. As suggested above, the *caudillo* initially was a regional political leader or boss who might exercise absolute or near-absolute power in his region. Often a local landowner or other local notable, he usually had an independent base for economic-political power. As time went on, the *caudillo* and *caudillismo* also came to refer to strong, if rather authoritarian, national political leaders such as Juan Perón of Argentina. In the rural areas of traditional Brazil, the large landowners, or *fazendeiros*, were often given the rank of colonel in the state militia. This also came to be an honorific title given to a powerful local notable. Like the colonels in the postbellum American South, *coronéis* were, and sometimes still are, powerful political players in much of rural Brazil. It would be difficult to understand politics in rural Brazil without referring to *coronelismo* or realizing the power and impunity of the *coronel*.

It is interesting to note that the sentiment in favor of strong man rule is sometimes manifest in the phenomenon of *continualismo*. This refers to continuing or remaining in office one term after another as Franklin Delano Roosevelt did in the 1930s and 1940s. This is ofter the avenue by which a strong leader cum caudillo morfs into a dictator as was the case with Porfirio Díaz who served as president of Mexico repeatedly from 1876 to 1910 and the beginning of the Mexican Revolution. In the 1990s, Alberto Fujimori's attempt to alter the constitution in Peru to allow for more than one term was one of the factors that led to his political demise. In 2008 and 2009, attempts by the presidents of Venezuela and Colombia to lenghten their terms in office caused concern in both countries.

CUARTEL, CUARTELAZO, GOLPE DE ESTADO, AND THE JUNTA

Political culture in Latin America is also influenced by the tendency of the military to leave their barracks, or *cuartel,* to intervene in the political process, the *cuartelazo.* Indeed, when the government is indecisive, ineffective, or overly

corrupt or leans too far to the left, many civilians call on the military to intervene. Military intervention has been an ongoing phenomenon in most Latin
American countries. With few exceptions, such as Costa Rica since the 1948 revolution and the subsequent abolition of the armed forces, and Mexico since the
1920s, the militaries have engaged in *golpismo.* They believe themselves to be
defenders of the constitution, upholders of national honor, or defenders against
subversion, corruption, or tyranny. The Latin American militaries have staged
some 250 coups d'état, or *golpes de estado,* since most of the nations became independent in the early part of the nineteenth century. After the successful *golpe,*
the dominant military coup makers, or *golpistas,* typically set up a military *junta*
to rule until civilian government is restored. Most commonly, the *junta* is comprised of upper-level officers from the army, navy, and air force. The period of
rule can range from the time it takes to elect or appoint a new civilian president (usually a few months) to more than a decade, as was the case in Brazil
(1964–1985) and Chile (1973–1990). This latter type of extended military governance came to be what Guillermo O'Donnell called "bureaucratic authoritarianism." As suggested above, it was used to refer to the extended period of military
rule where the military actively ran the bureaucratic governmental apparatus.
Such bureaucratic authoritarianism characterized many of the governments in
South America during the 1960s (beginning with the coup in Brazil in 1964),
1970s, and 1980s. Nations under such rule included not only Brazil, Chile, and
Argentina but also Bolivia and Uruguay. A progressive Nasserite (a nationalist
military government patterned after that led by Gamal Abdel Nasser in Egypt
from 1952 to 1970) ruled Peru from 1968 to 1980. A conservative form of extended
military rule characterized Guatemala from 1954 until 1985, and the military
dominated politics well into the 1990s. Since democratization has intensified and
has butressed continuing civilian rule in the 1990s, the tendency toward military
intervention and *golpes de estado* has diminished. It should be noted, however,
that a *golpe* was executed against Hugo Chávez in 2002 and the new government
was readily accepted by the Bush administration, which may have had some
role in facilitating it. This time, however, the coup was not accepted by the pro-
Chávez masses and younger military officers who mobilized to force the end of
the coup and Chávez's return to power.

   With the return to democracy and greater focus on civil society, democratic
(and authoritarian) attitudes are being explored and charted by a number of opinion polls and survey research organizations. Of particular interest are the regionwide surveys done by Latinóarometer (www.Latinobarómetro.org). Newer works
on *Democracy in Latin America* (both titles begin with this phrase) by George Philip
and Peter H. Smith also explore democratic attitudes in some depth.

OTHER *POLÍTICOS*

Professional politicians are *políticos.* In fact, all those who engage in politics could
be described as *políticos,* or *políticas* if they are women. One does not, however,
need to be authoritarian to qualify. Different countries have different political cultures. In Brazil, the tradition of the *chefe político* emerged. It came to have special

meaning and refers to a *político* with special powers and attributes who could best be described in English as a political boss. The figure of the political boss also exists in Spanish-speaking America and could be referred to as a *jefe político*, although the connotation of power might not be quite so strong. The *caudillo* would be more powerful, if even less likely to abide by the rule of law.

CORPORATE VALUES AND CORPORATISM

Another aspect of Latin American society that strongly influences the political system is corporatism. The concept dates back to the medieval Iberian Peninsula when society was conceived organically. The whole society was divided into different bodies (*corpus*) or corporations according to specific function or profession. The identification of individuals is oftentimes stronger to their particular body than to the nation. Church officials highly identify with the Catholic Church and display intense loyalty to it. Military officers in particular frequently display more loyalty to their military institutions than to civilian government or national civilian leaders. Thus, military officers often remain more loyal to their service branch, if not the military more generally, than to the government or civil society. Such feelings facilitate coups and narrow interpretations of the public interest.

PATRON-CLIENT, CLIENTELISM, AND OTHER SPECIAL RELATIONS

As was suggested earlier, there is often great disparity in power and prerogative in Latin America. Those who do not have power seek protection from those who do. Thus, alliances between the powerful and the not-so-powerful are often made. Indeed, this practice began on the large landed estates between the *patrón* and the *peon*, his humble employee. As with patrons and their supporters and followers elsewhere, this type of relationship spread throughout the society. The *patron-client relationship* refers to the special ties of personal loyalty and commitment that connect a powerful person with those below him. The *patrón* will look after his followers and personally intervene to make sure they are well treated or to assist them in a time of trouble, even paying for medical treatment for a family member from personal funds. As the *patrón* rises or falls, his retainers rise or fall with him. The followers give unswerving support to their leader and can always be counted on because of their personal loyalty. The practice is common in politics and the governmental bureaucracy, as well as society more generally. It has characterized many political movements as well. Indeed, it has been suggested that many Latin American political parties are personal parties grouped around the party leader. Many observers have also noted the existence of personal factions or groups within parties and government—public administration in particular is often rife with these personal groupings. Taken one step further, this can lead to *clientelismo*, which is the practice of filling governmental positions with one's friends and associates to the exclusion of other, often better-qualified job candidates.

TABLE 18. Satisfaction with Democracy by Country*

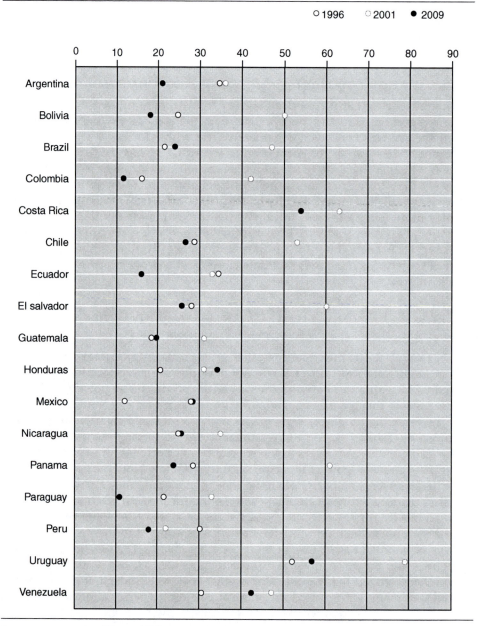

Responses to question: *"How satisfied are you with the way democracy works in your country?* Data indicate percent responding "very satisfied" or "somewhat satisfied."

*Chart compiled by Beverly G. Ward and Mark Grzegorzewski from data from Latinobarómetro.

Another important social relationship that spills over into business and politics is that of the *compadre* and the *comadre*, the godparents of one's children. Given the traditional importance of the Church, it is not surprising that those who stand with the parents at the christening of their child should play an important role in the life not only of the child but also of the parents. The *compadre* or *comadre* is someone with whom one's relationship has been cemented. Like a blood relative, they generally are people who can be trusted. *Compadres* protect each other, as do *comadres*. They can gain access or special favors and can always count on one's help. If amenable, a person of a higher social status, like the *patrón*, may be chosen as a *compadre* or *comadre*, thus creating a special tie to the *patrón* for the whole family. The terms can also mean a close friend who can be counted on.

Personal or professional networks are always, then, quite significant. The importance of the small group, or *grupito*, cannot be underestimated. The *camarilla*, or clique, is pervasive in Mexican society and politics. In the political context, it specifically refers to a self-promoting political group that maximizes the power and position of its members through concerted collective action. In Brazil, friends, political allies, or associates often form a *panelinha* so that they can do business with each other or be assured of contacts through people they know they can trust.

Finally, improvization and finesse are greatly valued. One hopes to move things along with the same deftness that world-famous soccer player Pelé moved the ball down the field. Indeed, the Brazilians have a special word for such adroitness, *jeito*. To give a *jeito* is to finesse something, to manage it, to make things happen. In a world where all is not always perfectly organized, the ability to move forward through improvization is of great importance and is greatly valued.

Conclusion

Democracy still competes with authoritarian values and elitist proclivities in Latin America. The military, save in Costa Rica, is still capable of intervening in the political process and deposing an elected president. The constitution is not always followed and many among the public do not think that such strict adherence to law is necessary during a time of crisis. Democracy is, then, not yet fully consolidated. Philip notes that problems with democratic consolidation in Latin America have a historic and institutional dimension, and are at least in part the result of previous authoritarianism. In Latin America the conduct of politics is a complex process that occurs in a reality far different from that found in the United States, Canada, Australia, Great Britain, or elsewhere. In political and social interactions, all the factors we have discussed—and many others—come into play. Ultimately, power rules; but it is exercised through the culturally based concepts, rules, and techniques that define the power game in Latin America. Further, the nuanced nature of the role these factors play is often the deciding factor in many key political and other events. Their importance in business or economics cannot be underestimated; in the game of politics, their comprehension is essential.

Bibliography

Almond, Gabriel, and Sidney Verba. *The Civic Culture*. Princeton, NJ: Princeton University Press,1963.

Almond, Gabriel, and Sidney Verba, eds. *The Civic Culture Revisited*. Boston: Little Brown., 1980.

Almond, Gabriel, G. Binghum Powell, Kaarne Strøm, and Russell J. Dalton. *Comparative Politics Today*. 8th ed. New York: Pearson/Longman, 2004.

Avritzer, Leonardo. *Democracy and the Public Space in Latin America*. Princeton, NJ: Princeton University Press, 2002.

Camp, Roderic Ai, ed. *Democracy in Latin America, Patterns and Cycles*. Jaguar Books on Latin America, 10. Wilmington, DE: Scholarly Resources, 1996.

Diamond, Larry, Jonathan Hartlyn, Juan J. Linz, and Seymoul Martin Lipset, eds. *Democracy in Developing Countries: Latin America*. 2nd ed. Boulder, CO: Lynne Rienner, 1999.

O'Donnell, Guillermo. *Bureaucratic Authoritarianism: Argentina, 1966–1973, in Comparative Perspective*. Berkeley: University of California Press, 1988.

O'Donnell, Guillermo. *Modernization and Bureaucratic Authoritarianism*. 2nd ed. Berkeley: Institute of International Studies, University of California, 1979.

Peeler, John. *Building Democracy in Latin America*. 23rd ed. Boulder, CO: Lynne Rienner, 2009.

Philip, George. *Democracy in Latin America: Surveying Conflict and Crisis*. Cambridge, MA/Oxford: Polity Press/Blackwell, 2003.

Silvert, Kalman. *The Conflict Society: Reaction and Revolution in Latin America*. New York: American Universities Field Staff, 1966.

Smith, Peter H. *Democracy in Latin America: Political Change in Comparative Perspective*. New York: Oxford University Press, 2005.

Touraine, Alain. *What Is Democracy?* Translated by David Macey. Boulder, CO: Westview Press, 1997.

Tulchin, Joseph S., with Bernice Romero, eds. *The Consolidation of Democracy in Latin America*. Boulder, CO: Lynne Rienner, 1995.

Vanden, Harry E., and Gary Prevost, *Democracy and Socialism in Sandinista Nicaragua*. Boulder: Lynne Rienner, 1993.

FILMS AND VIDEOS

Details of a Duel: A Question of Honor. Chile/Cuba, 1988.

Evita. United States, 1997.

Missing. United States, 1983.

The Revolution Will Not Be Televised. Ireland, 2004.

State of Siege. United States, 1982.

WEBSITES

Latinobarómeter.org.   An excellent source for recent survey research on Latin American political attitudes.

TEN

POLITICS, POWER, INSTITUTIONS, AND ACTORS

Power moves politics in Latin America, and naked power often rules. As we suggested in Chapters 5, 8, and 9, politics in Latin America has to do with powerful political and economic actors. Powerful *políticos* (and the occasional *política*) have dominated most Latin American societies since classical Mayan and Aztec times. Dictators such as Antonio López de Santa Anna in Mexico, Juan Perón in Argentina, and Anastasio Somoza in Nicaragua have ruled absolutely. Oligarchies such as the dominant fourteen families in El Salvador have dominated politics and brutally suppressed those who challenged them. Military juntas have monopolized power, cancelled elections, imprisoned and sometimes eliminated the opposition, and ruled for decades. The military and other groups have ignored constitutions and seized power forcefully, as when the Chilean military bombed the presidential palace to overthrow Salvador Allende in 1973. Also, power can come from the mobilized masses, demonstrations, or general strikes that force a government out of office or a dictator to resign. There have been more than 200 extraconstitutional assumptions of power in Latin America since the republics became independent. Indeed, it has been the constellation of power and not constitutional constraints that has conditioned the conduct of politics during most of Latin American history. It is the powerful individual, group, institution, or party that most often rules. Only those who know how to use power can be serious players.

Yet, as Latin American societies have become more complex, those who rule do so through the apparatus of the state and its interaction with political parties, political movements, individuals, and interest groups. Those who aspire to power must take over the apparatus of the state and use it to rule. This can be done by a coup d'état, a fraudulent election, a political agreement among political and/or economic elites to share power, or a relatively honest election with some real political competition. However the state apparatus is taken over, any discussion of the nature of political systems in Latin America must begin with a realization of the greater role that has been traditionally assigned to the state, particularly compared to classical models of liberalism. John Locke and other classical liberal thinkers believed that the best government was that which governed least. They were reacting to that absolutist configuration of the state that monarchies like Spain used to rule domestically and over their colonies in the sixteenth, seventeenth, and eighteenth centuries. Yet, it was precisely this absolutist state that served as the model for Latin American rule. Its use and misuse in Latin America have been quite different from the way the liberal state developed in Great Britain and the United States.

When the Latin American nations gained their independence in the early nineteenth century, there was a serious struggle over the political forms that would be adopted by the newly independent nations. During the colonial period, the region experienced different forms of authoritarian rule and state absolutism. The traditional elites who retained power, now independent from Madrid and Lisbon, had little, if any, democratic experience. Indeed, since the conception of the state that was projected from Madrid or Lisbon was absolutist during the colony, the elites had to find informal, noninstitutional (and not institutionalized), more personalistic ways to assert their authority and adapt to local conditions. There was almost no experience with institutionalized representative or popular democracy. The regional assemblies that were found in North America were absent in Latin America. Democracy was little practiced.The postindependence rulers were short on practical democratic models. Indeed, after independence, several countries experimented with monarchical and/or dictatorial rule.

The constitutional structures of the newly independent states were nominally democratic and modeled on the liberal constitutions of France, the United States, and the Spanish liberal constitution of 1812. Yet, political practice and political culture tended to be authoritarian and absolutist, even for committed democrats like Simón Bolívar. Gradually, new groups emerged and democratic practice engendered more democratic and less absolutist attitudes, although the latter have persisted to the present day. A strange hybrid resulted. Most countries adopted a republican, democratic form of government; but in reality, traditional authoritarian patterns were most often employed by the elites and suffrage was very limited initially. In the century and a half after independence, suffrage was gradually expanded, but there was frequent reversion to authoritarian politics and elitist, if not dictatorial, rule. As suggested in Chapter 9, much of the course of Latin American history has been an alternation between the authoritarian tendencies that were acquired during colonial and even precolonial times and the democratic ideas and ideals that were interjected at the time of independence. Democracy has been gaining ground in recent years, but reversions to authoritarian rule are frequent and decision-making practices continue to reflect the authoritarian aspects of the political culture. In his seminal work on Latin American democracy, George Philip observes that predemocratic patterns of political behavior (institutional, organizational, and cultural) have frequently survived democratization. Thus in the region "authoritarian legacies have survived the democratic transition. The bureaucracy remains patrimonialist, law enforcement is weak and public opinion will often support open law breaking by political leaders." He goes on to observe that there is more to succesful democracy than holding elections. Both he and Peter Smith frequently refer to unconsolidated democracy in Latin America.

Constitutions

Jurisprudence is a highly developed art in Latin America. Legal documents are beautifully written and comprehensive. Latin American constitutions are no exceptions. They tend to be long, detailed, flowery documents with a large number of articles (the Mexican constitution of 1917 has well over 100 articles) covering a great many specific situations. As such, they frequently need to be modified or replaced. Based on code law, they are not open to case-based interpretation, as is the case with Anglo-Saxon case law. Nor is legal precedent part of the judicial system. Constitutions have historically been more a norm to strive toward than a strict basis for the rule of law. Presidential power and prerogative are often more important than specific constitutional provisions or prohibitions.

Like the idealism of Don Quixote that permeates the culture, Latin American constitutions represent an ideal to which those who govern and are governed aspire. There have been times and places in Latin American history where the constitutions have been carefully followed (Costa Rica from 1950 to the present, Uruguay and Chile in the 1960s), but they are frequently subordinated to the power of the strong executive, dictator, or military junta. Those who rule have and use power and are less likely to be constrained by the constitution or other legal codes, although they may pay lip service to them. Like U.S. president Franklin Delano Roosevelt in the 1930s, they are more likely to find ways to massage the courts and the constitution to achieve desired policy results. The political tradition in most of Latin America is of strong-man rule and the subordination of law and the courts to the executive and other powerful political and economic actors. The concept of the rule of law and protection of the individual against the arbitrary power of the state (through government) that classical liberals from Hobbes on have espoused is not well developed in most of Latin America, although the process of democratization has begun to tentatively incorporate some liberal concepts of human rights and procedural protections. On the whole, though, power and the powerful have generally ruled. Historically, protection for specific groups often came from *fueros* or *amparos*, which protected specific rights—or privileges—for designated groups (rather than as a constitutional right that protected all).

Only in recent decades have supreme courts become apt at delimiting presidents' interpretations of what is permissible under the constitution. It should be noted, however, that the process of democratization based on Western concepts of classical liberal democracy that has recently spread through the region has strengthened democratic aspects of political culture in all countries where it is practiced and has begun to place a greater emphasis on the subordination of power and the powerful to the law. Nonetheless, practice is often contradictory. In 2000, the Chilean Supreme Court stripped former President Augusto Pinochet of his congressional immunity so that he could be tried for human rights violations committed during his brutal dictatorship—as had been the case earlier for a former general who ruled Argentina during the dirty war—but Peruvian president Alberto Fujimori was inaugurated for his third term after fraudulent elections were held when he forced the Peruvian Supreme Court to exempt him from a constitutional prohibition against third terms. He was later forced from office by political pressure that developed from an evolving corruption scandal and tried and convicted on his return to Peru in 2007. It is of interest to note that although President Hugo Chávez enjoys broad popular support, he could not quite muster the majority needed to remove presidential term limits from the constitution in a closely contested referendum in 2007 (49 percent in favor, 51 percent opposed).

Like the constitution in the United States, Latin American constitutions almost universally created three branches of government: executive, legislative, and judicial. However, very rarely are they coequal, even in the constitutions. Two realities common to Latin American systems are a granting of greater power to the executive branch over the legislative branch and a general lack of significant judicial review. Further, while most Latin American constitutions contain a significant listing of human, civil, and political rights, they also include provisions whereby those rights can be suspended in an emergency or time of crisis by the executive.

STATE OF SIEGE

A state of siege (*estado de sitio*) or state of emergency (*estado de emergencia*) may be invoked by most Latin American presidents (usually with the consent of the legislature) for a given period of time, normally ranging from thirty to ninety days. It allows the president to suspend most constitutional guarantees, such as freedom of speech and assembly as well as habeas corpus, and to legislate by decree. After the initial period runs out, it may be renewed. This has often been an avenue by which presidents acquired dictatorial powers. Latin American constitutions are also often contradictory on the question of the military, asserting in one place the primacy of civilian rule but in another granting the military a special responsibility for protecting national sovereignty and maintaining domestic order.

CODE LAW

The legal systems in Latin America are based on code law. Most analysts of Latin American constitutions and laws stress that the systems are based not on the flexible notions of British common law but rather on strict interpretation of extensive legal codes. Rather than building on a series of case law decisions, Latin American law is deductive. This code-based law has its origin in Roman law, Catholic traditions, and especially the Napoleonic Code. Much of the code law in place was inspired by the Napoleonic Code, which was promulgated in France in 1804, became the basis for the French Civil Code, and was copied across Continental Europe and in the state of Louisiana in the United States. The influence of Roman traditions can be traced to the long Roman domination of the Iberian Peninsula, which left more than just its language. This tradition emphasized the importance of a comprehensive, written law that is applicable everywhere, in contrast to the medieval traditions of law on which the English system is based, with its emphasis on limits. What was clearly missing from the Iberian ideas of law transported to the New World were the notions of social contract developed in the English ideas of Hobbes and Locke, which laid the groundwork for the idea of a rule of law based on the consent of the governed.

CORPORATISM

John Peeler argues that another feature of Latin American constitutionalism drawn from earlier traditions is corporatism. In contrast to the more individualist ideas of the social contract, the Iberian tradition is more corporatist, with a great emphasis on the sociability of humans and their collectivity. Latin American constitutions are more likely to acknowledge the legitimacy of the interests of collective groups than of individuals. It is therefore interesting that in contemporary Latin American politics the struggle is often over which groups should have their interests acknowledged. For example, some of the constitutions (Argentina, Brazil, Colombia, and Mexico) specifically acknowledge the rights of indigenous groups, children, senior citizens, workers, women, and so on (see Tables 19 and 20 on women's political rights).

TABLE 19. Women's Constitutional Guarantees

Country	Legal Text	Statement of Equality
Argentina	Political constitution of 1994	All inhabitants are equal before the law. No privileges of blood or birth are recognized, nor personal exceptions nor titles of nobility.
Bolivia	Political constitution of 1967	All human beings enjoy guarantees and rights regardless of race, gender, language, religion, or any other form of discrimination. Men and women are equal in rights and obligations.
Brazil	Federal constitution of 1988 and state constitutions of 1989	Men and women are equal in rights and obligations.
Chile	Political constitution of 1980	All are born free and equal in dignity and rights.
Colombia	Political constitution of 1991	All people enjoy the same rights, without discrimination based on gender or other reasons.
Costa Rica*	Political constitution of 1949	All are equal before the law and cannot commit any discrimination contrary to human dignity.
Cuba	Political constitution of 1976	Women enjoy the same rights as men.
Dominican Republic	Political constitution of 1966	Does not expressly relate the equality of rights between women and men.
Ecuador	Political constitution of 1979	Women have the same rights and opportunities as men.
El Salvador	Political constitution of 1983	All people are equal before the law.
Guatemala	Political constitution of 1985	Men and women have the same opportunities and responsibilities.
Honduras	Political constitution of 1965	All Hondurans are equal. Any discrimination based on gender is prohibited.
Mexico	Political constitution of 1917	Men and women are equal before the law.
Nicaragua	Political constitution of 1987	All people are equal. Discrimination based on birth, race, nationality, origin, or other factors is prohibited.
Panama	Political constitution of 1972	There are no personal exceptions or privileges, nor discrimination by reason of gender, race, social class, religion, or political beliefs.
Paraguay	Political constitution of 1992	Men and women have equal rights. The state should concern itself with making equality a reality and with facilitating the participation of women in all arenas of national life.
Peru	Political constitution of 1993	No one should be discriminated against for reasons of origin, gender, race, language, religion, or other.
Uruguay	Political constitution of 1967	All people are equal before the law.
Venezuela	Political constitution of 1961	Discrimination based on gender, race, creed, or social condition is prohibited.

*The constitution of Costa Rica establishes that mothers, children, and the elderly enjoy special protection by the state.

Source: Statistical Abstract of Latin America, Vol. 35. Los Angeles: UCLA Latin American Center Publications, 1999.

TABLE 20.   Women's Political Rights

Country	Year Right to Vote Granted	Right to Be Chosen through Popular Election	Year CEDAW* Ratified
Argentina	1947	Since 1991, candidate lists for popular elections must include women in a minimum of 30% of elected positions.	—
Bolivia	1952	Same for men and women.	1960
Brazil	1932	Same for men and women.	1984
Chile	1949	Same for men and women.	1989
Colombia	1954	Same for men and women.	1981
Costa Rica	1949	Same for men and women.	1984
Cuba	1934	Same for men and women.	—
Dominican Republic	1942	Same for men and women.	1982
Ecuador	1929	Same for men and women. The law establishes the obligatory inclusion of 25% of women on candidate lists in multiperson elections.	1981
El Salvador	1950	Same for men and women.	1981
Guatemala	1945	Same for men and women.	1982
Honduras	1955	Same for men and women.	1983
Mexico	1953	Same for men and women.	—
Nicaragua	1955	Same for men and women.	—
Panama	1946	Same for men and women.	1981
Paraguay	1961	Same for men and women.	1986
Peru	1955	Same for men and women.	1981
Uruguay	1932	Same for men and women.	1981
Venezuela	1947	Same for men and women.	1982

*Convention on the Elimination of All Forms of Discrimination Against Women, adopted by the United Nations in 1979.

Source: Mujeres Latinoamericanas en Cifras, 1995, pp. 138–139, as cited in *Statistical Abstract of Latin America,* Vol. 35. Los Angeles: UCLA, 1999.

Institutions

THE PRESIDENT

Latin American republics are based on the strong presidential form of government. Chile did experiment with parliamentary government around the turn of the twentieth century but has since employed presidential rule. Like France, Haiti does have both a president and a prime minister, but most power resides with the president, who appoints the prime minister. The single most distinctive political feature of Latin American rule is the power of the executive. Contemporary Latin American presidential power is deeply rooted in the autocratic traditions of the colonial period. Presidential power in the twentieth century has many different underpinnings that are post-colonial, including populist and revolutionary mobilizations, but the continuity with the past is strong. Also, the contemporary Latin American president wears many hats: chief executive, commander-in-chief, head of state, and head of party, to name a few. Multiple powers are not unique to Latin American presidents, just as U.S. and French presidents share similar multiple roles. In Latin America, these multiple roles only further strengthen an already strong presidency, especially because of the president's ability to invoke broad emergency powers. Even during the last decade, when democratic rule predominated in the region, ruling presidents have occasionally assumed dictatorial power, the most dramatic case being Peruvian president Alberto Fujimori's *auto-golpe* of 1992. Latin American presidents often tend to continue in office—*continualismo*. This is often how elected presidents have evolved into dictators. As a way of curbing this aspect of presidential power, many Latin American constitutions, including those of Peru and Argentina, limit the time in office to two terms. The Mexican constitution of 1917 goes one step further, limiting the president to one six-year term. Several other states also limit the president to one term. Others, like Costa Rica, specify that if a president serves more than one term in office, the terms cannot be consecutive.

The president is also the personification of the state, as manifest in the presidential sash worn on formal occasions. His or her figure commands a great deal of respect and authority. Some observers place considerable emphasis on the role of the Latin American president as the national *patrón*, replacing the local landowners and *caudillos* of the past, arguing that the president is the symbol of the national society, seen as being responsible for the well-being of the country. Consistent with the classic definition of personalistic politics, the president is seen as being responsible for the allocation of resources through presidential favors and patronage. Another side of this practice is that such a personification of power may lead to corruption; it is not unusual for Latin American presidents to leave the office considerably richer than when they arrived.

LEGISLATURE

As opposed to the parliamentary system of government, where the legislature is the dominant branch of the political system, or the government of the United States, where the legislature is coequal, in Latin America the legislative branch is seen as clearly subservient, often acting as an advisory body to the executive or occasionally as a rubber stamp. Most of the legislatures in Latin America are bicameral, with a chamber of deputies or chamber of representatives and a senate. However, almost all Central American states (not including Belize) follow the model of the Central American Federation and have unicameral legislatures, usually called "legislative" or "national assemblies." Venezuela and Cuba are also now unicameral. The legislatures' budgets are relatively small and their staff support, minimal. In many states, the legislators may have to share a secretary and basic office equipment. The committee system is neither strong nor well developed, nor have Latin American legislatures usually retained the ability to veto acts of the executive or to initiate programs. They have served more modest goals of providing a locus for the political opposition and special interests or for refining laws for implementation. It is too early to definitively declare a new trend for Latin American legislatures, but with the region's wide reestablishment of democratic rule in the 1990s, legislatures in some countries have begun to assert their power and independence. Most significantly, in 1992 and 1993, legislatures in Brazil and Venezuela removed sitting

Sample ballot from the 1998 presidential election in Venezuela. Thirty-six different parties competed, but Fifth Republic Movement candidate Hugo Chávez easily won the election with close to 60 percent of the vote.

presidents from office on the basis of official corruption while reasserting their prerogatives in countries such as Mexico, Argentina, Chile, and Uruguay. Such actions were virtually unprecedented. The Costa Rica Legislative Assembly has remained strong during past decades.

Legislators are most commonly elected to four-year terms for the lower house or unicameral legislatures and four- or six-year terms for the upper house. Legislators are usually elected from single-member constituencies, although there has been some experimentation with forms of proportional representation in countries such as Chile. The legislative sessions have historically been short and have been known to last as little as a month. Legislative debate is often acrimonious, with walkouts, protests, and sharp denunciations. Compromise and consensus are often in short supply. As a form of protection against abuse or coercion by the powerful, Latin American legislators enjoy a special right—immunity from arrest or prosecution while the legislature is in session.

COURTS

The organization of the legal system in Latin America is not unlike that of the United States, with a supreme court, appeals courts, and local courts. Judges are generally appointed, although the national legislatures may be involved through nomination or approval of presidential nomination or, in the case of Costa Rica, in the election of supreme court justices. Supreme court justices are not, however, appointed for life, as in the United States. Rather, they serve for a fixed term and must have their term renewed by appointment or election. A tradition of a strong, independent judiciary is not well developed in Latin America. From the supreme court down, the judiciary

The Brazilian Legislature in Session. *(Photo by Eraldo Peres/AP Images)*

has tended to be susceptible to political pressure from the executive or other power-ful groups. Further, certain crimes, such as terrorism or actions by military officers, may not be within the purview of civilian courts. Rather, such cases are referred to special military courts. In recent times, Latin American courts, although still weak, have begun to seek more effective ways of attacking official corruption and protect-ing individual rights. Symptomatic of this trend is the increasing use of *amparo*. The writ of *amparo* allows the individual to protect his or her rights by making a special appeal to the judicial system. It is one way the individual can protect himself or herself from the power of the state.

GOVERNMENT STRUCTURE AND LOCAL GOVERNMENT

Most Latin American states are unitary, meaning that there are no state-level governmental organizations with autonomous power or independence. The only federal states are Mexico, Brazil, Argentina, and Venezuela. The other nations are divided into provinces or departments. Traditionally the national government usu-ally appoints prefects or other administrative heads to rule over them. The process of decentralization has allowed for the elections of prefects or governors in many of the unitary states in more recent years. Municipalities exist at the lowest lev-els and may elect their mayors and councils (although the national government may appoint some council members as well). The organization of the four federal systems is similar to that in the United States, with elected state governors and legislatures and municipalities at the lowest level. Further, any discussion of the relative weights of central and local authorities in Latin American political systems must recognize a certain evolution over time. During the colonial period, the mon-archies were largely ineffective at controlling the interiors of their vast empires. Local authorities were generally appointed by the crown, but after appointment they largely functioned in an autonomous way. In rural Latin America prior to the middle of the nineteenth century, local landowners and *caudillos* were the de facto rulers. Later, the process of nation building in the last half of the nineteenth cen-tury focused primarily around the communication system—roads, rail, and so on. These systems allowed central governments to extend their authority over the hin-terlands, thus replacing the rule of the *caudillos*. As a way of centralizing power, most Latin American countries adopted unitary governmental structures with national/local relations similar to that of France, with almost all authority flowing from the top down—from the central government to local authorities. The local *caudillos* were eventually supplanted as national armies and bureaucracies were cre-ated late in the nineteenth century. Rudimentary systems of national taxation were established, although no formal authority to raise taxes was given to local authori-ties (this general lack of revenue-generating authority poses a major problem for local governments today, which most commonly must rely on funding from the national government).

CENTRALIZATION AND DECENTRALIZATION

This pattern of centralization was the clear intent of most national rulers in the nineteenth century, but three countertrends of the twentieth century must be men-tioned lest one be left with the impression that Latin American politics has been marked only by centralized rule. First, four countries have adopted federal systems that have devolved some powers to the states—Brazil, Argentina, Venezuela, and Mexico. (Much of the autonomy of the states in Brazil and Argentina was, however, undermined by the long periods of bureaucratic authoritarianism in the 1960s, 1970s, and early 1980s.) Second, the sheer remoteness of some regions in countries like Brazil, Mexico, Argentina, and Colombia has significantly slowed down the integration process, although much of this regional remoteness has disappeared in the last twenty-five years. Finally, local leaders ranging from revolutionary chiefs and guerrilla leaders to drug traffickers and entrenched large landowners have often used the remoteness of their zones of activity to maintain relative independence from the central government. That combination is probably most evident today in Colombia. Recent years have seen significant initiatives across the region to decentralize government. They have met with some success and have opened the way for local governments to tax and raise some of their own revenues. This has made for significant reform and renovation in some municipalities.

ELECTORAL TRIBUNALS

In that their electoral systems have at times been highly susceptible to influence and manipulation, many Latin American nations have established a separate branch of government to oversee elections. Called "supreme electoral councils" or "supreme electoral tribunals," these independent bodies are charged with overseeing the electoral process and guaranteeing honest elections. They have separate budgets and are not under the control of any other branch of government. In countries like Costa Rica, they have become quite strong and independent and have helped ensure electoral integrity. In other instances, they too proved to be vulnerable to powerful influences. As democracy continues to develop in the post-1990s period, their existence is a very positive factor in maintaining honest elections and open political competition.

THE BUREAUCRACY

Political scientists have long acknowledged the importance of another part of government—the administrative sector, or bureaucracy. Bureaucracies in Latin America have tended to be large, poorly paid and administered, and unmotivated. Staffing is often done as a form of political favor to supporters of winning candidates or ministerial or agency appointees (one form of quid pro quo in a patron-client relationship). Professionalism and motivation are low, and the susceptibility to corruption or being suborned is often great. Indeed, the bribe, or *mordida* ("little bite in the hand"), is frequent in Mexico and most other countries. Corruption and favoritism often permeate the bureaucracies and feed negative perceptions of government in the general population. Bureaucratic appointments are not always made on the basis of clear standards. Costa Rica is the only Latin American country to have a professional civil service system. Elsewhere, each ministry or agency may have its own recruitment criteria and job classification system, with no general standardization or means of doing cross-agency comparisons. Nor are programs or university training in public administration widespread. Government offices are often open only in the mornings or until one or two P.M., and many workers have other jobs in the afternoons. In most cases, resources are very scarce. Similarly, phones go unanswered, lines are frequently long, service is poor, and the ability to have a request processed or a problem resolved is minimal. One frequently hears stories of requests simply not being processed until an extra inducement is added to the application. A sense of professionalism based on high levels of training, adequate compensation, and good morale is hard to find among public employees.

Knowledge of the bureaucratic sector is absolutely crucial to an understanding of Latin American politics. The implementation of government policy and programs is totally dependent on different segments of the bureaucracy. Bureaucratic functioning needs to be understood because many casual observers of the region are unfamiliar with the extensive role of government entities in the economy. In reality, most of the large Southern Cone countries, in pursuit of national development in the twentieth century, established significant state sectors to control everything from steel mills to coffee plantations. As in a socialist system, state employees set wages, prices, and production quotas. In the case of Argentina under Juan Perón, a government corporation, Institute Argentino de Promoción del Intercambio (IAPI), was established to purchase all agricultural products from the farmers and then to sell them on the international market with all proceeds going to the government. In some instances, more than 50 percent of the gross national product (GNP) was generated in the public sector. Such large-scale government intervention in the economy allowed many governments to establish significant social welfare programs in education, health, and social services, each with its own administrative bureaucracy. These large bureaucracies provided central governments with vast amounts of patronage that could be used to reward friends and co-opt opposition groups. The bureaucracies generally have lacked significant legislative oversight and, in many cases, have been both highly inefficient and corrupt, allowing both bureaucrats and those who appoint them to become wealthy. The nature and efficiency of these organizations have helped to legitimize neoliberal characterizations of a bloated, inefficient government apparatus that needed to be downsized. In the last two decades, however, processes of privatization and downsizing of the state have resulted in a significant decline in the size and role of the bureaucracy in most of Latin America and in the loss of thousands of jobs.

NEW DIRECTIONS: DEMOCRACY AND DEMOCRATIZATION

As Latin America enters the twenty-first century, important questions are being asked about the direction of the region's political systems. The history of the region, as discussed in Chapters 2 and 3, saw the emergence of a wide range of governments: monarchies, rule by a *caudillo* or strong man, civilian and military dictatorships, oligarchic democracies, parliamentary democracies, populist-corporatist regimes, and, in the case of Cuba, a communist-led state. It is difficult to generalize about the location of the different types of regime except to say that the parliamentary or Westminster-style governments developed only in countries such as Belize and Jamaica, which were formerly under British rule. Monarchical rule had some presence in the immediate post-independence period in the Latin countries, but by the latter part of the nineteenth century, the trend toward republican forms of rule, albeit with limited suffrage and strong elite rule, was well established. However, for most of the twentieth century, the trend toward democracy in the major countries of the region was blunted by a series of countertrends. The most pervasive was the short-circuiting of democratic rule by powerful leaders, both civilian and military. Mexico is a good example of this pattern. After initial flirtation with monarchical rule in the 1820s, republicanism flourished in the middle of the nineteenth century under Benito Juárez as a system was established with limited suffrage and regular elections. However, in the late 1870s, this trend was blocked by the emergence of a classic *caudillo*, Porfirio Díaz, who gained power by legitimate electoral means only to terminate the process and be continuously reelected through fraud and repression. He ruled for over thirty years, only being defeated and driven from office in 1910 by the powerful forces of the Mexican Revolution. After years of turmoil in the wake of the revolution, Mexico returned to a form of democratic rule with a federal republic in the 1930s. However, Mexican democracy was limited over the ensuing decades by a form of populist and corporatist rule that maintained the same political party, the Institutional Revolutionary Party (PRI), in power through a combination of popular mobilization, clientelism, repression, and voting fraud.

However, the Mexican PRI is not the only twentieth-century example of limitations on democracy that have occurred from regimes operating on a populist and corporatist model. Such regimes have mobilized popular support behind the government from the masses, especially the urban dwellers and working class, by attacking the traditional elites and promising significant increases in the standard of living for the majority classes. The classic examples of such regimes are those of Getúlio Vargas in Brazil and Juan Perón in Argentina. It would be unfair to classify these regimes as simply a continuation of the Latin American trend of strong-man rule, although there clearly was an element of that in them. However, they often did operate within an electoral framework and did bring about significant democratic reforms in the areas of social welfare and education. At the same time, limitations on civil liberties and political opposition prevent the placing of such governments completely under the banner of democracy. Venezuelan president Hugo Chávez has managed to mobilize popular support under a strong presidency but has done so by remaining in the general confines of a democratic system. That fact was underscored when he accepted the defeat of a 2007 referendum that would have significantly expanded his power.

Yet, populist or corporatist rule has not been the primary impediment to democratic rule in Latin America in the last 100 years; that has come from the military. In virtually every country of the region, with the exception of the British colonies that became independent in the last forty years, the military has assumed dictatorial powers, short-circuiting democratic rule for shorter or longer periods of time. The most recent strong intervention of the military into the region's political systems came in the 1960s and 1970s in prominent countries in South America and the almost continual dominance over the last half-century of military regimes in most of Central America (except Costa Rica).

In the late 1950s, many analysts of Latin America were arguing that the era of tyrannical rule was coming to an end. They pointed to long-standing democratic regimes in countries such as Chile and Uruguay and to emerging democracies in

Venezuela, Brazil, and Argentina. However, these predictions proved to be short-lived. A military coup in Brazil in 1964 that would begin twenty-one years of dictatorship started a process that would be repeated in Argentina (1966 and 1976), Peru (1968), Uruguay, and Chile (both 1973). In addition, efforts at achieving political democracy in El Salvador, where the military had ruled for decades, came to an abrupt end in 1972 when the military blocked the election of the Christian Democrat José Napoleon Duarte. As the 1970s came to an end, the great majority of Latin American countries were under military dictatorships. The 1980s were dubbed the "lost decade" in Latin America because of dramatic economic declines and rampant social problems. Military rule came to an end throughout the region, in large measure because the military governments had proven themselves incapable of dealing with economic and social woes. In the first years of the twenty-first century, no country in Latin America was under military rule, the last regime falling in Haiti in 1995 under the threat of a U.S. invasion.

It is generally acknowledged that five countries in Latin America stand out for the length and stability of their democratic experiences—Chile, Uruguay, Costa Rica, Colombia, and Venezuela. However, only Costa Rica has not suffered a serious setback or rupture of democratic rule in the period since 1948. What these countries generally have in common is that at some point in their history the economic and political elites found a way to act cooperatively for the purpose of staving off more radical demands for political and economic restructuring. In fact, when democratic rule broke down, as it did in Chile and Uruguay in 1973, it was because the elites came to the conclusion that revolutionary forces could not be contained by constitutional means.

Liberal democratic regimes were established in Uruguay and Chile between 1918 and 1932; Costa Rica established its regime in 1948. Colombia and Venezuela came close to establishing democratic rule in the late 1940s but only fully succeeded a decade later. Peeler argues that the key to the establishment of democracy was an agreement among the competing elites on the process of expanding political participation. He argues by counterexample that the failure to achieve such an agreement in Argentina after Perón's fall in 1955, marked by the continued exclusion of the Peronists, doomed the democratic process in that country.

All five countries conducted elections in the nineteenth century, but these elections were not the principal means of changing governments. Once in power through elections, individuals or parties regularly manipulated the system to maintain themselves in office, often forcing their opponents to turn to force to remove them. If elections were not a sufficient condition for democracy in the nineteenth century, how did that change in these five countries in the twentieth century? Chile may provide the best example. In the nineteenth century, Chile did enjoy a high level of political stability, interrupted only by a civil war in 1891. The basis of the stability was the political domination of an agro-export oligarchy that ruled through a series of limited-suffrage elections. By the 1930s, Chile had developed a clear tripartite system of Liberals, Conservatives, and Radicals. Although some parties would change, this tripartite division has persisted to the present. Key to the system is a center party that often holds the presidency—the Liberal Party until 1912, the Radical Party from 1938 to 1952, and the Christian Democrats from 1958 to 1973 and again from 1990 to 2000.

Chile has had the most openly class-divided politics of any country in the region in the twentieth century. It is argued that the traditional Liberal/Conservative alliance ruled until 1920 and then regained power during Pinochet's military rule. Otherwise, in the twentieth century, the oligarchy has protected its interests not by direct rule of its political party but rather by maneuvering within Chile's tripartite system and using the checks and balances established in the 1925 constitution, which was not fully implemented until 1932. Such checks continue today through the Chilean senate, whose appointed Conservative faction acts as a check on radical action by the governing center-left administration. Various center and center-left governments ruled during the unbroken forty-one years of democratic rule between 1932 and 1973. These governments promoted a series of reforms supporting labor union organization and the creation of an extensive social welfare system. However, they never attacked the serious interests of the traditional oligarchy. There were never any actions to enfranchise rural workers or to redistribute rural property. In fact, the traditional landowners actually gained the cooperation of several reform governments in their efforts to directly obstruct the organization of the rural workers. A variety of constitutional means, including six-year presidential terms with no reelection, a congress chosen on proportional representation, and judges insulated from direct political control, served to deny any sector the possibility of centralizing power and implementing their full agenda. In essence, it was a guarantee for the traditional oligarchy that their fundamental economic power would not be challenged. In return, the oligarchy supported the democratic system and did not turn to the military to defend their interests. The limitation of this system as a guarantor of democracy was demonstrated in 1973 when the oligarchy supported a military coup out of the fear that Popular Unity President Salvador Allende had set in motion political forces that could ultimately lead to the expropriation of their wealth. Democracy was reestablished only in 1990 when the oligarchy was convinced that the radical left was in full retreat and that power could again be placed in a trusted center party, the Christian Democrats, which had successfully mediated class interests prior to Allende's rule. The Chilean example demonstrates that democratic rule in Latin America in the twentieth century has been based on cooperation among elites. Only when the traditional oligarchy has been willing to support democracy have there been long periods of rule without military intervention to protect their wealth and property. This also suggests the importance of the idea of "**pacted democracy**," whereby the political elites make varied agreements to share power or alternate rule for a given period, and thus discourage and exclude new political leaders or political movements from challenging their power. Whether this pattern will persist in the twenty-first century remains to be seen.

Political Actors

Powerful actors dominate the political game in Latin America. We would agree with the definition of these players offered by Gary Wynia: "any individual or group that tries to gain public office or influence those who do." In Latin America, as elsewhere in the world, the list of such actors is a long one—landowners, businesspeople, peasants, industrial workers, civil servants, and military officers, to name just a few.

However, these labels are not sufficient to fully understand the different groups or their interaction. It is important to analyze each and to ascertain the role of each within the Latin American context. Wynia also makes some important observations about Latin American politics in comparison to other parts of the world. For instance, he notes that Latin America's political systems are not replicas of those in North America and Western Europe. They have more varied rules, and there is often not as much consensus among the political actors. Further, many interest groups are not as strong or well financed as in the United States or Europe.

We have previously discussed individual actors like dictators and the strong president; next, we turn to groups. Looking at each group, we need to ask, Who are the people involved, and from what social class, region, or ethnic group do they come? It is also necessary to ask what, if anything, they want from the political process and when and how they hope to get it. We must also realize that there may be groups that largely wish to be left alone by the political process. However, by and large we will focus on groups that seek to utilize the political process to their advantage. Another important variable to be studied is the resources that are available to each group—those that can be utilized to influence the political process. Resources can range from sheer numbers and the ability to mobilize them, organizational cohesion, and dedication to wealth and strategic presence in the economy to the capacity to engage in violent activity.

Traditional Large Landowners: *Latifundistas*

In all of the countries of Latin America, with the exception of Costa Rica and Paraguay, the Spanish and Portuguese monarchies granted lands to a group of landowners during colonialization. Initially, the monarchies had primarily been interested in the extraction of gold and silver from the Americas, but as time passed the grant of royal lands for the cultivation of foodstuffs became more the norm for their penetration into the new world. These plantations took on some of the forms of the feudalism of medieval Europe. The local populations were forced to work on the land as virtual slaves. The workers were not paid in wages but rather lived on the *latifundio, hacienda,* or *fazenda* and were given a small piece of land to grow their own food in return for their free labor on the *patrón's* land. The *hacendados* and *fazendeiros* came to be the dominant class of the colonial period, both politically and economically. They were generally not interested in any significant involvement in the central national government or the distant monarchy in Lisbon or Madrid. All that they needed was the loyalty of local politicians and a local police force that could be called in case of worker unrest.

At the time of independence early in the nineteenth century, this group, made up of *criollo* descendants of the early European settlers, eventually took the lead in breaking ties with Spain and Portugal, taking advantage of the relative weakness of those governments at the time. In the years since independence, this once-dominant class has seen its political and economic power eroded throughout the region. In countries such as Mexico, Bolivia, and Cuba, dramatic twentieth-century revolutions almost eliminated this class altogether. In most countries, over the last century, the large landowners slowly lost political power to the emerging commercial farmers and industrial elites. Beginning in the latter part of the nineteenth century, land ownership and cultivation practices began to change, bringing forward a new class of commercial entrepreneurs who ran their landowning operations as businesses. In some instances, the traditional large landowners transformed themselves into commercial farmers; but in the majority of cases, their lands were eroded by land reform and the cultivation of new land by the commercial farmers reduced their political and economic influence. Changes in the rules of politics over time also cut into their power; but as long as dictatorship and military rule prevailed, the playing field favored the elites, especially the traditional landowners. Later, as republican forms of government emerged in the nineteenth century with greater and greater extension of suffrage, the influence of this group began to erode. However, this erosion of influence has been a slow one because of the enormity of the power once held. In countries where the large landholders continued to dominate the economic landscape, such as El Salvador, they have wielded significant political power to the present time. *Fazendeiros* still have tremendous power in much of rural Brazil, as do their commercial counterparts.

BUSINESS AND INDUSTRIAL ELITES

While it is correct that rural elites held a dominant position politically and economically in most of Latin America well into the twentieth century, wealth has never been monopolized by them. Beginning in colonial times, businesspeople who engaged in a wide range of commercial enterprises, from trading to banking, have been a part of the political scene. The turning point for the industrial elites came with the Great Depression of 1929. The depression devastated the region economically, but it also opened the door to entrepreneurs producing goods that were no longer being supplied by depressed European economies. Many of the emerging entrepreneurs in countries like Brazil, Argentina, and Venezuela were new immigrants who generated considerable wealth within one generation. In these large countries, the manufacturing sector began to grow and eventually contributed a greater share of national wealth than agriculture did. The process of becoming more economically independent from Europe was further enhanced by the isolation generated by World War II. As their contribution to national wealth grew, industrial entrepreneurs sought and gained important concessions from the national governments. Unlike the rural elites, who largely favored the import of foreign finished goods without any significant tariff protection, the burgeoning industrialists sought to have their growing industries protected from foreign competition. In addition to government subsidies, the industrial entrepreneurs sought government support for the subordination of organized labor. For obvious reasons, the entrepreneurs generally did not want the interference with their management prerogatives or profits that labor unions generally attempt. Industrialists have had only mixed success in this arena. While military dictatorships like those in Chile, Brazil, and Argentina in the 1970s and 1980s repressed the labor movement, other governments have been less willing to blunt the power of the unions because of their ability to deliver votes, engage in demonstrations, and disrupt the economy.

All members of the business elite do not have the same economic interests or policy agendas. Some elements of the commercial elite have been more engaged in buying and selling traditional primary goods and importing and distributing finished goods. Their interest in import substitution industrialization (ISI) was thus muted. Further, smaller national industries and banks were often at odds with those interests that allied themselves with multinational corporations (MNCs) engaging in manufacturing and finance. The specific financial interests of each group defined their political position. Such elites, since they are few in number, generally did not seek to influence the government through the traditional political process; rather, they served on government boards and commissions or appealed directly to government officials. In many instances, these entrepreneurs sought to bribe government officials for favors for their individual firms. Such bribes were often an accepted part of the political process; however, when such payments came to light, as in Brazil in the 1990s, officials were indicted or forced to resign, as was the case with President Fernando Collor de Mello. Industrialists also sought and gained such overt favoritism as easy credit, export subsidies, and government purchase of only domestically produced manufactured goods. Although some businesspeople espoused the ideology of free trade, very few were actually prepared to go without government subsidies. Until the 1980s, this protectionist mantra generated by the ISI model was largely accepted without question by the governments of the large countries of the region—Mexico, Brazil, and Argentina. This perspective was bolstered by the ideas of the economist Raúl Prebisch and the Economic Commission for Latin America (ECLA). However, the revival of the free trade ideology under the banner of neoliberalism resulted in some profound changes. Begun under the Chilean dictatorship of Augusto Pinochet in the 1970s and 1980s, neoliberal ideas took hold in Argentina, Brazil, and elsewhere in the 1990s. As a result, tariff walls have been lowered and government subsidies of industry have been reduced. New competition from North American, Asian, and European entrepreneurs has weakened the economic and political position of many of the local industrial elites or has forced them to become associated with foreign investors. Commercial business elites may be able to adapt to the new sources of supply, but they may also be challenged by foreign chains like Wal-Mart.

THE MIDDLE OR INTERMEDIATE SECTORS

This is an important and pivotal group in the Latin American political scene. We use the term *intermediate sector* to distinguish it from the concept of middle class, which is prominent in the analysis of North America and Europe. Unlike the middle classes in these countries, which gained prominence and stature through economic activity following the Industrial Revolution and industrialization, Latin American intermediate sectors were primarily professional functionaries such as government bureaucrats, doctors, lawyers, shopkeepers, managers, accountants, middle-level military officers, and some teachers. This group has expanded with urbanization and industrialization and is marked by a relatively high level of education and centrality to the functioning of modern society. Their numbers, small until Latin America began to industrialize and urbanize, have grown significantly in recent years. In comparison to the middle classes of Europe and North America, they generally developed less class consciousness and have remained a diverse and fragmented community. Their diversity and specific interests have at times made them forces for change, as was the case with their support for the reformist Radical Party in Argentina during the twentieth century. At other times, they have not been a force for societal change, being largely dependent on the landed and industrial elites that dominated. Most sought to emulate the lifestyle and consumption patterns of upper classes rather than to supplant them, and they have definitely been much less entrepreneurial than their counterparts in the north.

The relationship of the intermediate sectors to the political process has been an interesting one. Not surprisingly, what they have demanded from the political system are resources that further the position of their group—government funds for education, industry, and communication infrastructure. They can move into or out of a particular political camp depending on how well they think their goals can be achieved. They have not been universally consistent in their support of any particular form of government. However, in the twentieth century, more often than not the intermediate sectors have been strong supporters of political reform and multiparty democratic systems. In those situations where these movements have come to the fore, they have clearly favored the expansion of the franchise and the development of defined civil liberties. The intermediate sectors can be connected directly to the development and prosperity of such political parties as the Radicals in Argentina and the Colorados in Uruguay. However, their support for democracy has not been unflagging. The Mexican middle sectors have always given strong support to the one-party domination of the PRI, and in the 1960s and 1970s the middle sectors generally supported the military regimes of Chile, Brazil, and Argentina. Generally, they fear radical or revolutionary movements because the success of such movements might herald the end of their hard-won standard of living. They are horrified by the prospect of slipping into the poverty of the masses. Their ambivalence is partially the result of the resources they bring to the table. In most Latin American countries, this sector has not been large enough to act as a definitive voting bloc, although this is changing in some countries. Instead, they bring to the political process their organizing skills and their central position as cogs in the government, industrial, and business/financial bureaucracy. Such positions lead them to be more comfortable in bargaining with the elites than in mobilizing the masses to achieve their political ends.

ORGANIZED LABOR

Labor organizing began in Latin America in the 1890s but had relatively little success in its early years. Much as in the United States, it was hampered by divisions among immigrant workers, who often spoke different languages, and by opposition from government authorities, allied with entrepreneurial elites in their implacable opposition to workers' organizations of any kind. The workers' movement may have seemed even more threatening in Latin America than in the United States as it was led almost entirely by political radicals espousing either socialist or anarchist ideas for the complete reorganization of society and the expropriation of the property of the ruling circles. In Argentina, the labor movement organized hundreds of thousands of workers in response to the abysmal working conditions of the time. However, the strong influence of labor was broken by severe repression early in 1919. Hundreds of workers were killed by the police and the army, and the militant leadership was broken. A similar situation occurred in Brazil during the same time period as socialist and anarchist labor leaders were jailed and deported.

Regionwide there was little successful union organizing in the 1920s. Only in the 1930s did labor begin to become a large enough force in the most industrializing countries to become a significant political factor. During the 1930s, significant labor struggles emerged again in Brazil, Argentina, Colombia, El Salvador, Bolivia, and Venezuela. However, even as labor succeeded in organizing many workplaces, the owners of industry and their representatives in government refused to recognize the legitimacy of their organizations or to grant them a significant political role. One exception was Mexico, where the regime of Lázaro Cárdenas (1934–1940) included the labor movement as part of a wider populist strategy aimed at further transformation of Mexican society in the wake of the 1910 revolution. The labor movement has had significant influence to the present time within the PRI. Argentina is also an interesting case of labor influence. By 1943, Argentine labor had recovered from the earlier repression to organize 500,000 workers into its ranks. After initial attempts by the military to repress the movement, Colonel Juan Perón emerged to harness the power of the labor movement behind his nationalist and populist political program. With the support of the labor movement, Perón easily won the 1946 presidential election despite active opposition by the United States. Perón responded by delivering tangible benefits to Argentina's working class over the following decade in the form of higher wages and significant government spending on health care and education. Perón was removed in a 1955 military coup, but the party he created has retained significant labor union support to the present time. In other countries, unions have been allied with other parties.

In contemporary Latin America, the labor movement has many resources at its disposal. While the labor movement does not represent all of the working class, but rather its aristocracy, in a democratic context it has the ability to mobilize considerable votes for its candidates. Yet, women and racial minorities are often underrepresented in leadership positions (see Table 21). Between elections, organized labor exercises important economic influence through strategic control of industrial enterprises. Strikes in industries such as transportation, banking, and mining can have great leverage in a society. In extraordinary situations, the labor movement can also be a catalyst for a more far-reaching general strike or even an armed insurrection. Most labor unions are organized into national labor federations, like the General Federation of Labor or General Confederation of Labor, and are affiliated with the Communist, Socialist, or Christian Democratic parties or with strong nationalist parties like the PRI in Mexico or the Peronists in Argentina. A few unions have been formed with the help of the U.S. American Federation of Labor/Congress of Industrial Organizations (AFL/CIO) and are heavily influenced by the less political U.S. labor model.

Rural Poor

The rural poor have often received considerable attention from scholars, but historically this group has been the most marginalized from political power. First of all, it is necessary to state that this group is not homogeneous and that its role in Latin

TABLE 21. Women on the Main Executive Boards of Nationwide Unions, Selected Years, 1983–1994

Country	Year	Both Sexes	Women N	%	Level	Organization
Argentina	1994	24	0	0	National Directing Council	General Confederation of Labor (CGR)
Bolivia	1994	37	1	2.7	Executive Committee	Central Union of Bolivian Workers (COB)
Brazil*	1991	25	2	8.0	National Executive	Unified Central Union of Workers (CUT)
Chile	1992	59	5	8.5	National Direction	Unitary Central Union of Workers (CUT)
Cuba	1990	17	4	23.5	XVI Congress Secretariat	Central Union of Cuban Workers (CTIC)
Dominican Republic[†]	1991	11	2	18.2	Executive Bureau	Unitary Central Union of Workers (CUT)
Mexico	1991	47	2	4.3	National Direction	Confederation of Mexican Workers (CTM)
Nicaragua[‡]	1993	12	3	25.0	National Direction	National Confederation of Workers (CNT)
Paraguay[§]	1990	15	1	6.7	National Direction	Unified Central Union of Workers (CUT)
Peru[¶]	1983	41	1	2.4	National Direction	General Central Union of Peruvian Workers (CGTP)
Uruguay	1993	17	3	17.6	Executive Secretariat	Intersyndical Plenary of Workers National Convention of Workers (PIT-CNT)
Venezuela	1990	17	1	5.9	Executive Committee	Confederation of Venezuelan Workers (CTV)

*The main trade union.
[†]There are several other trade unions in the country.
[‡]Trade union with the longest history.
[§]Trade union with the most members.
[¶]Corresponding to the strongest trade union.
Source: Social Watch. *The Starting Point*, 1996, p. 41, as cited in *Statistical Abstract of Latin America*, Vol. 38. Los Angeles: UCLA Latin American Center Publications, 2002, table 606, p. 178.

American society has evolved over time as the result of both land reform programs and economic transformation. The term *campesino* has been used to label those low-income agricultural producers who have some attachment to the land in rural Latin America. *Rural laborers* comprise another group made up of landless agricultural workers. In many ways, the basic conditions of their lives have changed very little over the course of several centuries. The great majority of both groups have lived in dire poverty, barely earning enough for their survival and reproduction, with little chance for advancement. Most people born as *campesinos* or rural laborers died in the same social situation and passed that legacy on to their children and grandchildren. While having common characteristics, it is also important to see the significant differences between various groups of the poor based on their different circumstances of employment.

The first group is known as *colonos*. They work on the large plantations described earlier as the *haciendas* and *fazendas*. Whether they are tenant farmers or sharecroppers, they are all too often bound to the plantation by generations of debt. This group is generally not paid in wages but allowed a small plot of land to grow food for their sustenance and provided the other basic necessities of life by the owner of the plantation in return for labor. In the best of situations, this group can be said to be protected from the greatest uncertainties of harsh rural life by the *patrón*. As one might expect, their political position is especially precarious. Since they are wholly dependent on the *patrón*, they have often been either marginalized from politics or manipulated by the *patrón's* dictates. In the context of democratic elections, *colonos*, *campesinos*, or rural laborers can be coerced into voting for the chosen political candidates of the estate owner. Because of its numbers, this group could be a significant political force. However, because they were traditionally isolated from one another on different estates and in different villages, their organizing power was often muted. Organizing efforts were often resisted with force by local owners and their allies among the police and judiciary. Currently, better opportunities for exchange of information and interaction are offered by the expanding modern communication infrastructure, but the forced commercialization of farming is rapidly forcing this group either off the land and into the cities or to become landless rural laborers.

The second important group is the rural wage laborers, who have become increasingly dominant through the economic transformation of Latin America in the twentieth century. These are the workers on Latin America's commercial farms and plantations who are hired first to plant and then later to harvest the region's primary cash export crops: cotton, coffee, sugarcane, and bananas. Many wage laborers may own small plots of land but are forced to sell their labor to supplement their income in order to survive. In many places, they are migrants because they often have to travel great distances to find enough work to survive throughout the year. North Americans are somewhat familiar with this class of Latin Americans because many work each year, both legally and illegally, in the agricultural fields of the United States. Like the *colonos*, this group is largely marginalized from the Latin American political process. The combination of their constant travel and precarious economic situation makes it difficult for them to become involved in politics, either as voters or as protestors; but there are important exceptions. Banana workers in Honduras, Costa Rica, Panama, and Guatemala have been very political at times, with involvement in both elections and protest actions. In recent times, many rural laborers have joined the Landless Movement (Movimento dos Trabalhadores Rurais Sem Terra) in Brazil and have begun to exert greater political pressure. Likewise, much of the organizational base of the Zapatistas in Mexico and the Confederation of Indigenous Nationalities of Ecuador (CONAIE) is rural.

The third group are the subsistence farmers, the *minifundistas* and *microfundistas*. As was pointed out earlier, there may be overlap between the last two categories because many subsistence farmers supplement their income with wage labor. The land that they occupy, sometimes with legal title and sometimes as squatters, is usually less than 10 acres. The crops are grown largely without mechanization or fertilizers because the use of either is out of the financial reach of the cultivator. In good times, the farmer grows enough for the family to survive and sells a small surplus at a local market. If there is crop failure due to storms or drought, there may not be a surplus and the family is driven toward the wage labor–migrant situation. In difficult economic times, the small farmer is also vulnerable to foreclosure if money is owed. This category of existence is generally preferred to that of wage labor, but it faces pressures from many directions. Proponents of land reform programs have often viewed this group's level of economic production as marginal and inefficient, so they have been targeted for elimination, with the hope that their labor can become available for the more efficient larger farms. Others have argued that giving them more land, irrigation, agricultural credit, and technical assistance would resolve much of rural poverty and increase the efficiency of production.

The rural poor have definite grievances to pursue with the political authorities. The *colonos* generally want the opportunity to improve their own lives and those of their children, usually by gaining the opportunity to work their own land. The wage workers want higher wages but are generally frustrated with the government's unwillingness to help them. Those who own small farms seek credit and technical support from the government and protection from their creditors.

For most of Latin American history, the rural poor were not in a strong position to pursue their grievances, divided as they were by both geography and differing interests. However, the twentieth century has seen a significant change in their political importance. In Mexico and Venezuela, mass political parties succeeded in organizing the rural poor into the political process as voters behind a clear political agenda. They have been even more important in revolutionary movements, playing a key role in such movements in Cuba, Bolivia, El Salvador, Guatemala, Peru, Colombia, and Nicaragua. In addition, the growth of grassroots movements such as the Peasants League and Landless Movement in Brazil (MST) and the peasant unions and other organizations in Bolivia underscore their growing political importance.

THE MILITARY

The armed forces must definitely be treated as a singularly important group in the political history of Latin America, although that prominence needs to be tempered by the fact that as Latin America enters the twenty-first century, for the first time in its modern history, no country is under military rule. Such a situation represents a stark contrast to the 1970s and 1980s, when more than half the region's governments were military-led. However, a strong process of democratization beginning in the mid-1980s brought civilian governments to power across the region, led by Peru in 1980, Argentina in 1983, Brazil in 1985, and Chile in 1989. Today, the discussion of the role of the military in much of Latin America revolves around its role as a significant bureaucratic interest group. Acceptance of the legitimacy of civilian rule and the subordination of the military to civilian political rule has seemingly become the norm in much of Latin America. Yet, the military still holds veto power in countries such as Guatemala and is still able to operate with impunity in some aspects of civil society. The military remains an active force in contemporary politics, and its current position flows from its long-standing power. Indeed, it was the military that removed President Zelaya from office in the 2009 coup in Honduras.

Since World War II and with the strong backing of the government of the United States, Latin American militaries have been competent, professional organizations with considerable modern weaponry. Not surprisingly, the region's largest country, Brazil, has the largest armed forces, with close to 300,000 soldiers in uniform. Brazil spends over $3 billion a year maintaining its forces, which include an aircraft carrier and more than 200 combat aircraft. Other countries that have maintained significant military forces in recent years include Mexico, Argentina, Chile, and Cuba. (Cuba significantly reduced its forces in the 1990s after maintaining close to 50,000 soldiers in Africa, with Soviet help, during the 1970s and 1980s.) Yet, the primary role of most militaries in Latin America has been the maintenance of internal order. However, the size and sophistication of military forces are not in reality the prime determinants of political influence in Latin America or elsewhere. Throughout the twentieth century, the U.S. and British militaries have been powerful forces but have never challenged control by civilian authority. In contrast, relatively weak and small military establishments in Latin America have usurped civilian authority and sought to dominate the political process.

The involvement of the Latin American military in politics has its roots in the military nature of the conquest and early settlement, the class character of the military families throughout the course of Latin American history, and other factors. Over the course of Spanish and Portuguese colonial rule, the military officer corps were deeply intertwined with political rulers and the landowning elites. They were often one and the same as leading military people also controlled large tracts of land. If the military leaders did not happen in a given instance to own significant land, they acted as an important ally against any forces that sought to challenge the landed oligarchy. As a result, the military entered the age of democratic reforms in the twentieth century in a position deeply suspicious of forces that would have curtailed the political and economic power of the old political and economic elites through democratic political means. With few exceptions, the political stance of the military as an enemy of democracy and reform was well established entering the twentieth century. Understanding the military in the twentieth century and especially in the last fifty years becomes a more complex problem. During that time the class character of military officers has changed considerably as fewer of the children of the military continued the family tradition and as the modern, more professional militaries often became an important avenue of social mobility for those who aspired to become members of the middle class or to improve their relative standing in it.

The education system for military officers has long been an important determinant of their orientation toward politics. Military leaders have maintained their system of officer corps education independent of and isolated from the civilian education system. Traditionally, most military education focuses on technical warfare training with little time devoted to the humanities or the social sciences. The

Centro de Altos Estudios Militares (CAEM) in Peru, which trained the Nasserite military officers who formed the reformist government of Juan Velasco Alvarado (1968–1975), is an exception; likewise, the training at the National War College (Escola Superior de Guerra) of Brazil viewed strategy as involving some degree of social involvement. Yet, in all military schools, to the degree that matters of history and society are treated, the ideological content very often views the military as the only institution of society that is unambiguously dedicated to the nation's welfare. All civilian politicians are treated with some suspicion, especially those of a center or left persuasion. However, certain interest groups, especially labor unions, are viewed as detrimental to the national interest. At least until recently, there has been little or no shift in this approach to education, which has definitely contributed to the military's willingness to carry out coups against civilian governments.

If military education has provided an ideological justification for certain forms of military intervention, then their disciplined and hierarchical forms of organization provided both the ability to carry out the overthrow of civilian governments and the ability to place themselves at the head of government bureaucracies previously headed by civilians. Military leaders in the 1960s and 1970s in countries such as Brazil argued that their hierarchical forms of organization could bring new levels of efficiency to government bureaucracies previously plagued by bad organization and chaos. This type of military government came to be termed *bureaucratic authoritarianism*. In general, claims that the military could be more effective rulers than civilians proved untrue and contributed to the downfall of military governments in the latter part of the 1980s. It is unclear just how readily the military can exercise its power in the current democratized period in Latin America. Yet, they still have the power to replace a government if they choose to mobilize.

GOVERNMENT BUREAUCRATS

Some have suggested that government bureaucrats should not be treated as distinct and separate actors within the Latin American political process because they simply carry out the wishes of whatever political leaders are in power. However, this view is insufficient for Latin America or most any other region of the world. The key factor in understanding the significant power of government bureaucrats is that while elected politicians serve distinct terms and military leaders can be driven from power at any time, the great majority of bureaucrats stay in their positions for lengthy time periods. In Latin America, government bureaucrats have wielded considerable power because of the post–World War II trend of large-scale government involvement in the ownership of important economic enterprises—banks, airlines, oil refineries, railroads, steel plantations, and many more—leading to the emergence of the nation of "technocrats" who played important political roles, particularly during the authoritarian periods in the 1960s and 1970s, in countries like Brazil, Argentina, Chile, and Uruguay. Privatizations within the last decade have reduced the government's role in countries like Argentina and Brazil, but public ownership remains formidable. A recent acknowledgment of the power of one segment of bureaucracy came in Venezuela where in 1999 the elected populist president Hugo Chávez spoke of the need to trim the size of the giant bureaucracy of the state-run oil company PDVSA (Petróleos de Venezuela). Chávez acknowledged the power of its bureaucracy, calling it a "government within a government." Other presidents have talked of reducing the size of the bureaucracy at all levels.

This sector has engaged in a significant amount of self-promotion to boost its importance. In contrast to military officers, who stake their right to political office on their duty to country and their organizational skill, government bureaucrats advertise their skill as technocrats who can rise above the squabbling or corruption that may plague elected leaders. Increasingly, many Latin American technocrats are trained at foreign universities in Britain, France, and the United States. Oftentimes they return to their homelands with strong beliefs that their newfound technical skills have given them the right to a say in the political and economic direction of their nation, not just as administrators. In Mexico, the previous four presidents came from the ranks of these *técnicos*.

Government bureaucrats, like those in other sectors, may well be motivated by selfless and patriotic concerns; but those who manage government institutions share many interests. First, they desire to continue their influence over public policy. Second, they seek to administer their agencies with as little interference as possible. Third, they enjoy the power and, in some instances, the wealth that comes from providing goods and services that those in the private sector need.

The means to achieve these ends are fairly well known. The reality is that elected officials are dependent on administrators to carry out their economic and political development plans. If an administrator disagrees with a particular policy initiative, he or she definitely has the ability to sabotage its implementation. While such sabotage may need to be subtle to succeed, the elected officials usually lack the legal authority to remove recalcitrant officials from their posts. It is not yet clear whether the trend toward smaller government bureaucracies promoted by neoliberal reformers in the 1990s will significantly reduce the power of this sector. Ultimately, the sector may well turn out to be an insurmountable barrier to the full implementation of privatization plans or other government reforms. Likewise, oversized bureaucracies have become a fiscal problem that fuels inflation.

POLITICAL PARTIES

The role of political parties is evolving in Latin America. Wynia argues that political parties have traditionally played at least three separate and distinct roles in Latin American society. Like political parties in the United States and Western Europe, they participate in elections with the aim of gaining state power. In a few countries, like Costa Rica and Venezuela, political parties have played this role for decades, almost exclusively concentrating their energies on winning periodic contests for power. In countries where elections have been the norm, Ronald McDonald and J. Mark Rubl argue that parties tend to serve four functions: political recruitment, political communication, social control, and government organization and policy making. However, until the 1990s, this role was sporadic in many countries, either because there were no elections, only military rule, or because their role was limited by the lack of constitutional norms. Beyond elections, there are two other roles for political parties, that of conspirators and the creation of political monopoly.

The category of conspirator describes those parties that do not accept the results of elections or operate in the absence of regular elections. These parties generally operate in the extraparliamentary arena, often turning to the use of force to gain power. Such parties could be coming from a variety of political positions, but most often they are movements that have been denied power through legitimate channels and turn to armed struggle to achieve their goals. Classic examples of this form of political activity occurred in Cuba, when activists in the Orthodox Party, denied the opportunity of gaining power through the 1952 elections because of Fulgencio Batista's cancellation of those elections, formed an armed organization (the 26th of July Movement) that challenged Batista and eventually defeated him.

Parties creating a political monopoly are those that seek to remain in power on a permanent basis. Latin America has two excellent contemporary examples of this type of political movement, the Cuban Communist Party (CCP) and the Mexican PRI. Both have been very successful in their efforts but have used different methods. The Cuban communists have succeeded in part through the establishment of formal rules of the game whereby the constitution enshrines the CCP as the country's only legal party, through its legitimacy as the party of the 1959 revolution, and through its social achievements. The PRI dominated the Mexican political scene for over seventy years, keeping the presidency up to the year 2000, when it finally suffered its first defeat in a presidential election. The party constructed a system where opposition parties competed for power but were limited in their real opportunities for victory by a series of PRI policies, including patronage, co-optation, voter fraud, and occasionally repression. Both movements were born in revolutionary conflict and maintained power in part by presenting themselves as the party of the revolution and as the only political force capable of moving forward the ideals of their revolutions. The success of such movements is not easy and is usually dependent on some measure of popular support together with the support of the military, although in both Mexico and Cuba the military remained subordinated to civilian politics and heavily influenced by the dominant party.

Latin American political parties emerged in the nineteenth century when most of the region's nations adopted republican forms of government with limited suffrage. Two primary political currents emerged during this time period, the Liberals and the Conservatives. The latter were drawn primarily from the traditional rural elites of the *latifundio* system, who primarily sought from the government a preservation of the economic and political patterns that were established during the colonial period. The Liberals represented the emerging modern upper classes of the nineteenth century, the owners of commercial agriculture and other newly founded activities. The Liberals wanted the government to undertake a more active role in breaking up traditional landowning patterns, separating church from state, and promoting foreign commerce. Latin American Liberals were not as committed to the political side of liberalism with its emphasis on constitutional rule and freedom of thought. Elections in Latin America were largely an elite matter throughout the nineteenth century, involving only about 5 percent of the adult male population. These parties engaged in electoral contests but also were often the basis for armed conflict as both sides often refused to recognize the results and turned to violence to achieve their political ends.

Representative of elite dominance and patriarchy, women and minorities still struggle for adequate representation in party leadership positions (see Table 22). Internal decision making is frequently authoritarian and often based on *personalismo*.

TABLE 22. Women in National Directive Bodies of Selected Political Parties, Selected Years, 1990–1994

Country	Year	Party	Both Sexes	Women N	Women %
Argentina	1990	Radical Civic Union	24	0	0
Bolivia	1991	Movement of the Revolutionary Left	9	1	11.1
		Free Bolivian Movement	16	1	6.3
		National Democratic Action	13	2	15.4
Brazil	1991	Workers' Party	82	5	6.1
		Liberal Front	121	2	1.7
		Social Democratic Party	121	2	1.7
		Labor Democrats	119	11	9.2
		Brazilian Democratic Movement	121	4	3.3
		Brazilian Social Democratic Party	121	8	6.6
Chile	1991	Christian Democratic Party	40	5	12.5
		Socialist Party	19	4	21.1
		Party for Democracy	20	5	25
		Independent Democratic Union	26	2	7.7
		National Renovation	15	2	13.3
Colombia	1993	Liberal Party	3	1	33.3
		Democratic Alliance, M-19	5	1	20
Costa Rica	1990	Christian Social Unity	17	1	5.9
		National Liberation	25	3	12
Cuba	1991	Cuban Communist Party	25	3	12
Dominican Republic	1993	Christian Social Reform Party	39	10	25.6
		Dominican Revolutionary Party	297	30	10.1
		Dominican Communist Party	22	1	4.5
		Dominican Workers' Party	27	1	3.7
El Salvador	1993	ARENA	15	1	6.7
		Christian Democratic Party	40	3	7.5
		National Democratic Union	10	4	40
		National Revolutionary Movement	9	1	11.1
		Farabundo Martí Front for National Liberation	50	7	14
Mexico	1992	Institutional Revolutionary Party	34	4	11.8
		National Action Party	28	5	17.9
		Democratic Revolution Party	32	7	21.9
Nicaragua*	1994	Sandinista National Liberation Front	27	6	22.2
		Social Christian Party	58	12	20.7
		Liberal Independent Party	121	20	16.5
		Communist Party of Nicaragua	103	15	14.6
Panama	1991	Christian Democratic Party	4	1	25
		Authentic Liberal Party	14	0	0
		National Republican Liberal Movement	31	4	12.9
		Panamanian Party	9	1	11.1
		Labor Party	5	0	0
		Democratic Revolution Party	5	0	0
Paraguay	1994	National Republican Association	72	6	8.3
		Radical Authentic Liberal Party	46	5	11.1
		Febrerista Revolutionary Party	30	6	20

Country	Year	Party	Both Sexes	Women N	%
Peru	1990	Peruvian Aprista Party	4	1	25
		United Left	6	0	0
		National Front of Rural Workers	20	3	15
		Change 90 Now Majority	5	0	0
Venezuela	1992	Democratic Action	33	7	21.2
		Christian Social Party	35	3	8.6
		Socialist Movement	34	4	11.8

*Regional Directive Council.

Source: Social Watch. *The Starting Point*, 1996, p. 40, as cited in *Statistical Abstract of Latin America*, Vol. 38. Los Angeles: UCLA Latin American Center Publications, 2002, table 605, p. 177.

Traditional Parties. As pressure for increased suffrage succeeded in widening the electoral base and new immigrant groups swelled the Latin American population in the early part of the twentieth century, two distinct patterns of political party loyalty developed: the Liberals and the Conservatives. They have persisted to the present day. In some countries, Colombia and Honduras being the best examples, the Liberal and Conservative parties, despite being elite-driven, succeeded in gaining electoral support from the newly enfranchised rural and urban masses. The liberals stood for political and economic liberalism (thus greater political rights and the curtailment of church power on the one hand and free trade and free markets on the other). The conservatives stood for official religion, centralized government, and state-regulated trade and commerce. This political division basically continued throughout the twentieth century, leaving these countries with essentially two-party systems unchanged over time. The Liberals and Conservatives who succeeded in transforming themselves did so by a variety of means. *Hacienda*-owning Conservatives, using the strong bonds of the patron-client relationship, have often been able to secure the support of their *colonos* through a combination of reward and punishment. Wage-paying commercial farmers associated with the Liberals may not have had as direct control of their employees, but many did succeed in convincing rural workers that their self-interest lay with support for the Liberal cause. Both parties succeeded in gaining strong familial loyalty to their movements, a connection that has now been passed on through multiple generations.

However, the cases where Liberals and Conservatives succeeded in transforming themselves into broad-based electoral machines were the exception. In some cases, such as in Chile, Liberals and Conservatives were forced to unite (Chile's National Party) to be able to confront new challenges to elite domination. In the majority of countries, the traditional parties rebuffed the demands of the newly emergent groups with the result that new, **European-inspired political parties** emerged on the scene after 1900. The most interesting were the Chilean Radical Party, the Argentine Radical Civic Union, and the Uruguayan Colorado Party. Modeled after the French Radical Party, these movements stood for suffrage, expanding public education and other government services, and the protection of workers' rights from the power of oligarchies, both urban and rural. Radical politicians succeeded in getting themselves elected in all three countries, drawing primarily on an immigrant and urban constituency, including the emerging proletariat and intermediate (middle) sectors. The Radicals generally did greater damage to the Liberals, who in some ways had attempted to appeal to the same constituency. As the Radicals eclipsed the Liberals, in some countries it turned the primary electoral battlefield into one of Radicals against Conservatives. In some instances, the elite former supporters of the Liberals turned to the Conservatives to form an oligarchic alliance. The heyday of the Radicals was relatively short-lived, although the Argentine party has undergone a rebirth in the last fifteen years. The Radical parties faced increased pressure in the 1930s and, unable to deal with the economic challenges of the Great Depression, either were overthrown by the military representing the traditional oligarchy or faced increasing pressure from both populist and socialist movements. They are still important political actors in Argentina and Chile, and the Colorados won the presidential election in 2000 in Uruguay. The Liberals have remained relatively strong in Colombia.

Nationalist Populist Parties. The 1930s and 1940s saw the emergence of populist parties in both Brazil and Argentina. Each was organized around a single charismatic leader, Getúlio Vargas in Brazil and Juan Perón in Argentina. The populist movement founded by Vargas did not outlive him, but the Peronist Party still plays an influential role in Argentine politics to this day. It is important to understand that the roots of Latin American populism were clearly different from those in the United States, where the movement was primarily a rural-based protest against the railroad monopolies. The success of Latin American populists in the 1930s and 1940s was with the growing urban industrial working class, whose needs were largely ignored by the dominant parties of the time—Conservatives, Liberals, and Radicals. Unlike the other political parties discussed here, the populists are harder to pin down as the movements were uniquely shaped by their leaders. As movements, they did not concentrate as much as the other parties on building organizational entities. Instead, they depended on the mobilizing power of the leaders themselves and, in the case of Perón, on his popular spouse, Eva. To underscore the centrality of personal rule, Vargas did not launch his populist movement's political party until he had been in power for almost fifteen years.

The heterogeneous political philosophy of the populists concentrated its attacks on the old order, the traditional *latifundistas*, but also on the commercial elites that had come to the fore in the beginning of the century. The populists were not revolutionaries; rather, their philosophy was to gain a greater share of the national wealth for their supporters within the framework of capitalism. It was also a nationalistic philosophy that sought to achieve national development without significant involvement of foreign investors, a stance that angered the foreign powers who had long dominated the region and those who had hoped to capitalize on the new opportunities. They were also supporters of rapid industrialization and state intervention in the economy.

The populists saw themselves as the archenemies of the Socialist and Communist parties that were seeking to appeal to the same constituency—urban industrial workers. However, unlike the Conservatives and Liberals, the populists believed that it was possible to defeat the prospect of revolution by creating gov-ernment-sponsored worker organizations, which could yield worker discipline in return for better wages and working conditions.

Even before creating a populist movement, Vargas had linked Latin American populism with European fascism through his concept of the *Estado Novo* (new state), a corporatist idea that combined strong government involvement in economic activities with the organization of workers into government-controlled unions. In the case of Brazil, the *Estado Novo* meant a centralizing of political power against the interests of regional authorities who dominated the country's politics prior to 1930. Vargas organized the Brazilian Labor Party in 1945 as a mass organization when his opponents in the traditional oligarchy tried to drive him from power. The Labor Party proved to be an effective vehicle for Vargas, winning the presidency for him in both 1945 and 1950. However, his role as a ruler who sought to mediate the diverse interests of Brazilian society was a failure. Vargas was hounded into sui-cide in 1954 by his political enemies, especially the military. Successors of Vargas, such as Juscelino Kubitschek, sought to continue elements of the populist program; but the Brazilian Labor Party did not succeed in becoming a permanent feature of political life.

The populism of Juan Perón in Argentina had many similarities to that of Vargas, but there were also some differences. Perón also incorporated elements of Italian fascism, but, unlike Vargas, who first gained power and then later created a movement to sustain his power, Perón gained power through the transforma-tion of the Argentine General Labor Confederation into his personal instrument and the incorporation of conservative, radical, and socialist groups into his politi-cal movement. When the military and the traditional oligarchy sought to block his ascendancy to the presidency by arresting him, Perón and his future wife, Eva, mobilized his forces to gain his release and pave the way for his victory in the 1946 presidential election. In power, Perón's strategy was similar to that of Vargas. He implemented programs that delivered social services and a higher standard of liv-ing to the urban workers while guaranteeing entrepreneurs labor peace through tight control of the unions. Like Vargas, his rule took on strongly nationalist tones, and policies of economic protectionism were implemented. The government took a strong hold on the economy, the most dramatic example being the creation of a government monopoly over agricultural commodity trading, a strategy that cap-tured the considerable profits of this section entirely for the government. He also nationalized the railroads, airlines, public utilities, and financial system, among other strategic sectors. In typical populist fashion, Perón did not move in any way to redistribute rural land as a revolutionary would have done but, rather, to simply bring the rural elites under government control. Perón used the profits from this scheme to finance industrialization, social welfare programs, and the takeover of the country's utilities from foreign owners. Once the Peronist economic strategy began to fail in the early 1950s, Perón fell victim to the power of the old elites, who engineered a military coup in 1955 and sent him into exile.

However, unlike the populist movement of Vargas that largely ended when he fell from power, the Peronist Party remained strong, in part inspired by its leader in exile in Spain. Fearing their power, the military prevented the Peronists from

President Chávez speaks. *(Ministry of Information, Venezuela)*

competing in elections or nullified the results if they favored the Peronists throughout the eighteen years of his exile. Only in 1973 did the military allow a Peronist
candidate to run for president and Perón to return in a desperate attempt to stem
a growing revolutionary tide. His party swept the elections of 1973, only to have
him die a year later. The party continued under the leadership of Perón's third wife,
Isabel, but the military ended that rule with a coup in 1976 and seven years of subsequent dictatorial rule. However, the Peronist Party, retaining its working-class base
and nostalgia for the golden days of the late 1940s and early 1950s, succeeded in
winning back control of the political system in both 1989 and 1995 under the leadership of Carlos Menem. Ironically, Menem shifted the ideology of the party almost
completely away from that of its founder, embracing widespread privatization, free
markets, and large-scale foreign investment. As a result, other political movements
began to erode the electoral base of the Peronists, calling into question their influence into the next century. Returning to its populist roots, the Peronists successfully ran Néstor Kirchner for the presidency in 2003. It has also been suggested that
Alberto Fujimori represented a new type of right-wing populism in Peru. Likewise,
some see Hugo Chávez as representative of a type of leftist nationalist populism
that has come to dominate politics in Venezuela.

　　Reform Parties. Another type of political party that emerged during the same
era as the populists was the democratic reform parties. Basically there are two types
of reform party, secular and religious. The traits that they shared were based on a
rejection of both the populists and the revolutionaries. The democratic reformers
did not accept the tendency toward demagoguery and the use of strong-arm tactics
against political opponents but did embrace the populist strategy of maintaining

capitalist, free enterprise systems. The democratic reformers, while sharing some of the short-term desires for social justice with the Socialist and Communist parties, obviously broke with them over the vision of a classless socialist society.

APRA Parties. The secular reform movement began with the American Popular Revolutionary Alliance (**APRA**), founded by Peruvian Victor Raúl Haya de la Torre while he was in Mexico in 1924. The party was inspired by a range of political ideas, including socialism, indigenism, and anti-imperalism and was more radical in its early years. The charismatic Haya de la Torre led the party through the 1970s. Long persecuted and marginalized in Peruvian politics, APRA only achieved government power under Alan García for a brief period in the 1980s and again in 2006. The return to power has rejuvenated the party considerably. However, similar political movements inspired by Haya de la Torre in Venezuela and Costa Rica have enjoyed considerable long-term success. The Democratic Action Party (AD) of Venezuela first governed in the late 1940s and has held the presidency of the country for the great majority of the last forty years. In a similar fashion, the National Liberation Party of Costa Rica has held the presidency of that country five times since its founding at the time of the Costa Rican civil war in 1948. Similar parties developed in Bolivia (MNR), the Dominican Republic (Partido Revolucionario), and Puerto Rico (Popular Democratic Party).

Christian Democratic Parties. Religious reformers are grouped in the Christian Democratic movement, which originated in Western Europe after World War II. Drawing heavily on Catholic thought, the Christian Democratic parties emerged as alternatives to the powerful Communist, Socialist, and Labor parties. The rise of Christian Democrats was especially important in Germany and Italy, where earlier procapitalist parties had been irredeemably tainted by their association with fascism. In the Latin American context, these parties emerged in countries where populism never took significant hold and as an alternative to the revolutionary parties. Latin American Christian Democrats came to embody very similar political programs to the secular reformists, embracing political democracy in opposition to military rule and a package of reform proposals, especially in the agrarian sector. In contrast to the secular parties, they drew their inspiration from progressive papal encyclicals and reform movements within the Church. Christian Democrats sought to organize throughout the region but ultimately have achieved full success only in Chile and Costa Rica and limited success in Venezuela and El Salvador. In Chile, the Christian Democrats first gained power in the 1960s as a middle ground between the Conservatives and the Socialist-Communist coalition that became Popular Unity (UP). Defeated by the latter in 1970 and then driven underground by the 1973 military coup, the Christian Democrats emerged in a postmilitary period in 1989 as the country's leading political force in association with the moderate socialists. The party won reelection in 1993 and is positioned for long-term influence with its centrist reform-oriented policies and Chile's relative economic stability. Christian Democratic parties elsewhere have been less successful. Only in two other countries have they enjoyed political power—two presidential terms in Venezuela in the 1970s (Social Christian Party, COPEI) and brief rule in El Salvador in the 1980s under José Napoleon Duarte at the height of the civil war as the recipient of considerable U.S. economic and military aid.

Left Reform Parties. A contemporary reform party that clearly bridges the religious and secular boundaries is the Brazilian Workers' Party (PT). The **PT** emerged in the late 1970s during the growth of opposition to the military dictatorship. From the beginning, the PT had both Marxist and Catholic leadership, the latter being drawn from the powerful ecclesial base communities. The most popular leader was the leader of the resurgent metalworkers union, Luiz Inácio da Silva, known simply as "Lula." The PT grew in strength rapidly despite many obstacles thrown in its way, including the jailing of Lula in 1981. With the return of electoral democracy in 1985, the PT established itself as a primary opposition party, supplanting older, more established left parties. In November 1988, the PT's Luiza Erundina de Souza was elected mayor of São Paulo, Brazil's largest city. The party also demonstrated its mobilization powers through massive industrial strikes in 1988 and 1989. In the 1989 presidential elections, Lula nearly won the presidency in a runoff election against Fernando Collor de Mello, whose well-financed campaign defeated the PT leader by a scant 6 percent. The PT, seeking a more centrist image, voted at its 1991 convention to affirm its commitment to a mixed economy and democracy while retaining socialist ideals. Delegates representing the party's 600,000 members also voted to grant women a minimum of 30 percent of leadership positions. Initially favored in the polls leading up to the 1994 elections, Lula eventually finished a distant second to the well-funded campaign of the centrist Fernando Henrique Cardoso. He was defeated again when Cardoso was reelected in 1999. After moving toward the center and reassuring business interests, Lula finally won the presidency in 2002 and was easily reelected in 2006. The PT has succeeded in becoming the government party but does not hold a congressional majority. Similarly, the Revolutionary Democratic Party (**PRD**) in Mexico is also representative of this new brand of leftist party, as is the Frente Amplio in Uruguay, which won the presidency and a congressional majority in the 2004 and 2009 elections.

Revolutionary Parties. The final group of parties to be discussed are the revolutionary parties. Revolutionary movements are discussed in far more detail in Chapter 11, but it is necessary to briefly discuss the revolutionary parties in the wider context of other political parties. Two different types of revolutionary party are usually acknowledged in the Latin American context, those whose origins are in Marxist thought and those whose roots are elsewhere. However, it is also necessary to note that not all parties that begin their existence as revolutionary ones remain so. We must also discuss in this context those original revolutionary parties that have become thoroughly reformist in their behavior.

Communist and socialist parties had their roots in the ideas and political activities of Karl Marx and Friedrich Engels in the last few decades of the nineteenth century in Europe. Initially, the Marxist movement was united, but the 1917 October Revolution in Russia was a turning point. Most European socialist parties had abandoned the possibility of revolution in favor of the achievement of socialism by parliamentary means, but the success of the first socialist revolution in Russia under the leadership of the Bolshevik Party inspired the creation of an alternative set of revolutionary parties, called "communist," that accepted the international leadership of the Soviet Union. Because Latin America industrialized considerably after Europe, the development of socialist or revolutionary parties along Marxist lines was slow to occur. However, during the 1920s and 1930s, these parties did begin to emerge, largely among intellectuals, students, and industrial workers. Overall, these parties did not fare particularly well in the region as they faced wholesale repression from the established governments and fierce competition to organize workers from both the Radicals and the populists. The primary exception was in Chile, where the Marxist parties succeeded in gaining a large following in the working class and entry into coalition governments during the 1930s.

By the 1950s the Socialist and Communist parties had largely ceased to be revolutionary in orientation. Where possible, in countries such as Guatemala, they sought to work through the political process, working with non-Marxist reform parties to obtain programs for workers' rights and land reform. However, the conservatism of these Communist parties only served to open political space to their left, which was soon filled by a new generation of revolutionary parties inspired by the success of the 26th of July Movement in Cuba. Basing themselves on Marxist ideology and co-opting the old, reformist Cuban Communist Party, movement leaders were soon at the head of a new generation of revolutionary parties that came to include the Sandinista National Liberation Front (FSLN) in Nicaragua, the Farabundo Martí National Liberation Front (FMLN) in El Salvador, and the Revolutionary Armed Forces of Colombia (FARC).

The best example of a non-Marxist revolutionary party is the PRI of Mexico. Founded in 1929, twelve years after the triumph of the revolutionary forces over the traditional oligarchy, this party has been one of the most successful in the twentieth-century history of political parties. From its founding in the late 1920s, the PRI won every presidential election in the twentieth century and held an absolute majority in the national legislature until the most recent election in 1997. Some dispute whether the PRI was ever a revolutionary party, but during the rule of Lázaro Cárdenas (1934–1940), the party used tactics of mass mobilization of workers and peasants to secure the gains of the 1910 revolution in the face of continued oligarchic resistance. After the period of Cárdenas's rule, the party became more traditional, maintaining its power through a variety of means ranging from repression to voter fraud to co-optation to maintain its absolute domination of the Mexican political system. By the 1980s, most considered that it had lost any revolutionary orientation.

Common Characteristics. Despite their obvious ideological differences, McDonald and Rubl argue that Latin American political parties share some important characteristics, primarily elitism, factionalism, personalism, organizational weakness, and heterogeneous mass support. The elitism revolves around the centralization of decision making within a small core of (male and mostly European) party leaders who are usually drawn from the upper and middle classes. Some parties engage in a facade of democracy through the conduct of public primaries, but in reality decisions are retained by the core leadership. The latest party to follow this more transparent approach was the Mexican PRI with its first-ever presidential primary in 1999. New parties like the PT and PRD also display a greater degree of leadership diversity and internal democracy.

Factionalism has also been an enduring problem in Latin American parties. Such factionalism is often most associated with the left, but bitter splits among party leaders on both personal and ideological lines have been common across the political spectrum. Only in the case of the existence of a strong figure, such as Fidel Castro in the Cuban Communist Party, Juan Perón in the Peronist Party, or Haya de la Torre in the APRA movement was serious factionalism avoided. When the latter died, his party split into several warring factions.

McDonald and Rubl also argue that Latin American parties have tended to more often be organized around personalities than ideologies. The roots of personalism are deep in Latin American history from the era of the *caudillos*, but they have been sustained throughout the twentieth century despite the development of party ideologies and structures. Beyond the obvious examples of Vargas, Perón, and Castro, others abound, including former army officer Hugo Chávez in Venezuela. As party leaders, these personalities in some cases are willing to quickly change their party's position to ensure continuation in office. Identification with a single leader has often proven easier than connection to party symbols and doctrines, especially in the case of the less-educated populations.

Latin America does have some significant examples of well-organized parties—the Mexican PRI, APRA up to the 1980s, the Cuban Communist Party, Argentina's Radical Party, Uruguay's Colorado and Blanco parties, and Venezuela's Democratic Action, but these are the exception rather than the rule. Most Latin American parties are more similar to the U.S. Democratic and Republican parties, coming to life primarily at the time of election, lacking strong ties to grassroots movements, and without a large number of formal members. Some are sustained by a relatively high level of party identification among the voting public, but in general party identification is weak in Latin America compared to Western Europe and the United States.

Class characteristics do tend to carry some weight in Latin American party identification but less so than in Western Europe because of the relatively late development of labor unions. An obvious exception to this rule is the Brazilian PT, which has a very clear worker and peasant allegiance. However, more common in Latin American politics are parties like the Mexican PRI, the Uruguayan Colorados, the Chilean Christian Democrats, and the Argentine Peronists, whose long-running electoral success is based on the creation of a multiclass constituency. Another basis of party identification in Latin America is region. Regional party identification has its roots in the nineteenth century, when warring Liberal and Conservative parties developed regional strongholds. Such patterns continue today in countries like Colombia, Uruguay, Honduras, Peru, and Mexico. In the latter, the opposition National Action Party (PAN) has developed a power base in the states nearest the U.S. border, likely influenced by the tradition of the two-party system in its neighbor to the north.

As suggested in Chapter 11, mass organizations have also become important political actors as well and may be displacing some parties or revolutionary movements.

Conclusion

One of the most important issues facing Latin America today is whether or not democratic rule will continue. Can the large steps taken in the last twenty years be sustained? To do so would clearly represent a significant break with Latin America's past. The most daunting issue may be whether or not democratic governments can be maintained in the face of deep socioeconomic problems that will not be solved

overnight. As was discussed more fully in Chapter 8, in the 1990s most democratically elected governments carried out programs of economic neoliberalism that
sought to open the countries to imports and foreign direct investments. These programs had mixed results and as a result there has been a fundamental shift to the
left in the last ten years, beginning with the election in 1998 of Hugo Chávez in
Venezuela. In Argentina, Bolivia, and Ecuador, citizens protesting neoliberal governments took to the streets and forced those governments to step down. In the
new century the citizens of Chile, Argentina, Uruguay, Brazil, Ecuador, Venezuela,
Nicaragua, and Guatemala elected either socialist or progressive governments. In
addition, the neoliberal Calderón narrowly held on to power for the PAN in the face
of a strong challenge from the reformist PRD candidate López Obrador in Mexico.

A series of leftist victories in elections in the last few years have suggested a
new political orientation in Latin America. These elections are part of a trend where
new movements and social actors, especially from the indigenous peoples of the
region, have thrust themselves into power. These movements are taking advantage
of the democratic openings of the last twenty years and in the process are raising the
expectations of the poor masses. However, many of the governments elected have yet
to show that they are capable of meeting the high expectations of their people. In the
past such a situation often invited the intervention of the military to restore order but
that period of Latin American history may well be over. There is little appetite, even
among the business and financial elites for a return to circumstances of widespread
repression and denial of civil liberties. In Chile, the 2010 election of a center-right

Bolivian President Evo Morales. *(Photo by Pablo Aneli/AP Images)*

candidate and not machinations by the military charted a more conservative course. It is significant that in the cases of Argentina, Ecuador, and Bolivia where mass street demonstrations brought down governments in recent years there was no intervention by the military and eventually, following caretaker rule, new governments were elected and took power constitutionally. The 2009 coup in Honduras did, however, suggest that under certain circumstances the military and entrenched elites were still capable of mobilizing to remove a constitutionally elected leader.

Bibliography

Asturias, Miguel Angel. *El Señor Presidente*. New York : Atheneum, 1972.

Black, Jan Knippers, ed. *Latin America: Its Problems and Its Promise*. 4th ed. Boulder, CO: Westview Press, 2005.

Chávez, David, and Benjamin Goldfrank, eds. *The Left in the City: Participatory Local Governments in Latin America*. London: Latin American Bureau, 2004.

Cleary, Edward. *The Struggle for Human Rights in Latin America*. Westport, CT: Praeger, 1997.

Close, David, ed. *Legislatures and the New Democracies in Latin America*. Boulder, CO: Lynne Rienner, 1995.

Dominguez, Jorge. *Democratic Politics in Latin America and the Caribbean*. Baltimore: Johns Hopkins University Press, 1998.

Foweraker, Joe, Todd Landman, and Neil Harvey. *Governing Latin America*. Cambridge, MA: Polity Press, 2004.

Liss, Sheldon. *Marxist Thought in Latin America*. Berkeley: University of California Press, 1984.

Loveman, Brian, and Thomas Davies, eds. *The Politics of Antipolitics: The Military in Latin America*. Wilmington, DE: Scholarly Resources, 1997.

Mainwaring, Scott. *Building Democratic Institutions: Party Systems in Latin America*. Stanford, CA: Stanford University Press, 1995.

Mainwaring, Scott. *Christian Democracy in Latin America*. Palo Alto, CA: Stanford University Press, 2003.

Malloy, James, and Mitchell Seligson, eds. *Authoritarians and Democrats: Regime Transition in Latin America*. Pittsburgh, PA: University of Pittsburgh Press, 1987.

McDonald, Ronald, and J. Mark Rubl. *Party Politics and Election in Latin America*. Boulder, CO: Westview Press, 1989.

Peeler, John. *Building Democracy in Latin America*. 2nd ed. Boulder, CO: Lynne Rienner, 2004.

Philip, George. *Democracy in Latin America: Surviving Conflict and Crisis?* Cambridge, MA/Oxford: Polity Press/Blackwell, 2003.

Smith, Peter H. *Democracy in Latin America: Political Change in Comparative Perspective*. New York: Oxford University Press, 2005.

Tulchin, Joseph, ed. *The Consolidation of Democracy in Latin America*. Boulder, CO: Lynne Rienner, 1998.

Wiarda, Howard. *Dilemmas of Democracy in Latin America*. Lanham, MD: Rowman and Littlefield, 2006.

Wiarda, Howard, and Harvey Kline, eds. *Latin American Politics and Development*. 5th ed. Boulder, CO: Westview Press, 2000.

Wynia, Gary. *The Politics of Latin American Development*. 3rd ed. Cambridge, UK: Cambridge University Press, 1990.

FILMS AND VIDEOS

Confessing to Laura. Colombia, 1990.
Death and the Maiden. United States, 1994.
Death of a Bureaucrat. Cuba, 1966.
Doña Barbara. Mexico, 1943.
Evita. United States, 1997.
La Paz. Bolivia, 1994.
Missing. United States, 1983.
The Seven Madmen (Los Siete Locos). Argentina, 1973.
State of Siege. United States, 1982.

TABLE 23. Participation of Women in Government, 1994

Country	Ministers	Under-Secretaries	Provincial or Departmental Governors	Local Officers	Senators	Deputies	Single-House Congress	Supreme Court	Court of Appeals	Judges
Argentina	0.0	9.8	0.0	3.6	4.2	13.2	—	0.0	15.3	29.9
Bolivia	0.0	5.4	—	10	3.7	7.7	—	0.0	—	—
Brazil	3.7	—	3.7	2.4	6.2	7.4	—	0.0	—	—
Chile	14.3	7.1	9.8	7.2	6.4	7.5	—	0.0	20.2	45.8
Colombia	13.3	13	3.7	5.6	4.9	11.5	—	0.0	7.7	49.3
Costa Rica	9.5	26.3	71.4	0.0	—	—	15.8	9.1	30.1	45.7
Cuba	2.6	9.4	0.0	5.3	—	—	22.8	39.3	14.3	43.8
Dominican Republic	14.3	12.9	28	4.9	0.0	11.7	—	0.0	30.7	35.4
Ecuador	0.0	7.9	11.1	3.1	—	—	5.6	0.0	4.0	11.7
El Salvador	10	8.8	—	11.1	—	—	10.7	13.3	0	14.7
Guatemala	23.1	12.5	—	1.2	—	—	7.5	11.1	11.5	11.7
Honduras	7.7	29.4	11.1	12.7	—	—	7	11.1	11.1	63.5
Mexico	17.6	—	3.2	2.9	11.8	13.8	18.5	19.2	1.5	34.7
Nicaragua	10	10.3	—	9.8	—	—	9	11.1	25	46.2
Panama	16.7	0	22.2	9	—	—	—	22.2	26.3	40.7
Paraguay	9.1	8.3	0	4.9	11.1	2.5	—	0	9	12.8
Peru	13.3	20	0	6.2	6.7	5.6	—	8.3	20.1	17.5
Uruguay	7.7	7.7	0	15.8	6.5	7.1	—	0	16.3	52.8
Venezuela	8.3	0	4.5	6.3	6.1	6.5	—	26.7	30	53

Source: Social Watch. *The Starting Point;* 1996, p. 24, as cited in *Statistical Abstract of Latin America,* Vol. 35. Los Angeles: UCLA Latin American Center Publications, 1999.

TABLE 24. Overview of Latin American Electoral Systems

Country	Presidential System	Legislative System	Governors and Municipalities	General Electoral Information
Argentina	The president is elected for a four-year term with the possibility of one successive term. If none of the candidates receives 45% or more of the votes in the first round of voting, a second round is held.	Bicameral congress. The 257 deputies are elected for 4-year terms and may be reelected. Half the Chamber of Deputies is renewed every two years. The 72 senators are elected according to procedures established in local provincial constitutions. One-third of the Senate is renewed every two years.	Governors and local authorities are elected according to the 24 provincial constitutions.	In December 1983, Argentina returned to a democracy and since then has had free and fair democratic elections. In April 1994, elections were held to form a constituent assembly. The assembly modified the 1853 constitution with several reforms, including reduction of the president's term—from 6 to 4 years, with the possibility of a second term—and the adoption of a second round of voting if no candidate receives 45% in the first round. In addition, the reforms abolished the electoral college system.
Bolivia	Beginning in 1997, the president was elected for a 5-year term without the possibility of consecutive reelection. The president may run for office again after one term has passed. If no candidate receives a majority, the congress chooses the president from among the top two candidates in an oral, roll-call vote.	Bicameral congress. The 130 deputies and 27 senators are elected for 5-year terms with the possibility of reelection.	Bolivia is divided into departments; there is one *prefecto* (governor) per department. The *prefectos* are elected for 5-year terms and have general executive powers. Municipal councils and mayors are directly elected by the people to 5-year terms.	The terms of office for the president and both houses of congress were increased from 4 to 5 years . In April 1994, a "popular participation" law was passed that gave local governments more control over their communities. In December 1995, reforms were passed to give more power to the governors of the departments. Evo Morales was elected president in a special December 2005 election following a nationwide general strike in June 2005 that forced the resignation of Carlos Mesa. Constitutional changes were made in 2007 and Morales was reelected in 2010.

Country	Presidential System	Legislative System	Governors and Municipalities	General Electoral Information
Brazil	The president is elected for a 4-year term with the possibility of reelection to one additonal term. If none of the candidates receives a majority in the first round of voting, a second round is held between the top two candidates, 20 days after the first round.	Bicameral congress. The 513 members of the Chamber of Deputies are elected from party lists for 4-year terms and may be reelected. When elections are held, all the 513 seats are up for election at the same time. The 81 senators are elected to serve 8-year terms and may be reelected. Two- thirds of the Senate is renewed at one time and 4 years later the remaining one-third is renewed. Members of both houses are elected by a system of proportional representation.	All state legislators and governors are elected for 4-year terms. Mayors and city council authorities are directly elected for 4-year terms.	In 1993, a popular referendum was held to choose among moving to a parliamentary system, returning to monarchy, or keeping the presidential system. A great majority of those people who voted supported the existing presidential system. In 1994, an amendment to the constitution reduced the term of the president from 5 to 4 years and added the possibility of presidential reelection.
Chile	The president is elected for a 4-year term with no possibility of reelection. If no candidate receives a majority of the votes, a second round of voting is held.	Bicameral congress. There are 120 members of the Chamber of Deputies. They are elected from party lists for 4-year terms and may be	Chile is divided into regions with one *intendente* (governor) per region. *Intendentes* are appointed by the president for a 6-year term and may be replaced at	In October 1988, a plebiscite defeat ended Pinochet's military dictatorship. In July 1989, a referendum approved 64 reforms to the constitution. The measures increased the number of directly elected senators from 26 to 38, reduced

(Continued)

TABLE 24.   Overview of Latin American Electoral Systems   *(Continued)*

Country	Presidential System	Legislative System	Governors and Municipalities	General Electoral Information
		reelected. There are 38 members of the Senate. The senators are elected for 8-year terms and may be reelected. Every 4 years half the Senate seats are renewed.	any time during their tenure. Municipal authorities are directly elected for 4-year terms and appoint the mayors.	the president's term from 8 to 6 years. and prohibited reelection of the president. In September 2005, several other constitutional changes went into force, including the elimination of appointed senatorial positions and senators for life, granting the president the authority to remove commanders in chief of the armed forces, and reducing the presidential term from 6 to 4 years.
Colombia	The president is elected for a 4-year term with the possibility of reelection. If none of the candidates receives a majority of votes in the first round of voting, a second round of voting is held.	Bicameral congress. The 166 members of the House of Representatives and the 102 members of the Senate are elected for 4-year terms and may not be reelected to consecutive terms.	Governors are elected for 3-year terms. Since 1988, mayors have been elected for 2-year terms.	In July 1991, the new constitution was approved which granted rights to minorities and introduced many political reforms aimed at decentralizing authority. In May 1994, vice presidential elections were held for the first time. Indigenous peoples have been allotted two seats in the Senate. In 2005, the constitution was changed to allow for presidential reelection. The following year, Alvaro Uribe Pérez was reelected president in only one round of voting.
Costa Rica	The president is elected for a 4-year term with the possibility of reelection. If one	Unicameral congress. The 57 members of the National Assembly	Governors are named by the president for 4-year terms. Municipal	Elections have been regular and democratic in Costa Rica since 1949.

Country	Presidential System	Legislative System	Governors and Municipalities	General Electoral Information
	candidate receives more than 40% of the vote, no second round voting is held.	are elected for 4-year terms and may not be reelected for consecutive terms.	authorities are elected for 4-year terms.	
Dominican Republic	The president is elected for a 4-year term with the possibility of one consecutive reelection. If none of the candidates receives a majority of the votes, a second round of voting is held.	Bicameral congress. There are 178 members of the Chamber of Deputies and 32 members of the Senate. All members of congress are elected for 4-year terms and may be reelected.	The governors of the 31 provinces are appointed by the president. The *síndico* (mayor) of each province is elected. Both serve 4-year terms.	In May 1994, the Dominican Central Electoral Board declared President Balaguer the winner in a contest international observers cited as plagued by "serious problems and irregularities" that may have affected its outcome. PRD opposition candidate Francisco Peña Gómez officially lost by only 22,000 votes. After lengthy negotiations between parties and candidates, Congress reduced President Balaguer's term to 2 years and prohibited the consecutive reelection of future presidents. The Dominican Republic has existed under three different constitutions since 1990. The most recent form was ratified in 2002. One of the most significant changes is the return of presidential reelection, which had been outlawed since 1994 due to President Balaguer's victory in a faulty electoral process.

(Continued)

TABLE 24. Overview of Latin American Electoral Systems   (*Continued*)

Country	Presidential System	Legislative System	Governors and Municipalities	General Electoral Information
Ecuador	The president is elected for a 4-year term without the possibility of consecutive reelection. The president may run for office again after one term has passed. If no candidate receives a majority, a second round of voting is held.	Unicameral congress. The 100 deputies of the Chamber of National Represen-tatives are elected by a system of proportional representation. The national deputies are elected for 4-year terms at the national level and provincial deputies are elected for 2-year terms at the provincial level. All deputies may be reelected.	Governors and municipal authorities are elected for 4-year terms.	In May 1996, congressional elections were held and the Social Christian Party won a majority in congress. A party representing the indigenous groups in Ecuador also won 6 seats. Prior to 1995, two constitutional reforms passed that have influenced the election of the president. The first reform revokes a previous law, which required that candidates for political office must belong to a political party, now allowing independents to run for any office. The second reform allows the president to run for reelection after one term has passed.
El Salvador	The president is elected for a five-year term without the possibility of consecutive reelection. If none of the candidates receives a majority of the votes, a second round of voting is held.	Unicameral congress. The 84 members of the National Assembly are elected for 3-year terms and may be reelected.	At the municipal level, local authorities are elected for 3-year terms. Governors of departments are appointed by the president.	In 1994, national and international observers judged the elections as having been generally free, fair, and nonviolent despite some irregularities. The former guerrilla movement FMLN participated as a political party in the elections in alliance with reformist groups and it became the second-largest political group in congress. The FMLN won the presidency in 2008.

Country	Presidential System	Legislative System	Governors and Municipalities	General Electoral Information
Guatemala	The president is elected for a 4-year term without the possibility of reelection. If none of the candidates receives a majority of the votes, a second round of voting is held.	Unicameral congress. The 158 members of congress are elected by proportional representation. The candidates are elected by a national and a departmental list procedure. Of the 158 candidates in the last election, 29 were elected from the national lists and 129 were elected from the departmental lists. Votes are cast separately for the national and departmental lists.	Governors are appointed by the president. The duration of their terms is also decided by the president. Mayors are directly elected for terms of 4 years.	In 1993, former president Jorge Serrano was constitutionally deposed after he attempted to seize full power. As a result of the crisis, congress elected Ramiro de León Carpio to be president and finish out Serrano's term. In 1994, the president held congressional elections and presented a referendum of constitutional changes to the Guatemalan people. The level of voter participation in the referendum was extremely low, but the constitutional reforms were approved. These reforms reduced the president's term from 5 to 4 years and established the current list system in congress by population.
Honduras	The president is elected for a 4-year term during one round of voting and may not be reelected.	Unicameral congress. The 128 members are elected for 4-year terms and may be reelected. Members of congress are elected on a proportional basis, according to votes cast for the presidential	Governors are appointed for 4-year terms. Municipal authorities are elected for 4-year terms.	November 2001 marked the sixth consecutive election of a civilian president since 1982, when Honduras returned to civilian rule. In January 1995, the police force came under the direction of the civil government while the technical judicial police (i.e., federal investigative police) came under the direction of the attorney general. In

(Continued)

TABLE 24. Overview of Latin American Electoral Systems *(Continued)*

Country	Presidential System	Legislative System	Governors and Municipalities	General Electoral Information
		candidate of their party.		May 1995, an all-volunteer military was put in place that ended forced conscription. In addition to these changes, many judicial changes are also under way. The 2009 Coup threatened constitutional rule.
Mexico	The president is elected for a 6-year term and may not be reelected. There is only one round of voting.	Bicameral congress. The 500 members of the Chamber of Deputies are directly elected for 3 years; 300 are elected from single-member constituencies and 200 chosen under a system of proportional representation. The majority party will hold no more than 300 seats. In 1994, a 6-year period of transition began that culminated in the formation of a new system for electing senators in the year 2000. This new system guarantees that at least 25% of the seats in the	Governors are elected for 6-year terms according to the organization and calendar of each state. The constitution allows for the replacement of governors by reelection during the first 2 years of their terms and by presidential appointment after that time. Municipal authorities are elected for 3-year terms. The mayor of the federal district was elected, not appointed, for the first time in 1997.	Until 2000, the official party, PRI, had won every presidential election since 1929. Measures have been taken in Mexico to open up the electoral process to other political parties. In recent years, through the reforms to the Mexican congress in late 1993, as well as the creation of the autonomous Federal Electoral Institute (IFE) to oversee federal elections, opposition parties have steadily expanded their representation in the political system. The 1994 elections were seen as critical because prior to the election the country was plagued by a series of crises, including the assassination of PRI presidential candidate Luis Donaldo Colosio. For the first time, the Mexican government asked the United Nations to train Mexican electoral monitors.

Country	Presidential System	Legislative System	Governors and Municipalities	General Electoral Information
		Senate will belong to members of minority parties. In the 2000 elections three senators were elected by direct vote in each state, and a fourth senator was allotted to the majority opposition party within the state.		
Nicaragua	The president is elected for a 5-year term, and may not run for reelection.	Unicameral congress. The 92 members of the National Assembly are elected for 5-year terms by proportional representation and may be reelected.	The office of governor does not exist in Nicaragua except in the autonomous Atlantic and South Atlantic regions. Municipal authorities are elected for 5-year terms.	In March 1994, congress reduced the future terms of the president, members of congress, and mayors from 6 to 5 years. Congress has also prohibited the election of the president's close relatives.
Panama	The president is elected for a 5-year term and may not be reelected for two terms after his or her first term. There is only one round of voting; the candidate who receives a plurality of the votes becomes president.	Unicameral congress. The 78 members of the National Assembly are elected for 5-year terms.	Governors of the 9 provinces are named by the president and may be removed at any time. Municipal authorities are elected by the people and serve 5-year terms.	On May 8, 1994, Ernesto Pérez Balladares of the PRD defeated Mireya Moscoso, widow of former president Arnulfo Arias of the Arnulfista Party, and salsa singer Rubén Blades of the Papá Egoró Party. International observers found the elections to be free, fair, and nonviolent. Moscoso was elected in 1999.

(Continued)

TABLE 24.   Overview of Latin American Electoral Systems   (*Continued*)

Country	Presidential System	Legislative System	Governors and Municipalities	General Electoral Information
Paraguay	The president is elected for a 5-year term and may not be reelected. Only one round of voting is held.	Bicameral congress. The 80 deputies and 45 senators are elected for 5-year terms and may be reelected.	Governors are elected for 5- year terms. Municipal authorities are elected for 5-year terms.	In February 1989, the overthrow of General Alfredo Stroessner initiated a transition to democracy in Paraguay. The elections of May 1993 were the first free and uncontested elections with an all-civilian slate of candidates since 1928. On June 20, 1992, a new constitution was approved that created the office of the vice president and prohibits the president and vice president from succeeding themselves. The constitution also established an electoral tribunal headed by three ministers of electoral justice who must be confirmed by congress. Municipal authorities are now elected and no longer appointed by the president.
Peru	The president is elected for a 5-year term and may be reelected for a consecutive 5-year term. If no candidate receives a majority in the first round of voting, a second round is held.	Unicameral congress. The 120 members of Congress are elected for 5-year terms and may be reelected.	Presidents of Peru's 25 autonomous regions are elected for a 5-year term. Municipal authorities are elected for a 5-year term.	In April 1992, President Alberto Fujimori dissolved congress and called for new congressional elections. The new 80-member congress served for 2 years and drafted a new constitution approved by a nationwide referendum in October 1993 by 52% of voters. The new constitution dissolved regional government and created a larger 120-member unicameral congress.

Country	Presidential System	Legislative System	Governors and Municipalities	General Electoral Information
				The new constitution also permits the president to run for reelection. Since then, the constitution has been amended to allow for regional governance.
Uruguay	The president is elected by a party list procedure for a 5-year term without the possibility of consecutive reelection. The president may run for office again after one term. If no candidate receives the majority in the first round, a second round is held.	Bicameral congress. The 99 deputies and 30 senators are elected by a system of proportional representation for 5-year terms and may be reelected.	Governors and municipalities are elected for five-year terms.	Since the end of military rule in 1985, 5 presidents have been elected. In May 1996, the Senate voted on an amendment to the constitution that will change the process of electing the president by including a primary election. This change has not yet been approved.
Venezuela	The president is elected for a 6-year term by the people. The executive vice president is appointed by the president. There is no second round of election for president.	Unicameral Chamber of Deputies. The 167 seats are elected from the federal territories and various indigenous communities to 5-year terms. They may be reelected to two additional terms.	Governors and municipal authorities are elected for a 4-year term.	Venezuela has a long-standing history of democratic rule, which began in 1958. However, in 1992 there were two coup attempts and in 1993 President Carlos André Pérez was impeached. After Hugo Chávez was elected president in December 1998, a Constituent Assembly was convened to draft a new constitution which established a unicameral Chamber of Deputies and a 6-year presidential term. Chávez won new election in 2000 and his supporters

(Continued)

TABLE 24.   Overview of Latin American Electoral Systems   (*Continued*)

Country	Presidential System	Legislative System	Governors and Municipalities	General Electoral Information
				gained dominance in the Chamber of Deputies. In 2007, Chávez proposed two constitutional amendments: one to grant the president emergency powers and the other to abolish term limits. Although initially rejected by the voters, they were later approved.

Sources: Georgetown University and Organization of American States Political Database of the Americas, http://www.georgetown.edu/pdba/; Wilfried Derksen, "Elections around the World," http://www.agora.stm.it/elections/election.htm.

ELEVEN

STRUGGLING FOR CHANGE

REVOLUTION, SOCIAL AND POLITICAL MOVEMENTS IN LATIN AMERICA

Latin America has struggled with the need for fundamental change and socioeconomic restructuring from the time that Túpac Amaru and Túpac Katari led uprisings in 1780 and 1781. Most acknowledge the severe inequality that exists throughout the region and very much believe it needs to be changed. The means of doing so are, however, hotly contested. The term *revolution* is employed to evoke the fundamental restructuring that is so much needed in Latin America. Revolutions are, then, much touted and the term is often used to describe any power realignment in Latin America. Nonetheless, it could be argued that thoroughgoing revolutions are much talked about but little done in the region. Even the struggle for independence was more of a change in political elites than a comprehensive restructuring of the social-economic-political structures that the term *revolution* implies. Yet, the vision of a total transformation of oppressive societal structures that revolution involves has continued to inspire political leaders in Latin America. Indeed, many have argued that only through such a revolution can long-standing problems such as massive poverty, inequality, and malnutrition be remedied. Thus, each new revolutionary attempt at thoroughgoing change has been met with utopian enthusiasm by supportive sociopolitical groupings: in Mexico from 1910 to 1917, in Guatemala from 1944 to 1954, in Bolivia from 1952 to 1964, in Cuba from 1959 on, in Nicaragua from 1979 to 1990, in El Salvador during the revolutionary struggle from 1980 to the peace accords in 1992, and in Venezuela from 1999 on. But contradictions emerged in these processes as well. The resort to authoritarian methods and the many internal and external difficulties in achieving such revolutionary visions often dampened much of the initial enthusiasm and occasioned many defections from the revolutionary process.

To many analysts, the defeat of the Sandinistas in the 1990 Nicaraguan elections, coming in the context of the collapse of the Communist Party–led governments in Eastern Europe, marked the end of an era of radical revolution in Latin America that had begun with the triumph of the Cuban Revolution in 1959. Many of the same observers noted the flagging fortunes of the revolutionary movements in Guatemala and El Salvador in the early 1990s and predicted the early demise of Fidel Castro's government in Cuba. Others were far less certain that the era of revolution in Latin America had ended. Armed insurgencies intensified in Peru in the 1990s, reappeared in Mexico, and continued in Colombia. Further, in El Salvador and Nicaragua the revolutionary movements have not been destroyed. The Sandinsta National Liberation Front (FSLN) of Nicaragua and the Farabundo Martí National Liberation Front (FMLN) of El Salvador were still important political movements that could contest power in presidential elections and command an important bloc of votes in their national legislatures and local governments. Yet, such a position is far short of the revolutionary goals that each of them sought. By 2005, the dominant national economic and political elites, aided by a variety of direct and indirect actions by the United States, had been able to blunt the drive for revolutionary takeover outside of Colombia, even though the revolution was still in power in Cuba. Indeed, the struggle for revolutionary change has always been difficult in Latin America, given the forces that have been arrayed against it. By the beginning of 2008, new political and social movements and the leaders they supported were once again invoking the need for fundamental change and challenging the neoliberal agenda. This was particularly true with Hugo Chávez in Venezuela and Evo Morales in Bolivia, where socialist revolutions were once again being discussed. Further, the Sandinistas were able to recapture the presidency in Nicaragua in 2006 and the FMLN took that office in El Salvador in 2009.

In recent years, many seeking change and social-economic restructuring have begun to harness their vision and creativity to mobilize in less violent but highly effective ways. For instance, many had despaired of popular rule in Bolivia after the demise of the Bolivian revolution led by the Movimiento Nacionalista Revolucionario (MNR) in 1952 and ended by a military coup in 1964. Recent years had even seen the country led by a U.S.-educated member of the elite who seemed only too happy to bow to U.S. policy in such areas as the eradication of coca leaves. Thus, it was all the more remarkable that Bolivian President Gonzalo Sánchez de Lozada was forced out of office by massive displays of popular power by social movements, community organizations, unions, and students in October 2003. A staunch advocate of globalization and neoliberal policies prescribed by international financial institutions like the International Monetary Fund (IMF) and World Bank, he was also symbolic of the upper-class, Western-oriented political elite that have governed Latin America in an authoritarian manner since the Spanish conquest in the early 1500s. His tormentors were equally symbolic of those the political class had long ruled and repressed. They were small farmers, indigenous peoples, workers, miners, students, and intellectuals who dared to challenge the status quo. In 2005, successor president Carlos Mesa was also forced from office by the same forces. Later that year Evo Morales was elected to the presidency with their support. This was not, however, the first time people had arisen in the Andean highlands. There had, for instance, been an uprising in 1780 under the leadership of Incan descendant Túpac Amaru. The 1960s had seen the formation of Marxist guerrilla groups in both Bolivia and Peru. Like most other attempts at radical change from Túpac Amaru on, such attempts had been repressed, first by the European forces and then by the national military or the dominant political elite. This occurred in the central part of

Mexico in the early 1800s when the mostly Indian, mostly peasant masses answered the famous *grito de Dolores*—the cry for freedom and independence that rang out in 1810. There, a popular movement under the leadership of Miguel de Hidalgo began the struggle for popular control and Mexican independence. The movement was brutally repressed by the Spanish authorities, and Hidalgo and his successor, José María Morelos faced the same fate as Túpac Amaru: they were executed by the Spanish colonial authorities. The mass uprising was not successful. Rather, Mexican independence, like that in Bolivia and all of Latin America save Haiti, was won by *criollo* political elites who ruled in the name of the majorities but rarely for them.

Dissatisfaction with elite rule, exclusionary political projects, or policies that cause or perpetuate the economic or ethnic marginalization of the masses has continued in Latin America. There have been many other uprisings, like that led by Farabundo Martí in El Salvador in 1932. Indeed, it was the generalized dissatisfaction with Porfirio Díaz' political ruling class in *fin de siglo* Mexico that induced *los de abajo* (those on the bottom) to enroll in the various armies—and thus the revolutionary project—of the Mexican Revolution. Such dissatisfaction and its focus on the failure of the political elite have led to other less successful political rebellions as well. The *Bogotazo* and the ensuing violence in Colombia from 1948 to 1956, the Bolivian revolution in the early 1950s, the popular struggle in Guatemala from the 1960s to the 1990s, and the decade-long civil war in the 1980s in El Salvador are cases in point. Before the most current forms of radical political mobilization are examined, a more careful discussion of revolutions and revolutionary mobilizations must be undertaken.

It is necessary to review the development of previous movements, tracing the demise of the belief in violent revolution in Latin America to the ascendance of political democracy throughout the region to the temporary political dominance of the ideology of free enterprise embodied in the programs of structural adjustment and neoliberalism, and to the resurgency of more radical movements after 2000. As the new century began, prescriptions for revolutionary change needed to undergo some reexamination. The heady days that revolutionaries experienced in the late 1970s were clearly not in evidence, but radical movements, and new leadership were considering some of the same policies that they had advocated.

Cuba

The modern wave of revolutions in Latin America began in the Caribbean island of Cuba. That revolution, under the leadership of Fidel Castro and the 26th of July Movement, was a watershed event in Latin American revolutionary history. Following the cancellation of the scheduled 1952 national elections by Fulgencio Batista, Castro and several dozen followers organized an attack on an army barracks in Santiago, hoping to incite a nationwide uprising against the dictatorship. That attack failed, but three years later it led to the formation of the movement, named for the date of the 1953 failed attack. Drawing in part on the earlier experiences of Augusto César Sandino in Nicaragua in the late 1920s, the Cuban revolutionary movement based itself in the isolated Sierra Maestra mountains of eastern Cuba and sought to build a revolutionary army from the ranks of the local peasants. Given the history of rebellion of that region, the tactics proved successful as the rebel army flourished and eventually engaged in several successful battles against the conscript army of the dictator Batista. Aided by other revolutionary actions in Cuba's cities and the flagging support for Batista both domestically and internationally, the 26th of July Movement succeeded in taking power on January 1, 1959. In the ensuing months, the revolutionary government, with the support of mass mobilizations of workers and peasants, transformed Cuban society. The economy was placed largely in the hands of the state, and by 1961 Fidel Castro had committed Cuba to the socialist path of development, the first country in the Western Hemisphere to do so. Given the popularity of Fidel Castro and the other Cuban rebels, it is not surprising that there was soon a proliferation of self-declared Marxist guerrilla groups through much of Latin America. This proliferation of the Fidelista theory of revolution through armed struggle (*foquismo*) marked what Regis Debray termed the "revolution in the revolution" (a revolution in the Marxist theory of revolution in Latin America).

Although the subsequent wave of guerrilla activity in the region and the virtual canonization of Che Guevara helped free Latin American revolutionary thought

Ernesto Che Guevara, 1928–1967. (*Salas Archive Photos/Alamy Images*)

from the dogmatic, static orientation that had come to characterize it during Joseph Stalin's rule in the Soviet Union, the unyielding emphasis on armed struggle effectively foreclosed a broader examination of the doctrine and the search for more effective ways to mobilize the masses. This new vision of revolution effectively challenged the now bureaucratized orthodox communist parties, but it did not produce any successful guerrilla movements in the 1960s or well into the 1970s. It did, however, spawn a series of urban and rural guerrilla movements across Latin America and generated a great deal of literature by and about these new Marxist revolutionaries. The introduction of Maoism and Chinese-oriented communist parties in countries such as Colombia and Brazil further stimulated the development of new forms of radical Marxism. However, the subsequent growth in Marxist parties and movements also provided an excellent rationale for the creation and implementation of the U.S.-inspired national security doctrine, counterinsurgency training, and its concomitant strong anti-communism. The U.S.-inspired counterinsurgency defeated most of the original guerrilla movements by the early 1970s. Most significantly, Che Guevara was killed in Bolivia by U.S.-trained soldiers while fighting with a Bolivian revolutionary group in 1967. Guerrilla groups did, however, manage to struggle on in Guatemala, Colombia, and Nicaragua.

OTHER REVOLUTIONARY ENDEAVORS

By 1970, several innovative approaches to Marxist thought were emerging. In Peru, Hugo Blanco was breathing new life into the Trotskyist movement through his work with the highland peasants. In Chile, socialists and communists were contemplating the realization of a peaceful revolution under the leadership of constitutionally elected socialist president Salvador Allende. The far left Movement of the Revolutionary Left (MIR) did, however, argue that rightist forces would never allow such a transition. In Argentina, leftist theorists began to apply and adapt the theory to their own specific reality. A radical brand of Marxist-inspired Peronism (or Peronist-inspired Marxism) ensued and eventually led to a Marxist faction within Peronism (Juventud Peronista) and the formation of the radical Peronist Montonero guerrilla group. The Montoneros and the Revolutionary Army of the People (ERP) eventually confronted Argentina's military government in an intense struggle. In Uruguay, the Robin Hood–like Tupamaros hoped to foment a popular revolution. Although gains were made toward less dogmatic interpretations and in political education, the lingering emphasis on armed struggle over political education or organization eventually led to intense conflict and violent repression, which the left was ultimately unable to resist. Revolutionary and socialist movements were profoundly affected by the results of Allende's Popular Unity socialist experiment in Chile. Allende sought to make radical changes in Chilean society (land reform, wealth redistribution, increased political participation) within the parliamentary process. Some progress was made during the three years he was in power (1970–1973), but the reformist socialist experiment was largely thwarted by Allende's lack of majority control of the legislature. The entrenched power and opposition by the country's elites together with international isolation engineered by a hostile U.S. government disrupted the country's economy and set the stage for a military coup. Allende's rule came to a bloody end in September 1973 when the Chilean military stormed the presidential palace and killed Allende and thousands of his supporters. A military government under General Augusto Pinochet was established and held power for seventeen years. The primary impact of the Chilean events was to convince most of the Latin American left that reform-oriented efforts at achieving socialism were fruitless. These views were also bolstered by the 1973 military coup in Uruguay and the subsequent coup in Argentina in 1976. By 1976 military rule had become the norm throughout the region, and the combination of dictatorial rule and unsolved social and economic problems spawned a series of revolutionary upsurges, which were strongest in Nicaragua, El Salvador, Colombia, and Peru. Each had its own characteristics and should be viewed individually, although there were many similarities.

Nicaragua

Nicaragua's leading revolutionary movement, the FSLN, was formed in 1961 and was directly inspired by the success of the Cuban Revolution. Its early leaders, Carlos Fonseca and Tomás Borge, abandoned the reformist-oriented Nicaraguan Socialist Party (PSN) to form the FSLN. With direct Cuban assistance, the FSLN sought to replicate the Cuban experience and that of their namesake, Augusto Sandino, by establishing a guerrilla army in the mountains of northern Nicaragua that could eventually challenge the power of the dictator Anastasio Somoza. Another element crucial to the revolutionary philosophy of the FSLN was its emphasis on will and the belief that to some degree revolution could be improvised. They turned to the writings of Sandino, José Carlos Mariátegui, and the Italian Antonio Gramsci to craft a philosophy based on revolutionary action, the importance of the subjective factor in making revolution, and the role of ideology in motivating the masses.

In its early stages, the FSLN consisted of just twelve people, including Colonel Santos López, a veteran of Sandino's earlier struggle. Fonseca fought successfully for the inclusion of Sandino's name in the organizational label, but the lack of unanimity on this shows that a variety of revolutionary influences were at work in the early 1960s. Led by Fonseca, the small group studied Sandino's writings and tactics as they prepared for their first guerrilla campaigns in 1963. Those campaigns, like many other similar ones in Latin America at the time, were a failure. The new Sandinistas had failed to do what their namesake had done so well—mobilize the local populace on the side of the guerrillas through well-planned political and organizational activities coordinated with and part of the armed struggle. Over the ensuing years, the FSLN managed to survive by realizing its mistakes and broadening its political work to include neighborhood organizing in the poorest barrios of the capital, Managua. However, the National Guard of the Somoza dictatorship was a powerful force, and it exacted many defeats on the Sandinistas during the 1960s. The Sandinistas survived and slowly built their organization, especially by reaching out to progressive members of the Catholic Church who had been inspired by liberation theology. The FSLN was the first revolutionary organization in Latin America to welcome Christians within its ranks, a position that would bear considerable fruit in the late 1970s.

Between 1967 and 1974 the FSLN carried on what it termed "accumulation of forces" in silence, largely recruiting members in ones and twos and engaging in few armed actions. The silence was broken in a spectacular way with the December 1974 seizure of the home of a wealthy Somoza supporter. An FSLN commando unit held more than a dozen foreign diplomats and top Nicaraguan government officials for several days, finally forcing Somoza to release key Sandinista political prisoners, pay a large sum of money, and broadcast and publish FSLN communiques. This dramatic act reinserted the FSLN into the political scene at an important time. Popular sentiment against the dictatorship had been growing since it had greedily profited from the devastating 1972 earthquake that had further impoverished more Nicaraguans. However, even as the FSLN reemerged, its own divisions had become clear. By 1975 the organization had split into three tendencies on the basis of tactical differences. The Prolonged People's War group was basically Maoist in orientation. Their strategy and concrete work emphasized rural guerrilla warfare. Relatively isolated in the countryside, they were probably the slowest to realize that a revolutionary situation was developing in the country. The Proletarian Tendency based itself in large measure on dependency theory and the traditional Marxist emphasis on the industrial working class. This tendency saw the Nicaraguan revolution as unfolding along more traditional lines as a confrontation between the bourgeoisie and the proletariat. Nicaragua's urban working class, small as it was, was seen as the main motor force of the coming revolution. Political work in the cities was emphasized, and this group also built a base among students. The Insurrectionist, or Tercerista, tendency was the last to emerge. In reality, it did not represent an entirely new approach; rather, it served primarily as a mediator between the two existing tendencies. The Terceristas (or "third force") did not draw a sharp distinction between a rural and an urban emphasis, seeing the need for action in both arenas. Its main and most controversial contribution was its alliance strategy. While not the first group in the FSLN to propose such an orientation, they were the first in the era of Somoza's decline to place it at the center of political work. There was also ample historical precedent for it in the strategies of both Sandino and the 26th of July Movement in Cuba. Both earlier movements incorporated heterogeneous elements while maintaining a revolutionary position. The Insurrectionists believed strongly that it was necessary to mobilize a broad-based coalition to overthrow the dictatorship while maintaining the organizational integrity of the FSLN.

The separation into tendencies did not mean the disintegration of the FSLN. Each current pursued its political work in its own sector, and as the crisis of the dictatorship deepened, all achieved successes. Efforts by the leaders to reestablish unity did not cease, although they were hampered by the imprisonment of key figures such as Borge and the death of Fonseca in combat in November 1976. The three tendencies finally began to converge in the upsurge of mass antidictatorship activity in late 1977 and early 1978 in the wake of the death of popular opposition newspaper editor Pedro Joaquín Chamorro. In 1978, the three tendencies collaborated to establish the National Patriotic Front (FPN), which created an anti-Somoza front encompassing trade unions, the Moscow-oriented Nicaraguan Socialist Party, student groups, and some small middle-class parties like the Popular Social Christians—all under FSLN hegemony.

In September 1978, the FSLN, led by the Terceristas, carried out an insurrection which, while not successful, laid the groundwork for the dictatorship's defeat.

Drawing on the lessons learned from the September 1978 action and with the organization formally reunited in March 1979, the FSLN launched its final offensive in the late spring of 1979. Somoza's National Guard fought hard to defend the dictator, who desperately ordered the bombing of Sandinista strongholds in the cities; but in July 1979, Somoza fled the country and the FSLN assumed power at the head of a provisional revolutionary government. The success of the Sandinistas in defeating the dictatorship and embarking on the fundamental restructuring of Nicaraguan society was a watershed event for Latin America, a second potential socialist revolution. The Nicaraguan Revolution did not fulfill its promises, but that did not change the significance of the events that unfolded at the end of the 1970s in one of the region's poorest countries. The reelection of FSLN leader Daniel Ortega as president in 2006 once again challenged U.S. influence and opened the possibility for change.

El Salvador

Nicaragua was not the only Central American nation convulsed by revolution in the 1970s and 1980s. Neighboring El Salvador witnessed a bloody confrontation between the military and revolutionaries that cost 75,000 lives between 1975 and 1992 and sent more than 500,000 Salvadorans into exile in the United States. The revolutionary period ended with a United Nations–brokered peace agreement that rewarded the revolutionary coalition, the FMLN, with a prominent role in Salvadoran politics as the country's primary political opposition group. The Salvadoran military, while still a major political force, stepped down from the controlling position that it had held for more than half a century.

It is not surprising that revolutionary forces came to the fore in El Salvador, for no Latin American country better fit the profile for revolutionary change. The events of the 1970s and 1980s followed directly from dramatic confrontations of the early 1930s and the 50 years of direct military rule that followed. By 1932 Salvador was the most class-polarized society in the region. In the latter part of the nineteenth century, El Salvador had become one of the world's largest coffee producers, meeting the ever-growing European demand with the development of ever-larger coffee plantations dominated by a few wealthy families. The coffee boom enriched a series of oligarchic families, who came to dominate Salvadoran society, while it further reduced the peasant population to seasonal labor and marginal lands. From 1907 to 1931, political power rested in the hands of a single family, the Meléndez clan. The peasantry who were driven off their communal lands during the latter half of the nineteenth century did not accept their fate passively and engaged in several uprisings, both armed and unarmed, from 1870 onward. The conflict between the ruling oligarchy, made up of coffee farmers, foreign investors, military officers, and Church leaders, and the landless peasants came to a head in 1930–1932. The Great Depression had further impoverished both the remaining small farmers and the plantation laborers as the price of coffee fell precipitously. The possibility of revolution developed very quickly. In 1930, a May Day demonstration in San Salvador against deteriorating economic conditions drew 80,000. Liberal reformer Arturo Araujo won the presidential election in 1931 with the support of students, workers, and peasants. The new government attempted to broaden the political spectrum by announcing that it would permit the newly formed Communist Party, under the leadership of Farabundo Martí, to participate in the 1931 municipal elections. However, the military, under the leadership of Maximiliano Hernández Martínez, seized power in December 1931; and the following month, Martí led a premature, mostly peasant rebellion that succeeded in murdering a few landlords and seizing control of some small towns, primarily in the northwestern part of the country.

The response of General Hernández to the uprising was swift and brutal. Known ever since as *La Matanza* (The Massacre), the joint actions of the military and oligarchy killed between 30,000 and 60,000 people, a huge toll in a nation of only 1.4 million. The repression was both selective and widespread. Using voter rolls, the military hunted down and killed virtually everyone affiliated with the Communist Party, including Martí. At the time, the military's actions took on the character of a race war as indigenous people were also singled out for attack.

La Matanza did not end resistance to the rule of the oligarchy, but it reduced it significantly for the next forty years. A series of military leaders ruled the country into the 1960s without even the facade of democracy. In that decade, a reformist challenge to the military developed under the leadership of the Christian Democratic Party and José Napoleon Duarte. Duarte, educated in the United States and the spirit of Kennedy's Alliance for Progress, developed a strong following among intellectuals, students, and a growing middle sector. Duarte's reformist challenge ended with a probable victory in the 1972 presidential elections, but the military voided the results and continued in power. Duarte and other Christian Democratic leaders went into exile, but other, more radical leaders saw the military's actions as proof that the reformist path was not viable in El Salvador. This view was reinforced by the fact that the U.S. government did not intervene, even to promote its seeming prototype for a centrist reformer like Duarte against the Salvadoran generals. As guerrilla groups began to form in the rural areas of the country, other factors also promoted revolutionary prospects. By 1975, about 40 percent of the peasants had no land at all, compared to only 12 percent in 1960. The other surprising force for revolutionary change that developed in the latter half of the 1970s was the Roman Catholic Church. The combination of the reform-oriented ideas of the 1968 Medellín Conference of Latin American Bishops and the repression of the Salvadoran military against the Church itself propelled the clergy and its followers into a central role in the political opposition to the military. The leader of the Salvadoran Church, Archbishop Oscar Romero, was a conservative at the time of his leadership appointment; but the death of a close friend at the hands of the military combined with the growing polarization in the country led him to the unusual position of supporting the right of armed rebellion. In response, the military assassinated Archbishop Romero in 1980 in the midst of growing civil and revolutionary resistance to the military regime.

In 1980, most of the revolutionary guerrilla groups that had begun armed activities in the 1970s came together to form the FMLN. The two primary organizations in the FMLN were the ERP and the Armed Forces of Liberation (FAL). The ERP was founded in 1971 by Marxist and Christian forces that were motivated by the *foco* theory of revolution inspired by Che Guevara. The FAL was the armed wing of the outlawed Communist Party that developed into a significant force only in the late 1970s. The primary significance of the FAL was that it was one of the few cases where a reformist-oriented Communist Party opted to participate in an armed struggle. Also important in the revolutionary equation was the Democratic Revolutionary Front (FDR), an umbrella alliance also founded in 1980 that encompassed all major popular organizations, labor groups, and community groups. From the beginning it served as the political arm of the FMLN and after 1982 was recognized internationally as a legitimate political force. The heart of the FDR was the People's Revolutionary Bloc (BPR), the largest of the popular organizations. It was formed in 1975 by diverse organizations of shantytown dwellers, workers, students, teachers, and practitioners of liberation theology. By the late 1970s, despite the severe repression of the military, the organizations of the BPR had succeeded in many places in the country in establishing alternative governing bodies.

Following the decisive triumph of the Sandinista revolutionaries in the summer of 1979, the possibility of revolution in El Salvador seemed very real. Popular mobilizations spread throughout the country. Factories were occupied in San Salvador, and 1980 was declared to be the "year of the liberation." Fearing a repetition of the Nicaraguan Revolution, a section of the Salvadoran elites and the government of the United States carried off a military coup designed to forestall the revolutionary process by appearing to instigate significant reform. On October 15, 1979, a new military junta took power, promising reform. The new government even encompassed figures from the left, including Social Democrat Guillermo Ungo and a minister of labor from the small Communist Party. The new junta promised to reform the security forces, institute land reform, and recognize trade unions. However, the political practice of the new government was far different from its rhetoric. Within a week of taking power, the government security forces broke up strikes, occupied rebellious towns, and killed more than 100 people. In January 1980, Ungo and the entire civilian cabinet quit their posts, acknowledging that the military was already making all key political and security decisions. Three weeks later, the military opened fire on a massive demonstration of 150,000. In March, Romero was assassinated, and the military attacked his funeral procession of 80,000. Thirty people were killed. By March 1980 it was clear to most political activists in El Salvador that open, legal political activity in opposition to the military was impossible. Many political moderates, including a sizeable part of the Christian Democrats, joined with the revolutionary left. This movement soon coalesced into the FDR and FMLN. Christian Democrat Duarte assumed leadership of the junta, claiming to be in the political center between left- and right-wing forces. In reality, Duarte was a figurehead who ruled on behalf of the traditional elites.

In January 1981, on the eve of President Ronald Reagan's inauguration, the FMLN launched an insurrection that was intended to take power. However, the Salvadoran military, with significant resupply by the United States, defeated the offensive and set the stage for a protracted armed conflict. The FMLN had hoped to gain victory before the Reagan administration took office. It gambled that the Carter administration would not resume aid to the Salvadoran government, which had been suspended 1 month earlier in the wake of the killing of four North American churchwomen by Salvadoran security forces. However, the FMLN's judgment proved to be wrong.

Citing proof of Nicaraguan Sandinista support for FMLN rebels on January 17, 1981, President Carter authorized the shipment of $5 million of military equipment and twenty additional U.S. military personnel. Three months later, the U.S. ambassador in El Salvador at the time of the shipments, Robert White, revealed that there was no real evidence of Nicaraguan involvement but the announcement of the shipment had served its purpose. The Salvadoran military had been reassured that despite obvious human rights violations even against U.S. citizens, the government of the United States was fully committed to preventing a victory by the Salvadoran revolutionaries. There was not going to be another Nicaragua in Central America.

The civil war continued for ten more years. The FMLN showed considerable resilience in the face of a concerted effort by the Salvadoran army and its U.S. backers to eliminate the guerrilla challenge. At the high point of assistance in the late 1980s, El Salvador was receiving close to $1 billion per year in U.S. aid, ranking behind only Israel and Egypt. Total U.S. aid during this period exceeded $5 billion. The FMLN was a substantial force, with several thousand soldiers in arms. It controlled more than one-third of Salvadoran territory and carried out regular attacks in all but two of the country's fourteen provinces. However, throughout the 1980s, the Salvadoran revolutionaries faced the dilemma that even if they could mount an insurrection that challenged the hold of the Salvadoran military, they faced the prospect of a massive U.S. intervention that would deny them the victory that they sought. As a result, from about 1982 onward, the FMLN argued that the only solution to the civil war would be a negotiated settlement. Sporadic negotiations did occur throughout the 1980s, but the political situation both inside and outside of El Salvador prevented a successful conclusion. To ensure continued support from a reluctant U.S. Congress, the Reagan administration pressed the Salvadorans to hold elections, even though it was clear that these could not be fully democratic in the context of the civil war. There was little freedom of the press, and no candidates of the left could participate without risking assassination by right-wing "death squads." With significant U.S. backing, Christian Democrat Duarte won the 1982 presidential election but was largely a figurehead. Throughout the 1980s, real political power lay with the Supreme Army Council and Roberto D'Aubuisson's ultra-right National Republican Alliance (ARENA), which controlled the Salvadoran legislature. Duarte was allowed by the military to remain in power as long as he permitted them free reign against the FMLN. Obviously, such an arrangement did not allow for any real dialogue or hope for a settlement between Duarte and the FMLN. In 1989, with Duarte dying of cancer and the Christian Democratic Party deeply divided, ARENA candidate Alfredo Christiani won the presidency, further entrenching the hold of the far right on Salvadoran politics. The new ARENA government vowed a rapid campaign to defeat the FMLN, but the latter responded in the fall of 1989 with a significant military offensive that reached all the way into the capital. These events served to underscore the fact that after a decade of fighting, the civil war was a stalemate with no end in sight.

However, regional and international events intervened to bring about a negotiated settlement within 2 years. The electoral defeat of the FSLN in Nicaragua in 1990 and the rapid changes in the Soviet Union and Eastern Europe between 1989 and 1991 weakened the position of the FMLN but also put pressure on the U.S. government and its Salvadoran allies to come to the bargaining table. Under United Nations auspices, brokered settlements moved forward in Cambodia, Angola, Mozambique, and Namibia, placing additional pressure on Central America. In 1990–1991, the FMLN made several concessions toward peace that went largely unreciprocated. In the March 1991 national legislative elections, the FMLN and its sympathizers fielded candidates. Despite significant pressure against the left and intimidation of voters, the left managed to win eight seats and ARENA was denied majority control. In November 1991, the FMLN declared a unilateral cease-fire that was to last until a peace agreement was signed. In January 1992, under mounting international pressure, the ARENA government signed an agreement with the FMLN. The agreement called for the removal of more than 100 military officers implicated in human rights violations during the civil war. The army was to be reduced by 50 percent, the National Intelligence Directorate dismantled, a new police force created to include members of the FMLN, 1980 agrarian reform completed, democratic elections held, and the FMLN disarmed in exchange for land and resettlement compensation for its troops and the right to become a political party.

This agreement was clearly far short of the thoroughgoing social revolution to which the FMLN had committed itself a decade earlier, but it did represent a partial victory for the revolutionaries and a setback for El Salvador's traditional oligarchy. Since the signing of the agreement, El Salvador has remained a contradictory nation. The traditional oligarchy has worked hard to undermine the agreement. The Christiani government was reluctant to purge high-ranking military officers and to disarm the notorious army and police units. In March 1993, a U.N.-appointed truth commission named sixty-two Salvadoran officers responsible for the worst massacres, tortures, and murders of the twelve-year war and called for the immediate dismissal of forty of them. The U.S. Army School of the Americas had trained forty-seven of them. The officers were eventually dismissed but only after pressure from a united opposition within El Salvador and a temporary suspension of aid by the Clinton administration in 1993.

Elections held under the aegis of the accords, especially the first one in 1994, were marked by significant fraud emanating from the government and periodic armed attacks against candidates and supporters of the left. The Christiani government used its control of the Supreme Electoral Tribunal to prevent opposition voters from registering. Especially in the 1994 elections, this fraud definitely denied the FMLN several seats in the National Assembly and control of the local government in several cities. Despite these obstacles, the FMLN succeeded in creating political space for the left that was unprecedented in Salvadoran history. In the March 1997 national and municipal elections, the FMLN fared quite well. It won the mayoralty of San Salvador—the most important political office after the presidency—as well as other key departmental municipalities. Of the country's 262 municipalities, the FMLN governed fifty-three, covering 45 percent of the population. On the congressional front, the FMLN won twenty-seven out of eighty-four seats, just one fewer than ARENA, which was forced into a government coalition with other conservative parties. The FMLN achieved its success in local elections based on its work in the fourteen municipalities it controlled from the 1994 elections and the role it has played in the national legislature as an opponent of the government's unpopular economic policies. As a result of the 2003 elections, the FMLN emerged as the largest single party in the National Assembly, with thirty-one seats, three more than the ruling ARENA Party. In 2004, its presidential candidate, the former guerrilla leader Schafik Handal, lost his bid for the presidency to the ARENA candidate Tony Saca, but the party maintained a strong presence in the country and won the presidency in 2009.

Guatemala

A discussion of revolution in Guatemala must encompass a long period of time and does not involve transcendent events like the Cuban revolution of 1959 or the Sandinista revolution of 1979. The high point of revolutionary forces in Guatemala may well have been in 1944, when an armed uprising succeeded in driving the long-time dictator General Jorge Ubico y Castañeda (1931–1944) from power. The movement against Ubico began with a student strike and escalated into a general strike that forced Ubico's resignation in June 1944. However, the resignation was a front for the continuation of Ubico's system, and it soon led to an armed rebellion of students, workers, and dissident army officers. The rebel movement won an easy victory and set up a junta government known as the October Revolution. The rebellion paved the way for elections that brought Juan José Arévalo to power in 1945. Once in power the Arévalo government pursued a reformist strategy rather than a revolutionary one. There was unprecedented government spending on schools, hospitals, and housing; and workers were allowed to unionize and engage in collective bargaining. However, rural Guatemala, which held 90 percent of the country's population, was largely untouched by the reforms. Arévalo was followed in office by Jacobo Arbenz, who deepened his predecessor's reform program but maintained Guatemala fully within the framework of capitalism. In fact, in 1950, Arbenz declared that his primary intent was to make Guatemala "a modern capitalist country." His primary extension of Arévalo's reforms was to carry them to the rural sector by inaugurating a modest land reform that challenged the most blatant policies of the U.S.-owned United Fruit Company. Arbenz also legalized the Communist Party, a reform-oriented organization with significant influence among unionized workers. These reforms, although modest in character, were too much for the country's oligarchy and the government of the United States. In 1954, Arbenz was removed from power in a military coup strongly backed by the United States through the actions of the Central Intelligence Agency (CIA). The newly installed government of Castillo Armas cracked down on anyone suspected of revolutionary activity. This witch hunt succeeded in setting back the possibility of a Guatemalan revolution by many years. The military coup ushered in a 30,000-strong armed force that brutally repressed any opposition political movements over the ensuing forty years. Peaceful forms of protest were routinely outlawed, and rural villages were often attacked by army patrols seeking to capture "subversives."

The revival of an armed resistance to the Guatemalan military began with the November 1960 revolt of army officers against President Miguel Ydígoras. The revolt was crushed when the United States sent Cuban exiles being trained for the ill-fated Bay of Pigs invasion. However, several rebel leaders escaped and established low-grade guerrilla warfare against the regime. One of the guerrillas' first leaders was Marco Antonio Yon Sosa, originally trained by the United States. Yon Sosa was killed in combat, but guerrillas who survived helped form the Guerrilla Army of the Poor (EGP) in 1972. Inspired by liberation theology, they built a base among the highland Indians, the first revolutionary movement to do so. By 1980 the EGP and other smaller groups had more than 5,000 members. The growing strength of the rebel movement alarmed the Guatemalan oligarchy, and fierce repression was unleashed against the rural areas in the early 1980s. The military's strategy was to destroy the guerrillas' base of operations by terrorizing the civilian population.

During General Romeo Lucas García's rule (1978–1982), there were numerous massacres. With financial support from the U.S. government, the military evacuated Indians from the northern highland guerrilla strongholds in Quiche and Huehuetenango departments and organized them in "model villages," a strategy developed by the United States in Vietnam. The military offered the local population a stark choice: work with us and be housed and fed, or die. In 1982, Lucas García was replaced in a coup by General Efraín Ríos Montt, a "born-again" Christian. Montt declared a state of siege and dramatically increased the level of repression. On July 6, 1982, more than 300 Indian residents of Finca San Francisco in Huehuetenango were massacred outside of their local church. Between 1981 and 1983, it is estimated that 100,000 Indians in 440 villages lost their lives at the hands of government forces. More than 1 million people were displaced from their homes. The repression resulted in the growth of the revolutionary movement. In 1982, the four main guerrilla groups, headed by EGP, united to form the Guatemalan National Revolutionary Union (URNG). With stepped-up covert U.S. assistance, the Guatemalan military escalated its war against the guerrillas. Newer, more sophisticated weaponry, including helicopter gunships, forced the URNG into retreat by 1983, a move that the Guatemalan government falsely labeled as a defeat of the revolutionary forces. The revolutionary movement survived throughout the 1980s and was bolstered by the growth of strong social protest movements in Guatemala's cities led by labor unions and human rights organizations. In 1987, the labor organizations formed a coalition with the Group of Mutual Support (GAM, an organization of relatives of the victims of repression) and the Peasant Unity Committee (CUC) to demand improved wages, an accounting for the victims of the repression, and land distribution. These forces of civil society, viewed by the military as allies of the guerrilla movement, also faced harsh repression. Despite the repression, the civil society organizations survived and participated in the 1992 U.N.-brokered negotiations started between the URNG and the government and military. The negotiations occurred because the guerrillas, with their numbers reduced to less than 3,000, realized that military victory was unlikely and the Guatemalan government was under pressure from the administration of George H. W. Bush to reduce emphasis on military aid programs and increase emphasis on consolidating a regional trading bloc. However, given the depths of Guatemala's repression and the reluctance of the oligarchy to accept cooperation with the revolutionaries, the peace settlement did not come easily. In 1993, President Jorge Antonio Serrano attempted to reimpose military rule and return to tactics of harsh repression. However, his coup attempt was reversed by a combination of street demonstrations and opposition from the

Clinton administration. Serrano was replaced by Ramiro de León Carpio, the parliament's human rights advisor. His appointment put the stalled negotiations back on track, and a peace settlement was finally achieved on December 27, 1996, bringing an end to Central America's longest civil war. The peace agreement formally ended the civil war but did not end violent conflict in the country, nor did the settlement significantly address the long-standing social inequalities that have fueled the conflict. Most importantly, there was little change in the pattern of land tenure, with 65 percent of the country's arable land remaining in the hands of just 2.6 percent of the population. The peace agreements called for peaceful settlements of land claims and the return of thousands of displaced families, but the administration of President Alvaro Enrique Arzú Yrigoyen, with the support of the country's traditional oligarchy, did little to further those aspects of the accords. The former revolutionaries, the URNG, operating as part of the civil opposition, now use the courts and public protest to press their reform agenda; but at this time, the relationship of forces is against them.

Colombia

Another of Latin America's most important contemporary revolutionary movements is the Revolutionary Armed Forces of Colombia (FARC). In 2010, the FARC had a presence in more than 60 percent of Colombia's municipalities. Although under sharp attack from well-armed paramilitaries and the Colombian government, the FARC sustained itself for more than three decades and contributed significantly to that country's continuing political unrest. The origins of the FARC lie in the peasant struggles of more than a half-century ago. Facing harsh living and working conditions, the workers on coffee plantations began to organize around labor demands and broader political concerns. The movement was most active in central Colombia but faced brutal repression by the army. The peasants responded with armed self-defense groups as early as the 1940s. In 1948, a ten-year period known as *La Violencia* was sparked by the assassination of populist leader Jorge Gaitán. The Colombian Communist Party was very active in this time period and assisted in the organization of self-defense and guerrilla groups. With the triumph of the Cuban Revolution in 1959, the concept of self-defense began to be transformed into the idea of the pursuance of guerrilla warfare with the goal of achieving state power for the purpose of social revolution. It was in this political context that the FARC was founded in 1964.

The organization began among communities of displaced peasants who had settled uncultivated lands in the hope of fleeing the repression of the state. Those who were fleeing state violence traveled in large groups protected by armed self-defense units, a process known as "armed colonization." These settlements were strongly under the influence of the Communist Party. It was these communities that later became the base of the FARC. The nature of national politics in Colombia also contributed to the development of a revolutionary movement. Two political parties, the Liberals and Conservatives, totally monopolized political power and prevented the development of any role within the system for legal means of dissent. To move competition from more violent forms and share power through alternation, they signed a power-sharing agreement in 1956. This alliance, known as the National Front from 1958 to 1974, has dominated the Colombian political scene to the present. Until the implementation of a new constitution in 1991, these two parties ruled under a permanent state of siege designed to curtail virtually all social protest. By blocking almost all possibility of a democratic left, the state created conditions for the emergence of an opposition that was outside of the parliamentary framework.

The FARC was not the only revolutionary group to be founded in this context. The National Liberation Army (ELN) was formed in 1964, the Popular Liberation Army (EPL) in 1965, and the April 19th Movement (M-19) in 1973. Smaller urban groups were also formed in this time period. In its early years, the growth of the FARC was slow. By the late 1970s, it had established a marginal presence in the central and southern parts of the country; but in the early 1980s, the FARC grew rapidly as the result of a government crackdown on legal opposition. Up until that time it had operated primarily in the political arena but now began to more clearly articulate its role as a military vanguard. It acquired the organizational structure of an army and developed an autonomy from the Communist Party. By 1983, it had expanded its military activity to eighteen fronts.

The FARC was committed to fundamental societal transformation through the armed achievement of state power, but it also pursued a flexible tactical position. In 1983, the government of Belisario Betancur made a significant peace overture. Departing sharply from the political stance of his predecessors, Betancur acknowledged many of the socioeconomic demands of the FARC. A cease-fire was arranged, and the possibility of a political revolution of the conflict became real. In the context of the cease-fire, the FARC formed the Patriotic Union (UP), a political front in which the Communist Party played a significant role. The FARC

The late Manuel Marulanda Velez, also known as "Tirofijo" (sure shot) in the mountains of Colombia. He was the undisputed leader of the FARC, the oldest and largest guerrilla movement in Latin America. *(Printed with permission of Diego Giudice/Archivolatino.com)*

was preparing for a possible electoral role but did not dismantle its military apparatus.

The possibility of a political settlement was scuttled by Betancur's opposition in the congress, which rejected the reforms proposed in the accords. The political opposition represented the traditional oligarchy and its allies in the military. When a new government under Virgilio Barco came to power in 1986, the government's overture to the armed opposition officially ended. It refused to recognize the demands of the opposition as legitimate and immediately launched harsh repression against the rebels and their supporters in civil society. During 1988 alone, close to 200 UP leaders were assassinated; and in a decade of repression, nearly 3,000 UP members, including mayors, municipal council members, and senators, were killed, virtually eliminating the organization. Despite this repression, the FARC did not officially return to a stance of war until 1991, after the military occupied the town of Casa Verde, the home of the FARC leadership. Although brief peace talks were conducted in mid-1991, the war intensified from that time onward. A constitutional assembly convened in 1991, and the FARC blamed the government for missing an opportunity to incorporate the political opposition through that process.

As the decade of the 1990s wore on, the FARC and other armed rebel groups found themselves at the center of political unrest in the country. The central government in Bogotá was increasingly unable to govern the country effectively as it battled the increasing influence of both drug cartels and rebel political movements. Unable to control the country by normal means, the government turned to paramilitary organizations to deal with problems by sheer force. In essence, it privatized the war against the FARC and the ELN and in the process served to delegitimize the state. As a result, the 1990s saw great ongoing costs in terms of human lives and property. The weakness of the central government opened the door for the FARC to implement a strategy of undermining local ruling structures by its tactic of "armed oversight." By gathering detailed information on local government financing and spending, the guerrillas were able to both target and expose corrupt local officials while also steering some government revenues toward FARC-sponsored projects.

The ongoing crisis of agriculture also contributed to the growing strength of the FARC. As traditional agricultural production declined, the rebels built support among those sectors hardest hit by the decline. The FARC successfully attracted unemployed youth from the countryside into its ranks. As the peasants increasingly looked to coca production to make up for the decline in other production, the FARC stepped forward with protection for those communities. Such actions helped finance the FARC's activities while also raising its political legitimacy among the poorest sectors. The support of the coca growers has contributed to the growing polarization of the society as the government has ignored the real socioeconomic issues and sought with the support of the U.S. government to place the rebels' activities within the militarized scope of the War on Drugs.

The relationship between the FARC and the political process has been more problematic. In 1996, in the midst of sharp conflict between the coca growers and the central government, the FARC organized a highly successful boycott of the municipal elections in the areas where its influence was strongest. In some cities, mayors were elected by as few as seven votes but prevented from taking office by popularly convened local councils. However, the ability of the guerrillas to protect those communities that defied the central government was limited. The government authorized campaigns of terror against these communities, carried out by private paramilitaries. Such growing polarization and the growing importance of the ELN make the prospect of a political settlement to Colombia's long-running insurgent rebellion unlikely in the near future. Heightened U.S. involvement through Plan Colombia further escalated the conflict. The election of hardline President Alvaro Uribe in 2002 dashed any immediate hopes of a negotiated settlement of the long-running civil war. Uribe ruled out negotiations with the FARC and, with the support of the United States through Plan Colombia, vowed to militarily destroy the guerrilla movement. In 2003, the government won some significant victories over the FARC, including targeted attacks on its leadership; but the FARC escalated its own tactics with increasingly bold terror attacks on wealthy Bogotá neighborhoods, including the bombing of the El Nogal club that killed thirty-six persons in February 2003. With the war continuing in stalemate, negotiations between the FARC and Colombia resumed in 2004 over ending the conflict and the prisoners held by both sides. Aided by the Venezualan and other Latin American governments, a dramatic prisioner release was negotiated in 2007, but the process was stimied after the Colombian armed forces raided a FARC camp just inside Ecuadoran territory and killed the leader who was coordinating prisoner exchanges in 2008. Although suffering some loss of power, the FARC has continued to battle the government since then.

Peru

One of Latin America's most interesting revolutionary movements is Peru's *Sendero Luminoso* (Shining Path) of José Carlos Mariátegui. In the late 1980s and early 1990s, they were the most active rebels in Latin America and were seen as seriously challenging state power against an increasingly weak central government in Lima. A decade later, with most of its key leaders either in jail or dead, Shining Path was reduced to a marginal position in Peruvian politics. Its relative demise provided some interesting insight on revolution and revolutionary movements.

Shining Path was founded in 1980 by Abimael Guzmán, a philosophy professor at the university in Ayacucho. He had been doing preparatory work in the area for some years before. For the next thirteen years, the Communist Party of Peru, known as Shining Path, was a central actor in Peruvian politics. Founded on the Maoist principle of a peasant-based revolution that would gain control of the countryside and eventually encircle and overwhelm the central government, Shining Path was quite successful in reaching out from its original student base to gain widespread influence among the indigenous people of the Ayacucho region, long ignored by the central government in Lima. The rebels burst onto the scene by assassinating local officials who refused to cooperate with their efforts and by seeking to create armed, liberated communities out of the reach of the central government. Their political strategy was fiercely sectarian, rejecting all other political movements as part of the status quo. Shining Path was willing to use violence against any reformist forces that refused to cooperate with its strategy—trade unionists, neighborhood organizers, other leftists, or priests and nuns engaged in community organizing. This harsh sectarianism eventually contributed to the movement's decline. Initially, the government's response was almost entirely counterproductive. In the 1980s, the government carried out a military occupation of the highlands region where Shining Path was based. The army's draconian actions did not succeed in defeating the revolutionaries in their strongholds, and popular reaction to the government repression actually helped to spread the revolution to other provinces. Between 1989 and 1992, Shining Path stepped up its armed activity in Lima and engaged in a highly effective car- and truck-bombing campaign, badly shaking the government's confidence. However, upon a thorough review of its earlier counterproductive repression, the government began to reformulate its counterinsurgency strategy. Playing on the divisions in the rural communities that were created by Shining Path's sectarian tactics, the government began to succeed in getting rural inhabitants to join government-backed armed self-defense groups. It was a testament to Shining Path's brutality that the government began to succeed despite its own previous brutality. Shining Path's war became one of *campesinos* against *campesinos*. Shining Path's base of support generally did not grow beyond the most marginalized people—students, teachers, and unemployed youth from the shantytowns. It became more a sect than a broad-based popular movement.

In 1992, through stepped-up intelligence activities, the police were able to arrest a number of key intermediate-level officials, weakening the organization's internal structures. This increased repression occurred in the framework of President Alberto Fujimori's auto-coup, or assumption of dictatorial powers, under the guise of fighting Shining Path. Fujimori's efforts culminated later in 1992 with the arrest of Guzmán. Soon after his capture, Guzmán called off the armed struggle and sought political dialogue with the government. However, in 1994, several key Shining Path leaders denounced Guzmán's call for negotiations and vowed to continue the armed struggle. Most of them were later arrested. Shining Path has not been completely destroyed, but as the decade ended it sought to remain politically relevant in the wake of its disunity and numerous defeats at the hands of the government. By 2005, it had been reduced to a few small bands operating in remote areas where the production of coca leaves and the related drug trade could help to finance its existence.

New Social Movements

In recent years, protest and resistance have taken on different forms. New types of mobilization are developing all over Latin America. Unlike radical revolutionary movements of the last few decades, these new movements do not employ or advocate the radical, revolutionary restructuring of the state through violent revolution. Rather, their primary focus is to contest power by working through civil society to modify the existing political system and pushing it to the limits to achieve needed and necessary change and restructuring. Although there have been some exceptions, like the initial Zapatista uprising of early January 1994 and the very brief participation of the Confederation of Indigenous Nationalities of Ecuador (CONAIE) in a would-be junta that held the Ecuadorian Congress building overnight in January 2000, they were short-lived and both movements quickly moved from trying to insert themselves as the regional or national rulers to negotiating power with existing national political elites (while at the same time trying to change the composition of the national political class).

These new political movements all contest power but do so in a political environment that is substantially different from what it has been historically. National-level political participation was quite limited at the time of independence. As suggested above, mass political movements like that led by Hidalgo failed, while those led by the less popularly oriented members of the *criollo* elite, like Iturbide, succeeded and set the stage for the elitist politics of the nineteenth and much of the twentieth centuries. The franchise—and concomitant political participation—were widened in the nineteenth and twentieth centuries. This in turn challenged the political elite to seek mechanisms to incorporate (if not manipulate) ever wider segments of the population. This eventually led to the emergence of mass-based parties, reformist and revolutionary parties, and populism as a means of incorporating the masses into a national project led by a political elite. Some reformist parties, like Liberación Nacional in Costa Rica and Acción Democrática in Venezuela, were able to bring about some economic and political structural change and incorporate wider sectors of the masses into national society and competitive two-party dominant political systems. A few populist projects, like Peronism in Argentina, were also able to achieve significant economic redistribution, break the oligarchy's economic domination, and incorporate the laboring masses and segments of the middle class into the (one party-dominant) party system, albeit under the somewhat demagogic leadership of Juan and Evita Perón. On the other hand, the Cuban revolution challenged traditional elitist rule in a different way but left little space for the development of autonomous social movements, though it did respond to the needs of the masses and developed the mechanism of *poder popular* that fomented active participation at the neighborhood and local levels. The widespread rebellion against Anastasio Somoza in Nicaragua helped to make it possible for the Sandinista revolution to take power and for the FSLN-led government to begin an economic, social, and political restructuring of the Nicaraguan nation. Indeed, as we noted in *Democracy and Socialism in Sandinista Nicaragua,* the strength and relative autonomy of many of the mass organizations in Nicaragua in the early 1980s were significant and helped to show that new organizational structures and political movements that supported them could radically change the way power was exercised in Latin America. Likewise, the strength and dynamism of neighborhood- and community-based movements that began to flower all over Latin America in the 1980s (even under repressive military regimes) redefined the parameters of political activism and suggested new repertoires of action for emerging social and political movements.

The systems of mass communication and related communication technology as well as easy, low-cost access to the internet have combined with higher levels of literacy, widened access to higher education, and much greater political freedom under the democratization process. The result has been a new wave of political and social movements that are often different in their organization and strategy and endeavor to articulate popular needs in new ways. This has occurred when ideas of grassroots democracy, popular participation, and even elements of liberation theology and Christian base community organization have been widely disseminated.

Likewise, there is a growing belief that racial, gender, and economic equality should exist and that systems that perpetuate inequality need to be changed.

Ever since the *Caracazo* in Venezuela in 1989, there have been different forms of popular protest against austerity measures and elements of the conservative economic policies that came to be called "neoliberalism" in Latin America. These have been manifest in diverse forms: the Zapatista rebellion in Mexico in 1994; the neopopulist Movimiento V República led by Hugo Chávez in Venezuela from the late 1990s on; the national indigenous movement led by CONAIE in Ecuador, the growth of its related party Pachakutik, and, in the election of Rafael Correa, the Movement of Landless Rural Laborers (MST) in Brazil; the *Asambleas Barriales* and other protest organizations in Argentina; and the indigenous peasant unions and Cocaleros Federation and their linked political movement, the Movimiento al Socialismo (MAS) in Bolivia.

Argentine Manifestation

In Argentina, popular mobilizations, street demonstrations, strikes, and neighborhood *asambleas populares* (or *Asambleas Barriales*) shook the political system and the political class to the core at the end of 2001 and occasioned the resignation of the elected president Fernando de la Rua, and the rapid replacement of three other appointed presidents (the vice president had already resigned). In early 2002, a declared anti-neoliberal Peronist president, Eduardo Duhalde, was voted into office by the Argentine Congress. The unresolved economic crisis, default on the foreign debt, and Duhalde's perceived need to make some concession to the IMF, other international financial institutions, and U.S. policy kept the population angry and mobilized. Demonstrations and protests continued through early 2003 as the Argentine nation grouped to find a political force capable of ending the crisis. There was so little confidence in traditional parties or politicians that one could frequently hear a popular refrain among many Argentinians—*Que se vayan todos!* (Throw them all out!). However, the limitations of this movement were shown when the Argentine people elected Néstor Kirchner, a more traditional politician from the Peronist Party, to be president in 2003. He promised to move away from neoliberalism and dictates from the IMF and other international financial institutions and return to the traditional nationalist positions of the Peronists.

The nature of the protest in Buenos Aires and other Argentine cities suggests the political sea change that is sweeping across Latin America. Governance is breaking down, and traditional political institutions are losing legitimacy as new movements surge to challenge traditional political leadership. In recent years, a great many of the masses—and some of the middle class—seem to be hit by a feeling that the much touted return to democracy, celebration of civil society, and incorporation in the globalization process have left them marginalized economically, if not politically as well. The reactions in Argentina, Mexico, Ecuador, Bolivia, Brazil, and Venezuela are strong and significant and, in varying ways, represent a new means of pressuring for much needed restructuring, not from above but by the common people. It is also quite possible that the democratization and celebration of civil

society allow—some would say encourage—the political mobilization that is manifest in the widespread emergence of new social and political movements.

Dissatisfaction seems widespread. Selected abstention rates are indicative
of growing disillusion with government and the political system. In elections in
Argentina in 2001, some 41 percent of the voters abstained or cast annulled or blank
ballots. The 1998 national elections in Brazil saw a similar phenomenon, with 40.1
percent of the electorate either abstaining or casting blank or annulled ballots. In
the Mexican presidential election of 2000, the abstention rate alone was 36 percent.

As the continent democratizes, there is even greater discussion of the emergence
of a new(er) political class. Such talk is, however, coupled to a growing consensus
that the political class's new political enterprise is leaving behind the great majorities
and effectively further marginalizing specific groups within those majorities. Such
groups include indigenous people in southern Mexico and Ecuador, rural laborers
and the poor generally in Brazil, the rural peasants and indigenous people in Bolivia,

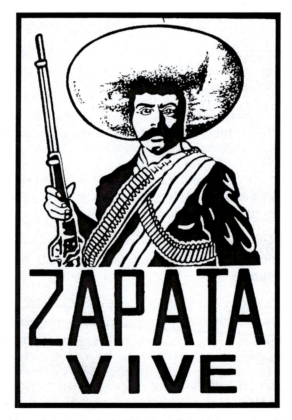

Zapata lives! Legendary figures such as Mexican Revolutionary Emiliano Zapata inspire
great admiration and emulation. After Zapata became the inspiration and namesake for the
Zapatistas, pictures and Zapata decals like this one were freely circulated in Chiapas and
other parts of Mexico.

those who live in the slums and who have been left out of the diffusion of oil wealth in Venezuela, as well as large segments of the lower and middle classes in Argentina. Major organizations include the national indigenous group CONAIE in Ecuador, the Cocaleros Federation led by Evo Morales in Bolivia, and the MST in Brazil. Smaller groups include social movements like the Madres de la Plaza de Mayo in Argentina.

Chiapas: Regional Victory

In southern Mexico, local and community organizations began to resist the dire economic consequences engendered by globalization and globalized integration through free trade and the North American Free Trade Agreement (NAFTA). It is argued that similar forms of resistance have occurred throughout the hemisphere since the region was interjected into the international capitalist economic system. Yet, these previous struggles were more akin to traditional peasant or indigenous rebellions in that they did not spawn strong national or international links and as such were easily marginalized or defeated. Indeed, localized resistance had bubbled to the surface sporadically since the time of the conquest, if not before. This certainly had been the case in southern Mexico and the Yucatan. Perhaps stimulated by this tradition of rebellion, in the 1980s the indigenous rural population in Chiapas began to resist and organize against the traditional land inequity and the hardships that the commercialization of agriculture and Mexico's further integration into the global market structure caused them. Racial identity and unequal land distribution helped to solidify the movement and led to the formation of a social movement that eventually spawned the Zapatista Army of National Liberation (EZLN). Unlike some other groups, the Zapatistas were successful in linking their struggle to a growing continental indigenous identity and the disastrous effects of globalized free markets on local small farmers. Their ingenious use of the internet, the mountain or ski mask, public relations, marches, and mobilizations kept their cause before the Mexican nation and the international community. They were able to create a highly politicized movement with considerable regional power and national visibility. They were not, however, able to link their struggle to other large politicized social movements to form a national coalition. Nor were they able to mobilize their support behind a nationwide new political party or political movement (as was done in Ecuador and Brazil) that would be sympathetic to their demands once it achieved national power or that would at least ensure them adequate space in civil society to continue to mobilize support and pursue their demands (as would be done in Bolivia in 2003 and 2005).

Ecuador

Southern Mexico was not the only place where the effects of neoliberal policies and the globalization process generated innovative responses. Since Incan times, local indigenous communities have been marginalized from important decision-making processes in Ecuador. This practice was extended to virtually all indigenous people after the conquest and continued during the republic. Yet, by the 1990s, the traditional struggle for land, power, and some modicum of justice for the indigenous, mostly peasant masses, was gradually transformed from a local, community-based one to a national one coordinated by CONAIE. CONAIE had become a national organization that was able to mobilize thousands of its people in land takeovers and marches. It connected different ethnic and regional groups and used modern means of communication to forge a national social movement. In the process, it became a major power contender that could challenge governmental action by the late 1990s. After the disastrous dollarization of the economy and imposition of other neoliberal economic policies by President Jamil Mahuad, CONAIE was able to mobilize tens of thousands of its constituents for a march on Quito that culminated in the taking of the congress building and—backed by a few progressive army officers and civilian politicians—the formation of a short-lived junta in January 2000. This was the first time indigenous people had governed substantial parts of Ecuador since the conquest. Their victory was, however, brief. Although some horizontal contacts with other organizations had been made, the CONAIE militants were not part of a broad-based national coalition that could retain power. With the support of the United States, the traditional political class was able to retake power and negotiate the exit of Mahuad by placing Vice President Gustavo Noboa in power. Once mobilized, CONAIE, learning from the experience, initiated a national political strategy and even started an affiliated political party, Pachakutik, in 1995. In the 2002 elections, they continued to cultivate their now highly politicized national social movement but were also able to field successful local and congressional political candidates. Eventually, they threw their support behind Lucio Gutiérrez, the army colonel who had been part of the short-lived junta in January 2000. Thus, they helped to elect Gutiérrez to the presidency, though their support was not unconditional. They maintained their autonomy but ensured that their demands would at least receive a hearing at the highest level and might even be received with some sympathy. This stance became important because, once in power, Gutiérrez moved away from his anti-neoliberal positions to the point of seeking a free trade agreement with the United States. CONAIE led the opposition against the turn in the president's politics, and in early 2005, he was forced from office amid large street protests. The support of CONAIE and other indigenous movements was fundamental for the 2006 election of left-leaning candidate Rafael Correa to the presidency, and his pursuit of a more progressive political agenda. Later, they would criticize the Correa government for its willingness to extend mining concessions that endangered indigenous communities.

New Social Movements and New Politics: The MST

The radically different nature of these new social movements and the new politics can perhaps best be seen in the largest of the new social movements in Latin America, the MST in Brazil. Their ranks exceed 1 million, and on one occasion they were able to mobilize 100,000 people for a march on Brasília. In a pamphlet titled *Brazil Needs a Popular Project*, the organization calls for popular mobilizations, noting that "All the changes in the history of humanity only happened when the people were mobilized" and that, in Brazil, "all the social and political changes that happened were won when the people mobilized and struggled." Their political culture and decision-making processes break from the authoritarian tradition. The movement has been heavily influenced by liberation theology and the participatory democratic culture that is generated by the use and study of Paulo Freire's approach to self-taught, critical education.

The MST itself was formed as a response to long-standing economic, social, and political conditions in Brazil. Land, wealth, and power have been allocated in very unequal ways in Brazil since the conquest in the early 1500s. Land has remained highly concentrated, and as late as 1996, 1 percent of the landowners who owned farms of over 1000 hectares owned 45 percent of the land. Conversely, as of 2001, there were some 4.5 million landless rural workers in Brazil. Wealth has remained equally concentrated. In 2001, the Brazilian Institute of Government Statistics reported that the upper 10 percent of the population averaged an income that was nineteen times greater than that of the lowest 40 percent. The plantation agriculture that dominated the colonial period and the early republic became the standard for Brazilian society. The wealthy few owned the land, reaped the profits, and decided the political destiny of the many. Slavery was the institution that provided most of the labor on the early plantation system and, thus, set the nature of the relationship between the wealthy landowning elite and the disenfranchised masses who labored in the fields. Land has stayed in relatively few hands in Brazil, and agricultural laborers continue to be poorly paid and poorly treated. Further, after the commercialization and mechanization of agriculture that began in the 1970s, much of the existing rural labor force became superfluous. As this process continued, not only were rural laborers let go but sharecroppers were expelled from the land they had farmed and small farmers lost their land to larger family or commercial estates. This resulted in increases in rural unemployment and the number of rural landless families. Many were forced to migrate to the cities to swell the numbers of the urban poor, while others opted for the government-sponsored Amazon colonization program whereby they were transported to the Amazon region to cut down the rain forest and cultivate the land. Few found decent jobs in the city, and the poor soil of the former rain forest allowed for little sustained agriculture. As conditions deteriorated, the landless realized that they were fighting for their own existence as a group and, as such, were the authors of their own destiny. The origins of the organization go back to the bitter struggle to survive under the agricultural policies implemented by the military government. The landless in the southern Brazilian state of Rio Grande do Sul began to organize to demand land. Other landless people soon picked up their cry in the neighboring states of Paraná and Santa Catarina. They built on a long tradition of rural resistance and rebellion that extends back to the establishment of *palenques* or large inland settlements of runaway slaves and to the famous rebellion by the poor rural peasants of Canudos in the 1890s. In more recent times, it included the famous Peasant Leagues of Brazil's impoverished northeast in the 1950s and early 1960s and the "grass wars" in Rio Grande do Sul and the southern states in the 1970s. When the MST was founded in southern Brazil in 1984 as a response to rural poverty and lack of access to land, wealth, and power, similar conditions existed in many states. Indeed, there were landless workers and peasants throughout the nation. Thus, the MST soon spread from Rio Grande do Sul and Paraná in the south to states like Pernambuco in the northeast and Pará in the Amazon region. It rapidly became a national organization with coordinated policies and strong local participation and decision making, with frequent state and national meetings based on direct representation. By 2001, there were active MST organizations in twenty-three of the twenty-six states.

This type of national organization had not been the case with the Zapatista movement because conditions and identity were much more locally rooted. Yet, in both cases, traditional politics and traditional political parties had proven unable and unwilling to address the deteriorating economic conditions of the marginalized groups who were suffering the negative effects of economic globalizaton. Their response was grassroots organization and the development of a new repertoire of actions that broke with old forms of political activity. Developing organization and group actions began to tie individual members together in a strongly forged group identity. The MST decided from the outset that it was to be an organization for the landless workers that would be run by the landless workers for their benefit as they defined it. They engaged in direct actions such as land takeovers from large estates and public lands, construction of black plastic-covered encampments along the side of the road to call attention to their demands for land, and marches and confrontations when necessary. They even occupied the family farm of President Fernando Henrique Cardoso to draw attention to his landowning interests and the consequent bias they attributed to him. They were at times brutally repressed, assassinated, and imprisoned; but they persevered, forcing land distribution to their members and others without land. Their ability to mobilize as many as 12,000 people for a single land takeover or 100,000 for a national march in 1997 suggested just how

MST Militants on the move. *(Photo by Paulo Santos-Interphoto/AP Images)*

strong their organizational abilities were and how well they could communicate and coordinate at the national level. They also created a great deal of national support and helped to create a consensus that there was a national problem with land distribution and that some substantial reform was necessary. Struggles that were once local and isolated were now international and linked. The news media and growing international communications links, like cellular phones and especially electronic mail, greatly facilitated the globalization of struggle and of awareness of local struggles as well as support and solidarity for them. This and the dramatic actions like massive land takeovers by the MST also generated considerable support at the national level and helped to define what might have been considered a local problem as a national one that required national attention and national resources to remedy it.

The interaction between the MST and the Workers' Party (PT) is also instructive. Although relations between the two organizations are generally excellent at the local level, with overlapping affiliations, the national leaderships have remained separate and not always as cordial. The MST has maintained a militant line in regard to the need to take over unused land and assert its agenda, whereas much of the PT leadership has wanted to be more conciliatory. Thus, the landless backed and supported Luiz Inácio "Lula" da Silva and the PT in most local campaigns and the national campaign for the presidency. In this way, they helped to achieve significant regime change in Brazil, where Lula was elected with 61.27 percent of the vote in the second round of voting in 2002. Indeed, realizing the PT's historic challenge to neoliberal policies and elitist rule, the landless turned out heavily in the election to join some 80 percent of the registered voters who participated in the voting in both rounds. The Landless again supported Lula in the 2006 election, but were even more critical after major land reform initiatives failed to materialize in his second term. Once the elections were over, the MST did not press to be part of the government. Rather, they continued to press the government for a comprehensive land reform program and redistribution of the land and the wealth. There would be no return to politics as usual. The PT would press its "0 Hunger" program and other social and economic initiatives, and the MST would press the PT government for the structural reforms (e.g., comprehensive agrarian reform) that it considered necessary.

Conclusion

Political scientist Eric Selbin has suggested that, given Latin America's 500-year-old tradition of rebellion and revolution, we should be wary of dismissing the possibility of future revolutions there. An understanding of why revolution and serious study of it must remain integral to our study of Latin America is rooted in the fact that the recent growth of democratic political forms and economic restructuring have done relatively little to eliminate the social inequalities and political disenfranchisement that plague Latin America in the twenty-first-century. The greater harbinger for the continued probability of revolutionary upsurges and movements for radical change in Latin America comes from the fact that as the region begins the new millennium more people live in poverty than was the case twenty years ago and the fact that the gap between the richest and poorest grows wider. Nearly half of the region's more than 580 million people are poor, an increase of more than 70 million in one decade. Most of the regimes that took power during Latin America's recent turn to democratic rule did not seem to make any significant progress in the arena of social justice, with the result that the neoliberal economic models triumphant at the start of the 1990s were increasingly being called into question. By 2008, politics were once again changing. There were myriad new social and political movements that were pressing hard for structural change and were democratizing the decision-making process if not the political culture itself. New leftist presidents had been elected throughout the region and many were beginning to implement projects for radical change. As U.S. President John F. Kennedy observed in the formulation of the Alliance for Progress, the stifling of reforms makes the violent struggle for change inevitable. Contemporary democratic regimes, as Selbin notes, rely far too often on pacts among elites (pacted democracy) and the marginalization of the indigenous population and masses generally. It would seem that social change will remain on the agenda in the twenty-first century in Latin America. It would also seem that new means of organizing for such change are being developed in communities and new social and political movements throughout the region.

Yet, Latin America's ruling elites have rarely demonstrated great tolerance for such political opposition, and it is unclear whether that will change overnight. The social movements themselves, often with a single-issue focus, are not necessarily capable of articulating the broader vision for societal change that the region's social and political inequalities demand. It remains to be seen if these new, highly politicized movements or new political parties, like Brazil's PT or Bolivia's MAS, will be able to remedy the region's problems through massive mobilizations and concerted political action. The extent to which they can achieve genuine change and socioeconomic restructuring remains to be seen. If they cannot, then the next question to be asked is whether or not the traditional forms of revolution and rebellion will remain relevant or whether yet other forms of struggle will replace them.

Bibliography

Alvarez, Sonia, Evelina Dagnino, and Arturo Escobar, eds. *Cultures of Politics/Politics of Cultures: Revisioning Latin American Social Movements*. Boulder, CO: Westview Press, 1998.

Arnson, Cynthia. *Comparative Peace Processes in Latin America*. Palo Alto, CA: Stanford University Press, 1999.

Bradford, Sue, and Jan Rocha. *Cutting the Wire, the Story of the Landless Movement in Brazil*. London: Latin American Bureau, 2002.

Broad, Robin, ed. *Global Backlash, Citizen Initiatives for a Just World Economy*. Lanham, MD: Rowman & Littlefield, 2002.

Colburn, Forrest. *The Vogue of Revolution in Poor Countries*. Princeton, NJ: Princeton University Press, 1994.

Debray, Regis. *Revolution in the Revolution?* New York: Grove Press, 1967.

della Porta, Donatella, and Sidney Tarrow, eds. *Transnational Protest and Global Activism*. Lanham, MD: Rowman & Littlefield, 2005.

Eckstein, Susan, ed. *Power and Protest: Latin American Social Movements*. Berkeley: University of California Press, 2001.

Ellner, Steve, and Daniel Hellinger. *Venezuelan Politics in the Chávez Era: Class, Polarization and Conflict.* Boulder, CO: Lynne Rienner, 2003.

Escobar, Arturo, and Sonia E. Alvarez. *The Making of Social Movements in Latin America: Identity, Strategy and Democracy.* Boulder, CO: Westview Press, 1992.

Hodges, Donald C. *The Latin American Revolution: Politics and Strategy from Apro-Marxism to Guevarism.* New York: William Morrow, 1974.

Kampwirth, Karen. *Women and Guerrilla Movements: Nicaragua, El Salvador, Chiapas, Cuba.* University Park: Pennsylvania State University Press, 2002.

Lefeber, Walter W. *Inevitable Revolutions: The United States in Central America.* 2nd ed. New York: Norton, 1994.

Liss, Sheldon. *Marxist Thought in Latin America.* Berkeley: University of California Press, 1984.

McClintock, Cynthia. *Revolutionary Movements in Latin America.* Washington, DC: United States Institute of Peace Press, 1998.

McLaren, Peter. *Che Guevara, Paulo Freire, and the Pedagogy of the Oppressed.* Blue Ridge Summitt, PA: Rowman & Littlefield, 2000.

Montgomery, Tommie Sue. *Revolution in El Salvador: From Civil Strife to Peace.* 2nd ed. Boulder, CO: Westview Press, 1995.

Palmer, David Scott. *Shining Path of Peru.* 2nd ed. New York: St. Martin's Press, 1992.

Selbin, Eric. *Modern Latin American Revolutions.* Boulder, CO: Westview Press, 1993.

Skocpol, Theda. *States and Social Revolution.* Cambridge, UK: Cambridge University Press, 1979.

Stahler-Sholk, Richard, Harry E. Vanden, and Glen Kuecker, eds. Special issue: "Globalizing Resistence: The New Politics of Social Movements in Latin America." *Latin American Perspectives* 34, no. 2 (March 2007).

Stahler-Sholk, Harry E. Vanden, and Glen Kuecker, eds. *Latin American Social Movements in the Twenty-First Century: Resistance, Power and Democracy.* Lanham, MD: Rowman & Littlefield, 2008.

Stedile, João Pedro, and Bernardo Mançano Fernandes. *Brava Gente: a Trajetórai do MST e a Luta Pela Terra no Brasil.* São Paulo: Fundacão Perseo Abramo, 1999.

Vanden, Harry E. *Latin American Marxism: A Bibliography.* New York: Garland, 1991.

Vanden, Harry E. "New Political Movements, Governance and the Breakdown of Traditional Politics in Latin America." *International Journal of Public Administration* 27, 2004. no. 13–14, 1129–1149.

Vanden, Harry E. "Globalization in a Time of Neoliberalism: Politicized Social Movements and the Latin American Response." *Journal of Developing Societies.* 2003. 19, no.2–3, 308–333.

Vanden, Harry E., and Gary Prevost. *Democracy and Socialism in Sandinista Nicaragua.* Boulder, CO: Lynne Rienner, 1993.

Wickham-Crowley, Timothy. *Guerrillas and Revolution in Latin America.* Princeton, NJ: Princeton University Press, 1992.

Wright, Angus, and Wendy Wolford. *To Inherit the Earth: The Landless Movement and the Struggle for a New Brazil.* Oakland, CA: Food First, 2003.

FILMS AND VIDEOS

A Place Called Chiapas. Canada, 1998.

Americas in Transition. United States, 1982.

El Salvador: Another Vietnam. United States, 1981.

Grass War! Peasant Struggle in Brazil. United States, 2001.

1932: Scars of Memory. United States, 2002. (The 1932 Matanza in El Salvador)

Raiz Forte/Strong Roots. Brazil, 2000.

Romero. United States, 1989.

Seven Dreams of Peace. United States, 1996.

Tupamaros. United States, 1996.

Ya Basta! The Battle Cry of the Forceless. United States, 1997.

WEBSITES

www.mst.br/   Landless Workers Movement in Brazil (MST).

http://conaie.nativeweb.org/   The Confederation of Indigenous Nationalities of Ecuador (CONAIE).

TWELVE

U.S.–LATIN AMERICAN RELATIONS

There are many ways of seeing the relationship between the United Sates and Latin America. That most commonly voiced in North America is that the United States, Canada, and the Latin American nations are sister republics who share a common identity in the Western Hemisphere. This vision is most often expressed as Pan-Americanism and is based on the premise that all the American republics have common interests and objectives no matter their place, power, or national identity within the Western Hemisphere. Accordingly, the Latin American republics are expected to willingly enroll in foreign policy initiatives championed by the United States, be it the fight against fascism during World War II, anticommunism, the war on drugs, free market initiatives, or the war on terrorism. Latin Americans, somewhat like Canadians, do not always see such a commonality of interests and are often resentful of pressure and cajoling by a powerful neighbor. Indeed, they often bemoan their proximity to the colossus of the north as suggested by an adage often heard in Mexico and smaller nations in Central America and the Caribbean—"so far from God and so close to the United States."

One of the earliest statements of the potential conflict with the United States was made by the hero of the struggle for independence from Spain and Liberator of South America, Simón Bolívar. His keen awareness of the developing strength of the United States and prescient vision of the need for Latin American strength and unity prompted him to organize an important hemispheric conference that was convened in Panama in 1826, two years after the now famous declaration of President James Monroe (the Monroe Doctrine) on the need to keep the former colonial powers out of Latin America. This concern could be construed in itself as a tacit recognition of the relative weakness of the Latin American states before the colonial powers of the day, and also a reaction to the United States' troubles in its fight with Britain in the War of 1812.

The 1826 Congress of Panama, as it came to be known, was to bring all the independent Spanish-speaking republics of the hemisphere together to discuss common interests and chart a common course. Brazil and the United States were invited (over Bolívar's objections) only at the last minute and the U.S. representatives never arrived while the congress was in session. The congress was poorly attended and never achieved its aims, though it did set forth a Latin American position—one that assumed Latin American interests were different from—and perhaps conflicting with— those of the United States. Fully aware of this developing disparity in power, Bolívar later wrote, in a letter to the British chargé d'affaires in Bogotá dated August 5, 1829, that the United States "seem destined by Providence to plague America with torments in the name of freedom."

As Peter Smith argues in *Talons of the Eagle*, the earliest years of the North American republic reflected the development of the "age of imperialism" and imprinted on U.S. attitudes toward Latin America a sense of superiority and domination that has persisted through more than two hundred years down to the present. In *Beneath the United States*, Lars Schoultz notes that in the first half of the nineteenth century, officials in Washington began to create a mind-set that would continue to influence U.S. policy toward Latin America down to the present. From this perspective, the neighbors to the south were inferior to their English-speaking northern neighbors, plagued with problems, and in need of assistance from the United States. Their territory was seen in the context of U.S. security interests and thus might need to be taken, bought, invaded, or otherwise controlled according to U.S. needs.

Imperialism, defined as the quest for land, labor, and resources through empire, fostered a great rivalry among the European powers that lasted for over 200 years and culminated in the cataclysmic world wars of the twentieth century. Thus, by 1898 most of the Western European powers, including tiny Belgium and The Netherlands, had established empires in different parts of what we now refer to as the third world or global south. They used their control to extract wealth for the metropolitan, colonizing country by obtaining cheap raw materials, markets for their manufactured goods, or investing large amounts of capital. The United States seemingly broke free from this system at its beginning through the successful eighteenth-century war of independence. In reality, the newly independent colonies almost immediately joined that system by looking southward for land and resources. As a result, U.S. behavior in Latin America from the nineteenth century onward would closely resemble the penetration of the region that marked three centuries of Spanish and Portuguese colonial domination (described in Chapter 2). The reality of the U.S. assumption of an imperial role is often overlooked because of the popular myth that U.S. foreign policy was established as a reflection of President George Washington's famous farewell address wherein he warned the new republic to avoid "foreign entanglements." The spin placed on this advice to avoid permanent military alliances suggested that the United States adopted an anticolonial, isolationist stance that would dominate U.S. foreign policy well into the twentieth century. The reality was far different, especially regarding U.S. relations with Latin America. First of all, Washington's views were countered by Alexander Hamilton and others, who argued that the United States should not ignore the conflicts in Europe but rather utilize them to its advantage as the colonies had done during the Revolutionary War, when they gained French assistance for the military defeat of the British at Yorktown. The differences between Hamilton and Washington were real and have often been manifested in U.S. foreign policy over the decades, but they were not significant in regard to Latin America. The development of that empire, sometimes defined as a U.S. sphere of influence, was done in stages that reflected the ever growing power and confidence of the United States. Not surprisingly, the first priority of the new republic was territorial expansion. Thus after purchasing Louisiana (formerly West Florida) after it had been transferred by Spain to France, the U.S. enunciated the No-transfer Doctrine in 1810 whereby it stated that the transfer of any part of (East) Florida into the hands of a foreign power would be troubling and under certain circumstances, would compel the United States to temporarily occupy that territory. There was considerable uneasiness that Spain would transfer part of Florida to Great Britain, which would in turn use it for bases in the growing conflict with the United States that would become the War of 1812. The political leaders of the new nation were in agreement that European influence in Latin America should be reduced and that there were long-term political and commercial opportunities in the region. From the beginning, the United States did not see Spain and Portugal as long-term threats, but rather believed that their declining colonial control would yield great opportunities for the expansion of the British and French empires. As a result, the United States came reluctantly to support the independence of the former Spanish and Portuguese colonies as a way to reduce European influence in the region.

In the early years of the nineteenth century, beginning with Thomas Jefferson, a policy for Latin America was crafted that culminated in the statement of the Monroe Doctrine in 1823 as official U.S. policy. Still adhered to almost two centuries later, the essence of the doctrine is that the regions of North, Central, South America and the Caribbean represent a hemisphere "unto itself" naturally dominated by the United States and largely free of significant influence from any other region of the world, especially Europe. Stated by a small young nation at the time, it was an attempt to neutralize European influence in the region that might threaten U.S. interests and a bold declaration representing much more hope than reality. It was the claim of an empire without any real substance that would take decades to realize.

As time went on, U.S. leaders looked southward to Florida, Mexico, and Cuba for new territories. Florida was the first prize to be taken from Spain through a combination of military force and negotiation. After opening negotiations with the Spanish in 1817 General Andrew Jackson seized Spanish forts at Saint Mark's and Pensacola, on the pretense that the Spaniards had failed to control Indian tribes in the territories. Failing to win British backing for its position, Spain agreed to cede Florida to the United States in return for freedom from claims by U.S. citizens against Spain and U.S. recognition of Spanish control over Texas. The British did not support Spain, fearing that its colonies could eventually fall into French hands, their chief imperial rival. U.S. control was a lesser evil. Of course, the latter concession on Texas would not be honored over time.

Territorial Expansion: Confrontation with Mexico

By the mid-nineteenth century the United States, often motivated by the concept of Manifest Destiny, began to expand its economic and political power into Latin America. U.S. nationals flocked to the Mexican territory of Texas and soon pushed for independence from Mexico joining *tejanos* (Texas Mexicans) who were already pressing for autonomy. Of great significance was the desire of the United States to obtain territory from Mexico, as it held the vast territories comprising what are now the current states of Texas, Arizona, New Mexico, California, Nevada, Colorado, and Utah. To achieve the dream of Manifest Destiny and realize its potential as a nation from the Atlantic to the Pacific, the acquiring of this vast territory from the Mexicans and the defeat of Indian tribes who lived in the region was seen as essential to the success of the United States if it was to take its rightful place in the imperial world order. The first step in the process was the annexation of Texas in 1845 by President James Polk. Colonists, many of whom were slaveholders from the U.S. south, had declared an independent Lone Star Republic in 1836. However, they were defeated by the Mexican army under the command of Antonio López de Santa Anna at the Alamo and their declaration was never recognized by the Mexican government. At the time of the annexation, Mexico considered Texas a renegade province and severed diplomatic ties with the United States upon Polk's declaration.

In 1846 Polk sent General Zachary Taylor south to claim the Rio Grande River as the southern border of the United States rather than the traditional Nueces River. After initial border skirmishes, tensions quickly rose between the two parties as the United States stationed a naval fleet off the Mexican coast at Vera Cruz. Diplomatic efforts to settle the dispute included U.S. demands that the acquisition of New Mexico and California, not just Texas be on the table. Rather than continue to negotiate, Santa Anna instructed his delegation to refuse these terms and war began. From the beginning the war went badly for Mexico and as a result of the Treaty of Hidalgo, signed in 1848, Mexico ceded more than a million square miles, nearly half its national territory, for the sum of $15 million. Several years later in 1853 under strong U.S. pressure, additional Mexican territory in what is today Arizona and New Mexico was transferred to the United States in the Gadsen Purchase. Ironically, it is to this vast territory that millions of Mexican workers have migrated in the last fifty years, thus reshaping its culture and language and, in the eyes of some, reclaiming lost lands.

As westward expansion increased, the U.S. showed more interest in Central America as a transit point to the United States' newly acquired west coast. As the California gold rush started to increase the demand for an easy route to California, Cornelius Vanderbilt established a trans-isthmus transportation route through Nicaragua. This began a period of increasing interest in the Central American isthmus and a U.S. canal through it, and would include numerous armed interventions in Nicaragua and the orchestration of the creation of the Panamanian state and the construction of the Panama Canal.

Dreams of Cuba

The United States also coveted Cuba throughout the nineteenth century and there was frequent talk of annexation. From Jefferson onward U.S. presidents viewed Cuba as a natural extension of U.S. territory. U.S. strategy came to be known as the "Ripe Fruit Theory" from a quote by John Quincy Adams:

> …there are laws of political as well as physical gravitation; and if an apple severed by the tempest from its native tree cannot choose but to fall to the ground, Cuba, forcibly disjoined from its own unnatural connection with Spain, and incapable of self-support, can gravitate only towards the North American Union, which by the same law of nature cannot cast her off from the bosom.

The press to annex Cuba reached its zenith in the 1840s and 1850s following the success of the war with Mexico as James Polk authorized negotiations with Spain to purchase the island. Ultimately these plans failed due to Spain's unwillingness to cede its last remaining major colony in the Americas, northern fears of the admission of a new slave state, and the opposition of the British and French, who were wary of expanding U.S. power. U.S. designs on Cuba would be placed on hold until 1898 but in the interim U.S. commercial interests reached out to Cuba and by the end of the century the United States had surpassed Spain as the island's leading trading partner.

Economic Transformation

With the economic growth and industrialization of the U.S. and its transformation into a capitalist power on the rise, trade, commerce, investment opportunities, and markets in Latin America became ever more important. As Lars Schoultz notes, from 1865 to 1896, the value of imports from Latin America more than doubled. The consumption of coffee and sugar alone rose sixfold. In the 1880s, Secretary of State James Blaine began a series of initiatives to revive the idea of hemispheric cooperation linked to Bolívar and his exclusively Hispanic America focus in the Congress of Panama in 1826. This new formulation of hemispheric unity would include—despite Bolívar's warnings—the now even more powerful United States. By the end of the decade, commerce and trade became the focus of U.S. interests. Thus, in 1889 U.S. Secretary of State James Blaine created the International Bureau of American Republics, which in turn was transformed into the Pan-American Union in 1890, as a mechanism to facilitate commercial and other interactions between the United States and the Latin American states. Located in Washington and sometimes pejoratively referred to as the "U.S. Colonial Office for Latin America," the Pan American Union would become the symbol of "Pan-Americanism" and U.S.-dominated hemispheric relations. Half a century later, it would in turn engender the Rio Treaty (the Inter-American Treaty of Reciprocal Assistance, 1947) and the Organization of American States (1948).

The end of the nineteenth century saw an important shift in U.S. policy toward Latin America and the simultaneous emergence of the United States as a significant international player. The defeat of the slave-owning South and the subsequent victory of the northern captains of industry, combined with the conquest of the American West set the stage for the emergence of the United States as a major industrial power in need of raw materials, markets, and places to invest capital. This transformation of the United States in the final third of the nineteenth century meant that the newly industrialized nation turned from the acquisition of new territory to the creation of a U.S. sphere of influence based on economic and political ties, backed by military force. As Peter Smith observes, this shift at the end of the nineteenth century was based in part on the growing racism of that era which acknowledged that bringing territories such as Puerto Rico and Cuba directly into the United States would clash with the predominantly Anglo-Saxon character of the nation. Second, there was a reevaluation by the Europeans of the utility of holding colonies and greater emphasis on commercial advantage. The United States, late to the imperial game, would seek to gain from its newfound position without the costs of maintaining an empire shouldered by the Europeans. In many ways this approach had been successfully utilized in South America in the nineteenth century where the British and French gained significant commercial advantage in Brazil and Argentina without establishing a colonial relationship.

The primary test for the new U.S. strategy came with Cuba in 1898. By that year Cuban independence forces, having relaunched their fight in 1895, were gaining significant ground against the Spanish. Not wanting the independence forces to triumph on their own and sensing Spain's likely defeat, U.S. forces entered the war on the side of the independence forces and secured a quick victory. The imperial nature of the U.S. intervention was made evident when U.S. forces did not allow Cuban independence leaders to be present at the surrender of Spanish forces in Santiago, Cuba in 1898. Through this act the United States made clear that it would determine the future status of Cuba. Some elements in the United States favored annexation as it had been desired for a century, but the new imperial strategy won the day. Following a brief U.S. military occupation, Cuba was granted its nominal independence in 1902. The island became a virtual protectorate of the United States over the next fifty-plus years down to the triumph of the Cuban revolution in 1959. Symbolic of this domination was the Platt Amendment, written by U.S. Senator Orville Platt, and inserted into the Cuban constitution, it granted the right of the United States to intervene on the island "for the preservation of Cuban independence and the maintenance of a government adequate for the protection of life, property, and individual liberty." It remained in effect until 1934 and subordinated Cuban sovereignty to U.S. control. The amendment also provided for a North American naval base at Guantanamo, a site still occupied by the United States against the objections of the Cuban government. Cuban products now went almost exclusively to the United States. U.S. companies invested in all aspects of the Cuban economy—sugar farms and processing plants, mining, communication, and railways. The U.S. Federal Reserve Bank established its only foreign branch in Havana. By 1926, U.S. direct investment on the island totaled nearly $1.4 billion. The Cuban events underscored the importance of the Caribbean basin, including the Central American mainland in United States foreign policy.

Gunboat Diplomacy, the Big Stick, and Dollar Diplomacy

In the period from 1898 to 1933 this region proved to be an important testing ground for the development of twentieth-century U.S. military, economic, and political power. The U.S. leaders sought to reduce European influence in the region, protect important commercial shipping lanes for expanded U.S. trade and to build an interoceanic canal that would facilitate commerce between the west and east coasts of the United States. This period came to be known as the Era of Gunboat Diplomacy and Dollar Diplomacy and would see more than thirty armed interventions.

The most important armed intervention after the Spanish-Cuban-American war came in Panama in 1903. In that year U.S. forces intervened to quell unrest and ultimately an agreement, the Hay and Herran Treaty, was signed with Colombia allowing the construction of a canal through its Panamanian territory. However, the Colombian legislature, fearing violation of its territorial sovereignty refused to ratify the agreement. The United States responded by inciting a rebellion for independence in Panama and then supporting the independence movement by recognizing the new state of Panama. When Colombia tried to intervene, Teddy Roosevelt ordered the stationing of U.S. warships off the coast to prevent Colombian troops from entering the rebellious province. The United States then arranged an agreement with Panama for a ten-mile-wide Canal Zone to be subject to U.S. control through a long-term lease so that the Panama Canal could be build. The zone would remain in U.S. hands until the 1977 Panama Canal treaties were negotiated under U.S. President Jimmy Carter and Panamanian president Omar Torrijos and full control of the Canal Zone was subsequently returned to Panama. The canal was opened in 1914 and immediately became a major international waterway. Protection of the shipping lanes in the Caribbean leading to the canal became a major focus of U.S. policy in the region and Panama became a long term compliant ally, opening the Canal Zone to several U.S. bases and the U.S. military's School of the Americas, which engaged in the controversial training of Latin American military officers for decades.

THE ROOSEVELT COROLLARY

The actions in Cuba and Panama became part of a broader U.S. strategy in the region. Theodore Roosevelt declared following European intervention in Venezuela in 1902 what became known as the Roosevelt Corollary to the Monroe Doctrine, that the United States, to avoid pretext for European intervention would maintain order in

Marines during 1915–1934 U. S. military occupation of Haiti. *(Bettmann/Corbis)*

the hemisphere. The doctrine had little real meaning beyond the U.S. sphere of influence in the Caribbean Basin, but it would be the basis of many armed interventions over the next thirty years in Nicaragua, El Salvador, Haiti, the Dominican Republic, and Cuba to name a few.

Although no longer interested in Nicaragua as the preferred location for a transoceanic canal, U.S. involvement continued there with a Marine incursion in 1909. The Mexican Revolution prompted renewed involvement in Mexico, including the naval bombardment of Vera Cruz in 1914 and military incursions in northern Mexico in pursuit of Pancho Villa, the Mexican revolutionary. Theodore Roosevelt's "big stick" became legendary in the Caribbean basin, and was a symbolic manifestation of gunboat diplomacy. The U.S. proclivity to send in naval gunboats and marines to sanction, control and direct the affairs of sovereign nations in Central America and the Caribbean became commonplace. The marines were not only in Nicaragua again (1912–1925 and 1926–1933) but also in Haiti (1915–1934) and the Dominican Republic (1916–1922). As witness to—and participant in—such actions, U.S. Marine Corps Major General Smedley Butler noted that

> I spent thirty-three years…being a high-class muscleman for Big Business, for Wall Street and the bankers. In short, I was a racketeer for capitalism…I helped purify Nicaragua for the international banking house of Brown Brothers in 1909–1912. I helped make Mexico and especially Tampico safe for American oil interests in 1916. I helped make Haiti and Cuba a decent place for National City [Bank] boys to collect revenues in. I helped in the rape of half a dozen Central American republics for the benefit of Wall Street.

DOLLAR DIPLOMACY

As financial interests intensified, these more primitive instruments of U.S. policy were replaced by "dollar diplomacy," where financial inducements and pressure became the most common means of influencing Latin American nations and favorable financial connections to the United States were emphasized. The United States was concerned that European powers under the guise of collecting debts would intervene militarily in the region, as they had done in Venezuela. In response, the United States developed the new policy which emphasized the support of private financial interests through U.S. government intervention. U.S. banks were encouraged to assume the debt of countries in the Caribbean basin with the promise that the U.S. government would use whatever means necessary to collect the debts. It was presented by President Howard Taft as representing a shift from "bullets to dollars" but in reality the guarantee to collect debt often resulted in direct military intervention to guarantee payments to the U.S. banks. The Dominican Republic was a good example of this scenario. In 1907 that government signed a fifty year agreement with the United States to assume control of its debts owed to European powers. Within a decade, in 1916, the United States Marines had occupied the island to deal with an armed rebellion against the government and in the process asserted its control over the country's treasury, army, and police in addition to the customs houses. U.S. occupation of the island only ended in 1924 when the local government agreed to keep its army under the command of U.S. officers.

LATIN AMERICAN REACTION

Such heavy handed interventionist policies on the part of the United States began to elicit considerable Latin American reaction. More removed from the Caribbean Basin and the United States' direct sphere of influence, Argentina chaffed under the United States' heavy handed relations with its fellow Latin American Republics. A prominent Argentine jurist, Carlos Calvo articulated what came to be known as the Calvo Doctrine. In his seminal *Derecho Internacional Teórico y Práctico de Europa y América* (*European and American Theoretical and Practical International Law*, Paris, 1868), he argued that jurisdiction over a dispute involving a foreign company must be resolved in the courts of the nation where the investments were made. It further prohibited military intervention or even any diplomatic intervention before all recourse to the local courts was exhausted. This doctrine became widely applied throughout Latin America and is at times manifest in a Calvo Clause along these lines inserted in a national constitution. The Drago Doctrine is a narrower application of Calvo's principle. Announced in 1902 by Argentine foreign minister Luis María Drago, it stipulated that no foreign power could use force against a Latin American nation to collect debts owed.

By the end of the 1920s, it became clear that better relations were needed if the United States was going to continue to have extensive foreign relations with its Latin American neighbors. The forces of fascism were also on the horizon and this helped to further convince the United States that it needed to improve Latin American–U.S. relations. In 1933, the Seventh International Conference of American States was convened in Montevideo, Uruguay. This meeting, which was attended by all the Latin American States as well as the United States, elaborated what would become one of the most comprehensive statements of modern international law regarding states and their rights. Signed at Montevideo on December 26, 1933, the Montevideo Convention on the Rights and Duties of States, stipulates some of the fundamental rights that the Latin American nations considered essential to protect their sovereignty and that were necessary to reign in the actions of their northern neighbor.

Article 1 defines what is necessary to be a state (population, defined territory, a government with capacity to rule and conduct international relations). Reacting to U.S. practice of withholding recognition, Article 3 states that "The political existence of the state is independent of recognition by the other states." Article 4 speaks to equality—"States are juridically equal, enjoy the same rights, and have equal capacity in their exercise. The rights of each one do not depend upon the power which it possesses to assure its exercise, but upon the simple fact of its existence as a person under international law." Key to the convention and as a decided reaction to U.S. interventions, Article 8 states clearly that "No state has the right to intervene in the internal or external affairs of another."

Consistent with the aforementioned Calvo and Drago doctrines, Article 9 notes that "The jurisdiction of states within the limits of national territory applies to all the inhabitants. Nationals and foreigners are under the same protection of the law and the national authorities and the foreigners may not claim rights other or more extensive than those of the nationals." Taking advantage of the changing winds in U.S. policy, and using their majority and developing concepts in public international law, the Latin American states were thus able to fashion known as *La Violencia*. It was finally ended by the formation of the National Front, a common front based on a political pact between the elites in the Conservative and Liberal parties whereby they agreed to share power among the mainstream elements of the two parties. A clear example of politics by pact among the elite, the agreement lasted until the early 1970s.

In the meantime, those desiring more fundamental change gravitated to a variety of guerrilla groups that began to operate in Colombia from the 1960s onward. Many of these gained such power that they were able to negotiate special agreements with the government; one of the original and surviving guerrilla groups, the Fuerzas Armadas Revolucionarias de Colombia (FARC), even managed to negotiate a temporary cease-fire with the Colombian government that gave them control over part of Colombian territory. They and other guerrilla groups had been greatly strengthened in the 1990s by agreements with several Colombian drug cartels that guaranteed protection and economic well-being for the peasants in their areas and gave the cartels certain protection from the armed forces as long as they paid their taxes to the guerrilla organization. By 2000, the eroding power and legitimacy of the government and the growing strength of FARC and the Ejército de Liberación Nacional (ELN) suggested that change in Colombia could still come through a revolutionary takeover. This and the continuing power of the drug cartels prompted the United States to greatly increase military, antidrug, and economic aid to Colombia in 2000. The U.S. war on drugs and the continued existence of FARC prompted the Clinton administration to create Plan Colombia, the multibillion-dollar plan to eradicate coca fields and stop the production of illegal drugs in Colombia. Conflict continued, but by 2007 the level of U.S. funding for Plan Colombia was being reduced despite President Alvaro Uribe's hard line with guerrilla groups and close cooperation with the United States. Yet, Colombia remained the United States' closest ally in South America and agreed to allow the United States to use sections of several Colombian military bases for military activities. Uribe's defense minister, Juan Manuel Santos, was elected in 2010 as a continuation of the hard line, pro-U.S. policies, but guerrilla activities, high unemployment, and great income disparity continued.

BRAZIL, U.S. FOREIGN POLICY AND THE NATIONAL SECURITY STATE

Like Cuba, change and social restructuring came late to Brazil. From independence in 1822 until 1889, Brazil was an empire under the control of emperors from the Portuguese royal family. Brazil did not see the consolidation of the modern nation-state until Getúlio Vargas's takeover of the federal government in the revolution of 1930 and his subsequent establishment of the "new state" in 1936. Vargas and his personal style of populism dominated Brazilian politics until his suicide in 1954. Through the efforts of many progressive political movements, change again occurred in the late 1950s. Juscelino Kubitschek was elected in 1955 by promising to move the country forward. His dynamic approach to government action and the founding of the new capital of Brasília helped heighten expectations for a brighter future.

After 1960, the United States became increasingly concerned with political mobilization of the masses and political movements that might, as had occurred in Cuba, movements like the Frente Sandinista de Liberación Nacional (FSLN) in Nicaragua, the Armed Forces of National Liberation (FALN) in Venezuela, the Revolutionary Armed Forces of Colombia (FARC), and the Movement of the Revolutionary Left (MIR) in Peru and Chile began to operate from Mexico and Guatemala in the north to Argentina and Chile in the south. Radical change and socialist revolution through violent struggle were now added to the political mix. The revolutions were not led or fomented by Latin American Soviet-oriented communist parties, which generally had very limited success, frequently criticized the young Fidelista revolutionaries, and often did not support the movements. Cuba became the revolutionaries' mecca and source for moral and sometimes material support. The radical regime continued in power into the twenty-first century and proved to be one of the longest lasting socialist governments. Although many expected a radical restructuring of the government when Fidel Castro was no longer the president, 2008 saw a stable, relatively effortless presidential transition to Fidel's brother, Raúl Castro.

EARLIER ATTEMPTS AT CHANGE: BOLIVIA AND COLOMBIA

Before the Cuban Revolution, other less radical attempts at change had been made in Latin America in the post–World War II period. The MNR in Bolivia was inspired by the philosophy and example of the Peru-based APRA and the Mexican Revolution. Led by Víctor Paz Estenssora, National Revolutionary Movement (MNR) radicals had led the strongly indigenous and heavily unionized radical tin miners, indigenous peasants, and middle-class supporters to seize power in 1952. They soon nationalized the tin mines and engaged in a major agrarian reform that distributed large amounts of land to impoverished peasants. Difficult economic conditions and the hostility of the United States made it difficult to maintain the reformist project. The experiment was cut short in 1964 when the vice president took power through a military coup. A series of military governments followed, but the masses mobilized once again in late 2003 to force the U.S.-linked president to resign. The mostly indigenous masses and their social and political movements again mobilized in 2005 to force the former vice president and now president to resign to pave the way for the new elections in December 2005. Indeed broad indigenous support facilitated the election of Evo Morales as president. He was the first indigenous Bolivian to hold that post, and was reelected in 2010 with 64 percent of the vote. He has joined with other progressive political leaders such as Venezuelan president Hugo Chávez, presidents Rafael Correa of Ecuador, Daniel Ortega of Nicaragua, and Raúl Castro of Cuba to chart a new course for his and other Latin America nations.

The movement to enfranchise the masses in Colombia was manifest in the figure of progressive liberal politician Jorge Gaitán. He represented the progressive wing of the Liberal Party and promised better conditions for the labor movement and for peasants. Before he could mobilize support for such badly needed reforms, he was assassinated in Bogotá in April 1948. Those committed to change took to the streets, and days of violent rioting followed. Known as the *Bogotazo*, the violent actions in the capital soon spread throughout the country, where bands of liberals attacked conservatives, whom they believed had denied them the change they so badly needed. Soon, the entire country was caught up in a decade of fighting a clear normative guide to state practice. One that would, they hoped, moderate U.S. actions.

GOOD NEIGHBOR POLICY

The Era of Gunboat and Dollar Diplomacy came to an end in 1933 with the new administration of Franklin Delano Roosevelt and his declaration of a Good Neighbor Policy for Latin America (the term was first used by President Hoover). In the ensuing years U.S. policy in the region would undergo a significant shift. As suggested in the Montevideo meeting, the repeated armed interventions and occupations were ending and would be replaced with nominal recognition of the sovereignty of Latin American countries and the view that the security of the region was a collective responsibility.

The Good Neighbor Policy also contained a commitment to shared democratic values and cooperative negotiation of disputes. The policy shift is credited with giving Washington near unanimous support from the region during World War II. However, the shift was a tactical one, not strategic. In reality the costs of maintaining constant armed interventions had become too costly and U.S. leaders sought new methods to maintain U.S. hegemony in the region. The high cost of intervention was epitomized by the case of Nicaragua. From 1909 onward the U.S. Marines were in almost constant occupation of the nation to deal with liberal challenges to U.S. dominance of the country. The occupation turned highly problematic in the late 1920s when a Nicaraguan rebel leader, Augusto César Sandino, fought the marines to a standstill in a bloody seven-year war. The war generated antiwar sentiment in the United States, anti-Yankee sentiment throughout Latin America and contributed significantly to a reconsideration of U.S. policy in the region by the Hoover administration.

Nicaragua under the Roosevelt administration also became a model for the Good Neighbor policy, revealing its dark underbelly. Not wishing U.S. troops to be bogged down in the country, the United States worked with the country's elites to create a new force, the Nicaraguan National Guard that would be funded and trained by the United States and replace the duties of the marines. The guard's leader, Anastasio Somoza, chosen by the United States in 1933, also became the country's leader. One of the guard's first acts was the assassination of Sandino after a meeting with the new president in 1933 and the defeat of his remaining rebel army. Somoza and first one son (Luis) and then the other (Anastacio Jr.) would establish a forty-five-year family rule that would last until the Sandinista Revolution of 1979. That rule was validated by elections every four years hailed by the United States as evidence of Latin American democracy in spite of the fact that radical parties were outlawed and the opposition conservatives accepted their permanent subordinate position. The Somoza family responded as dutiful U.S. allies setting an example for neighboring countries.

Democracy and World War II

In spite of U.S. lip service to democracy, by the time of the World War II, many countries in the Caribbean basin had fallen under dictatorial rule. Democracy was, however, advocated during the war. It should also be pointed out that not all of the Latin American countries followed the United States into World War II. Chile was hesitant and remained neutral for a time after the United States declared war on the Axis Powers and Argentina observed neutrality throughout the conflict. Conversely, both Mexico and Brazil collaborated in the war effort and sent contingents of troops to fight. Brazil also opened her territory to U.S. bases to facilitate the ferrying of U.S. planes to North Africa and Europe. In the process, many women U.S. pilots became active in the transfer of aircraft through Brazil and the Brazilian military established a working relationship with their counterparts in the U.S. military.

The Good Neighbor Policy also had an important economic dimension. In what became the mantra of bipartisan trade policy of the United States for the ensuing decades, Roosevelt argued that the United States could best enhance its world position through skillful economic diplomacy. Commercial ties with Latin American countries needed to be a higher priority than military interventions. The depression years, 1929–1932, were a disaster for U.S. trade within the region with both exports and imports falling more than 50 percent. Cordell Hull, the new secretary of state appointed by Roosevelt put liberalization of trade at the top of his agenda and over the next several years established trade agreements with several Latin American countries, including Colombia, Cuba, Honduras, Costa Rica, and Guatemala. Though the United States was not successful in negotiating other agreements due to Latin American resistance, by 1938 the United States, through its emphasis on commercial ties, had succeeded in becoming the largest trading partner for every Latin American country with the exception of Argentina. This was accomplished in spite of a vigorous move into the region by Germany in the 1930s. Of course, that German campaign would end with the beginning of World War II, leaving the region more dependent on the United States.

World War II completely restructured the character of international affairs. The formerly dominant powers of Britain and France lost their positions forever and would be forced to relinquish almost all their colonial possessions after the war. The defeated powers of Germany and Japan would recover quickly as economic powers, but in 1945 only the United States and the Soviet Union stood as superpowers. Their inevitable rivalry soon crystallized into the Cold War with its competing nuclear arsenals. For Latin America the emergence of the United States as a superpower presented a challenge that has now remained in place for over sixty years, notwithstanding the end of the Cold War in 1992.

The Rio Treaty and the Organization of American States

Probably the most important result of the expanded U.S. power after World War II was that the United States to a greater degree sought dominant influence beyond the Caribbean basin to all of Latin America. To this end, continental wide structures were set up, beginning with a comprehensive collective security agreement, the Inter-American Treaty of Reciprocal Assistance, or Rio Treaty (1947). Article three lays out the main thrust of the treaty obligations: the parties agree that, "an armed attack by any State against an American State shall be considered an attack against all the American States and, consequently, each one of the said contracting parties undertakes to assist in meeting the attack in the exercise of the inherent rights of individual or collective self-defense recognized by Article 51 of the Charter of the United Nations." Article 6 also gives the body the right to convene for possible action if a party is "affected by an aggression that is not an armed attack." Thus the United States individually or with the help of other sympathetic American states, could become involved with the affairs of her fellow republics if any perceived threat were registered. The following year, the old Pan American Union was updated and transformed into a new hemispheric organization. The new organization was named the Organization of American States (OAS in English, OEA in Spanish, Portuguese, and French) and was conveniently headquartered in the old Pan American Union building in Washington, D.C. It incorporated some functions of the old Pan American Union, added others and was premised on collective action. As a regional organization under the United Nations Charter, it too could employ collective security in the case of attack on a member state, and could engage in "common action" in the event of aggression (Article 4). Thus a U.S.-dominated coalition of American states could be legally empowered to act against an aggressor state, or sanction a member state for its actions that were short of direct aggression. This would from time to time, be used to sanction U.S. led intervention in Latin American countries, such as the invasion of the Dominican Republic in 1965 or the invasion of Grenada in 1983. Although not always vigorously implemented, much of the thinking of the Montevideo Convention was also reflected in the Charter of the OAS. Thus there was a strong prohibition against intervention: "No State or Group of States has the right to intervene, directly or indirectly, in the internal or external affairs of any other state (original Article 15)." Further, Article 17 states that "The territory of a State is inviolable; it may not be the object, even temporarily, of military occupation or other measures of force taken by another State, directly or indirectly, on any grounds whatsoever." But "measures adopted for the maintenance of peace and security in accordance with existing treaties do not constitute a violation of the principles set forth in Articles 15 and 17." Thus, a strong coalition of Latin American and Caribbean states could, at least, condemn U.S. intervention when it occurred in Panama in 1989 (even though they were hard put to find means to enforce their decision), but could also sanction sending in a U.S.-led OAS mission as was done in Haiti in the early 1990s after President Aristide was overthrown by a military coup. The OAS itself consists of an *Assembly* of all the states that meets annually, a *Permanent Council of Ambassadors* appointed by member states, and a *Secretary General*. Meetings of consultation are also called as needed and several specialized agencies exist, such as the *Inter-American Commission on Human Rights* and the *Pan American Health Organization*, which is affiliated to the World Health Organization.

Guatemalan Case

After World War II, the renewed power of the United States severely constrained the options open to the Latin American countries. Protection from a European power was no longer an option and the creation of regional alliances to combat the power of the United States was problematic, especially in light of the above-mentioned hemispheric organizations. However, even more difficult was the pursuit of an alternative path of economic and political development that in the lenses of the Cold War could be seen as socialist or Marxist in its orientation. These constraints did not prevent Latin Americans from trying to pursue alternative forms of development but most of these efforts, with the dramatic exception of the Cuban revolution, met with determined and successful resistance by the United States during the era of the Cold War, and sometimes often employed the structure of the Organization of the American States to do so.

Early in this era, the most dramatic example of the price that Latin Americans paid for pursuing a path unsupported by the United States was in Guatemala (see the section on Guatemala in Chapter 3). After the 1944 revolution put in place Juan José Arévalo (1945–1950), the democratically elected government of Jacobo Arbenz (1951–1954) pursued a project of radical reform based primarily on indigenous and worker rights and land reform aimed at lands unused by wealthy landowners and the U.S.-based United Fruit Company. Beyond the challenge to U.S. economic interests, U.S. government officials were alarmed by the presence of a few Guatemalan Communists at high levels of influence in the Arbenz government. After an extensive lobbying campaign by the United Fruit Company and the resultant heightened Cold War hysteria, the Eisenhower administration began to view the Guatemalan situation as a dire threat to U.S. security and soon mounted a major CIA operation to overthrow Arbenz. The orchestration of the overthrow was not dissimilar to a successful operation in Iran in 1953 (that overthrew the popular constitutional government of Mossadeq, reinstalled the shah, and set the stage for the rise of the Islamic revolution later). The U.S. operation led to the overthrow of the Guatemalan government in 1954 by General Castillo Armas and the imposition of military dictatorship. The cost of this intervention would be long standing for Guatemala. For most of the forty years following the 1954 coup, heavy repression and brutal violent conflict characterized the nation. The struggle was so intense that some 200,000 people (mostly civilians killed by government forces) lost their lives. Only in the last fifteen years has the country moved away from this era and haltingly readopted reformist and democratic principles. Guatemala paid a high price for its reformist path and the lessons weighed heavily on Latin Americans for decades.

However, one case stood out as a different result. In the 1950s, the 26th of July Movement under the leadership of Fidel Castro, Camilo Cienfuegos, and Che Guevara carried out a successful armed rebellion against the Cuban dictator, Fulgencio Batista. The revolutionaries succeeded in gaining power because U.S. political leaders abandoned Batista in the final months of the rebellion, believing that the rebels, not avowed communists, could be controlled and moderated much like the Bolivian revolutionaries after 1952. This proved to be a major miscalculation by Washington as the revolutionaries moved quickly to institute a series of radical reforms. As the revolutionary government began to implement reforms, the United States responded with harsh sanctions, including the embargo on goods to Cuba. Finally, the new Cuban leaders reached out to the Soviet Union for support and quickly received it, sharply reducing the options available to Washington. Over the ensuing years the United States would engage in numerous efforts to reverse the Cuban revolution, including the 1961 Bay of Pigs invasion, but none would prove successful and fifty years later Cuba stands independent of the Inter-American system dominated by the United States.

Alliance for Progress

The U.S. setback in Cuba resulted in a fixation by U.S. policy to avoid another Cuba. The immediate response of the Kennedy administration to Cuba was the formulation of the Alliance for Progress. Acknowledging that the Cuban Revolution was born of conditions of dictatorship and poverty on the island, Kennedy argued that the United States needed to promote peaceful reform in the region to forestall violent revolution. Thus U.S. policy and aid in the region needed to emphasize democracy, land reform, and industrialization. In many ways it was a restatement of the most idealistic principles of the earlier Good Neighbor Policy. In a few Latin American countries the spirit of the Alliance would be carried out, but the realities of the Cold War and U.S. instincts for hegemony in the hemisphere trumped the high-minded principles of the Alliance. Thus a growing emphasis on counterinsurgency, military missions, training members of the Latin American armed forces in the U.S. School of the Americas and the national security state. Betrayal of the Alliance was especially sharp when viewed against the background of armed U.S. intervention in the Dominican Republic in April 1965. This was done as a democratic movement under Juan Bosch was beginning to consolidate its power in the island nation.

National Security Doctrine

In reality U.S. policy in Latin America after the Cuban revolution was dominated by a military and security focus that placed the promotion of reform and democracy in a secondary position. The centerpiece of this approach was the concept of national security doctrine developed jointly by the U.S. policy makers and their counterparts in the Latin American elites to counter the possible influence of the Soviet Union in the region through the repression of all potentially revolutionary forces. The most prominent national security doctrine developed in Brazil through the Superior War School (ESG) founded in 1949 with French and U.S. advisors. As the Cold War escalated, the doctrine viewed Brazil in a state of permanent war where revolutionary forces that could ally with the Soviet Union must be defeated at all costs, including the suspension of civil liberties and democracy. The doctrine was Brazilian nationalist in its orientation but accepted that close ties with the United States and Western Europe were necessary.

In Brazil the primary manifestation of the national security doctrine was the military coup of 1964 against President João Goulart and the twenty years of military rule that followed. Fearing that Goulart's policies of reform, especially in the rural areas, were fomenting unrest and encouraging revolutionary forces, the generals seized power to "eliminate the danger of subversion and communism." In a short time, more than 50,000 people were arrested and the country's democratic institutions suspended. The Brazilian coup was a key test of the Alliance for Progress. In many ways Goulart's programs of reform were modeled after the alliance, yet the United States, now under the leadership of Lyndon Johnson, raised no objections to the coup and quickly developed strong ties with the ruling generals. Acceptance of the Brazilian coup established an important precedent that would see subsequent U.S. presidents either accept or support military rule throughout the region. In 1972 in El Salvador, the Nixon administration stood on the sidelines when the military voided an election won by José Napoleon Duarte, a reform-minded Christian Democrat, who symbolized a decade of the Alliance for Progress programs in that small, Central American country.

September 11 Coup in Chile

U.S. support for military rule was even better demonstrated on September 11, 1973, when the Chilean military forces removed President Salvador Allende from power in a coup that took his life. The United States was complicit in the coup through a range of measures instituted following Allende's election in 1970. It embargoed the country, stating explicitly that the Chilean people would suffer for electing a "Marxist" as their leader. The U.S. economic measures severely damaged the Chilean economy and behind the scenes the U.S. government maintained military aid and close ties to the Chilean military and urged them to overthrow Allende. For fifteen years after the 1973 coup the Chilean military governed by brutal, dictatorial means and carried out policies in the framework of a "national security doctrine" similar to that of the Brazilian generals. In spite of international outcry against its violations of human rights including the death and disappearance of at least 10,000 people, the generals maintained the support of the United States until they were defeated in a referendum in 1988, and democracy was returned in 1990.

Counterinsurgency

The long era of the Cold War deepened the willingness of the United States to place the defense of the status quo in Latin America ahead of all other objectives. The different guerrilla insurgencies that broke out all over Latin America after the Cuban revolution and challenged traditional oligarchic rule and U.S. domination were seen as a direct threat that, if unchecked, could lead to the implantation of communism all over the region. These insurgencies needed to be stopped, and the United States developed the doctrine of counterinsurgency to do so, often copying counterinsurgency techniques developed in the U.S. war against the Viet Minh and Viet Cong in Vietnam. U.S. military and financial missions carried this doctrine throughout Latin America and invited members of the Latin American militaries to learn it. Through support for such extensive training in counterinsurgency, military coups, the training of Latin American officers at the School of the Americas in Panama and later at Fort Bragg in North Carolina, and cozy relationships with Latin American financial elites, the leaders of the United States placed themselves in contradiction to not only radical change, but to decades of efforts by Latin Americans of many different political orientations to alter that status quo and build more equitable societies. This and the generous military aid that accompanied it, strengthened the Latin American militaries in their fight against different guerrilla groups, but also encouraged the militaries to resist many legitimate reform efforts and overthrow civilian governments that were not of their liking. This was a major factor in the long periods of often brutal military rule (bureaucratic authoritarianism) that developed in Latin America in the sixties, seventies, and eighties.

Cold War in Central America

The final chapter of the U.S. Cold War policies in Latin America came in response to the Central American revolutionary movements of the 1970s and 1980s. By the mid-1970s strong revolutionary movements had developed in Guatemala, El Salvador, and Nicaragua. In each case the revolutionary movements faced off against military dictatorships that had long received significant U.S. backing under the Cold War National Security doctrine. The assistance was significant, including military and economic aid and military training. The Central American events presented a special challenge to the administration of Jimmy Carter, which came to office pledging a foreign policy based on human rights. With regard to Latin America, Carter had completed the negotiation of the Panama Canal treaties, reopened diplomatic relations with Cuba, and condemned U.S. support for the coup in Chile. In Central America, Carter distanced himself from the military governments, including Somoza in Nicaragua. The Carter administration worked behind the scenes to prevent the triumph of the Sandinista revolutionaries, but once the FSLN was in power in 1979 it recognized the new government and sought to moderate its course through limited U.S. aid.

In El Salvador the United States supported a progressive coup in the fall of 1979 that briefly brought to power a figurehead civilian government. However, traditional right-wing military forces quickly reestablished control and carried out the assassination of the progressive archbishop Oscar Romero in March 1980. Romero's assassination spurred the further development of the revolutionary forces united under the banner of the Farabundo Martí National Liberation Front (FMLN) and, by early 1981, they were seemingly on the verge of power. One of Carter's last acts was the sending of military aid to the Salvadoran generals to successfully fend off an FMLN offensive.

The Reagan administration came to office in January 1981 critical of the Carter approaches in Latin America which he judged to have been soft on communism. Though he did not reverse the Panama Canal treaties, he had been critical of Carter for that initiative. He ended the overtures to Cuba and reimposed the ban on most U.S. citizen travel to the island. However, the greatest change in policy came in Central America where Reagan committed himself to the defense of the Salvadoran government with a massive package of economic and military aid (approved by a Democrat-led Congress) and a covert plan to overthrow the Sandinista government in Nicaragua through the funding of a rebel army that came to be known as the "contras." The latter program was part of a worldwide initiative that came to known as the Reagan Doctrine also involving support for anticommunist rebels in Afghanistan, Cambodia, Angola, and Mozambique. The doctrine was part of a broader reigniting of the Cold War against the Soviet

Union following years of detente under Nixon, Ford, and Carter. The Reagan policies in Central America ultimately fostered significant civil society opposition in
the United States as tens of thousands of civilians died in wars in Nicaragua, El
Salvador, and Guatemala. In the latter case, the Reagan administration did not
openly support the Guatemalan military but did nothing to stop the Ríos Montt
dictatorship from killing thousands of peasants in an early 1980s' counterinsurgency campaign. In the face of citizen pressure the U.S. Congress cut off aid to
the Nicaraguan contras in the mid-1980s, but Reagan continued the operation in
secrecy resulting in his near impeachment in the Iran-Contra affair. Ultimately,
the U.S. Central America policies of the 1980s achieved their primary objectives,
notwithstanding the devastation that occurred in the three countries (more than
100,000 people killed). The Salvadoran government fended off the revolutionary
efforts of the rebels forcing the FMLN to sign a 1992 peace agreement that converted it into a reformist political movement that has gone on to be a significant
force in Salvadoran politics and finally win the presidency in 2009. In Nicaragua
the Sandinistas militarily defeated the contras in 1989 but were driven from office
by election in 1990 by a war-weary populace. The conservative governments that
followed reversed the revolutionary course of the FSLN and brought the country back under U.S. influence. The FSLN could not return to power until Daniel
Ortega negotiated a questionable pact with conservative forces and subsequently
retook the presidency in 2006. In Guatemala the rebels were also forced to sue for
peace and eventually in 1994 a peace deal brought an end to the country's forty-
year civil war.

Latin America and the Post-Cold War World

Ten years into the new century, relations in the Western Hemisphere are at a crucial juncture. For the first time in decades there is the possibility of a fundamental
shift in the balance of power between the United States and its southern neighbors.
What are the key elements in hemispheric affairs at this juncture in the twenty-first
century? To answer this question it is necessary to step back twenty years, to the
end of the decade of the 1980s, the time of the end of the Cold War. At that moment
a variety of factors worldwide and in the Western Hemisphere came together to
favor the interests of the United States. The demise of Eastern European socialism, epitomized by the fall of the wall in Berlin in November 1989 and later the
unexpected collapse of the Soviet Union, delivered to the United States an unprecedented opportunity to wield its power in international affairs. The renewed ability of the United States to project its military power in world affairs was evidenced
in the Persian Gulf War in early 1991, the first major use of force by the United
States since its political and military defeat in Vietnam nearly twenty years earlier.
U.S. leaders spoke openly in the wake of their easy military victory against Iraq
that the "Vietnam Syndrome" had been broken and that the American people had
once again sanctioned the use of military power to defend U.S. interests abroad.
U.S. leaders were also clear that the changed stance of the Soviet Union had been
crucial to the success of its operation in the Persian Gulf. Less than a year after the
war, the Soviet Union departed the scene, no longer threatening the United States

with its nuclear weapons and leaving the United States as the world's sole military superpower.

Beyond military superiority the United States also took the ideological offensive. In 1991 President George H. W. Bush declared that the world was entering a new era that would be dominated by democracy and free enterprise. In this perspective the demise of the Soviet Union proved once and for all the bankruptcy of socialism and dictatorship. President Bush made such self-serving declarations in spite of the fact that the Persian Gulf War had been fought in the interests of Saudi Arabia and Kuwait, two long-standing monarchical dictatorships. While the events in Eastern Europe and the Middle East transformed world affairs, there were important companion developments in Latin America that also favored the interests of the United States. As the events were unfolding in Eastern Europe, two watershed elections occurred in Latin America that served U.S. interests. In Argentina Carlos Menem won the presidency and pledged a new direction for Argentina friendly to the United States and its economic ideology, a reversal of forty years of Peronist ideology and less than a decade after the United States sided with Britain in its war with Argentina over the Falklands-Malvinas. In Brazil, the right-wing candidate Fernando Collor de Mello defeated Workers Party candidate Luis Inácio (Lula) da Silva in an election that had been predicted to go Lula's way until the collapse of Eastern European socialism in the middle of the campaign. In December 1989, the United States, in its first major military action in the hemisphere since Grenada in 1983, invaded Panama and removed its former ally Manuel Noriega from power on the pretext of being involved in the drug trade. The invasion of Panama was followed in February 1990 by the electoral defeat of the Sandinistas in Nicaragua, an election they had been expected to win prior to the events in Eastern Europe and Panama. The Sandinista defeat was crucial because it marked the end of an era of revolution in Central America that had begun fifteen years earlier and placed the United States on the defensive in Nicaragua, El Salvador, and Guatemala. The Sandinista defeat was especially bitter because the revolutionaries had been successful in defeating the U.S.-backed contras in a ten-year war. Many believe these victories by the United States emboldened U.S. policy and led to a much more aggressive policy in Iraq and Afghanistan.

These political developments also allowed the United States to go on the political and economic offensive in the hemisphere, arguing that the triumph of capitalism was complete and that Latin America had to end its decades of economic nationalism and protectionism and open its markets to U.S. goods and investment. This economic penetration had always been true in Central America and the Caribbean but now was to be extended to South America, especially Brazil and Argentina. The centerpiece of the U.S. strategy was the Free Trade Area of the Americas (FTAA) launched with great fanfare by U.S. President Bill Clinton at the Summit of the Americas in Miami in December 1994 and scheduled to be implemented by 2005. It was to be a hemisphere-wide free trade area and was supported with enthusiasm by all of the Latin American presidents invited to Miami. At that time in the middle 1990s, momentum for the FTAA and the wider U.S. agenda for Latin America seemed unstoppable. However, more than a decade later, the FTAA project was basically dead and the United States was on the defensive in many parts of the region. What transpired in the intervening years and what are the prospects for the future?

In some ways it is not complicated to understand what happened in Latin America over the last decade to change the political landscape. The political and economic promises made by Latin American political leaders with the support of Washington espousing neoliberal principles were not met. Throughout the region economic programs that cut government services, encouraged the privatization of utilities and other government owned entities, and opened Latin American economies to more foreign investments and foreign goods proved to be a disaster for the region's majority poor. Macroeconomic growth rates increased and the wealthier segments of Latin American societies benefited, but overall the Washington-imposed policies proved to be a failure for the region. The varied manner in which Latin Americans have responded to the policy failures of the last twenty years have framed the present state of hemispheric affairs.

In many ways Venezuela has been at the center of the Latin American resistance to U.S. policies and therefore it is not surprising that in 2010 Venezuelan President Hugo Chávez, following in the footsteps of Simón Bolívar, is a leader of renewed Latin American efforts to reshape their relationship to the United States. In reality, Latin American resistance to the U.S. neoliberal agenda began in 1992 in Venezuela with a militant revolt against Carlos Andres Pérez and his policies. A leader of that revolt, army officer Chávez, was jailed but the seeds of resistance were sown. After his imprisonment, Chávez formed the Fifth Republic Movement, which had a strong populist, anti-neoliberal platform. He continued his political struggle as a candidate for president in 1998, winning with some 58 percent of the vote. The traditional parties won only single-digit support which in turn greatly diminished the power of the Venezuelan political elites. In the decade since, Chávez has won reelection twice and survived a recall vote, an attempted coup, and an owners' lockout to remain firmly in power and serve as the leading Latin American voice for a change in historic hemispheric relations.

Chávez's 1998 electoral victory foreshadowed a series of election victories by candidates of the left who have since triumphed in Argentina, Brazil, Uruguay, Ecuador, Chile, Nicaragua, Paraguay, and El Salvador. The victories by Lula in Brazil in 2002 (and his subsequent reelection in 2006) and Kirchners in Argentina in 2003 and 2007 were especially significant because of the weight of their countries in hemispheric politics and the commitment of their immediate predecessors to definitive neoliberal strategies. Ultimately, it was the opposition of Lula and Kirchner to the completion of the FTAA treaty that doomed the project. When U.S. President George Bush took office in 2001, he made completion of the FTAA a priority of his first administration and had the backing of the U.S. Congress to complete the deal. The treaty was to have been finalized at a meeting of the hemisphere's finance ministers in Miami in November 2003 but events played out in a very different manner. One month earlier, Lula and Kirchner met in Buenos Aires and solidified their opposition to the FTAA and at a special ministerial meeting convened in Washington prior to the Miami conference the project was placed on indefinite hold over the strong objection of the United

States. U.S. efforts to revive the treaty at the Summit of the Americas in Mar de Plata, Argentina in November 2005 failed as Hugo Chávez led a rally of 50,000 against the FTAA outside the presidential meeting. Faced with the failure of the FTAA project, the United States has been forced to retreat to the more modest project of the Central American Free Trade Agreement (CAFTA) and selected bilateral agreements with countries such as Chile, Peru, Colombia, and Panama. These agreements, if fully implemented, are not unimportant to U.S. interests in the region, but they fall far short of the U.S. domination that could have resulted from the FTAA.

Latin American Initiatives

The major Latin American countries, Argentina, Brazil, and Venezuela, wary of U.S dominance of the region have pursued a series of initiatives over the past fifteen years to create greater cohesion, especially among the countries of the Southern Cone. The initial major effort, the Common Market of the South (*Mercosur*) was a trade pact between Brazil, Argentina, Paraguay, and Uruguay formed in 1994. *Mercosur* has its origins in the neoliberal era of the 1990s but in the new century it took on a new role as an alternative to the U.S.-led FTAA. It remains an important project that has facilitated greater trade among its members. Venezuela is currently seeking full membership in the pact but its long term viability as the building block toward a South American Free Trade Agreement remains limited by trade disputes between Argentina and Brazil.

Meeting of the Bolivarian Alliance *(ALBA)* Countries. Presidents in photo, left to right: Daniel Ortega (Nicaragua), Raúl Castro (Cuba), Hugo Chávez (Venezuela), Rafael Correa (Ecuador), Evo Morales (Bolivia). Other member country presidents not pictured. *(Photo by Jairo Cajina/Xinhua/Photoshot)*

Bolstered by its strong oil and gas revenues in recent years, the Venezuelan government has embarked on a path of challenging U.S. hegemony in the region through a series of well-funded initiatives headlined by the Bank of the South and the Bolivarian Alliance for the People of Our America (ALBA). The Bank of the South initiative, formally launched at the end of 2007, is aimed at ending or reducing Latin America's dependence on loans from the World Bank, International Monetary Fund, and Inter-American Development Bank along with their stringent neoliberal conditionality. The Bank has seven initial members (Venezuela, Argentina, Brazil, Ecuador, Bolivia, Paraguay, and Uruguay) and an initial capital base of $7 billion. All twelve South American countries are eligible to receive loans from the bank. The founding of the bank came after successful bilateral assistance that Venezuela provided to Argentina in the last five years that allowed the latter to pay off its IMF debts and reverse the neoliberal economic policies that had been imposed on it. Independence from the IMF has proven to be positive for the Argentinean economy and to the recovery of its social indicators. However, the dramatic drop in world oil prices in the latter half of 2008 and continuing into 2009 and 2010 may limit Venezuela's promotion of the bank. In March 2009, Venezuela, Argentina, and Brazil agreed to contribute $2 billion each to the bank's start-up capital and the other four members a total of $1 billion.

Another project challenging U.S. hegemony in the region under Venezuelan and Cuban leadership is the Bolivarian Alliance for the People of Our America (ALBA). Launched in 2005 as a bilateral project then called the Bolivarian Alternative, it has been broadened to include Bolivia, Nicaragua, Ecuador, and the Caribbean island nations following the election of progressive presidents in those countries. Presenting itself as an alternative to the neoliberal model of the FTAA, ALBA involves the exchange of energy producing products for services, primarily in the field of health care and education. Cuba contributes its human resources, cultivated over the long years of the Cuban revolution in return for oil and gas from Bolivia and Venezuela. The exchange is also especially important for Venezuela as Chávez seeks to deliver on his promises to improve the daily lives of poor Venezuelans.

Venezuela is not alone in projecting Latin American independence from the United States in the new century. President Lula of Brazil has pursued that country's natural leadership of the region warranted by its sheer size and economic potential. That potential has never been more evident as Brazil dramatically expands its agricultural output and announces important new off-shore oil discoveries. Brazil is poised to become a major international player in the twenty-first century as it increasingly plays a leadership role in the nations of the global south, pressing at the United Nations for the restructuring of the Security Council and taking a leadership role in the World Trade Organization (WTO) negotiations. Brazil's stance lacks the radical rhetoric of Chávez' Venezuela, but may prove in the long run to be the greatest barrier to long term U.S. dominance of the region. Brazil, together with Argentina and other Latin American countries have also strengthened their ties in recent years with the People's Republic of China. The Chinese, eager to purchase raw materials and food stuffs, have raised their level of trade in the region by more than tenfold in the last decade. Trade with China gives the Latin American nations an additional option in international trade thus reducing their traditional reliance on the United States and Europe.

Prospects for the Future

What are the prospects for U.S.–Latin American relations in the coming years? There are a series of potential conflicts over resources such as oil and water that can bring the United States and key Latin American countries into confrontation. These conflicts could prove to be significant because now more than ever before Latin Americans are mobilized at the grassroots level to prevent the taking of their resources by powerful European and North American interests that have triumphed so often in the past. This resistance has been best symbolized in Bolivia and Ecuador where grassroots movements, mainly indigenous, have removed presidents from power through street demonstrations when they perceived that their natural resources were being auctioned off by their leaders to foreign interests. In both countries there are now presidents in office, Evo Morales and Rafael Correa, placed there by the votes of these movements and vowing to protect their natural resources. Other areas of strong contention include the U.S. desire for additional permanent U.S. bases in the region and its continuing desire to use the issue of drug interdiction as a wedge for U.S. intervention. U.S. efforts to expand its military bases in the Latin America suffered a setback when the new Ecuadoran government refused to renew the lease for a U.S. base at Manta that had been agreed to by the previous pro-U.S. government. Similarly, the Paraguayan government has successfully fended off U.S. overtures for a permanent military presence near its border with Bolivia. In 2009, the United States used its ties to the conservative Uribe administration in Colombia to add bases there.

For more than twenty years drug interdiction has been the rationale behind U.S. military presence in the Andean region, especially in Peru and Colombia. Pro-U.S. governments in those countries will likely continue to accept a U.S. presence, but the ability of the United States to extend its military power on the pretext of drug interdiction is limited. An exception to this trend of limited influence based on drugs may be Mexico where the Mérida Initiative, sometimes called Plan Mexico, is resulting in greater cooperation than ever before between the U.S. military and police establishment and their Mexican counterparts. Such cooperation became possible when violence stemming from the flow of illegal drugs through Mexican territory to the United States reached extremely high levels in the new century. The cooperation was also facilitated by the election of successive pro-U.S. National Action Party (PAN) governments in both 2000 and 2006.

Latin American–United States relations have not yet been fundamentally transformed and current initiatives may pass without that transformation. The United States still has many important factors to its favor, including dominant military power and economic investments throughout the region. Key Latin American countries, including Peru and Colombia, have strongly pro-U.S. leaders. The election of Barack Obama, a Democrat, to the presidency, offers the opportunity for the United States to reverse the dramatic fall of its Latin American influence that

President Obama at the Summit of the Americas meeting in Trinidad in 2009. *(Photo by Andrea Leighton/AP Images)*

occurred under George W. Bush. Obama has spoken of a "partnership for the Americas" and has declared that "what is good for the Latin Americans is good for the United States." His limited statements on Latin America, harkening back to John Kennedy and Franklin Roosevelt, place an emphasis on poverty reduction, including debt relief for most needy countries. However, Obama's priorities are likely to reside elsewhere so it is unclear whether the new administration will have a significant impact on the region. This tone was repeated by President Obama in his participation in the Summit of the Americas in Trinidad in April 2009 but no new initiatives of significance from the United States emerged at the meeting or subsequently. Soon after the Trinidad Summit a military coup in Honduras challenged the Obama administration to support broad Latin American opposition to the coup leaders, but ultimately the U.S. government did little to reverse the coup and it became a fait accompli. This policy revealed that the new administration was not prepared to initiate a fundamentally different Latin America policy and, in the process, regain lost credibility in the hemisphere. In spite of such obvious U.S. power and the plans of a new U.S. administration, the current period represents an important opportunity for Latin America to carve out a political space with renewed independence from its most powerful neighbor to the north. The success of that project for greater independence will likely rest on the ingenuity and strength of the working masses of the region and the resourcefulness of their leaders.

Bibliography

Arévalo, Juan José. *The Shark and the Sardines.* Whitefish, MT: Kessinger, 2007.

Blasier, Cole. *The Hovering Giant: U.S. Responses to Revolutionary Change in Latin America.* Pittsburgh, PA: University of Pittsburgh Press, 1976.

Butler, Smedly D. *War Is a Racket.* Los Angeles: Feral House, 2003.

Cameron, Maxwell A., and Brian W. Tomlin. *The Making of NAFTA: How the Deal Was Done.* Ithaca, NY: Cornell University Press, 2002.

Carothers, Thomas. *In the Name of Democracy: U.S. Policy toward Latin America in the Reagan Years.* Berkeley and Los Angeles: University of California Press, 1991.

Cooper, Andrew Fenton, Thomas F. Legler. *Intervention Without Intervening?: The OAS Defense and Promotion of Democracy in the Americas.* New York: Palgrave Macmillan, 2006.

Gleijeses, Piero. *Shattered Hope: The Guatemalan Revolution and the United States, 1944–1954.* Princeton, NJ: Princeton University Press, 1991.

Grandin, Greg. *Empire's Workshop: Latin America and the Roots of U.S. Imperialism.* New York: Henry Holt, 2006.

Holden, Robert H., and Eric Zolov. *Latin America and the United States, a Documentary History.* New York and Oxford: Oxford University Press, 2000.

LaFeber, Walter. *Inevitable Revolutions: The United States in Central America.* 2nd ed. New York: W.W. Norton, 1993.

LeoGrande, William M. *Our Own Backyard: The United States and Central America, 1977–1992.* Chapel Hill: University of North Carolina Press, 1998.

Lowenthal, Abraham F. *The Dominican Intervention.* Cambridge, MA: Harvard University Press, 1972.

Lowenthal, Abraham F., ed. *Exporting Democracy: The United States and Latin America.* Baltimore: Johns Hopkins University Press, 1991.

Martz, John D. *United States Policy in Latin America: A Decade of Crisis and Challenge.* Lincoln: University of Nebraska Press, 1995.

Mora, Frank O., and Jeanne A. K. Hey. *Latin American and Caribbean Foreign Policy.* Lanham, MD: Rowman & Littlefield, 2003.

Nef, Jorge, and Harry E. Vanden, eds., *Inter-American Relations in an Era of Globalization: Beyond Unilateralism?* Whitby, ON: de Sitter Publications, 2007.

Pike, Frederick B. *FDR's Good Neighbor Policy: Sixty Years of Gently Chaotic Chaos.* Austin: University of Texas Press, 1995.

Schmitz, David F. *Thank God They're on Our Side: The United States and Right-Wing Dictatorships, 1921–1965.* Chapel Hill: University of North Carolina Press, 1999.

Schoultz, Lars. *Beneath the United States: a History of U.S. Policy Toward Latin America.* Cambridge, MA: Harvard University Press, 1998.

Schoultz, Lars. *Human Rights and the United States Policy toward Latin America.* Princeton, NJ: Princeton University Press, 1981.

Sigmund, Paul E. *The Overthrow of Allende and the Politics of Chile, 1964–1976.* Pittsburgh, PA: University of Pittsburgh Press, 1977.

Sikkink, Kathryn. *Mixed Signals: U.S. Human Rights Policy and Latin America.* Ithaca, NY: Cornell University Press, 2004.

Smith, Gaddis. *The Last Years of the Monroe Doctrine, 1945–1993.* New York: Hill and Wang, 1994.

Smith, Peter H. *Talons of the Eagle: Latin America, the United States, and the World.* 3rd ed. New York: Oxford University Press, 2008.

FILMS

The Battle of Chile. Chile, 1976.

Bloqueo, Looking at the U.S. Embargo against Cuba. United States, 2005.

Missing. United States, 1982.

Origins of the OAS Charter. United States (OAS), 2007.

Panama Deception. United States, 1992.

Websites

http://www.alternativabolivariana.org/   ALBA (in Spanish)

http://www.bancosur.org/   BancoSur

http://cidh.oas.org/DefaultE.htm/   Inter-American Commission on Human Rights

http://www.mercosur.int/msweb/portal%20intermediario/pt/index.htm/   Mercosur (in Spanish)

http://www.oas.org/   Organization of American States

http://www.paho.org/   PanAmerican Health Organization

Authors

Gary Prevost is Professor, Department of Political Science, St. John's University/
College of Saint Benedict, Minnesota. He received his Ph.D. in political science from
the University of Minnesota and has published widely on Latin America and Spain.
His books include *Democracy and Socialism in Sandinista Nicaragua*, coauthored with
Harry E. Vanden; *The 1990 Nicaraguan Elections and Their Aftermath*, coedited with
Vanessa Castro; *The Undermining of the Sandinista Revolution*, coedited with Harry E.
Vanden; *Cuba: A Different America*, coedited with Wilber Chaffee; *The Bush Doctrine
and Latin America*, coedited with Carlos Oliva Campos; *Revolutionaries to Politicians*,
coedited with David Close and Kalatowie Deonandan; and *United States-Cuban
Relations—A Critical History*, coauthored with Esteban Morales, in addition to numer-
ous articles and book chapters on Nicaragua and Spanish politics. His research on
Latin America has been supported by a number of grants, including a Fulbright
Central American Republics Award.

Harry E. Vanden is Professor of Political Science and International Studies at the
University of South Florida, Tampa, where he was the founding director of the Latin
American Studies Center. He received his Ph.D. in political science from the New
School for Social Research and also holds a graduate Certificate in Latin American
Studies from the Maxwell School of Syracuse University. He has lived in several
Latin American countries, including Peru, where he was a Fulbright Scholar and later
worked in the Peruvian government's National Institute of Public Administration, and
in Brazil, where he held a second Fulbright and taught at the State University of São
Paulo. His scholarly publications include numerous articles and book chapters and the
following books: *Mariátegui, influencias en su formación ideológica*; *National Marxism in
Latin America, José Carlos Mariátegui's Thought and Politics*; *A Bibliography of Latin American
Marxism*; *Democracy and Socialism in Sandinista Nicaragua*, coauthored with Gary Prevost;
The Undermining of the Sandinista Revolution, coedited with Gary Prevost; *Inter-American
Relations in an Era of Globalization. Beyond Unilaterialism?* coedited with Jorge Nef; *Latin
American Social Movements in the Twenty-First Century*, coedited with Richard Stahler-
Sholk and Glen Kuecker; and *Politics of Latin America, the Power Game*, coauthored with
Gary Prevost, also published by Oxford University Press and now in its third edition.

INDEX

Index

CPSIA information can be obtained at www.ICGtesting.com
Printed in the USA
BVOW061203100812

297589BV00003B/4/P